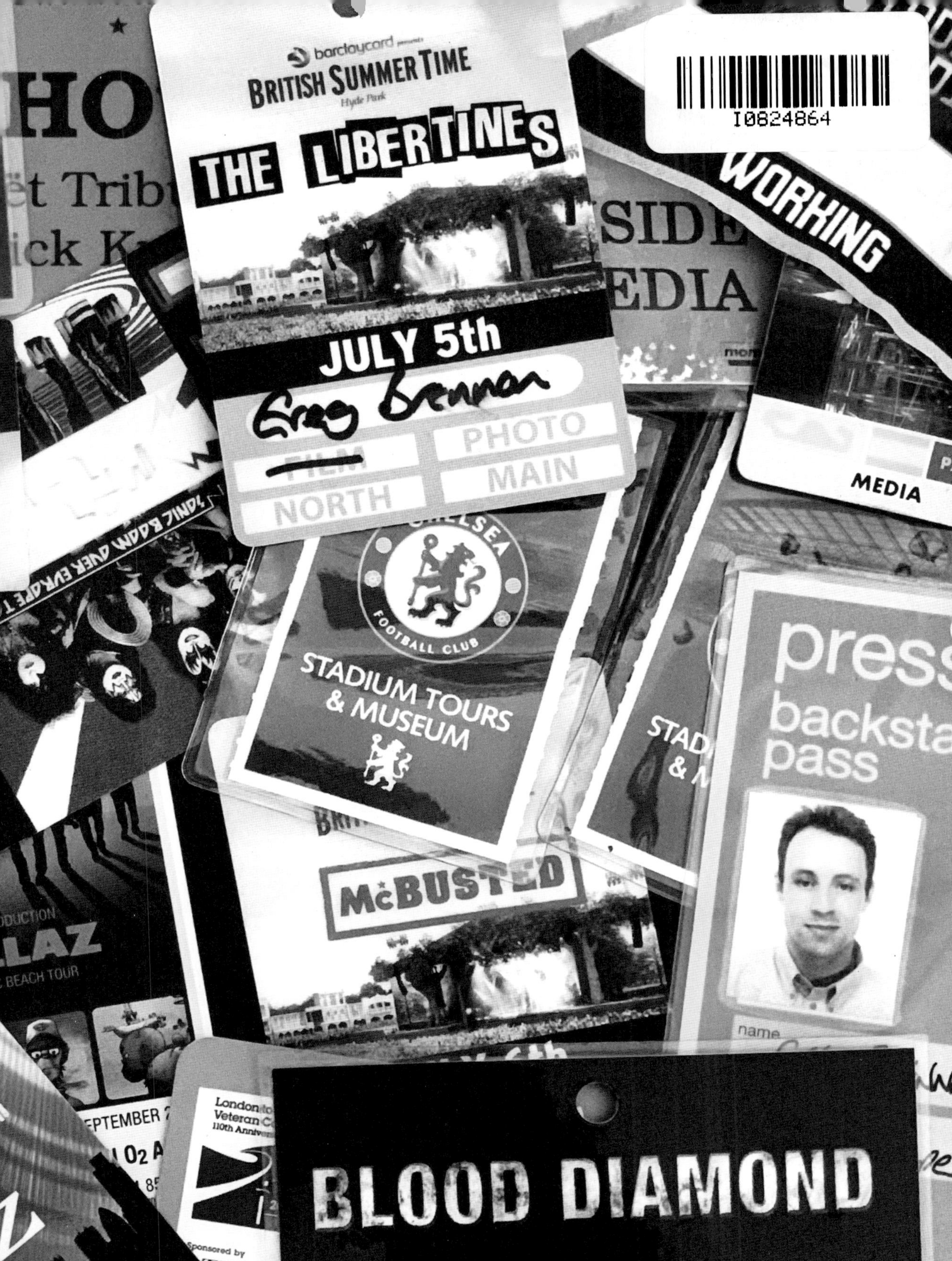
barclaycard presents
BRITISH SUMMER TIME
Hyde Park
THE LIBERTINES
JULY 5th
Greg Brennan
FILM
PHOTO
NORTH
MAIN
WORKING
MEDIA
CHELSEA FOOTBALL CLUB
STADIUM TOURS & MUSEUM
press
backsta
pass
name
McBUSTED
BLOOD DIAMOND
PHOTOGRAPHER
005
Sponsored by
Associate sponsor
RENAU
I0824864

THE BIG SHOT

PHOTOGRAPHS BY GREG BRENNAN

WRITTEN BY DYLAN BRENNAN

ACC ART BOOKS

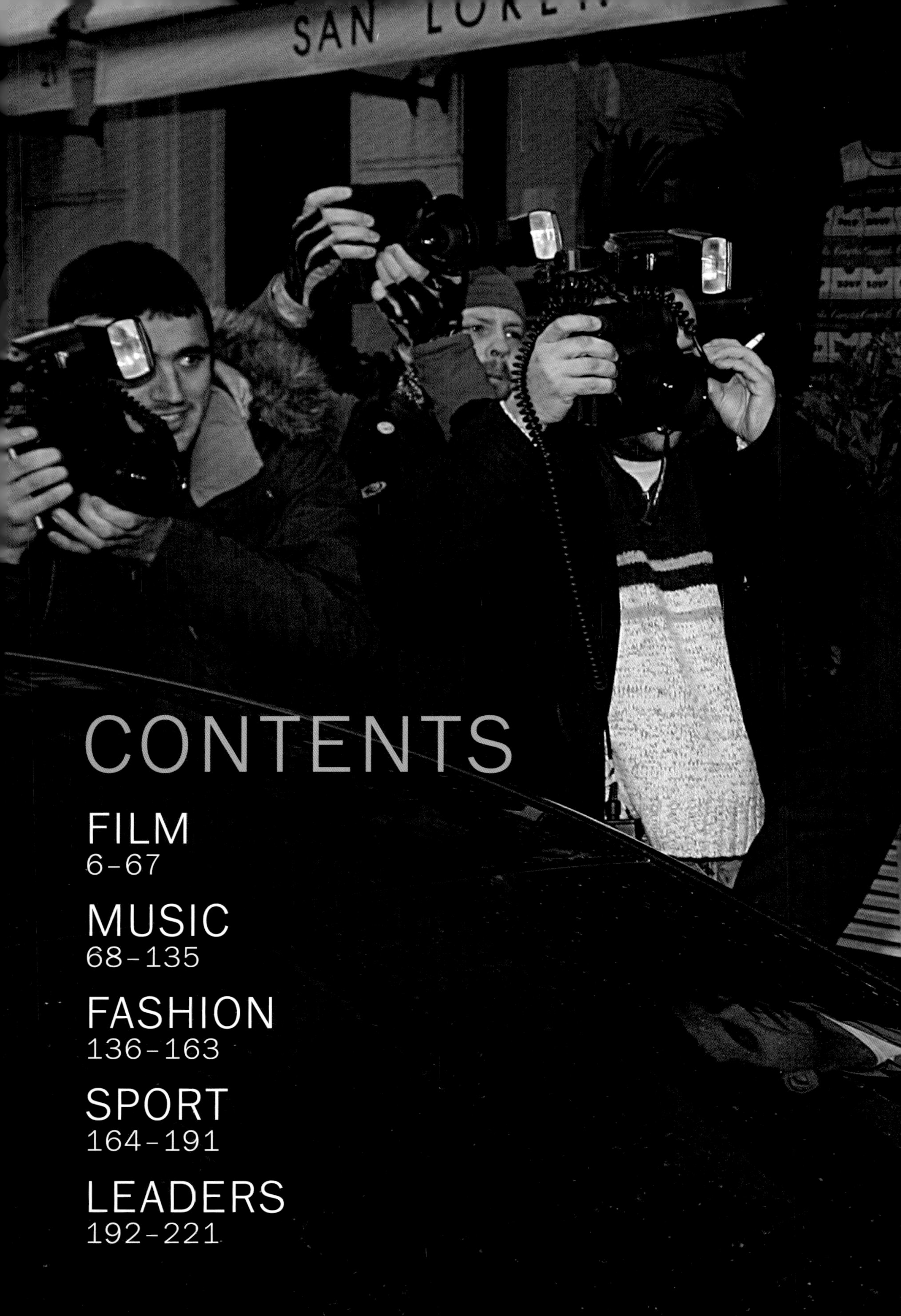

CONTENTS

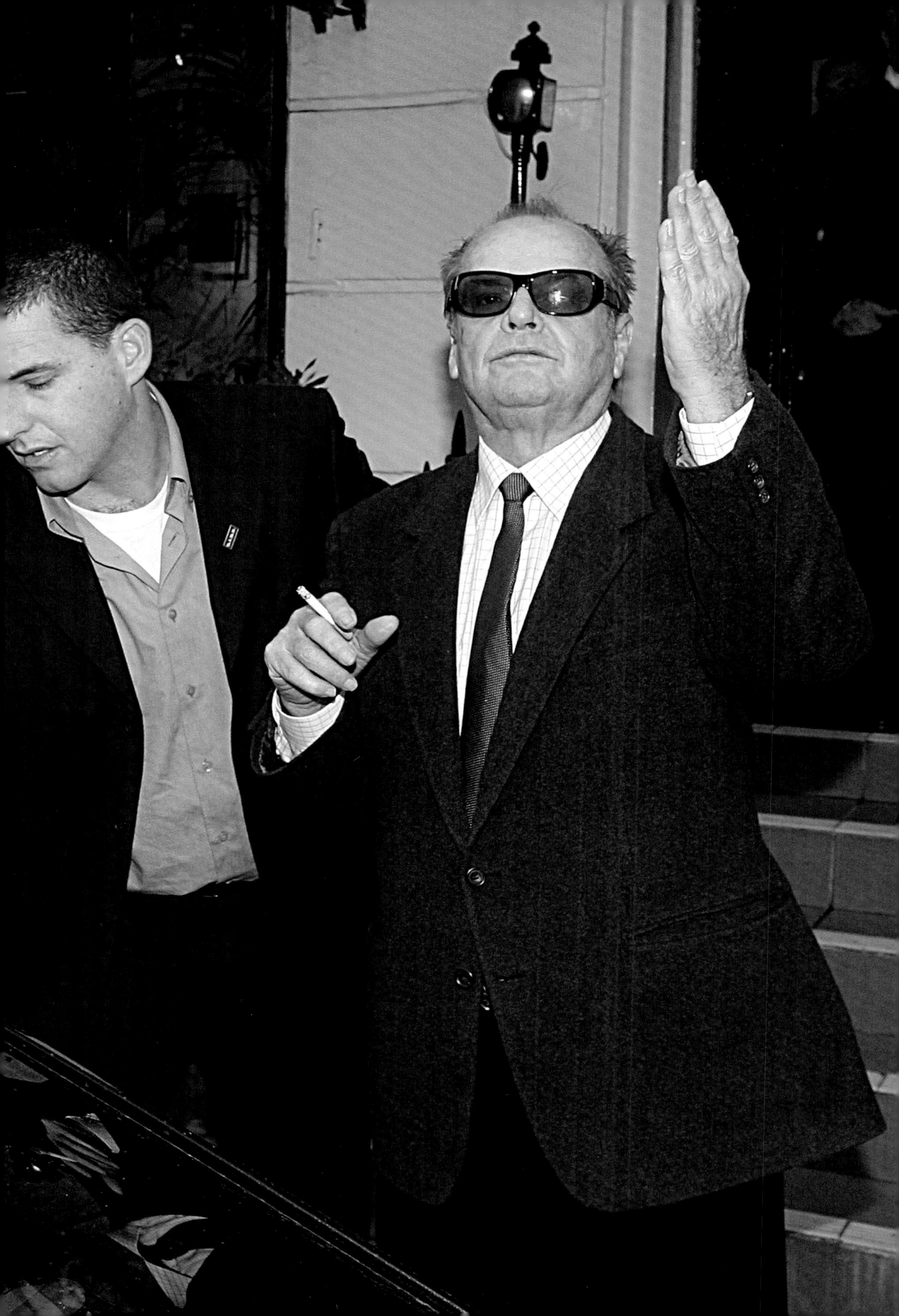

INTRODUCTION

When I bought my first camera in 1991, I could hardly have predicted where it would take me. The truth is, although I knew I had an appreciation for the art, I never had any grand designs of rubbing shoulders with the world's biggest names, nor did I imagine I'd eventually get frames that would stand the test of time. But as life often proves, the unexpected paths are sometimes the most rewarding.

I've always believed that good photography is about more than just snapping away and hoping for the best. Sure, you've got to have the technical know-how – proper lighting, framing, all that. But what really makes a photograph sing is its ability to tell a story, to catch something no one else has. Some might say it's about being in the right place at the right time. I'd argue it's also about knowing how to be that fly on the wall, while also ensuring everyone is comfortable and enjoying themselves.

I cut my teeth, not just on glamorous red carpets or carefully orchestrated press events, but also by hanging around where the real stories were happening – outside, where the air was fresh and the expressions were too. Rather than jostling with a sea of lenses all pointed at the same face, I tried a different approach: patience, charm, and a touch of wit. My tried-and-true method has always been to get them smiling first, and everything else will fall into place. People are at their most natural when they're having a good time; when the mask slips for a brief moment – that's when I hit the shutter. And that's when you get something special.

"There I was, camera in hand, capturing them at their most candid."

Now, it's funny to think about all the portraits that have come and gone through my camera's eye over the years. Musicians like Eminem and Lady Gaga, actors like Jack Nicholson and Clint

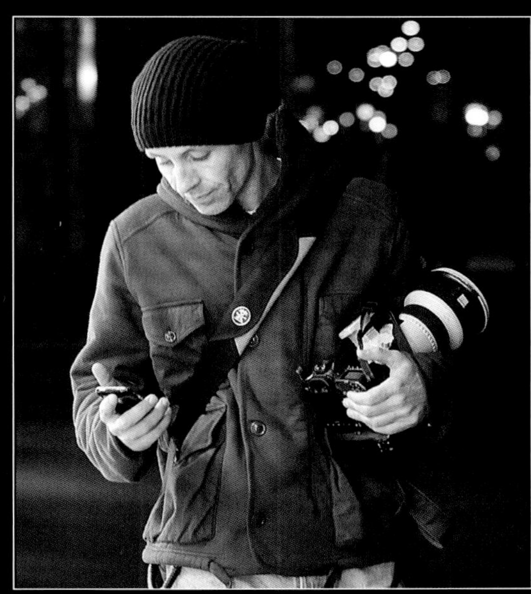

Eastwood, world leaders like Barack Obama and Nelson Mandela, royalty from across the globe – even the late Queen Elizabeth herself. I'll admit, seeing one of my portraits held in the Royal Photographic Collection still gives me a bit of a thrill. It's not every day you can say The Queen requested one of your pictures, is it?

London, with all its eclectic characters and a never-ending parade of famous faces, proved to be the perfect stage. There was always someone making history, someone about to shake the world; and there I was, camera in hand, capturing them at their most candid. Over the years, black-and-white photography became my signature style. It strips away the distractions. No flashy colours; just the raw, unfiltered essence of the subject. In a way, I think it brings us closer to the truth of the person in front of the lens. You see the rebel, the visionary, the human being behind the title.

But enough of the heavy stuff. What's photography if you can't enjoy it? I've had a grand old time photographing some of the most well-known figures in the world. Some of them even asked for copies – Michael Jackson, Bill Clinton, and yes, even the British Royal Family, to name a few. Still, it's never really been about the fame for me. It's about that connection, that brief instant when the world around you fades and all that matters is capturing the moment, the story in front of you.

So, here I am, many years later, with a library of memories spanning decades. Each image in this book is more than just a picture – it's a snapshot of history, of people who've made their mark, often in ways we never quite expected. And for me, it's been an absolute pleasure to be behind the lens for so many of those moments.

Now, let me show you some of my favourites.

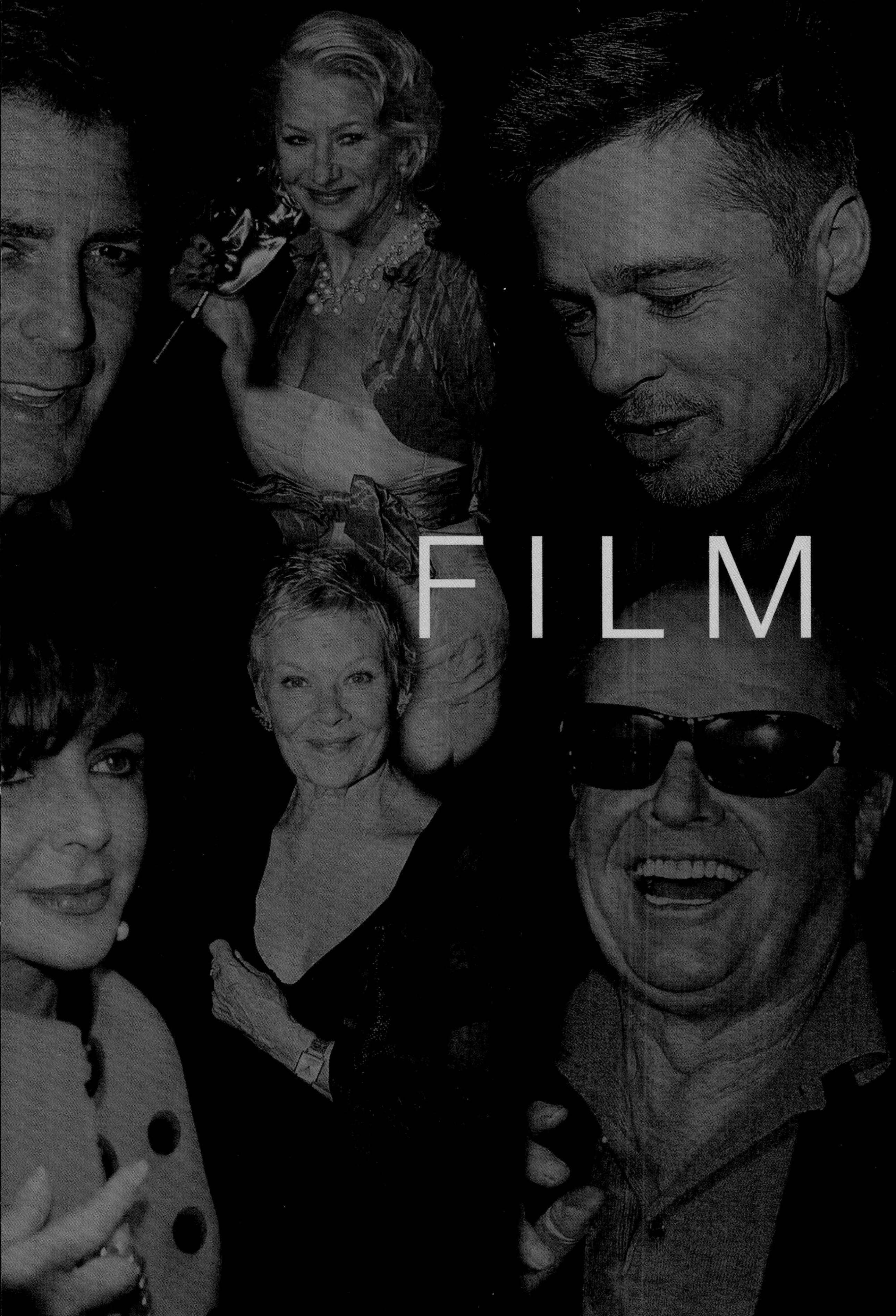

FILM

JACK NICHOLSON

January 2008

A question I have frequently encountered in my line of work is a deceptively simple one: "Who was your favourite subject to photograph?" Without hesitation, my answer will always be Jack Nicholson. He was, without a doubt, the best subject I ever had the privilege to shoot. More than that, he was a masterclass in the art of being looked at. He didn't just pose; he performed. Every glance, every smirk, every movement was delivered with the same effortless magnetism he brought to the screen. He had an innate understanding of the camera, and he played to it beautifully.

One thing I remember vividly is his annual pilgrimages to Wimbledon. He was a huge tennis enthusiast and made it a point to come every year for the tournament. During these visits, he always stayed at the same hotel in Mayfair, and whenever he was in London, it was a guarantee that he'd hit the town and shenanigans would occur.

One such instance occurred on St James's Street, just a stone's throw from the Ritz, at a quaint hat shop. Nicholson had just arrived in London and was gearing up for a round of golf. He walked in, tried on a few bowler hats and, as always, left an impression that far outlasted his visit. Like moths to a flame, a small crowd gathered around him. As he was leaving the shop, two builders working nearby spotted him and couldn't resist the opportunity to grab an autograph. One of them boldly stepped forward, but neither had a pen. The first man, clutching a hammer, looked around frantically, while the other, holding a brush dipped in white paint, thrust it towards Jack with a hopeful grin and said, "Use this". With his trademark grin and utterly unphased by the unusual request, Nicholson obliged. He took the paintbrush, gave it a thoughtful twirl, and then, with a flourish, signed his name in white paint across the builder's back. The man turned to his friend, awestruck – I wouldn't be surprised if he never washed that shirt again. Afterwards, Nicholson wandered around the corner for brunch, which saw him send sandwiches and drinks to the media waiting outside. Jack thrived in the spotlight, relishing the attention that followed him.

Some nights, usually whenever he was leaving a restaurant surrounded by admirers, he would spontaneously begin kissing people on the street and slipping bills into the hands of the homeless as though he were some old Hollywood Robin Hood. One night, while leaving his hotel, a woman walking by stopped, frowned slightly, and asked him who he was. Jack looked her straight in the eyes, flashed that iconic smile, and declared, "I'm Jackie Baby!" From that moment on, I'd always address him as "Jackie Baby" whenever I photographed him, a nickname that never failed to bring out his infectious grin.

"Then, with a flourish, signed his name in white paint across the builder's back."

He has this uncanny ability to make everything feel larger than life, to turn the mundane into the extraordinary. Always, unequivocally, Jack Nicholson. Sadly, those vibrant encounters have become a rarity. Jack hasn't graced us with his presence in a while, and his absence is felt.

To me, he remains one of Hollywood's truest legends. He just has a certain way about him that nobody else has – boundless in his charisma, effortlessly cool and completely devious. Exactly like he is in his films. Some people act like stars. Jack simply is one.

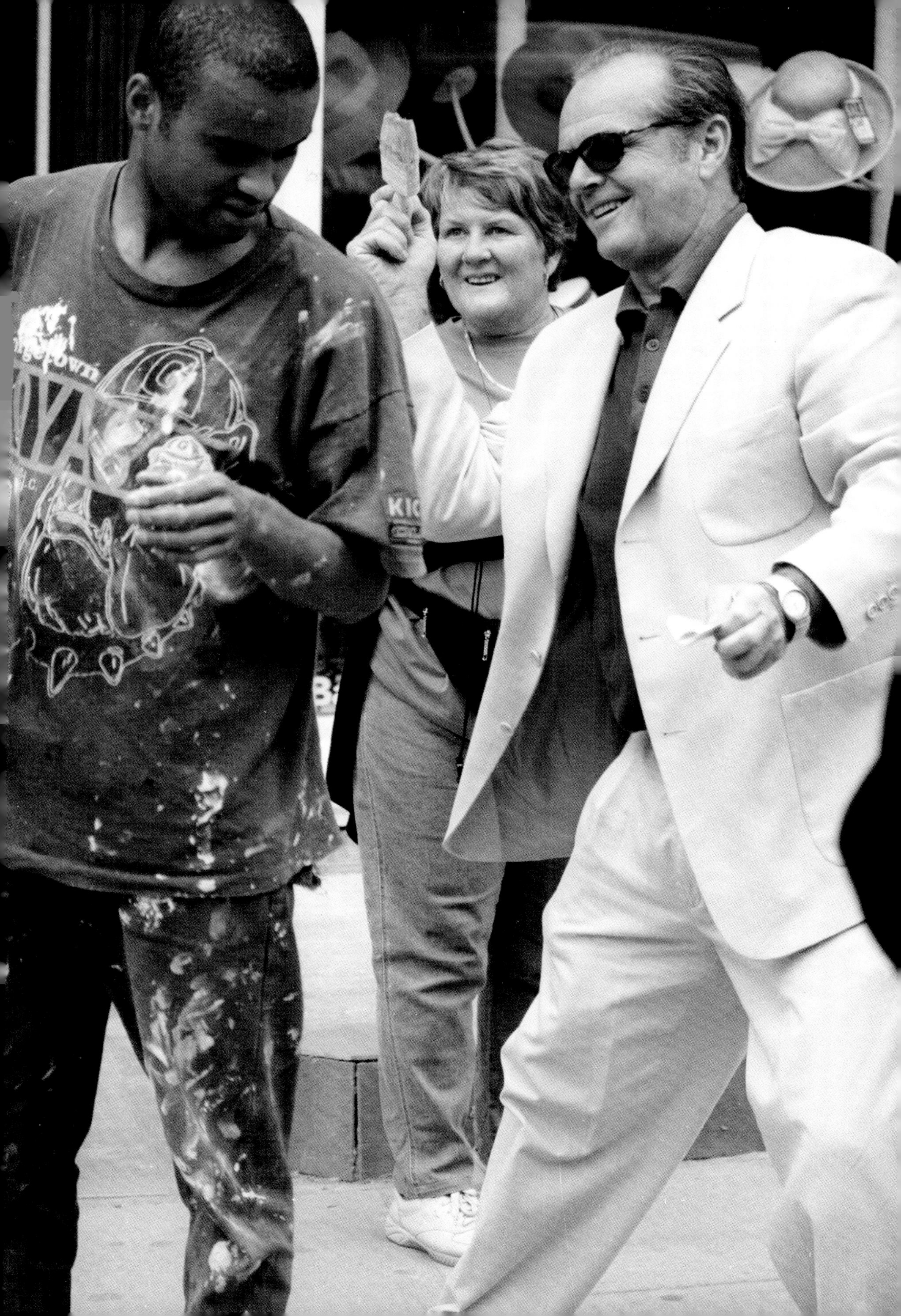

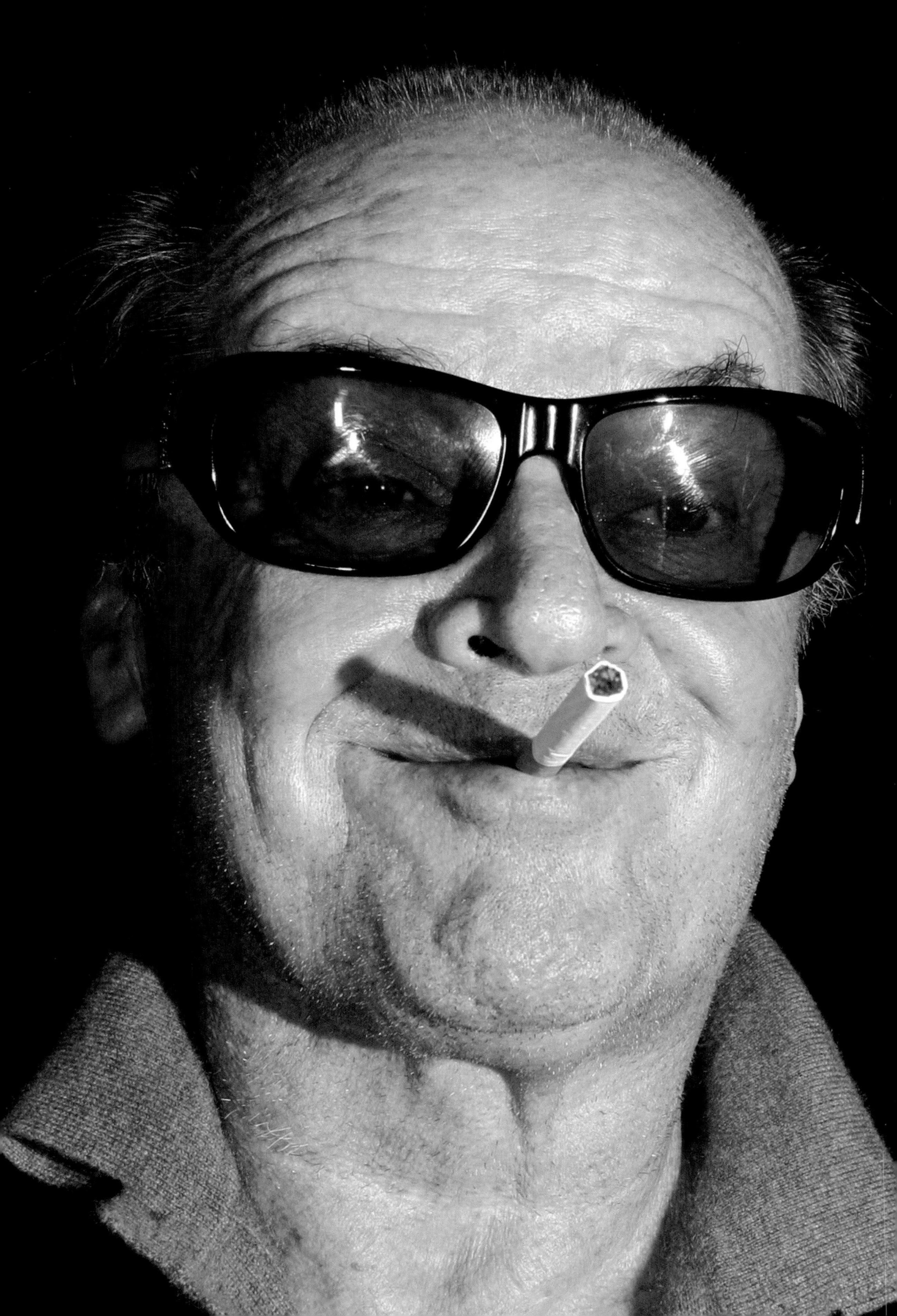

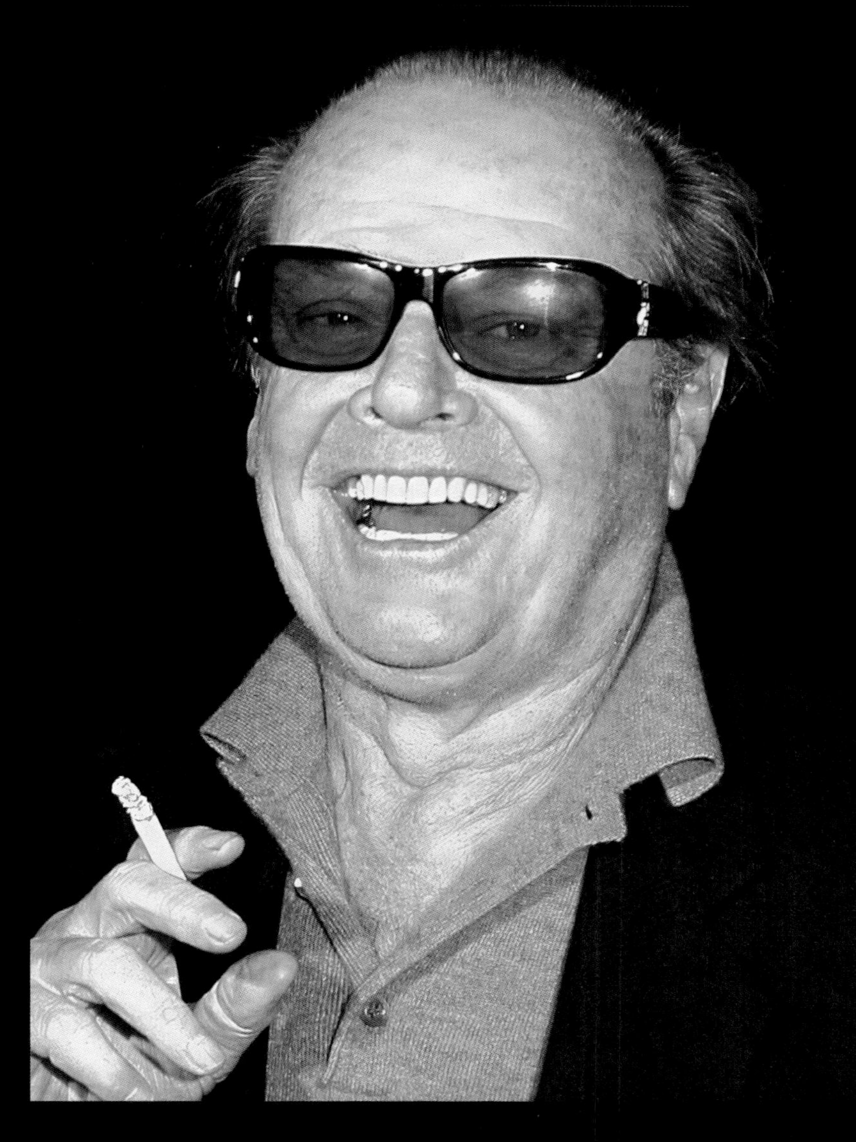

Jack Nicholson
The Wolseley, Piccadilly
January 2008

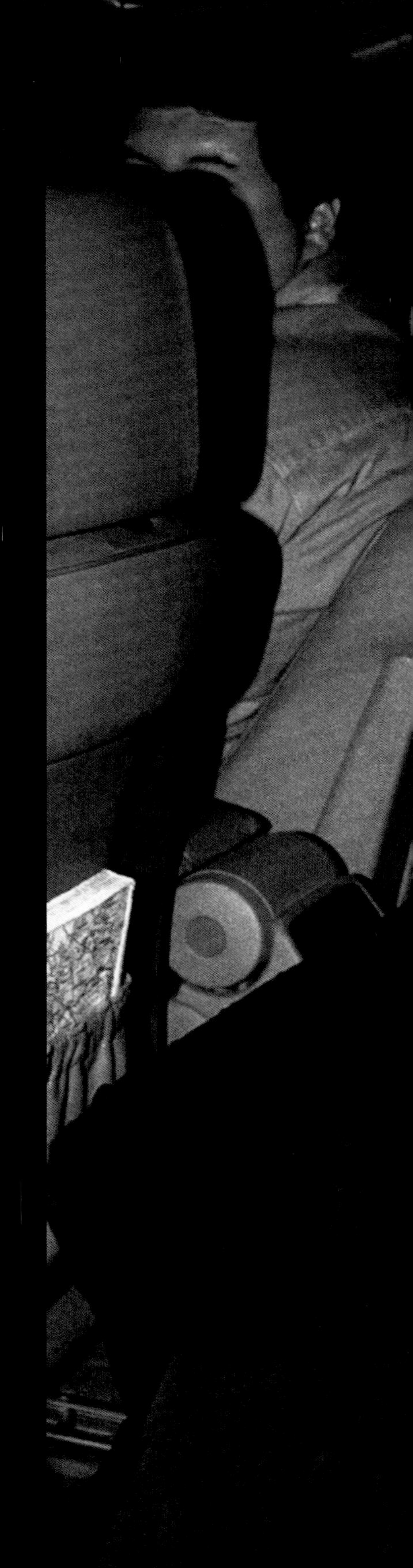

Angelina Jolie and
Billy Bob Thornton
The Ivy, Covent Garden
July 2001

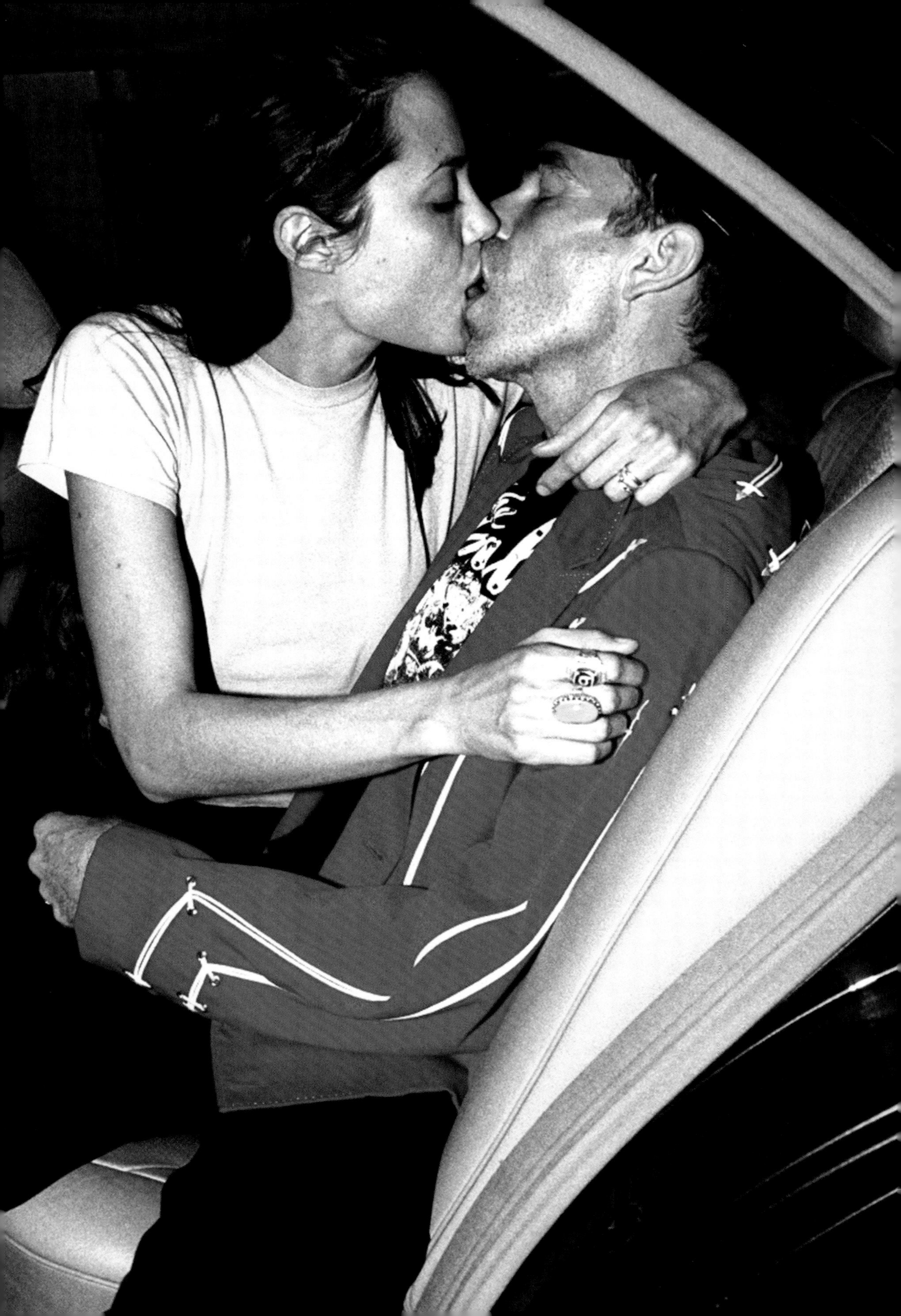

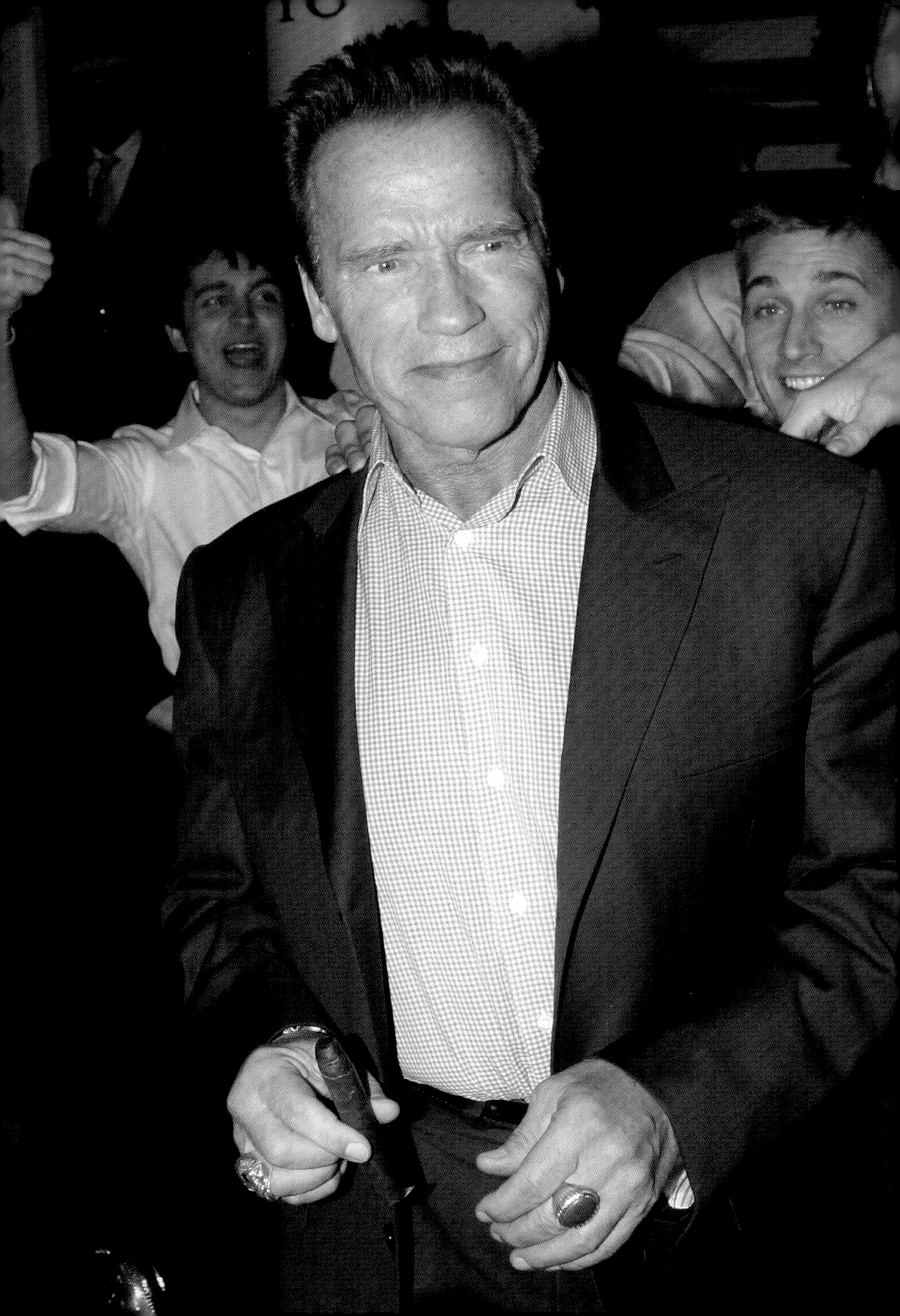

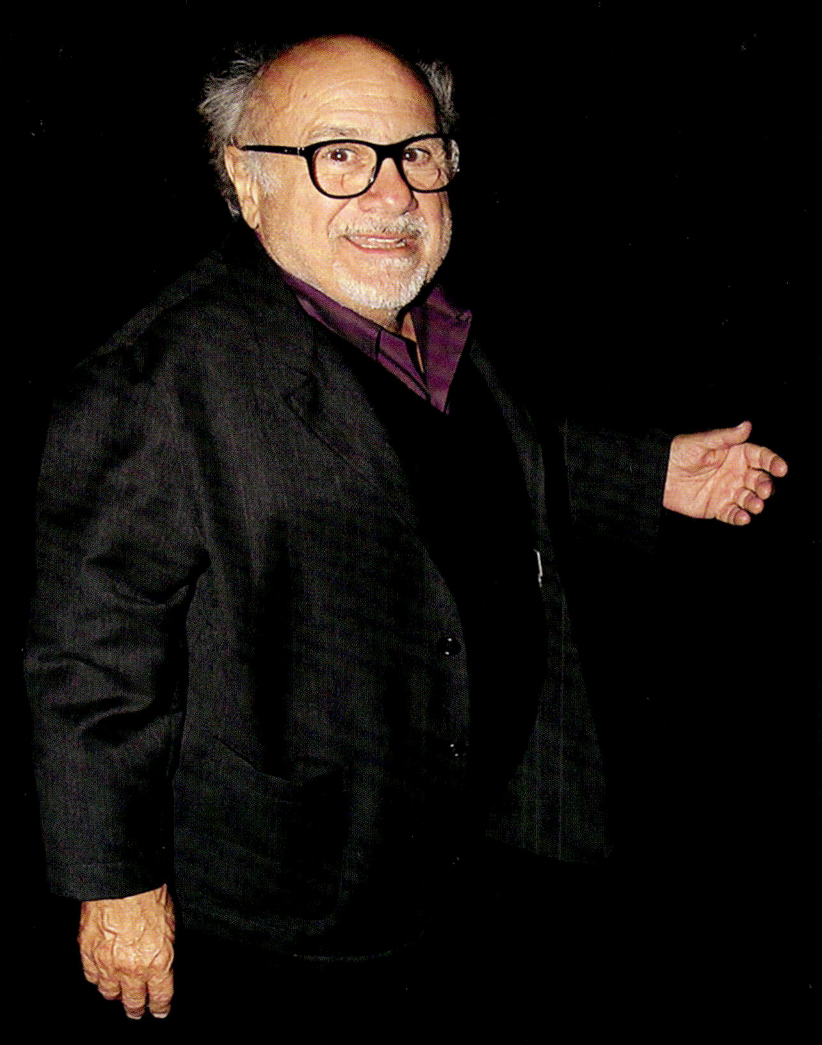

Arnold Schwarzenegger
The Arts Club, Mayfair
March 2012

Danny DeVito
Soho Hotel
October 2016

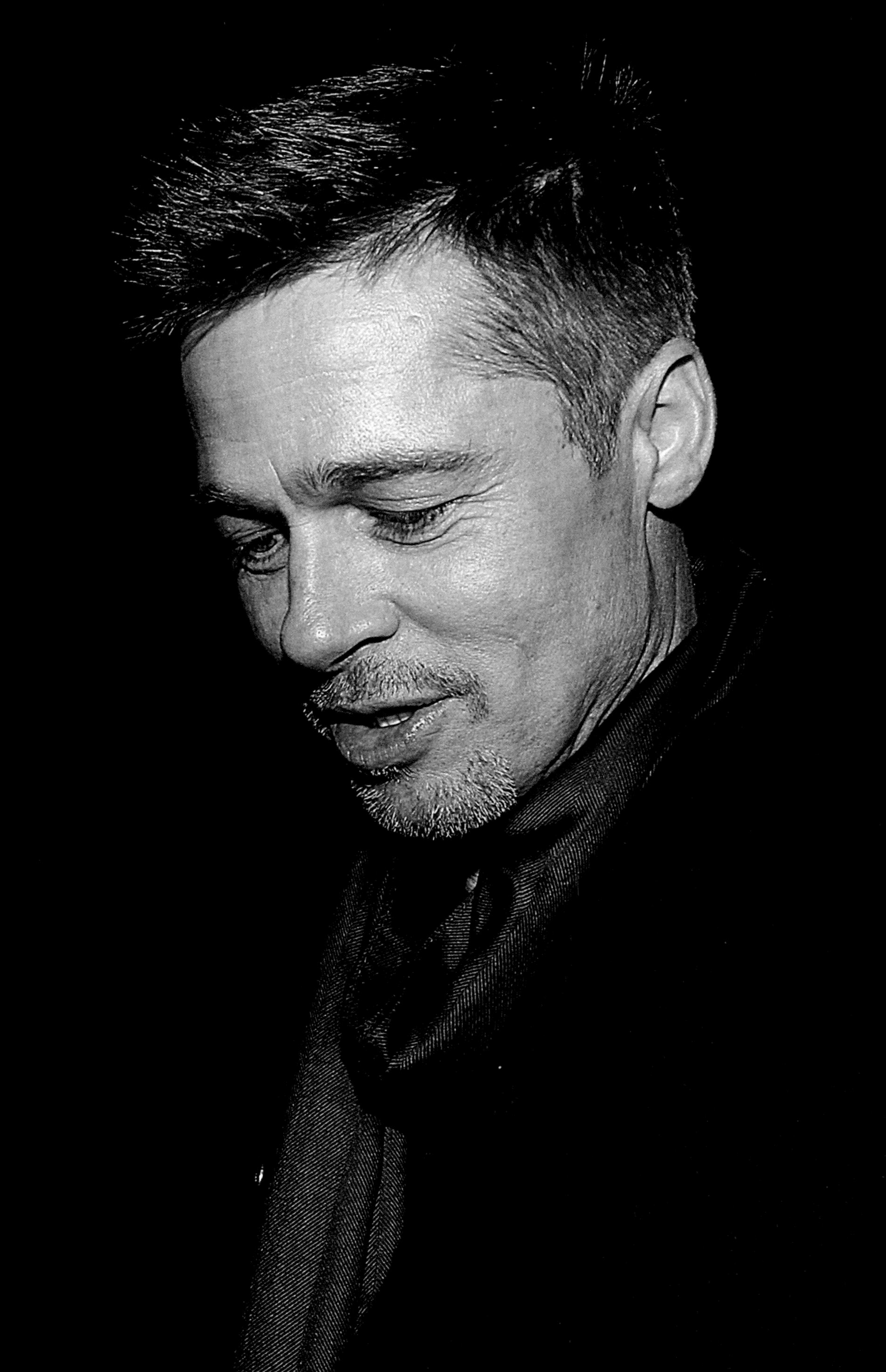

Brad Pitt
Leicester Square
November 2016
Premiere for 'Allied'

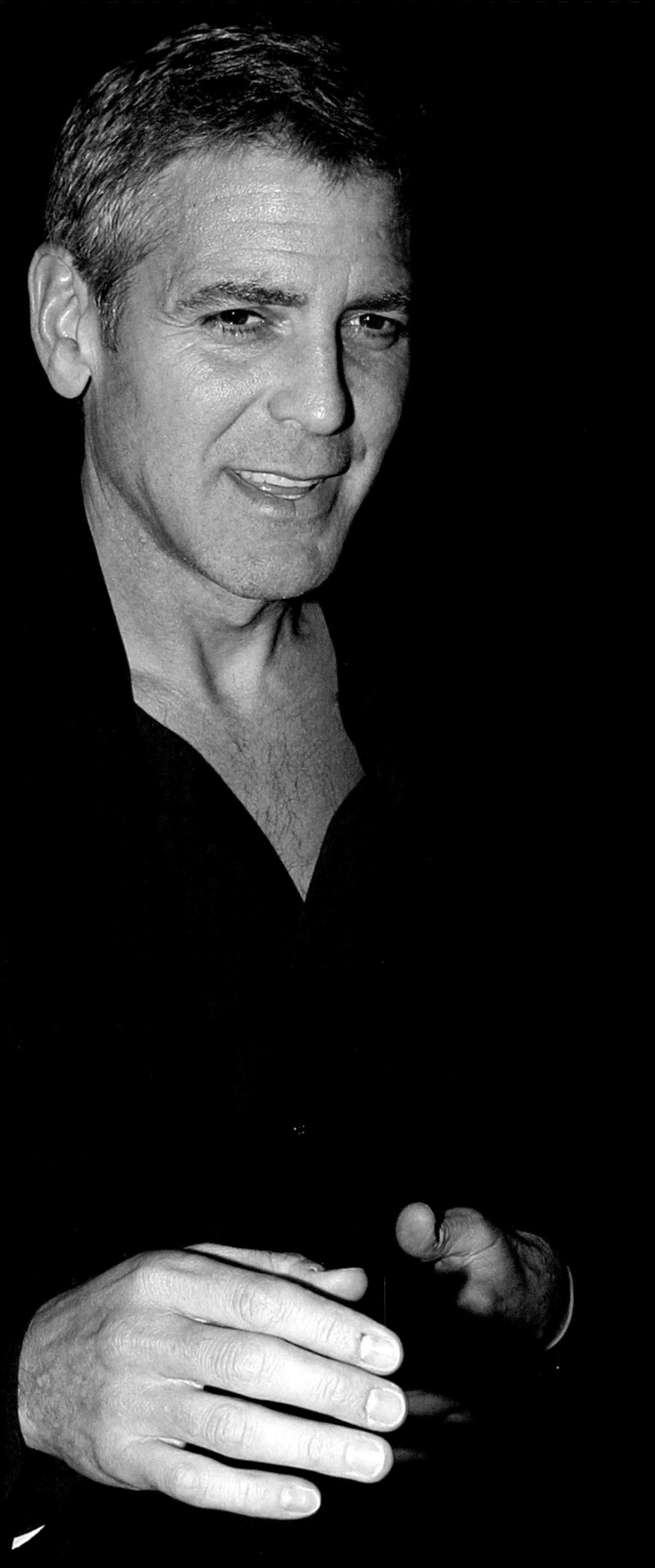

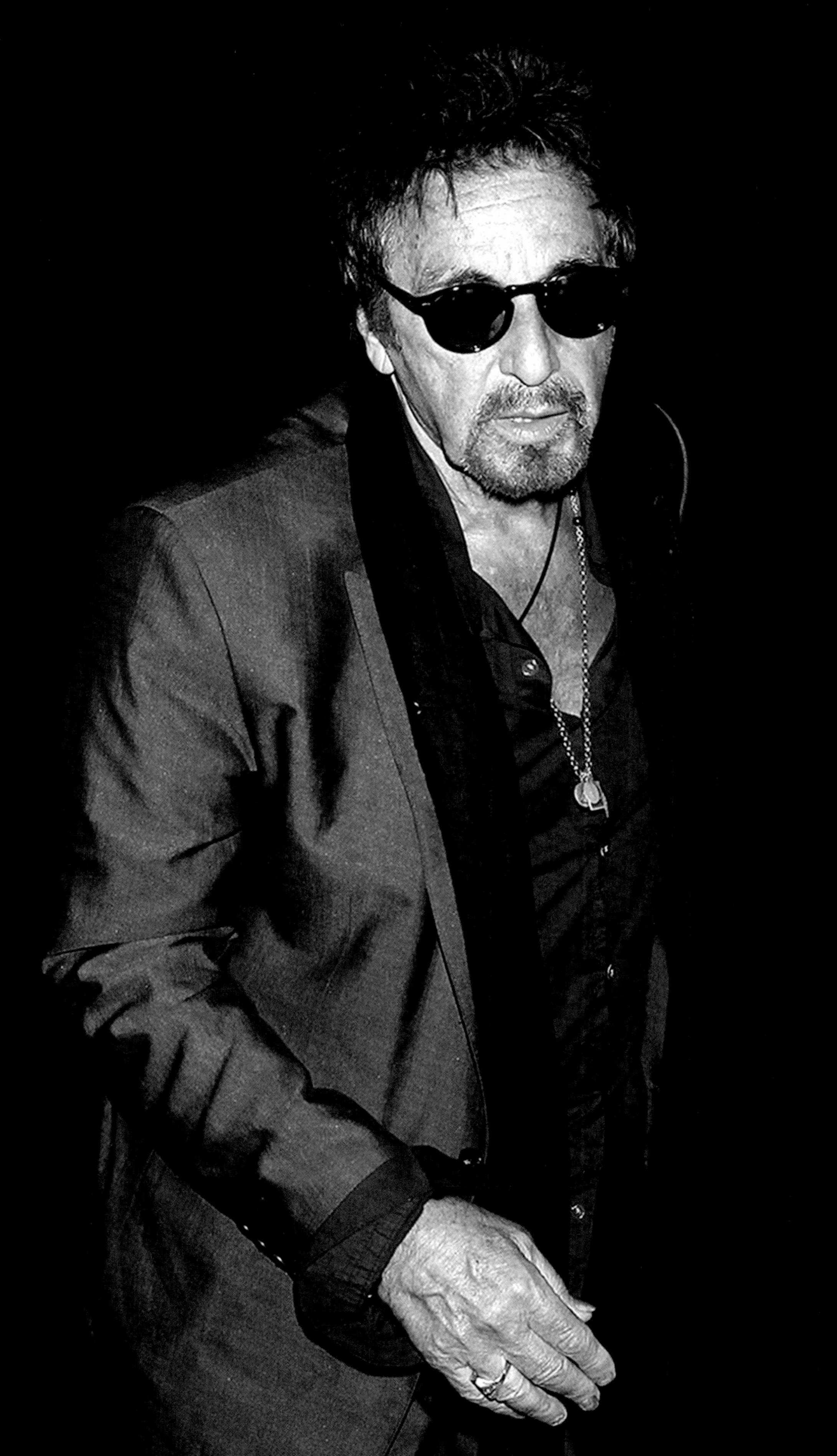

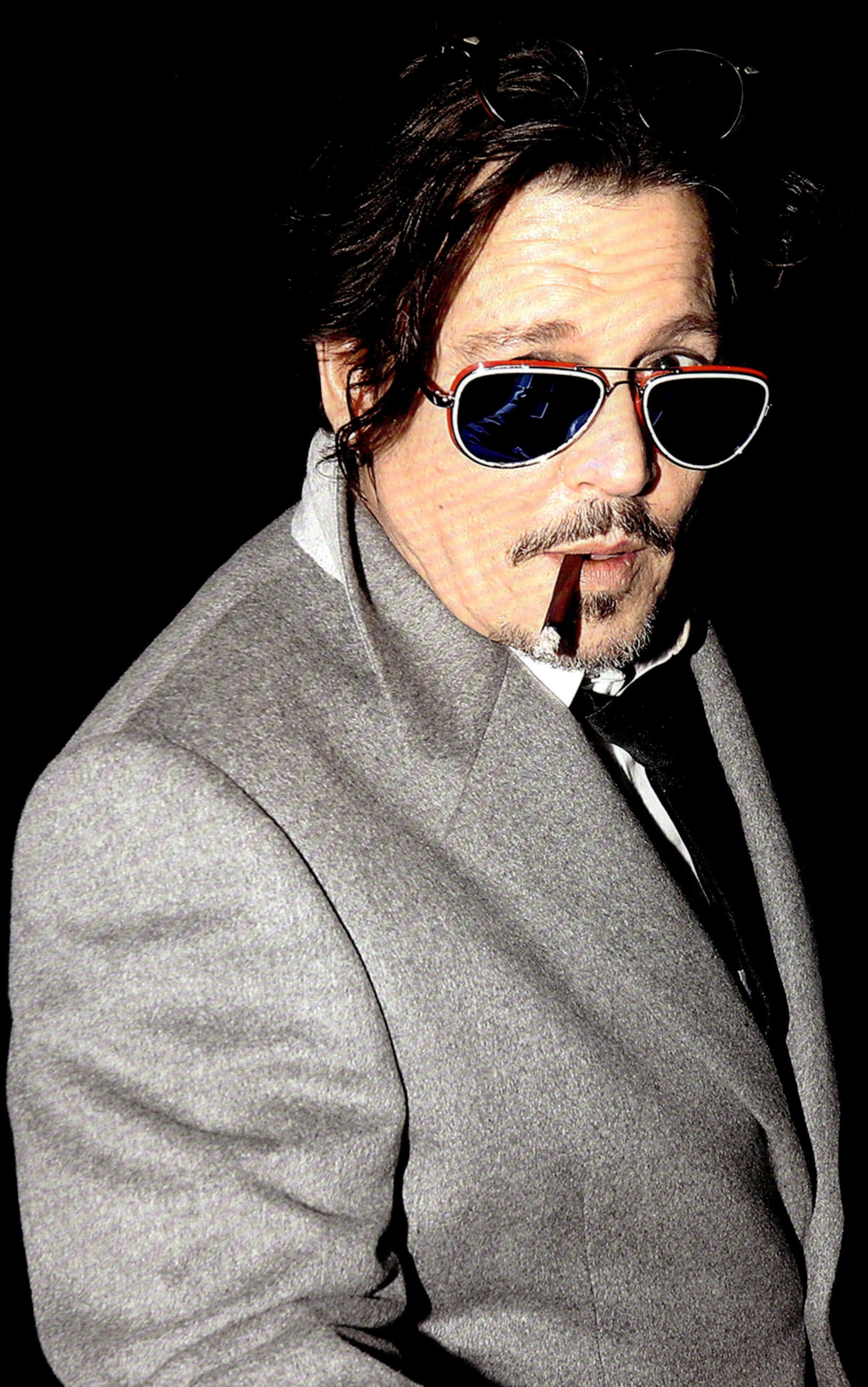

Johnny Depp
Novikov Restaurant & Bar, Mayfair
April 2024

Previous pages:
George Clooney
St Martins Lane Hotel, Soho
April 2008

Al Pacino
Chiltern Firehouse, Marylebone
September 2014

ROBERT DE NIRO

May 2002

It was early evening, the golden hour when London's streets begin their transition from daytime bustle to nighttime mystery. I was at home, camera bag half-packed on my bed, mentally plotting the evening's photographic excursion, when my phone's shrill ring cut through my concentration. On the other end, a voice, breathless with urgency, informed me that 'The Ghost' had arrived at the Dominion Theatre. I knew exactly who they meant and instantly abandoned my careful packing, grabbing lenses and stuffing them haphazardly into my bag. Time was of the essence. In my early days, during a conversation with another photographer, I'd confessed my ambition to capture Robert De Niro. He chuckled and responded, "You mean The Ghost?" When I questioned the moniker, he leaned in conspiratorially: "In the trade, he's known as The Ghost. You always know he's there, but you never see him." I laughed at the time, but now it felt like a challenge.

Arriving at the theatre, I was met with the usual chaos – a writhing mass of autograph hunters pressed against barriers, journalists with notepads at the ready, photographers with their lenses pointed expectantly at the main entrance like artillery. Minutes stretched painfully as the evening air grew cooler and optimism waned. The crowd's energy began to ebb, replaced by murmurs of speculation. Had De Niro already slipped in through some hidden entrance? The Ghost, living up to his reputation? My shoulders sagged as I turned away, camera bag suddenly feeling twice as heavy, as I momentarily believed he had eluded me once more.

I traced the theatre's perimeter, my footsteps echoing against the building's stone façade, when the unmistakable creak of rarely used hinges stopped me in my tracks. A service door, previously invisible against the wall's texture, swung open just an arm's length away. I glanced up and, to my astonishment, out popped Robert De Niro himself. For a moment I couldn't believe my eyes. There he was, Jake LaMotta, eyes scanning the alley for lenses, just a few feet away and walking straight towards me, accompanied by none other than Brian May and Roger Taylor from Queen.

Time compressed into a photographer's usual decision tree: move too quickly and risk alerting the 30-odd fans and photographers still waiting around the corner; hesitate too long and watch the moment dissolve. My hands found my camera with muscle memory that bypassed conscious thought. The viewfinder came to my eye as naturally as blinking. Fortunately, the stars aligned in that instant, and as a triumphant payoff for all the times The Ghost had evaporated before I could capture him, I managed to get these incredible shots.

"In the trade, he's known as The Ghost. You know he's there, but you never see him."

That night marked the beginning of what would become many encounters with Robert De Niro over the years. With each subsequent meeting, the man behind the enigma revealed himself in quiet increments. Beyond the fortress of his public persona – built on intensity and inscrutability – existed a man of surprising gentleness. His legendary status almost seemed incidental to him, worn not as armour but as a slightly ill-fitting coat to which he'd grown accustomed. The Ghost, as it turned out, was a lot more visible than we thought!

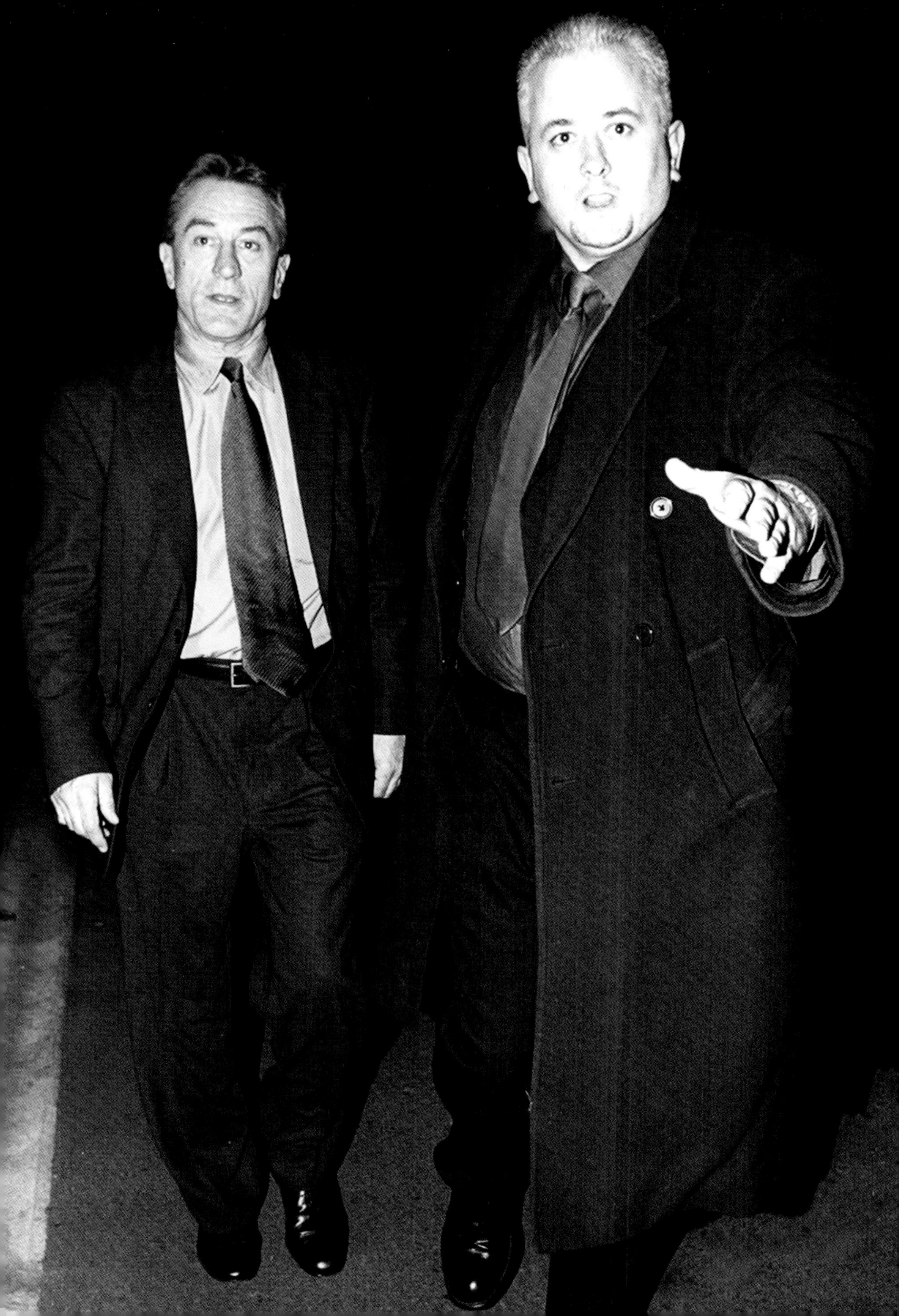

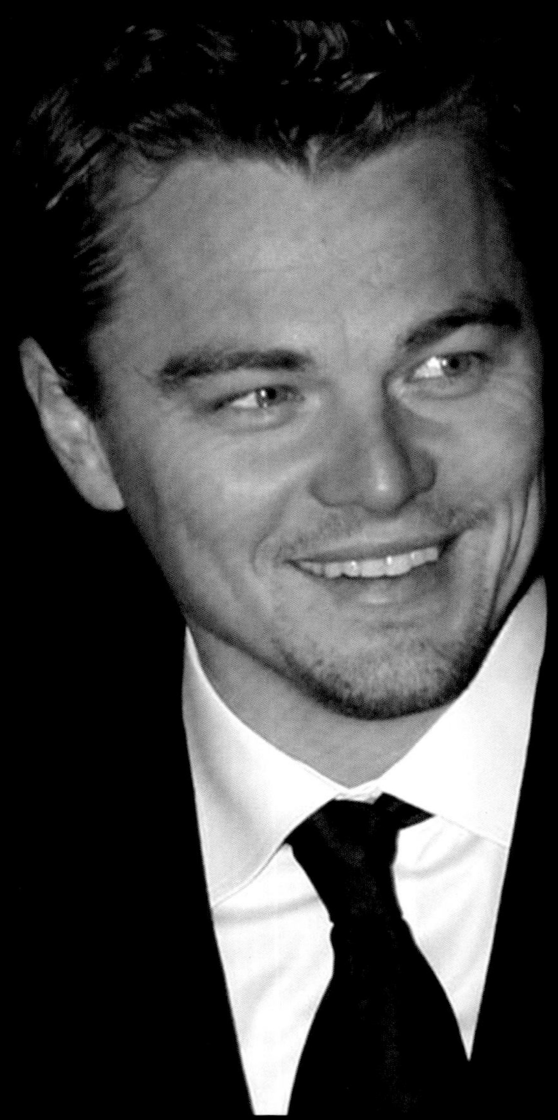

Leonardo DiCaprio
Leicester Square, January 2007
Premiere for 'Blood Diamond'

Kate Winslet
Locanda Locatelli, Marylebone
October 2011

Following pages:
Elizabeth Hurley
Royal Courts of Justice, Westminster
October 2009
Leaving Andy and Patti Wong's Chinese New Year celebrations

Sir Ian McKellen and Ruby Wax
Royal Courts of Justice, Westminster
October 2010

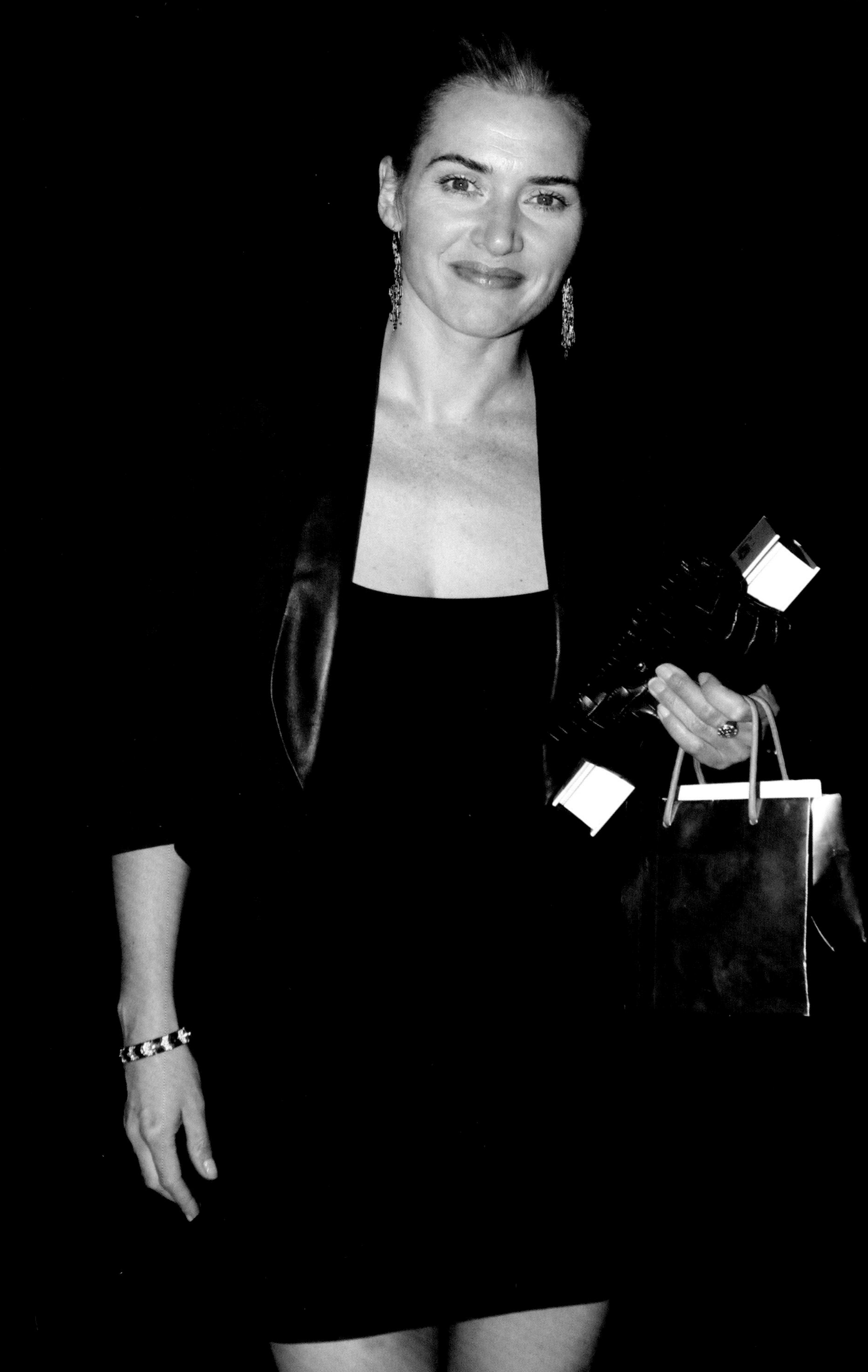

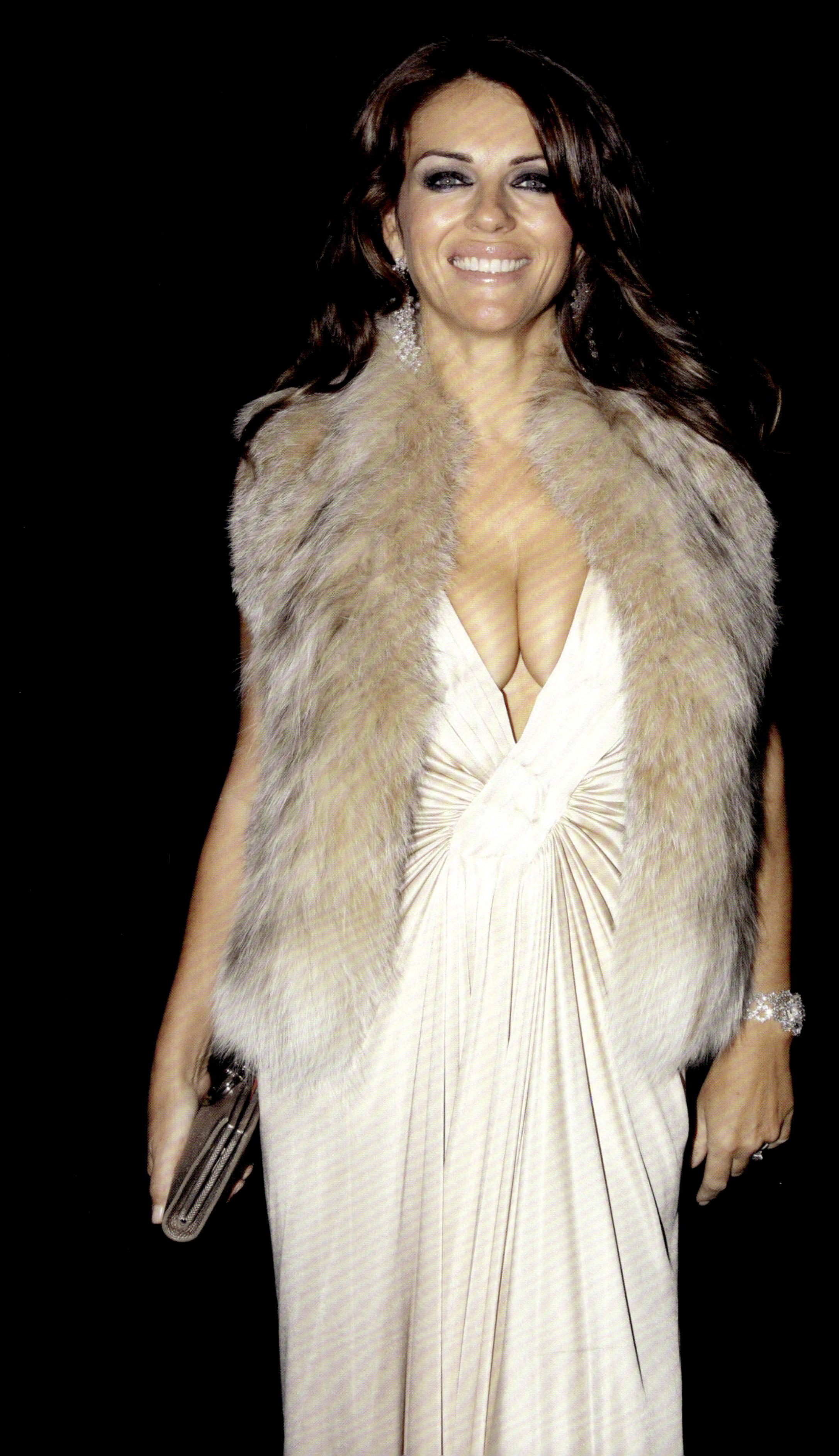

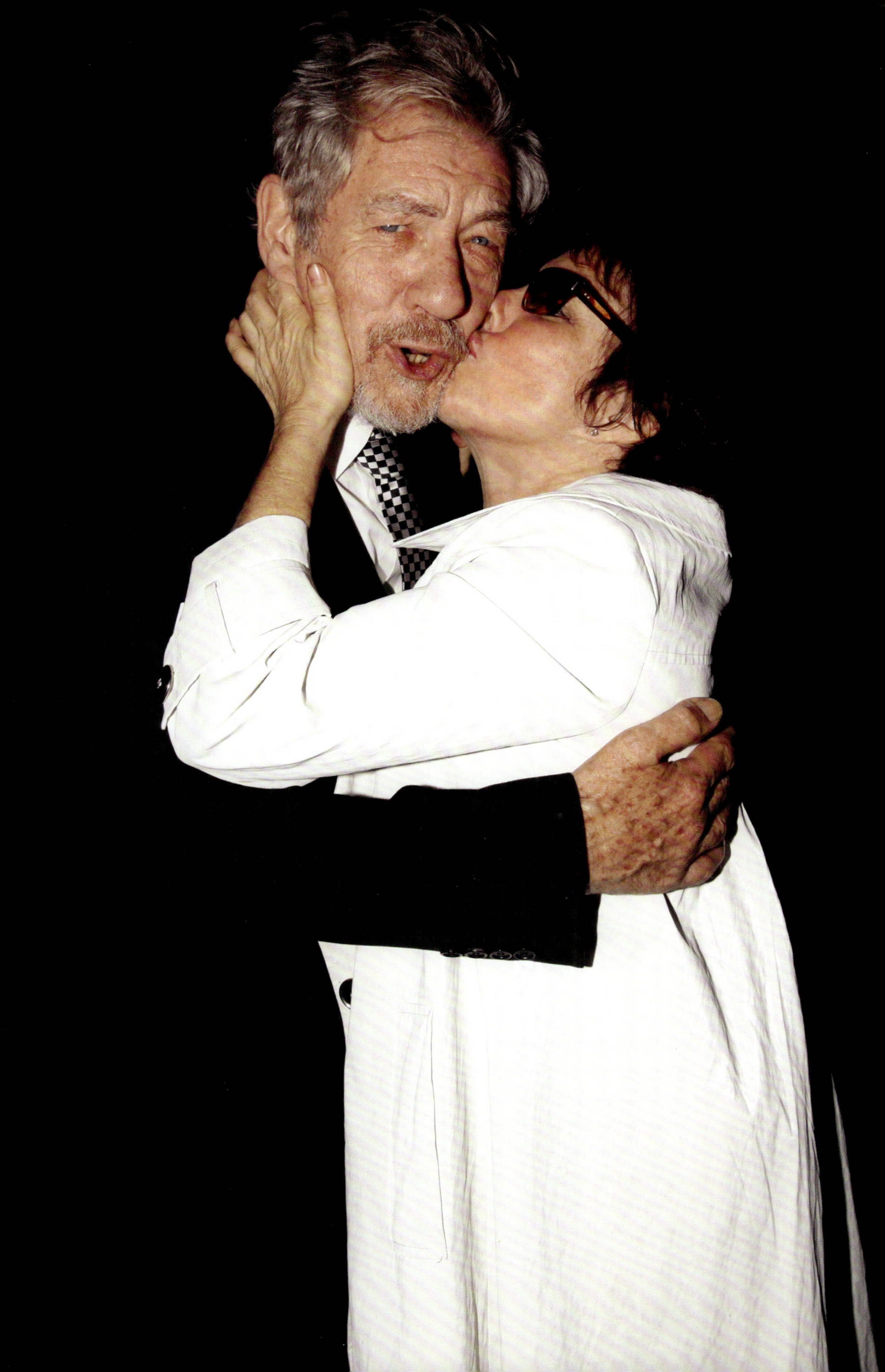

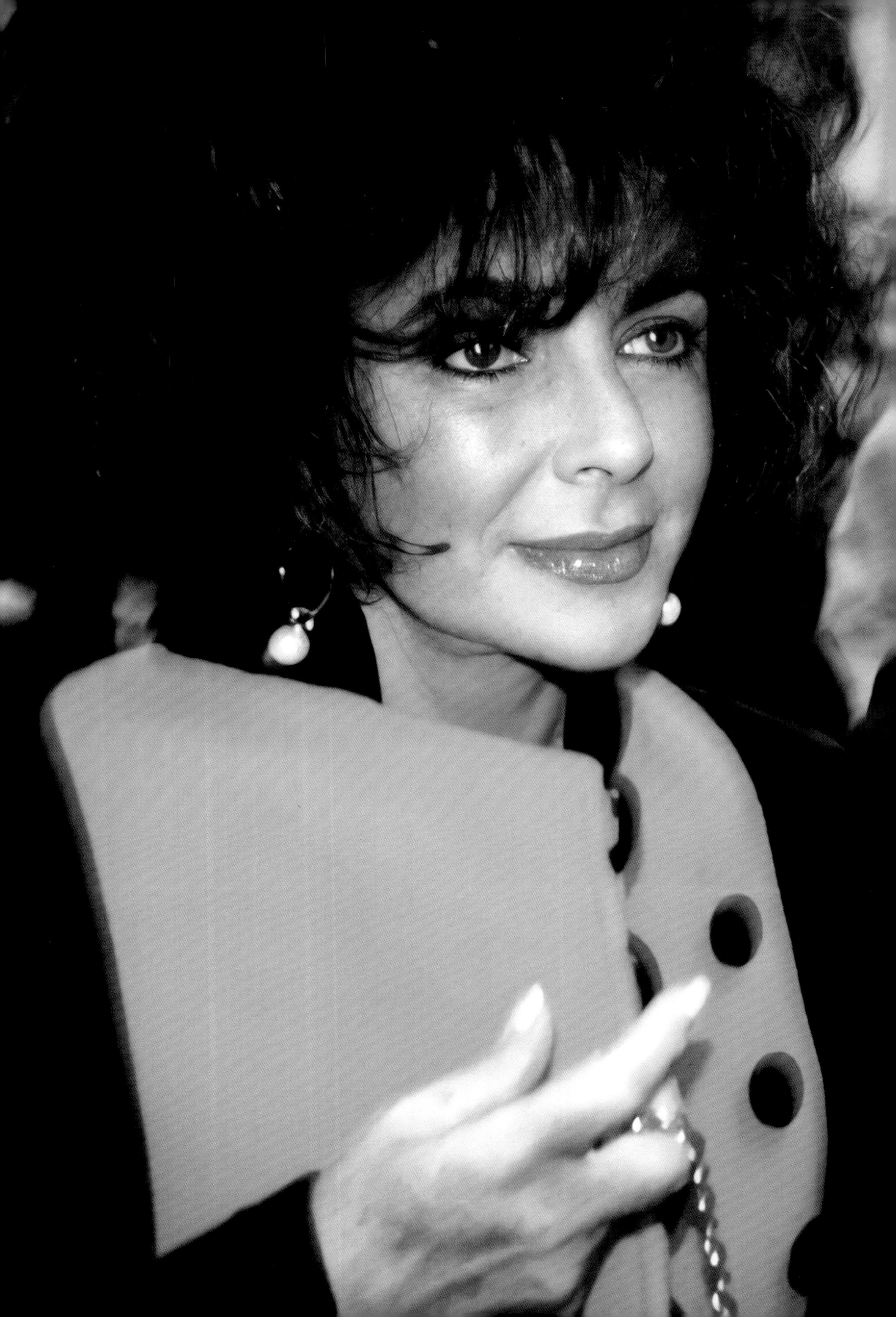

ELIZABETH TAYLOR

November 1991

I grew up in California. My family had a home that was situated beside a drive-in theatre, and I loved the view of the screen from my bedroom. Occasionally I even set my radio to the same frequency as the sound. Classic movie nights were on Wednesdays. I used to arrange pillows, unwind, and spend the late hours of the night watching masterpieces from my window. Hollywood has always captivated me: the stars, the glitz, the flashbulbs – everything about it was pure excitement, the kind that captivated teenagers like me. I never would have imagined back then that I would soon be standing in front of my own camera, taking pictures of the greatest men and women in history. I saw all of Elizabeth Taylor's films, from *Cat on a Hot Tin Roof* (1958) to *Cleopatra* (1963), thanks to these movie evenings. She has always been my favourite leading lady in cinema.

After I eventually left the drive-in behind and relocated to London, it was time for me to start planning my future. I decided to concentrate on the many chances I had to view and take pictures of well-known people, which at the time made London such a fantastic city. I jumped right in, purchased my first camera, and began doing freelance work for local newspapers, which quickly led to national publications and magazines. Though I was well aware of the intense competition and hundreds of photographers vying for the same shot of the same subject in an attempt to sell it first for a quick penny, I never attempted red carpets or other major events. I tried to be different. Get something that nobody else would. Instead, I tried my luck outside of the events by employing a specific strategy: always be courteous, keep them smiling, crack a few jokes, and give them a few compliments. It was a hit, so I used my wonderful technique every single time, incorporating the traditional black-and-white Hollywood aesthetic for the best pictures of the lot.

I went to a brunch at the Mirabelle in Mayfair back in November of 1991. A star-studded lineup of celebrities, including Princess Diana, Elton John, Elizabeth Taylor and Michael Caine, graced the luncheon portion of an HIV fundraiser event. Since the HIV/AIDS epidemic aroused intense media interest, it was nearly impossible to get anywhere near them. But after the luncheon, Taylor was to visit the London Lighthouse hospice in Notting Hill Gate, so I decided she was the one I wanted to photograph and waited for our first meeting to happen. She exceeded all of my expectations. Incredibly eager to pose for every photo I took, she was charming and patient but still possessed that star aspect one would expect from a person of such celebrity.

Over time, I switched between icons. When Michael Jackson visited town in May 2000, his manager urged me to meet with him outside the Royal Albert Hall following a night of shopping at Harrods, even though the lunacy around him was a continual source of inconvenience. As I stood outside waiting for him to show up, Jackson got out of a Mercedes van with Elizabeth Taylor. They stood and posed for photos, which shocked me, and Michael even asked for a printed copy! It was an incredible privilege for me to stand in front of two of the most renowned celebrities in the world.

"She should be remembered for what she was: the True Queen of Hollywood."

The second time I saw Elizabeth was when she arrived at the Regent Street Café Royal for dinner in October of 2002. Her health had started to deteriorate, and it was obvious that she was having difficulty walking. Still, we got a few pictures with her sons. When I last saw her, it was by total coincidence in 2008 as she was leaving through the back door after a private visit. I declined to take pictures of a woman's failing health out of complete respect for her.

Who wishes to be remembered as they were just before death? She should be remembered for what she was: the True Queen of Hollywood, who I used to watch on a screen outside my bedroom window.

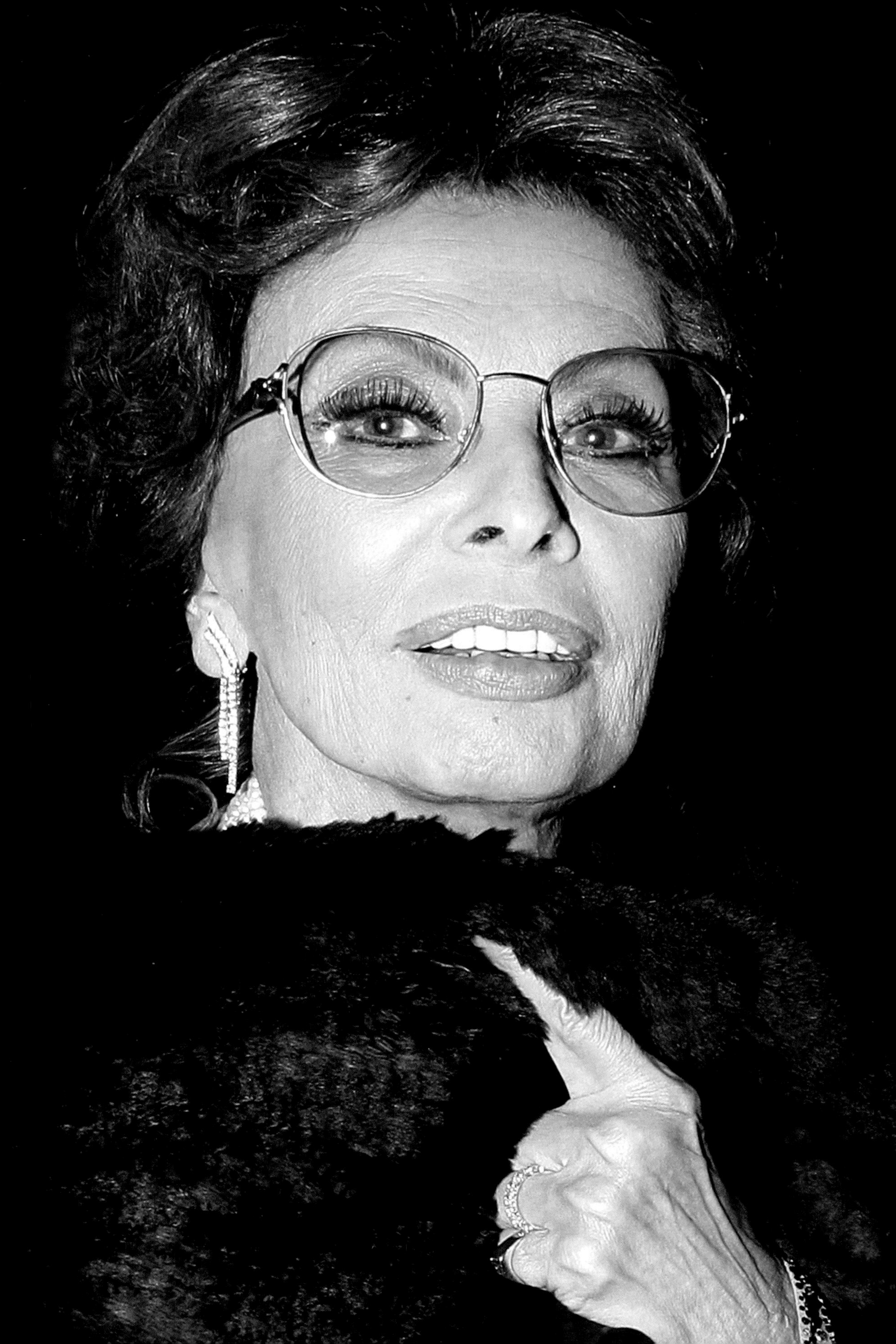

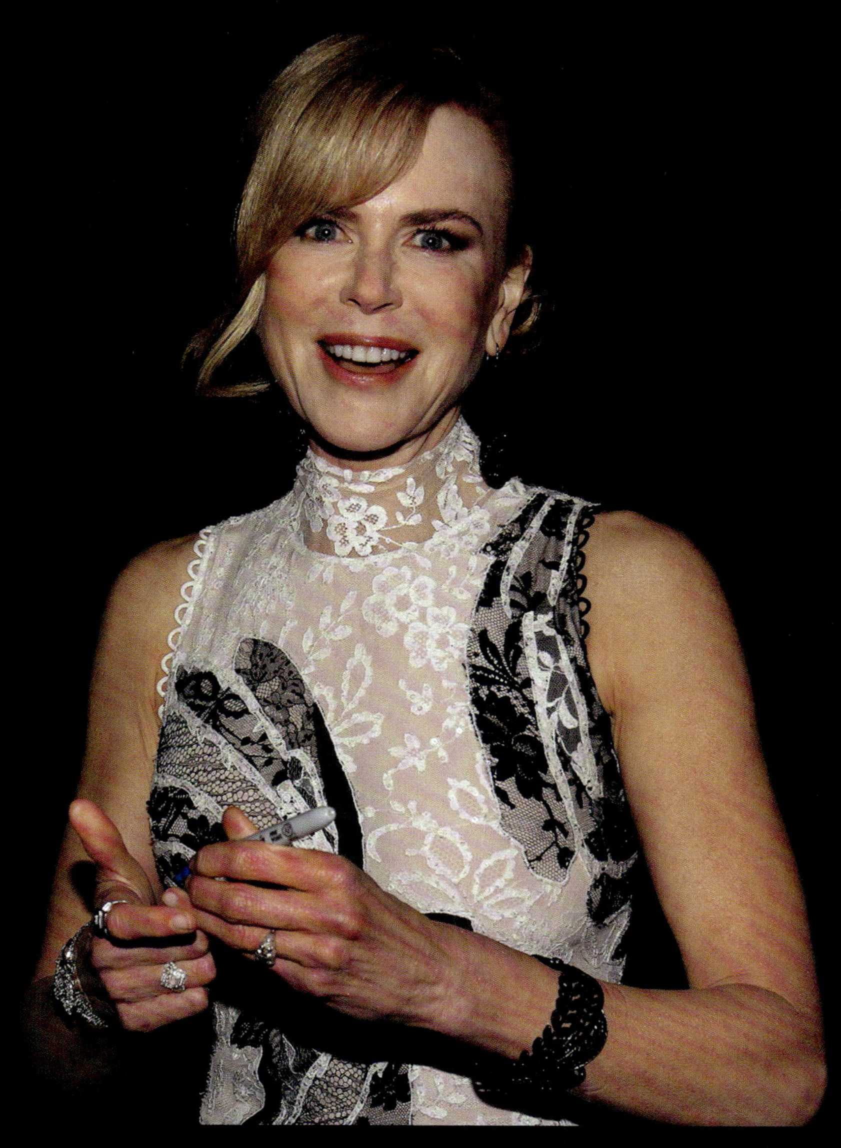

Sophia Loren
The Dorchester, Mayfair
November 2009
Leaving the party celebrating the release of a new issue of the Pirelli calendar

Nicole Kidman
The Old Vic theatre, Waterloo
November 2015
Leaving the Evening Standard Theatre Awards where she won Best Actress for her role in 'Photograph 51'

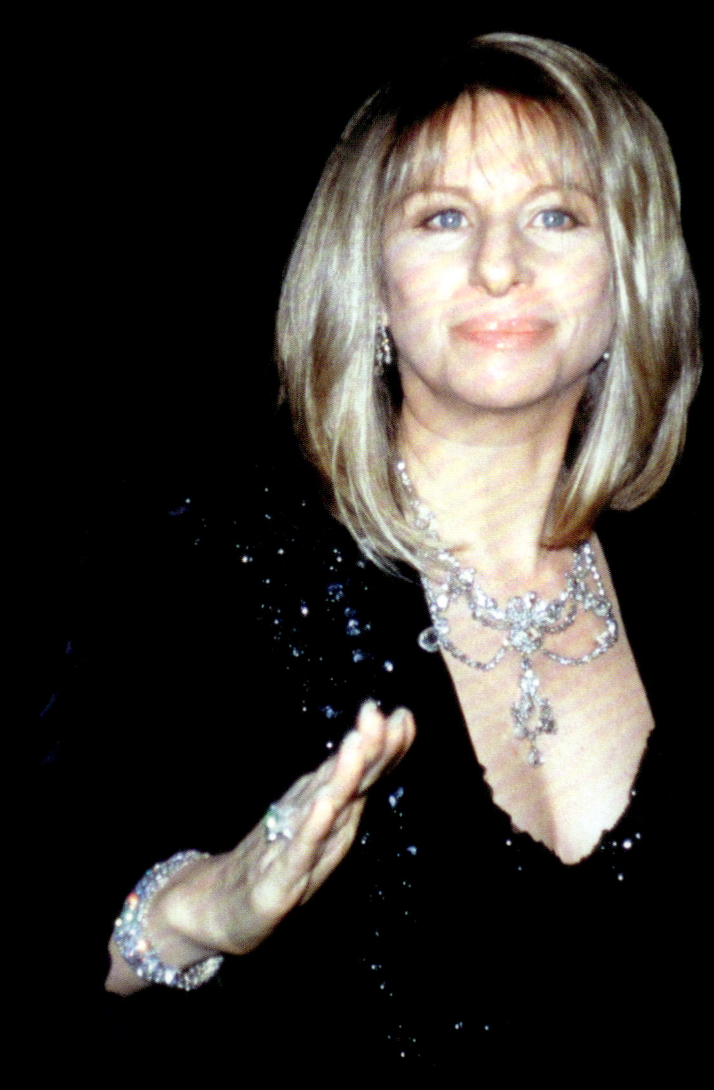

Barbra Streisand
Mirabelle, Mayfair
February 1992
London premiere for 'The Prince of Tides'

Robert Redford
The Ivy Soho
December 2005

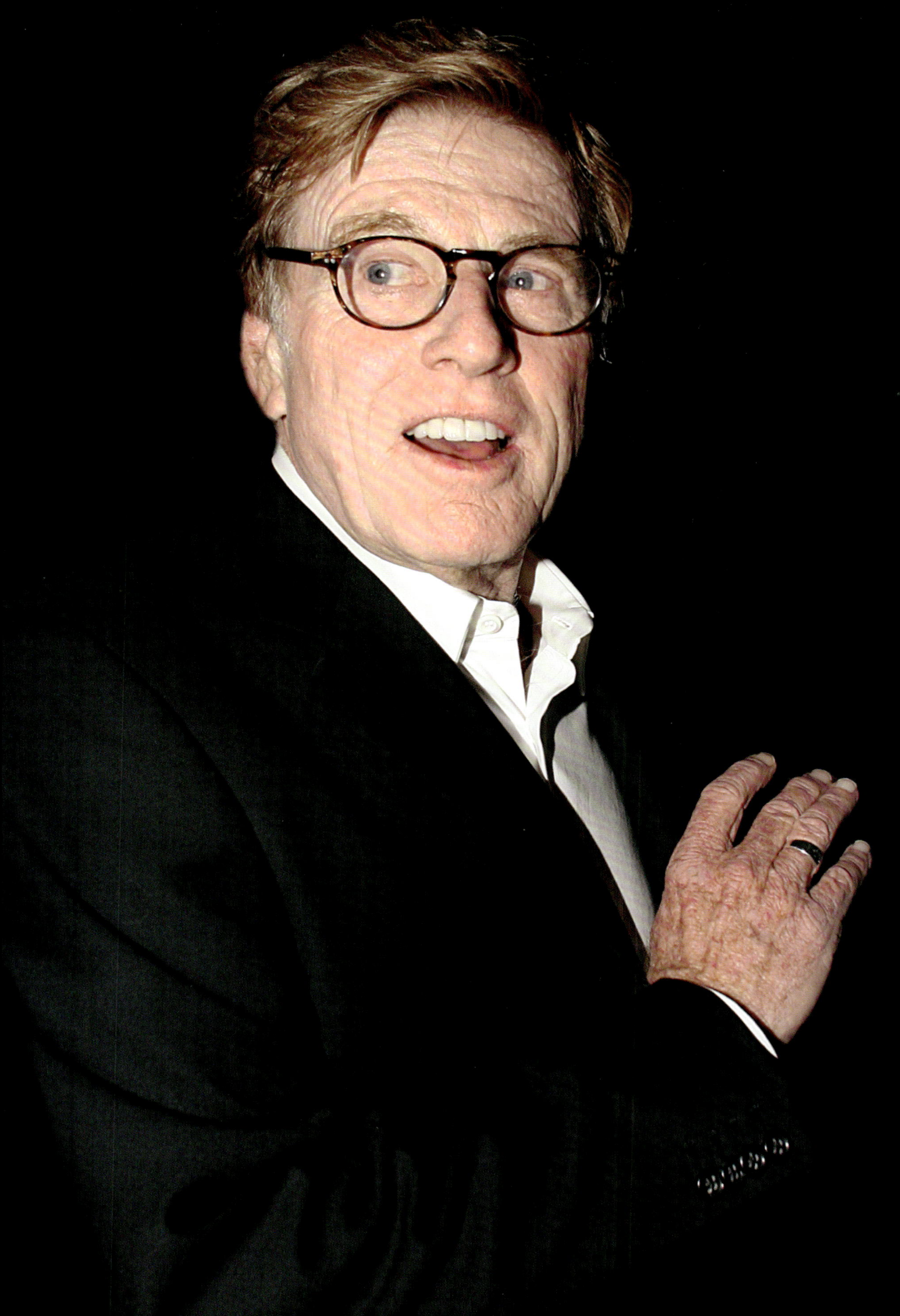

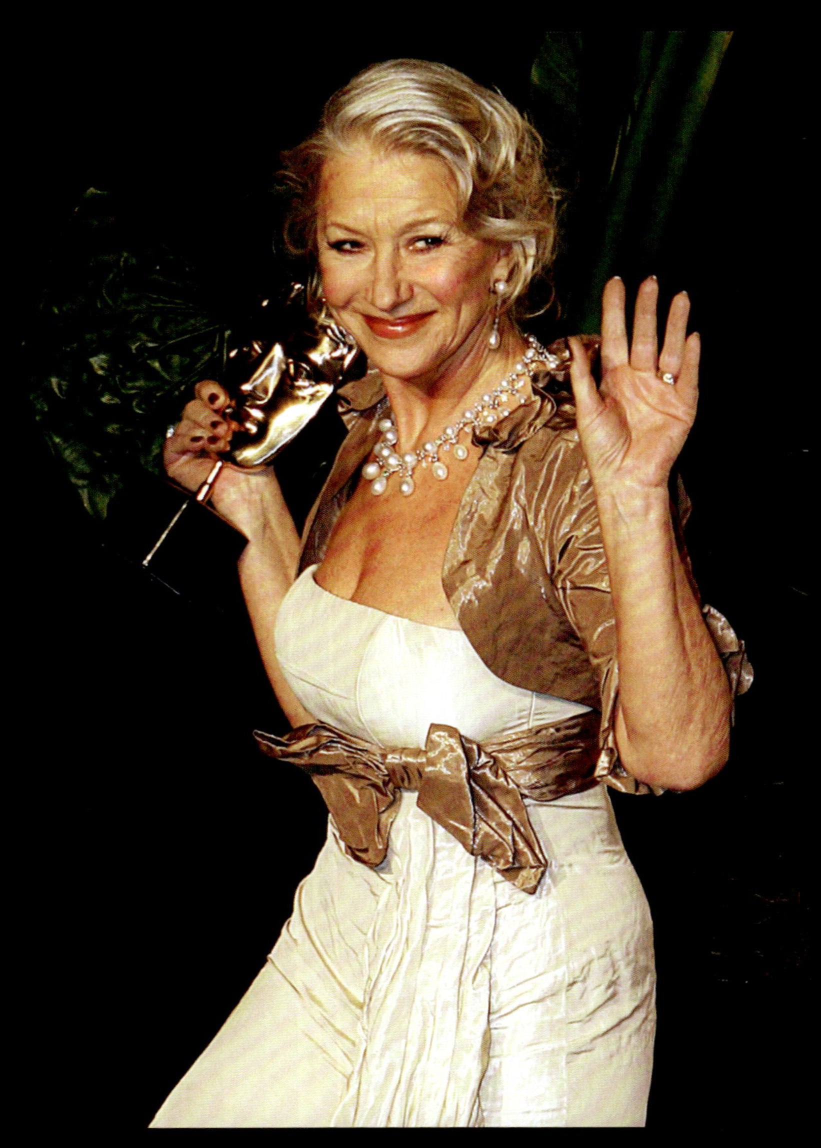

Dame Helen Mirren
Royal Opera House, Covent Garden
February 2007
After receiving her BAFTA for her role in 'The Queen'

Dame Judi Dench
Berkeley Square
November 2006
Afterparty for 'Casino Royale'

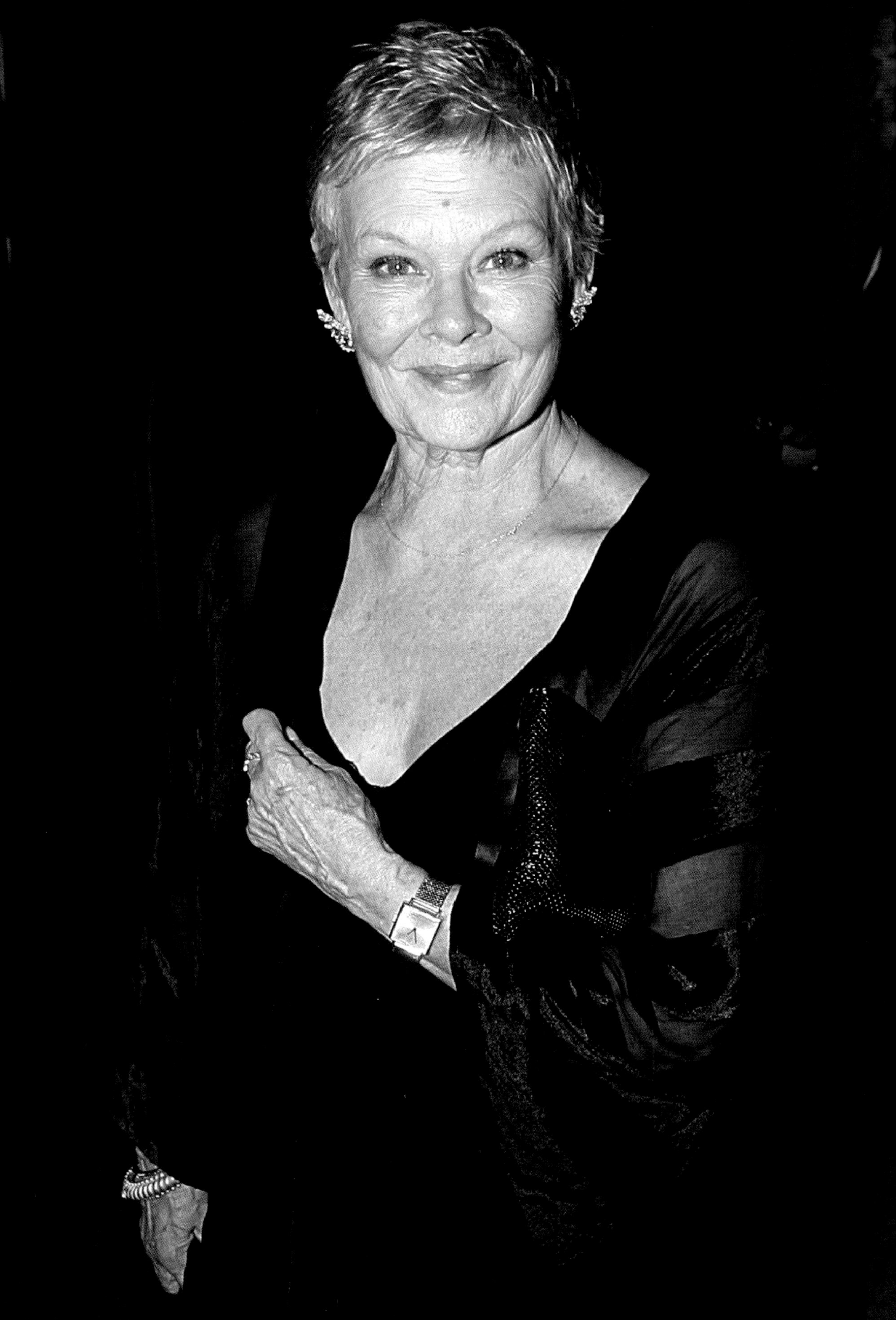

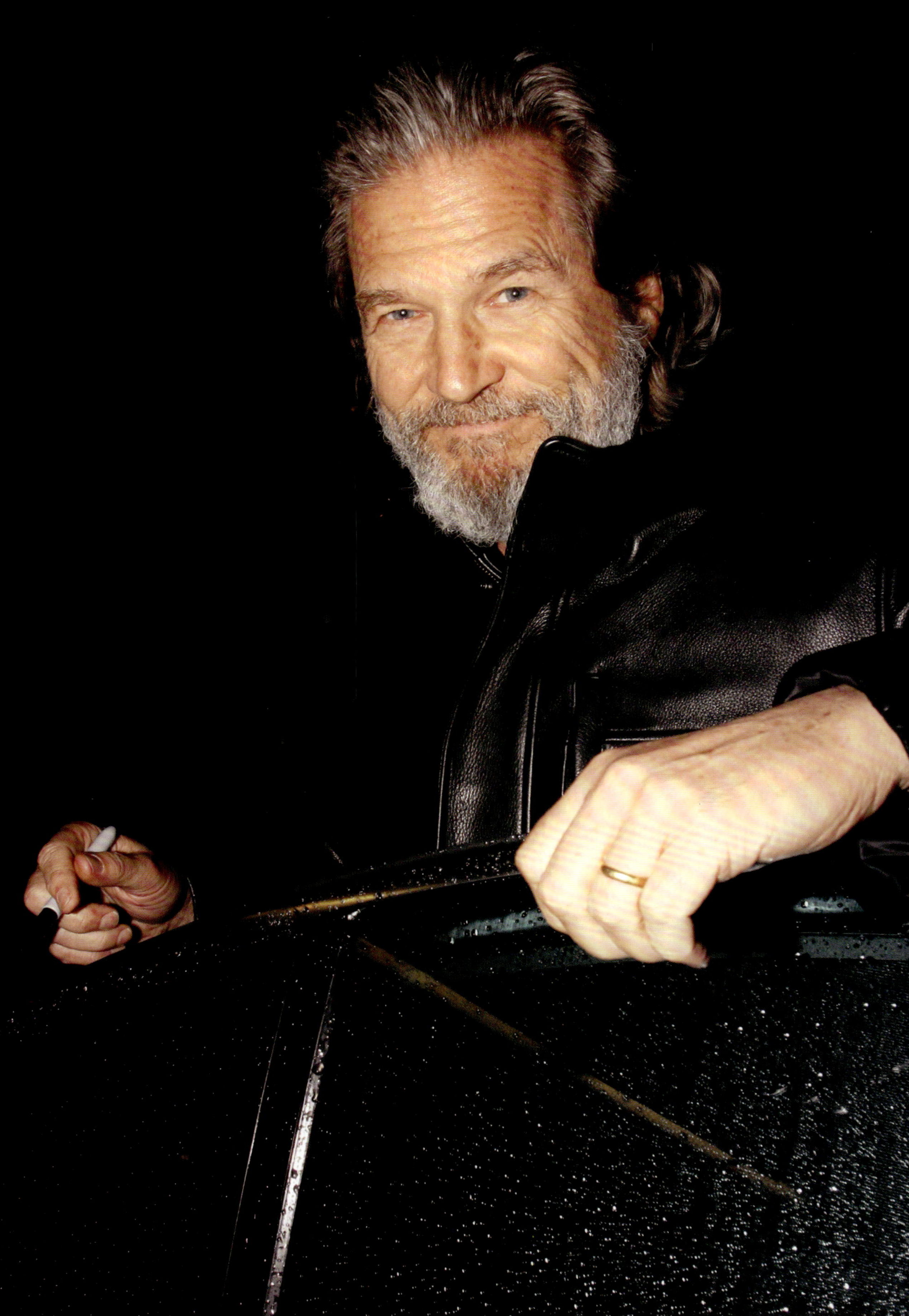

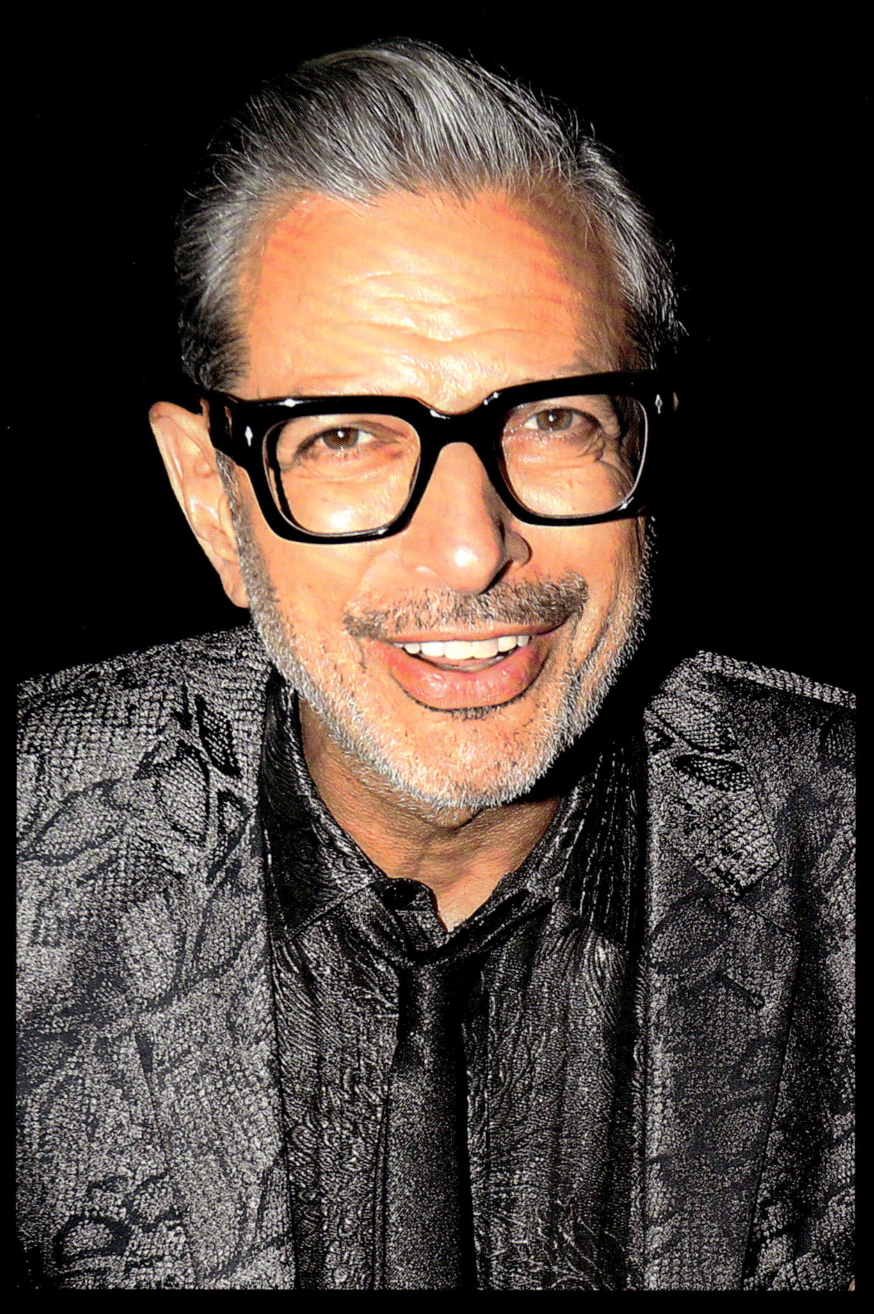

Jeff Bridges
Claridge's, Mayfair
December 2009
On his way to record 'The Graham Norton Show'

Jeff Goldblum
Corinthia Hotel London, Whitehall
October 2018

"I have an idea. How about I take a picture of you taking a picture of me?"

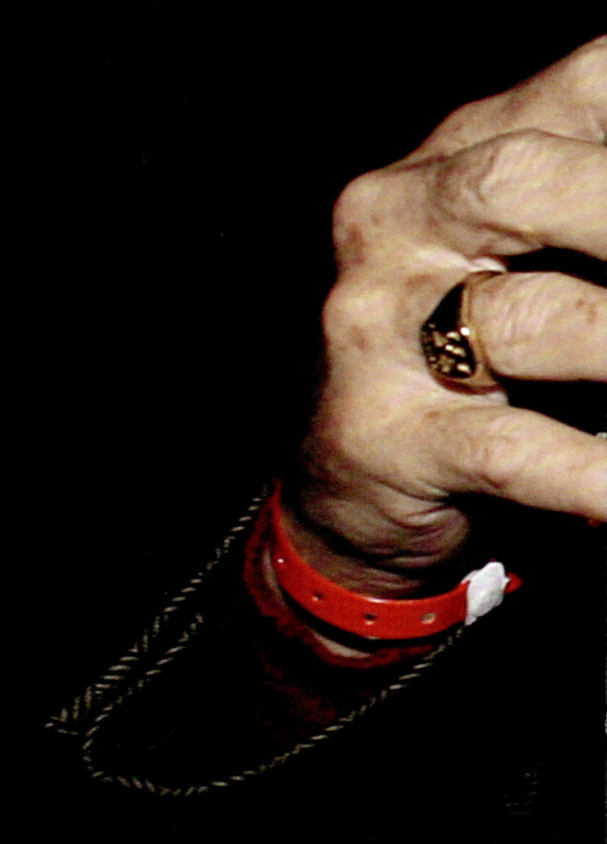

For this picture I found myself at Soho's The Shadow Lounge, ostensibly attending an art sale buzzing with whispers that the phantom of the contemporary art world, Banksy, might materialise. Everyone was scanning the room, speculating in hushed tones whether the artist had already infiltrated the crowd in some unassuming disguise. While the mysterious street artist never showed up, I can hardly call it a disappointing evening. Among the curated crowd of art collectors, culture vultures, and beautiful people whose profession seemed simply to be beautiful, I spotted a man whose presence immediately recontextualised the room: Dennis Hopper.

As a long-time admirer of Hopper's work, I seized the opportunity to approach him. What struck me immediately was the contrast between his screen presence and his actual being. He had none of the volatility, none of the wild-eyed chaos of his characters. Instead, his voice was gentle, almost musical in its soft articulation, and his attention was always on you rather than scanning the room for more important conversations. A familial connection gave me an easy way in – my father and uncles had walked the same high school hallways as Hopper in San Diego decades earlier. His eyes brightened with genuine interest when I mentioned this. "What

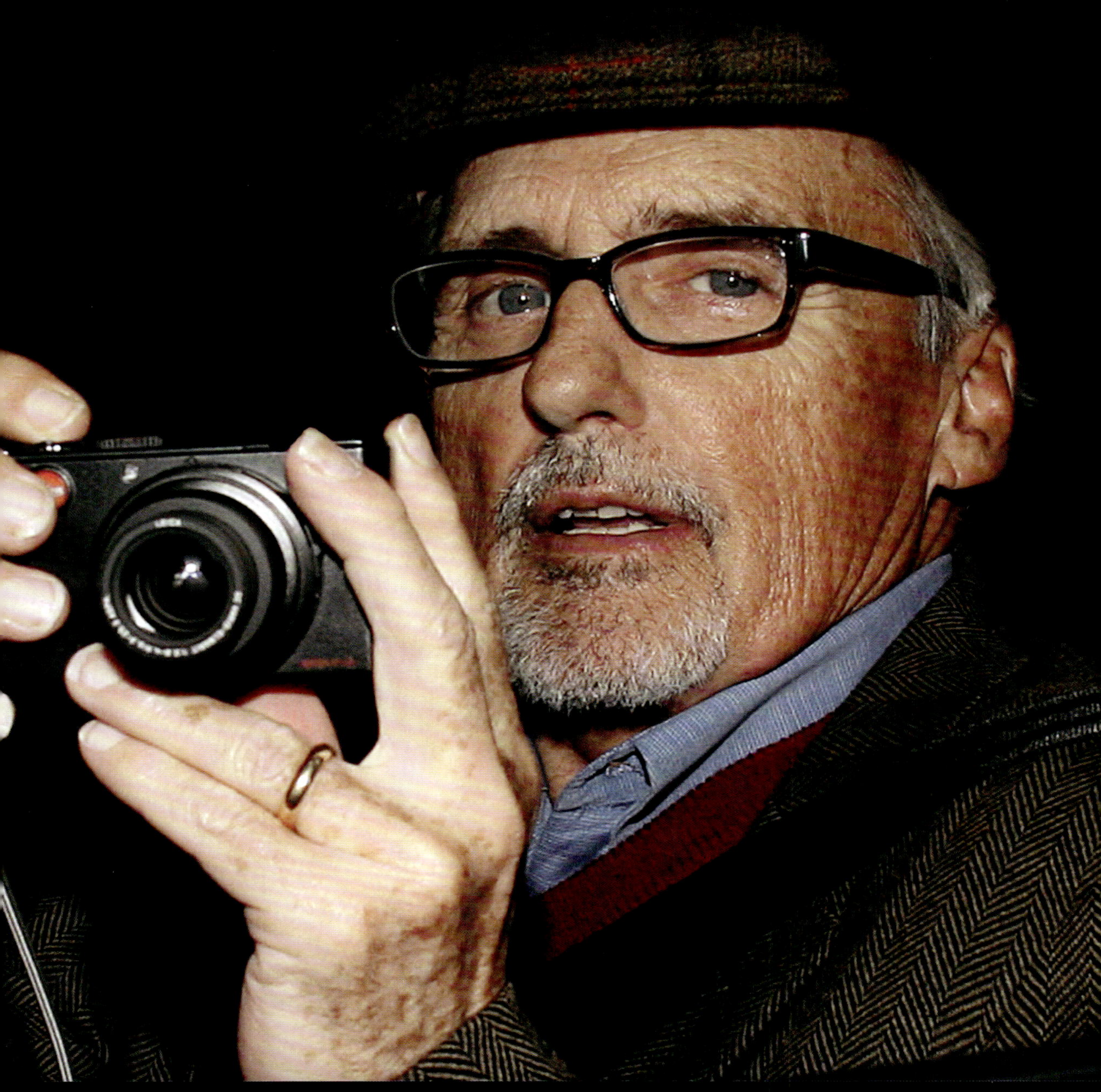

were their names?" he asked, and I could see nostalgia sparking across his features.

Our conversation naturally shifted to one of Hopper's greatest passions, one that ran parallel to his cinematic career but remained less known to the general public – photography. I expressed my admiration for his visual documentation of America's cultural upheavals in the 1960s: his iconic images of Martin Luther King Jr during the March on Washington; of Warhol and Fonda; of Paul Newman with that quiet, introspective stare. It was all about timing. About knowing when to be there.

As the evening wound towards its conclusion, with gallery assistants beginning the subtle choreography that signals closing time, Hopper prepared to leave. But first he paused, a playful spark animating his gaze, and suggested something unexpected: "I have an idea. How about I take a picture of you taking a picture of me? You can send it to both me and your father."

This was the result. I love it for how meta it is – the photographer becomes the subject, the observer the observed, and all filters of celebrity momentarily dissolve in service of a shared creative impulse.

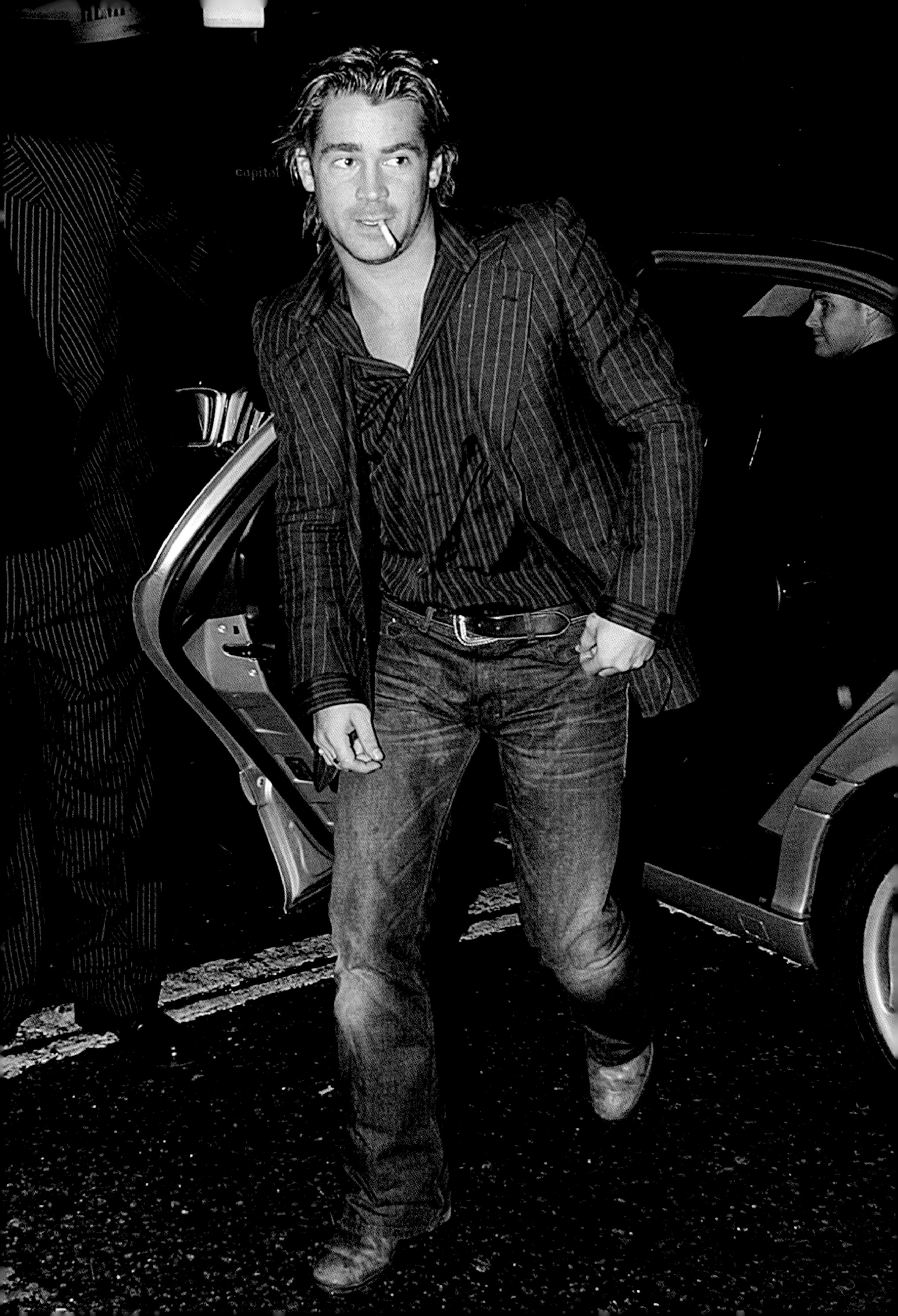

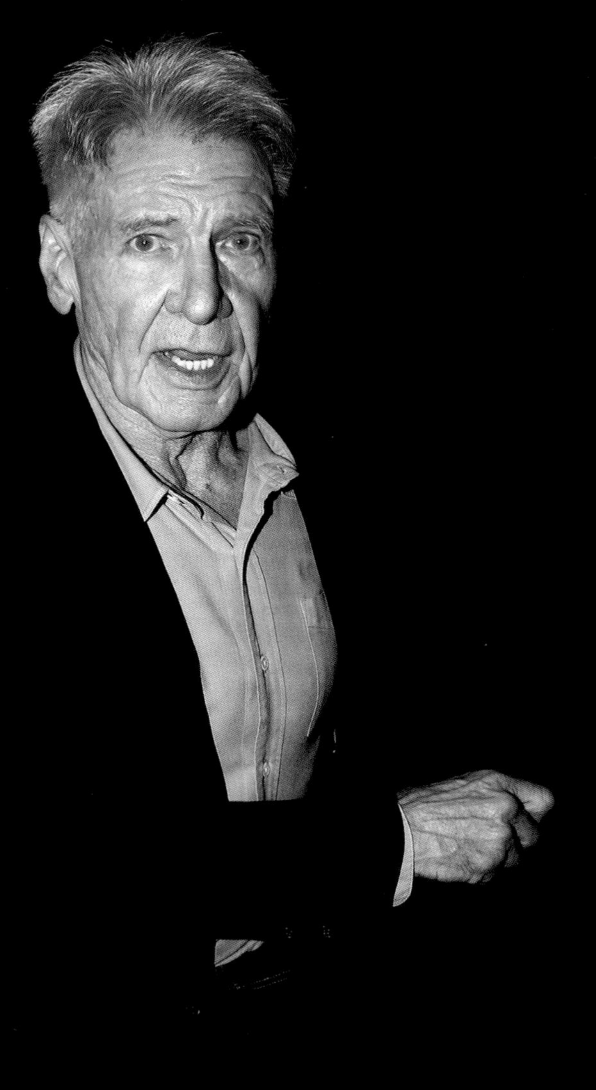

Colin Farrell
Annabel's, Mayfair
November 2003
Afterparty for the London premiere of 'Intermission'

Harrison Ford
Kai Mayfair
June 2023

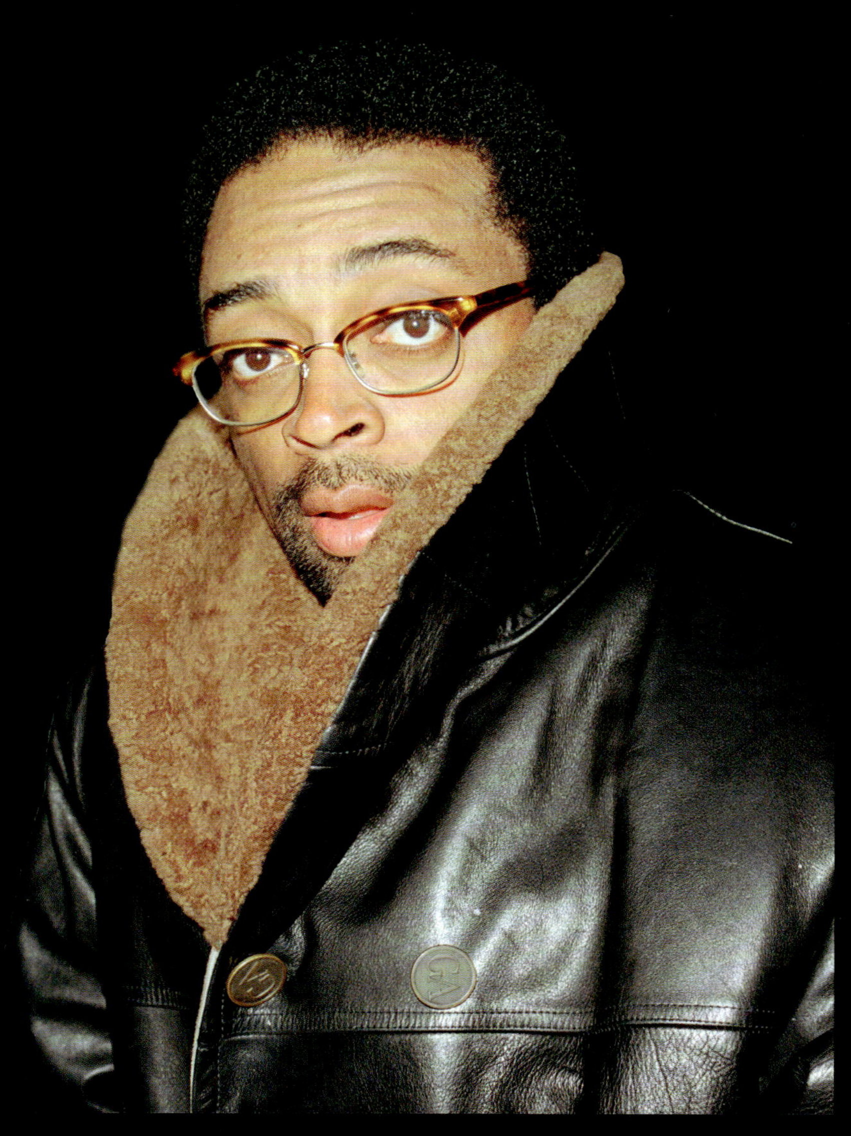

Spike Lee
The Ivy, Covent Garden
December 1998

Laurence Fishburne
Hyde Park Hotel, Knightsbridge
September 1993

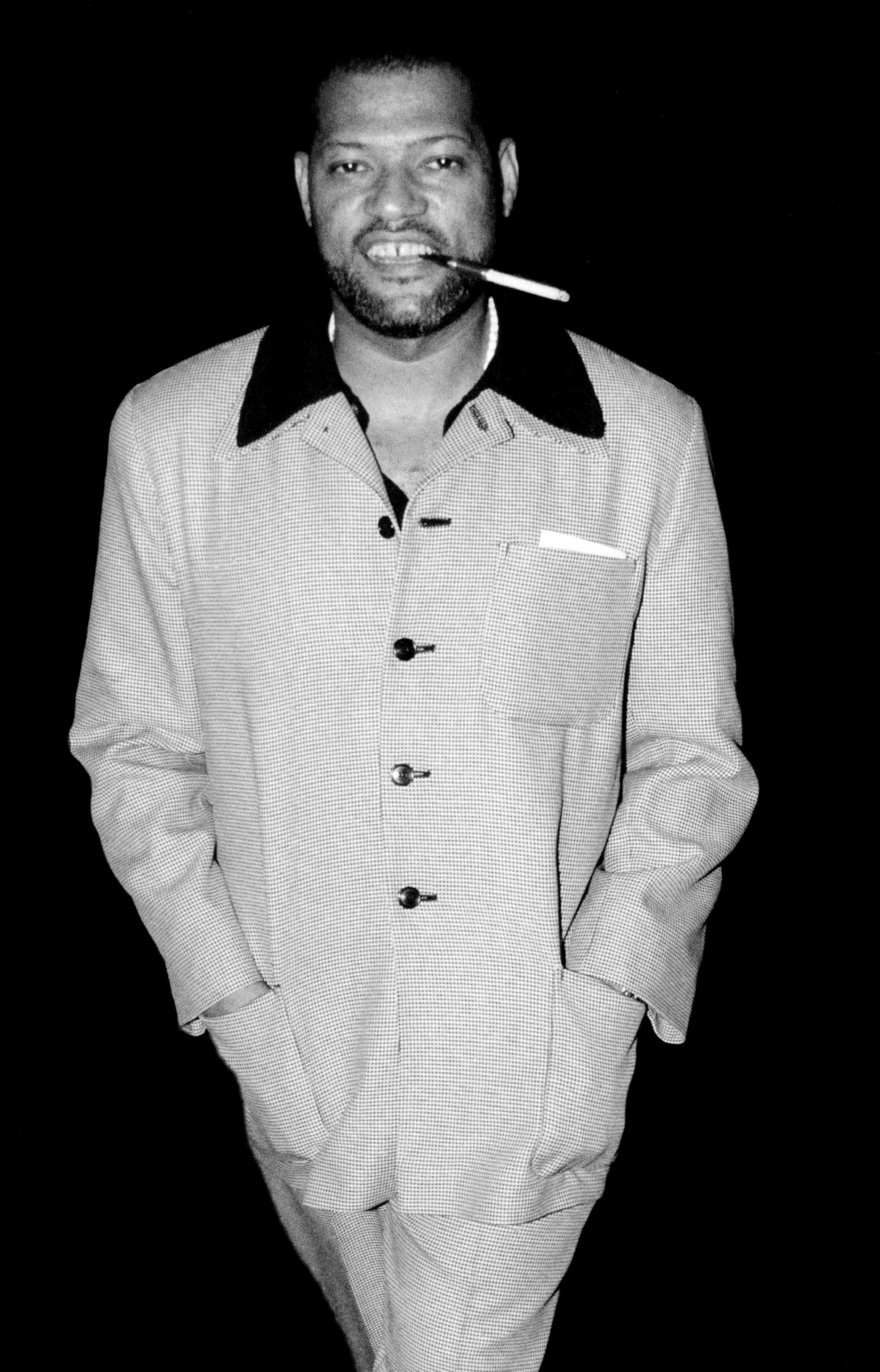

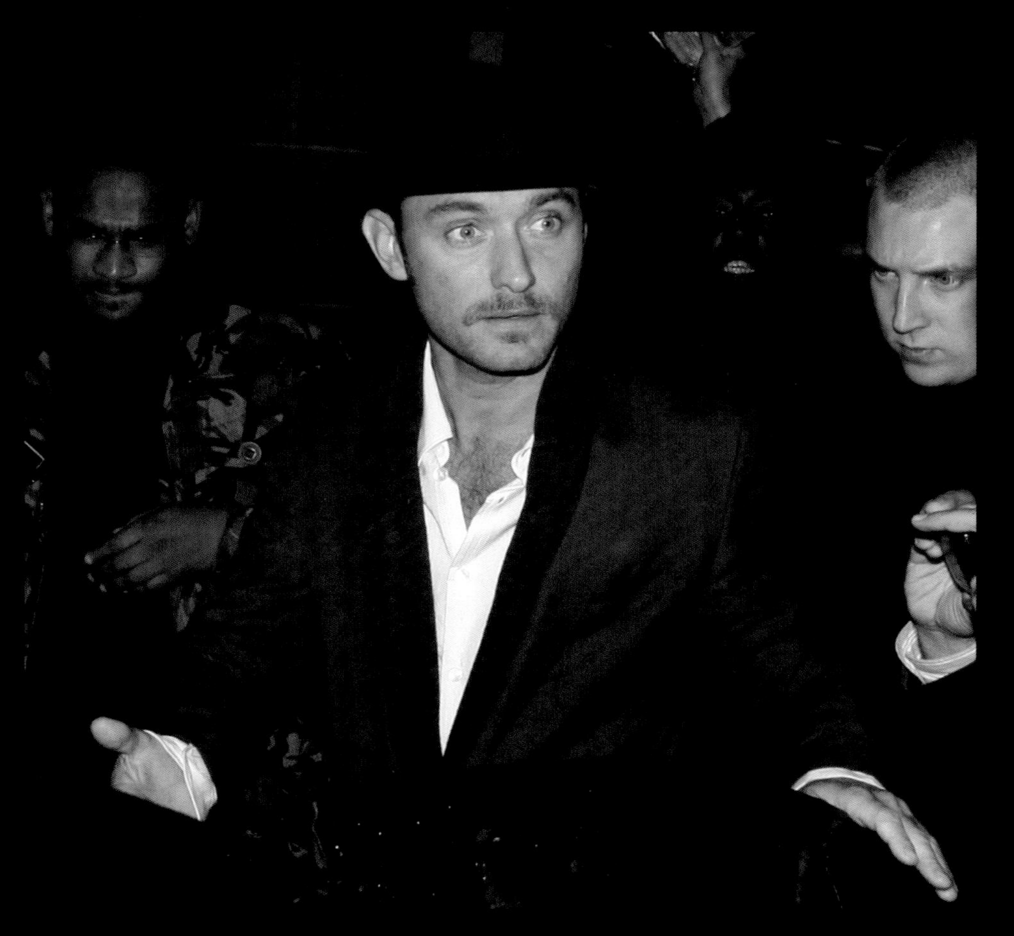

Jude Law
Cipriani, Mayfair
September 2010
Dinner with Sienna Miller

Daniel Craig
Scott's, Mayfair
October 2005
Taken the day before he was announced as the new James Bond

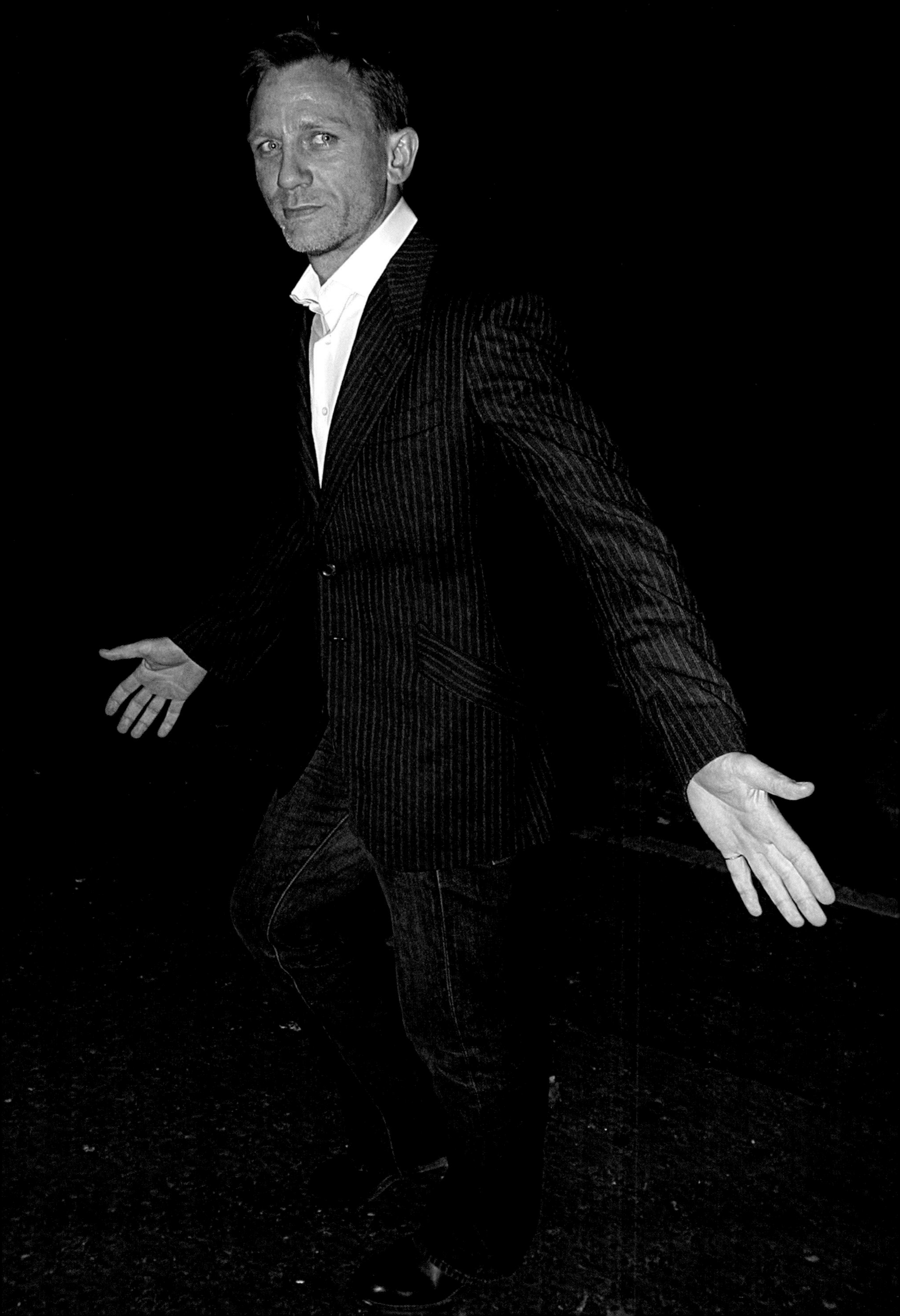

HARVEY KEITEL

February 2008

"He broke into a wide smile, pressed his lips to the cold glass of the window and blew a playful kiss."

The Royal Albert Hall shimmered like an amber jewel in London's February darkness, its neoclassical columns aglow for the BAFTAs – British cinema's top night for polished shoes and speeches. As always, I was there among the press pack, camera strapped around my neck, tasked with immortalising the procession of stars as they navigated the red-carpet gauntlet.

Among the constellation of celebrities expected that evening, there was one name that particularly resonated with me: Harvey Keitel, the Hollywood classic. From *Mean Streets* (1973) to *Reservoir Dogs* (1992), Keitel had built a career on characters whose emotional wounds were visible just beneath the skin – a photographer's dream subject.

Despite the excitement, the evening did not unfold as I had hoped. Due to a mix-up with my press credentials, I found myself on the wrong side of the red carpet. This bureaucratic hiccup quickly became photographic quicksand for me as I watched, helplessly stationed behind the wrong barrier, as Keitel made his entrance on the opposite side. However, I wasn't ready to accept defeat. Experience had taught me that red carpets were generally just the opening act; as with most of these events, there's always a second chance to catch up with your favourite celebrities at the after-party, which in this case was at the Grosvenor House Hotel. I arrived there breathless and slightly dishevelled, a regular consequence of navigating the congested arteries of London. I caught sight of Keitel through a glass partition, mingling with the other guests. As he began descending the staircase, moving further from my sphere of influence with each step, an idea took shape. I positioned myself outside a large window that offered a direct line of sight, raised my camera, and did something no photography school teaches: I knocked on the glass, much like a kid at an aquarium.

Keitel turned, momentarily startled, his eyes finding mine. What happened next transcended all expectation. To my astonishment, he broke into a wide smile, pressed his lips to the cold glass of the window and blew a playful kiss in my direction, before recoiling with laughter. It was spontaneous, ridiculous, and utterly perfect. That brief, impromptu interaction resulted in a photograph that was picked up by numerous publications the following day, turning what could have been a disappointing night into a career highlight.

In the end, Harvey Keitel proved to be quite the sport, and not such a bad lieutenant after all.

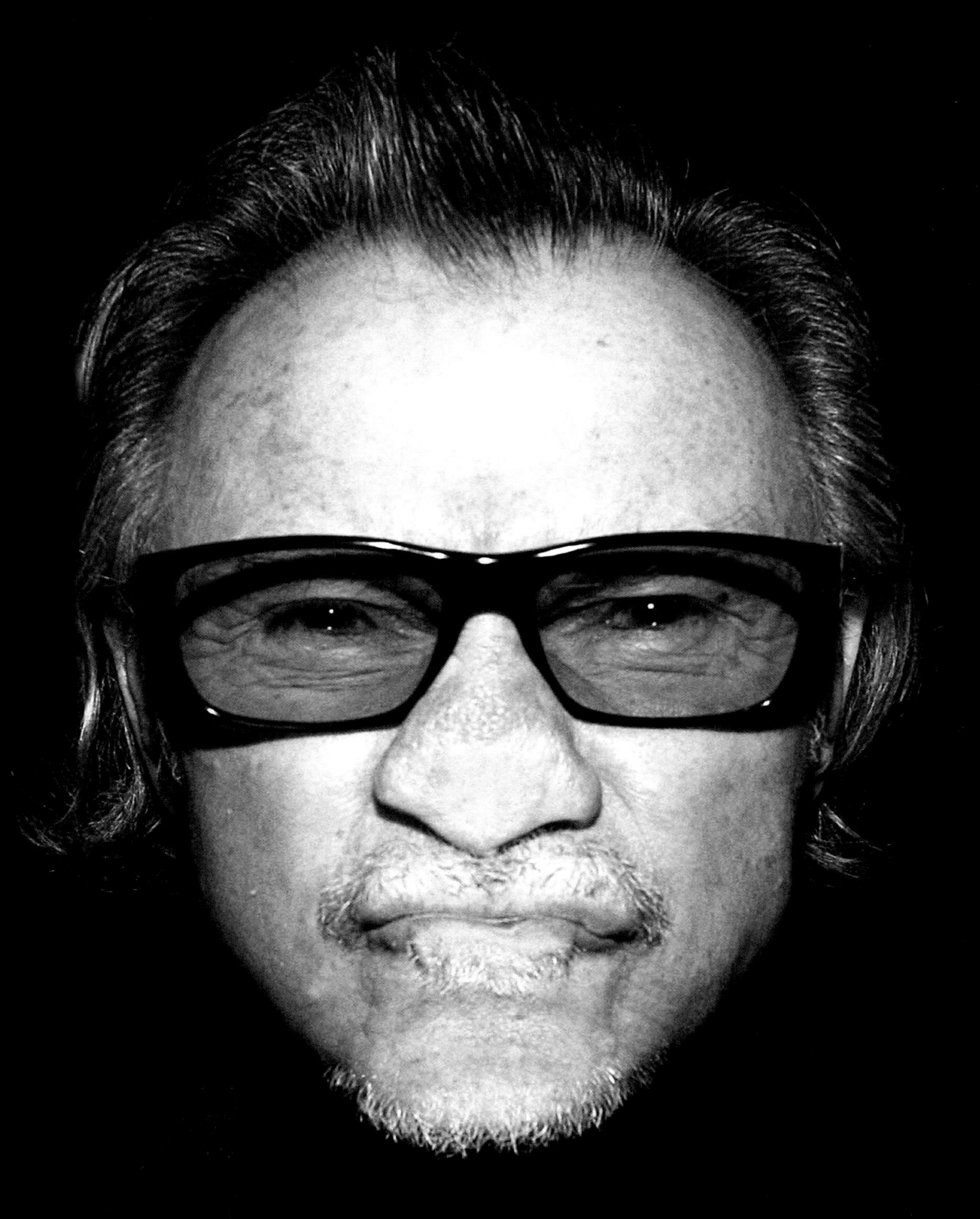

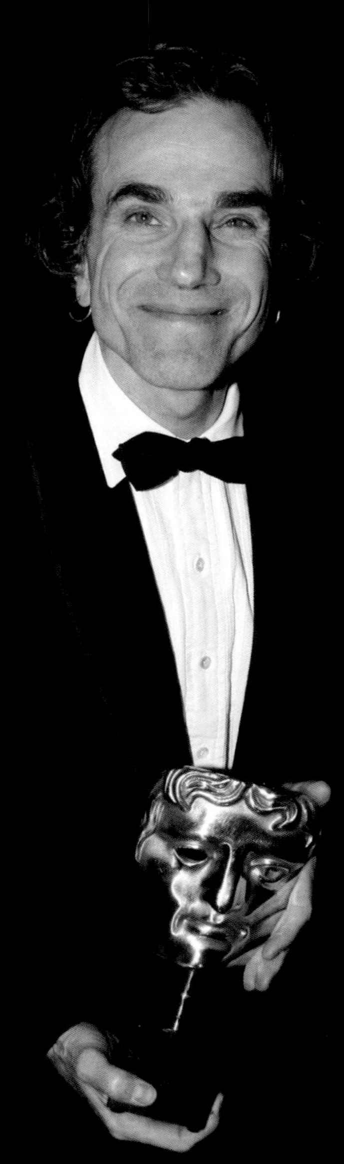

Daniel Day-Lewis
Grosvenor House Hotel, Mayfair
February 2008
BAFTA afterparty, celebrating his win for his role in 'There Will Be Blood'

Tilda Swinton
Grosvenor House Hotel, Mayfair
February 2008
BAFTA afterparty, celebrating her win for her role in 'Michael Clayton'

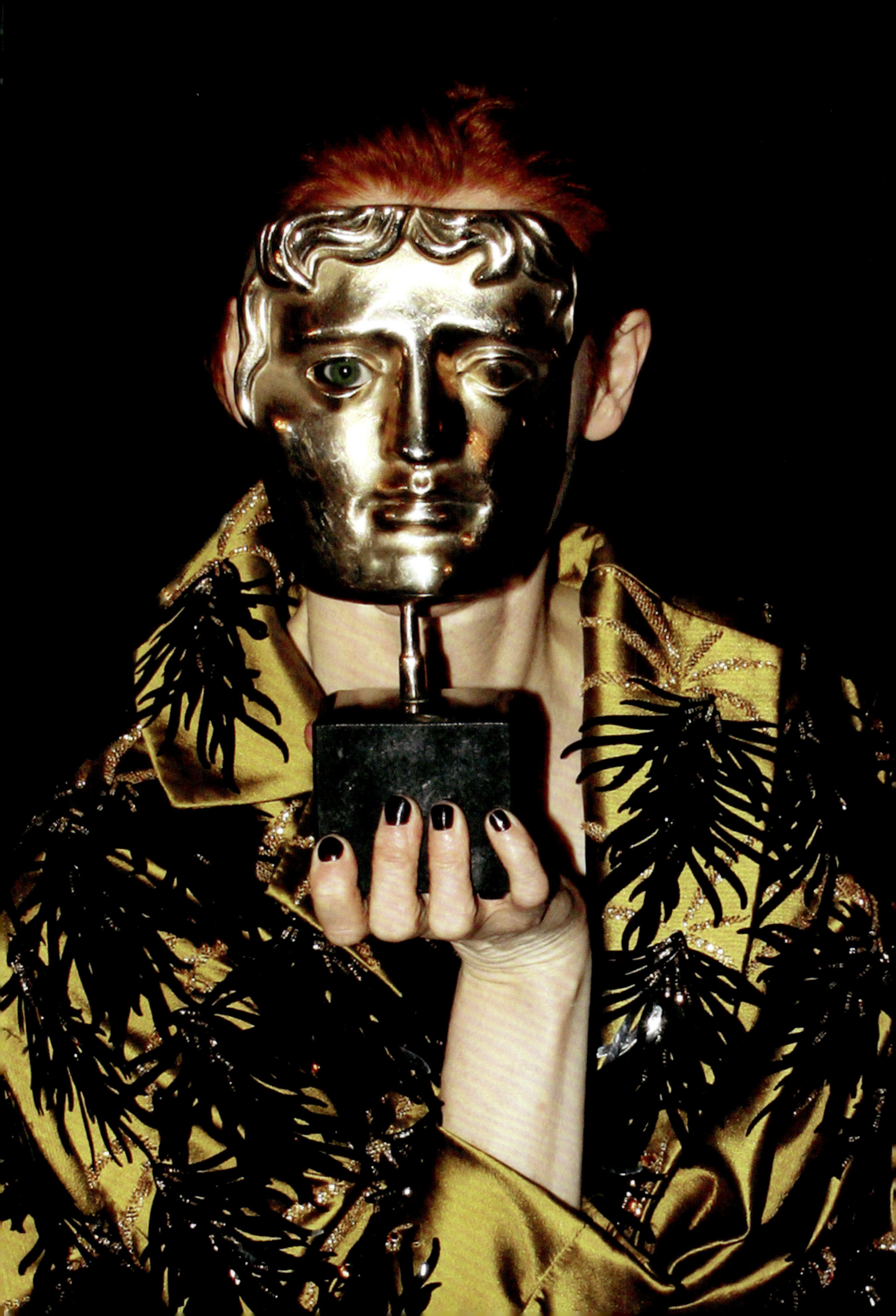

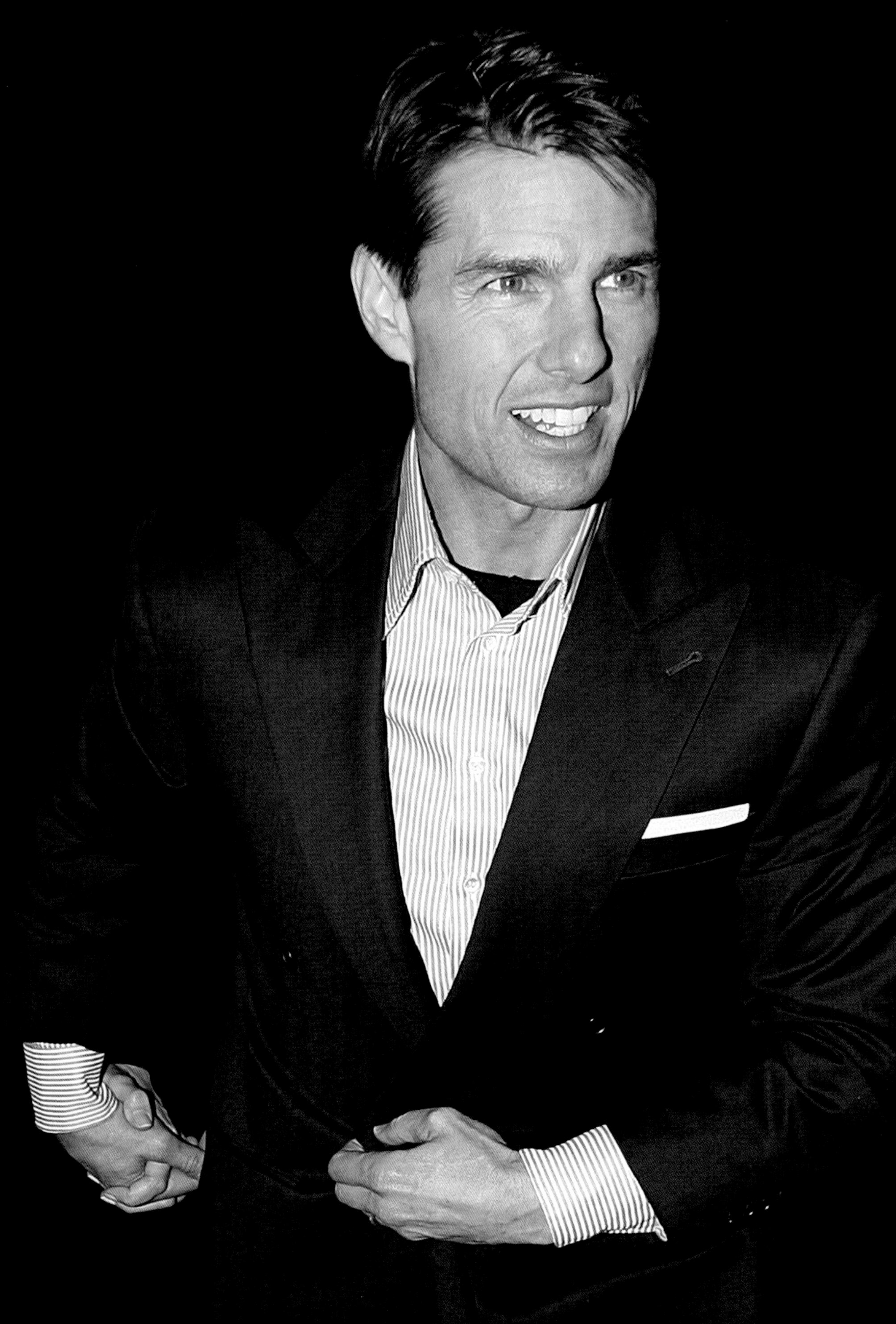

TOM CRUISE
September 1998

Some stars shine, then fade. But a rare few seem stitched into the very fabric of cinema itself, as if they were never meant for anything else. Tom Cruise is one of those. He doesn't just make movies. He is movies. And after decades of photographing him, catching glimpses of his life through my lens and from the pavement's edge, I can say this with certainty: Tom Cruise is exactly what we all hope our idols might be – warm, generous, and unfailingly human, even in spite of his position as fame incarnate.

My first time photographing him was at the *Far and Away* (1992) premiere in Leicester Square. He and wife-at-the-time Nicole Kidman met Princess Diana that night – royalty greeting royalty, in a way. They made space for everyone around them. And the cameras, mine included, couldn't help but follow.

The Ivy was London's North Star in the '90s. On any given night, you'd walk in and spot two, three, sometimes a dozen world-famous faces. Tom was a regular, and so was Nicole. One time, they were in the thick of filming Stanley Kubrick's fever dream, *Eyes Wide Shut* (1999). They were staying just down the road at The Dorchester, yet for all the mystique, Tom didn't vanish behind tinted windows or bodyguards. He stepped out. He strolled. He signed everything. You'd see him gently laughing as he chatted with someone's mum on the phone; or hear him record a voicemail for a stranger's answering machine. "Hi, this is Tom Cruise – leave a message after the tone." It was surreal, sincere, and weirdly comforting. He knew what it meant to people. And he leaned into it, not out of obligation, but joy.

Another of my favourite memories is from an unassuming Italian restaurant. He stepped out with Russell Crowe and Iain Glen, long before Glen's role as Ser Jorah Mormont in *Game of Thrones* (2011–19). The three of them were laughing like schoolboys and playing to the lens as if the night was theirs alone. I even have an image somewhere of Tom grinning as he grabbed my camera and snapped a photo of me for once.

Over the years, I have photographed him more times than I can count. Decades have passed, but something in him has remained fixed – not ageless, not untouched by time, but somehow unchanged in spirit. Just recently, I saw him again, helicopter blades carving the air above Battersea. He flew himself in, because of course he did. Who else but Maverick would pilot his own chopper into London, soaring over traffic like a blockbuster lead chasing daylight?

> *"Tom has always understood the contract of celebrity, but he's never treated it like a burden."*

Because here's the thing: Tom has always understood the contract of celebrity, but he's never treated it like a burden. He wears it like a second skin – one he crafted himself through sheer will and relentless devotion to the spectacle of cinema. He's the last of a dying breed of true icons in film. There are actors, there are celebrities, and then there is Tom, still spinning across the sky like a comet that will never burn out. There may be louder stars now, and newer ones, and stars built to vanish in a season. But for me, there's never been anyone quite like him. He's the last one standing. And the truth is, he never sat down.

Denzel Washington
Curzon cinema, Mayfair
November 2007
After a screening of 'American Gangster'

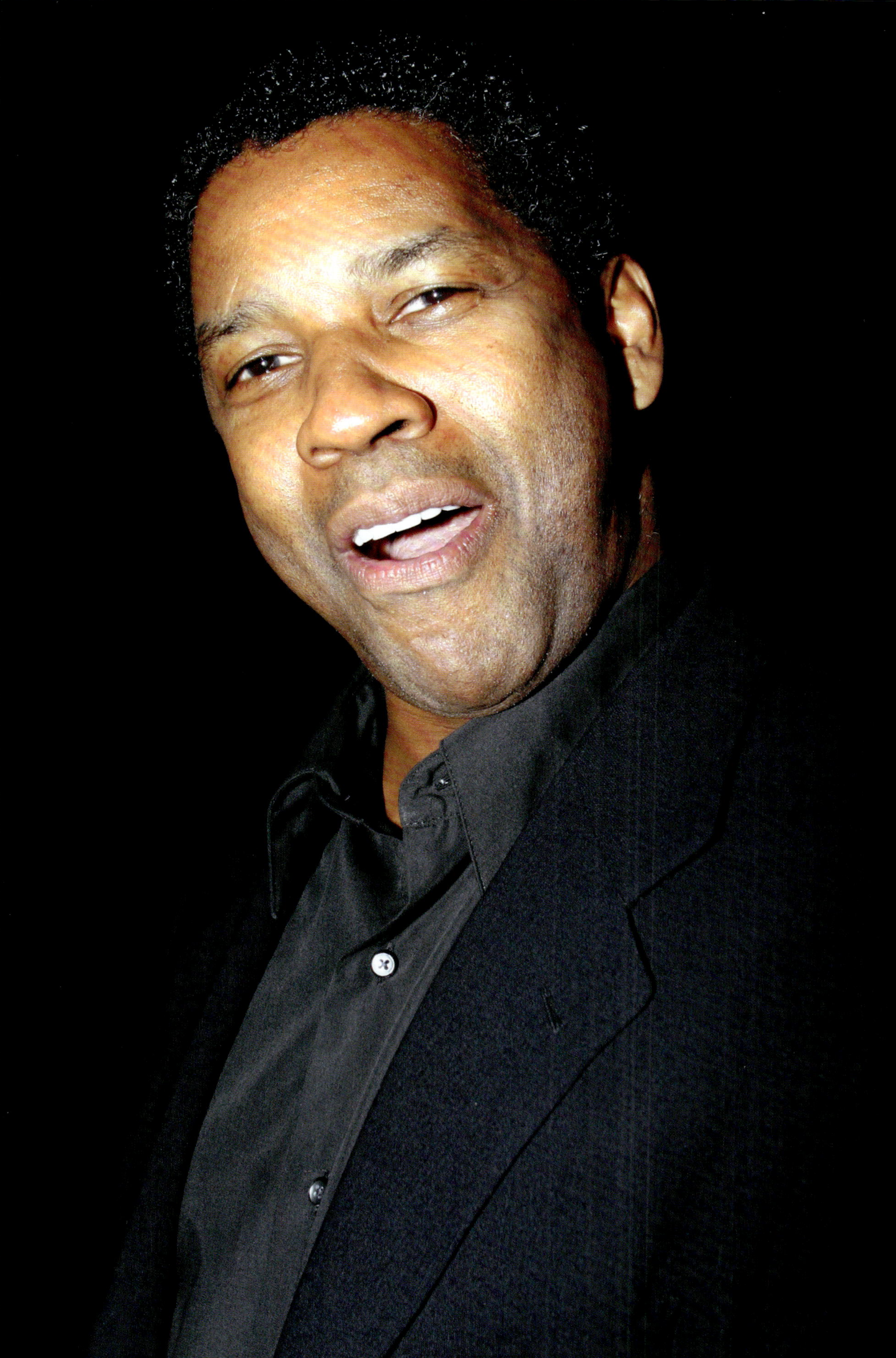

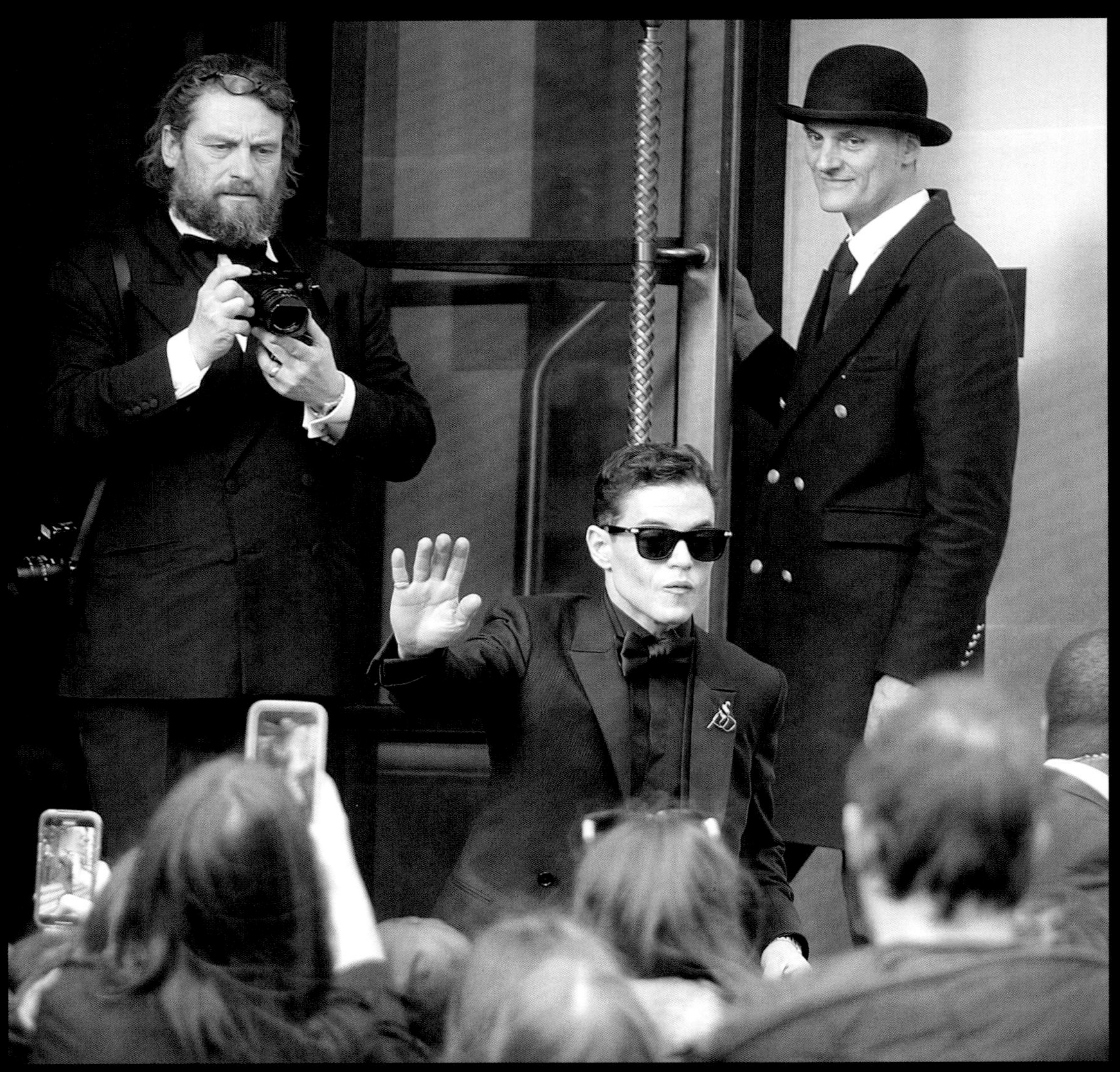

Rami Malek
Corinthia Hotel London, Whitehall
February 2024
On his way to the BAFTAs

Pedro Pascal
London Palladium, Soho
July 2025
After watching 'Evita' starring Rachel Zegler

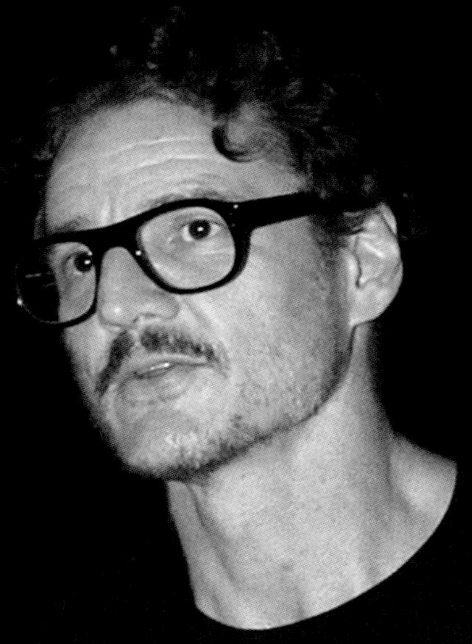

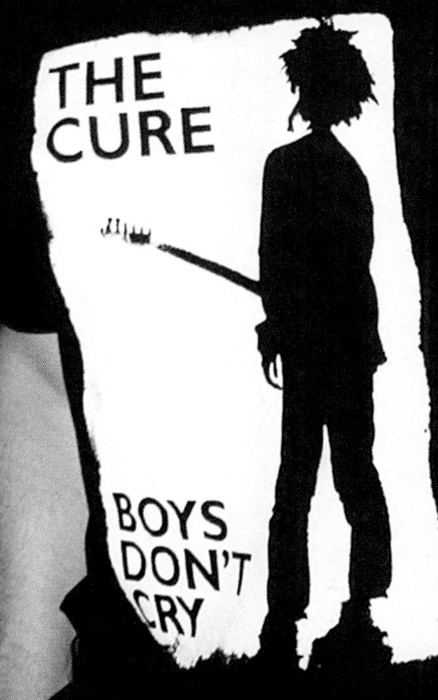
THE
CURE
BOYS
DON'T
CRY

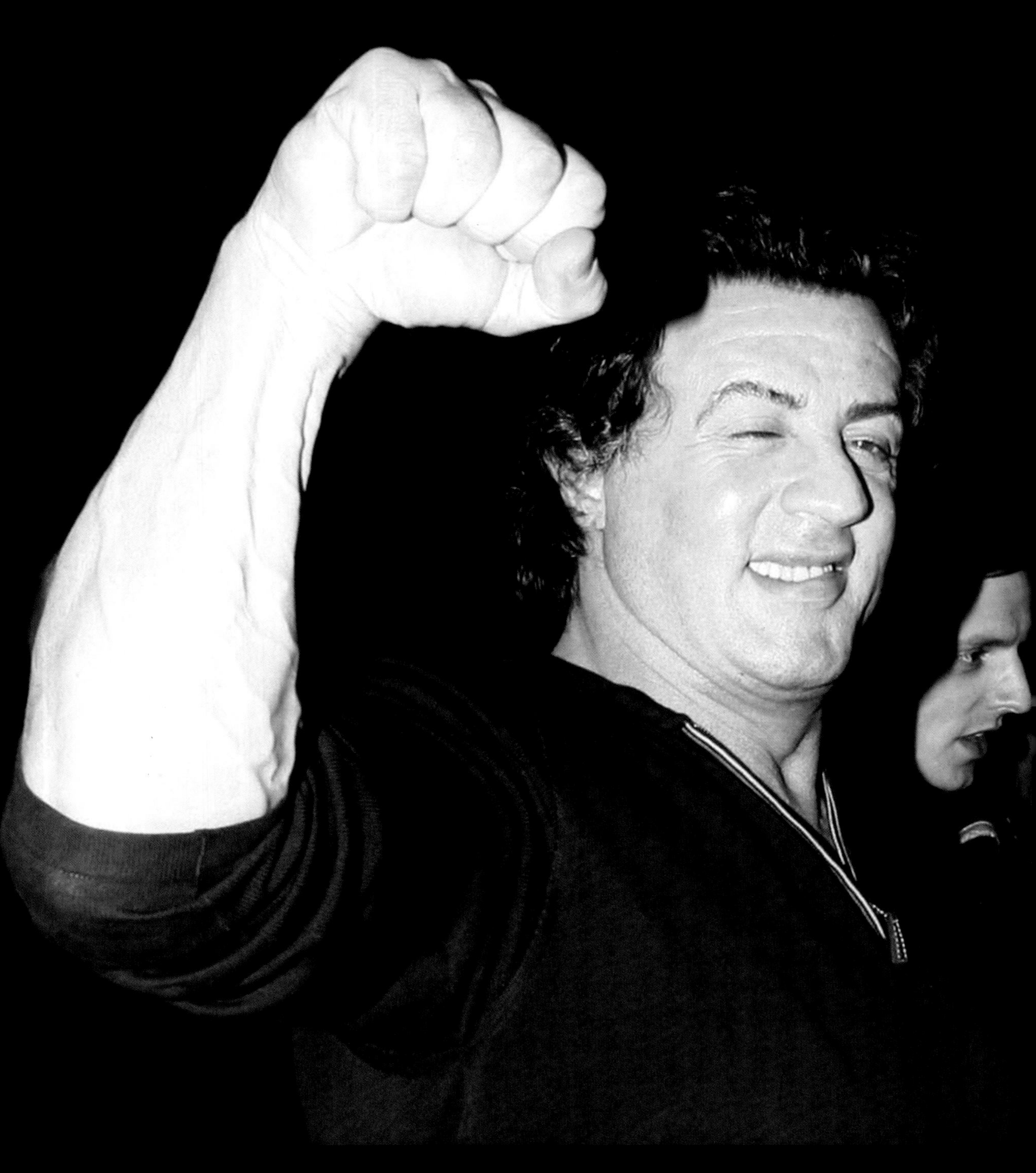

Sylvester Stallone
The Dorchester, Mayfair
March 2005

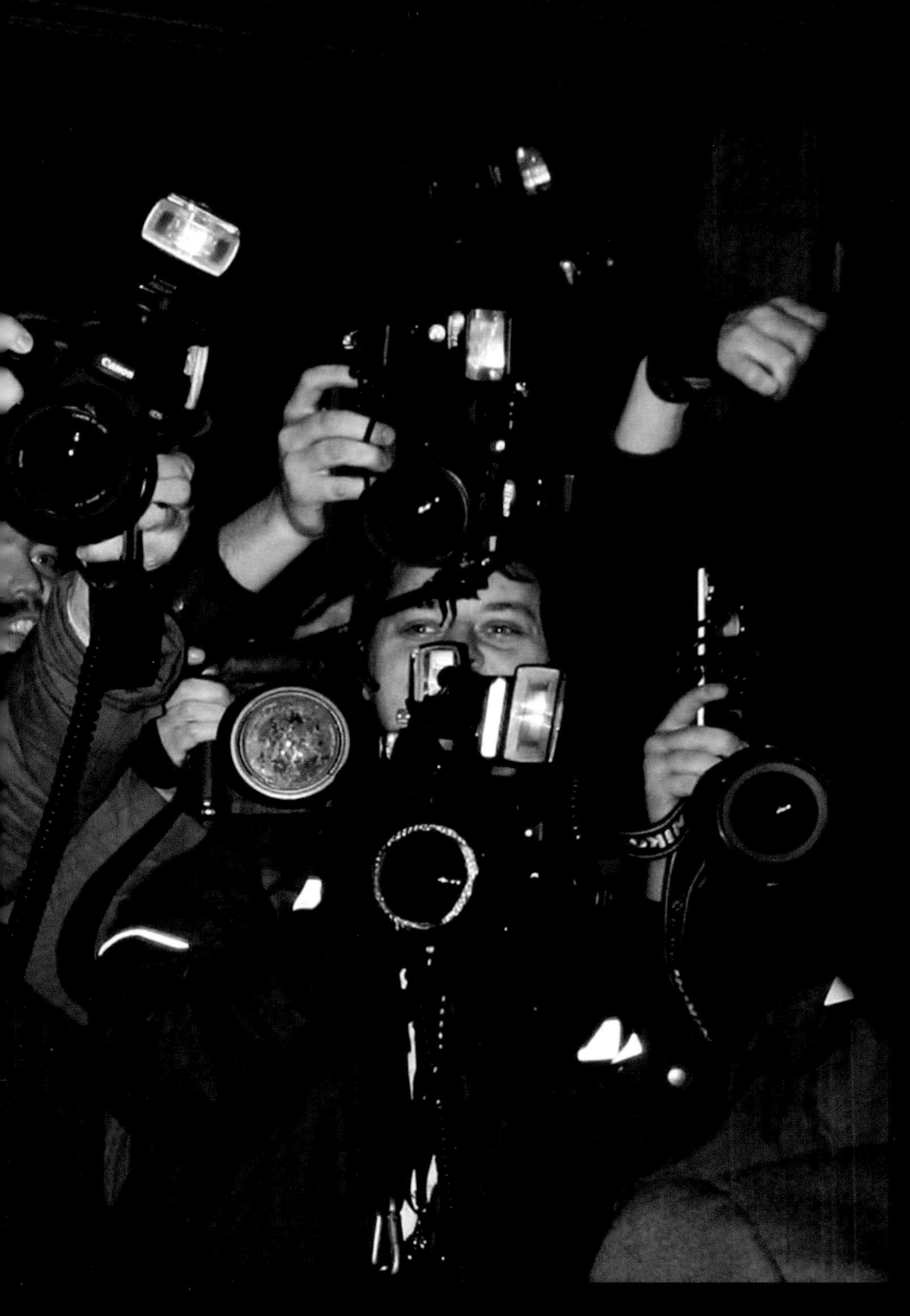

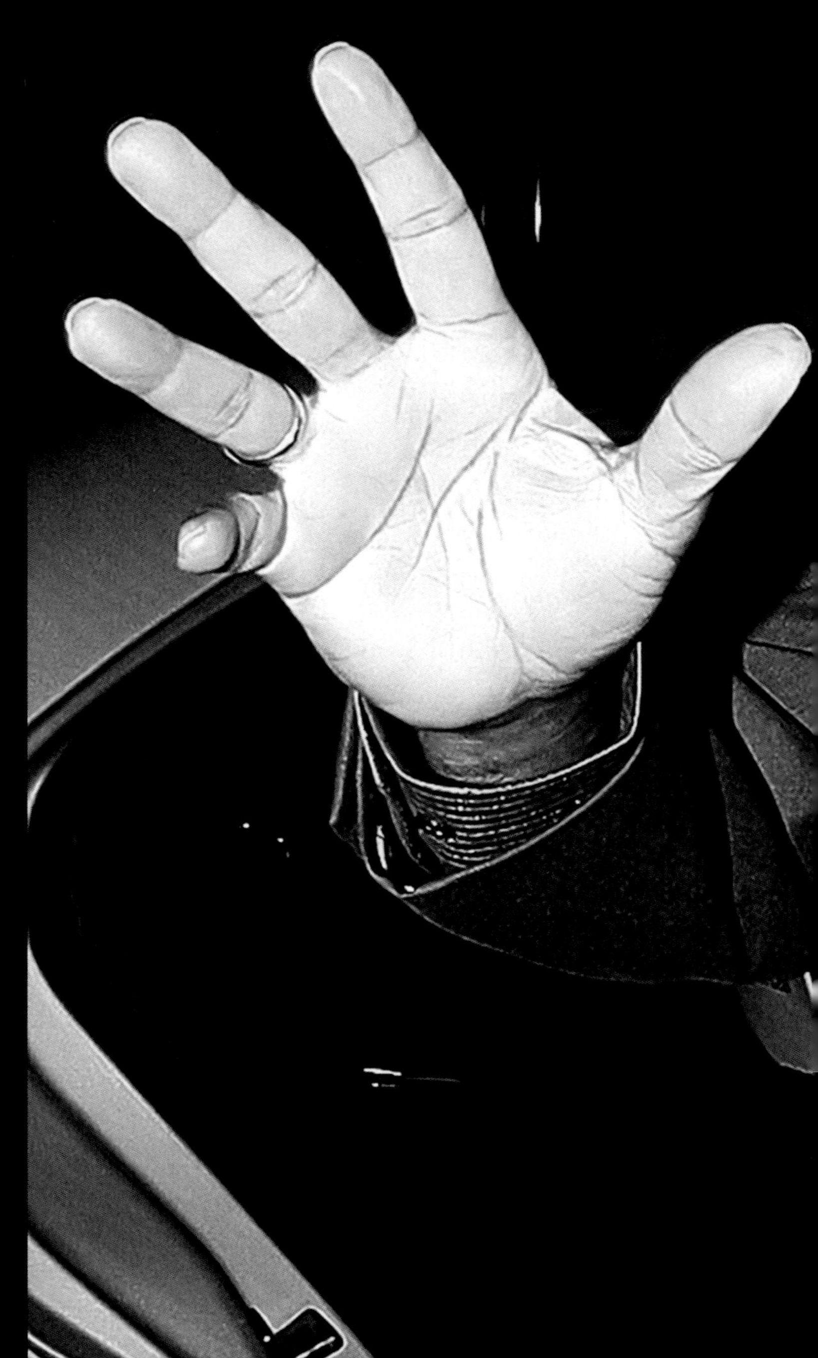

Morgan Freeman
The Ivy, Covent Garden
January 2008

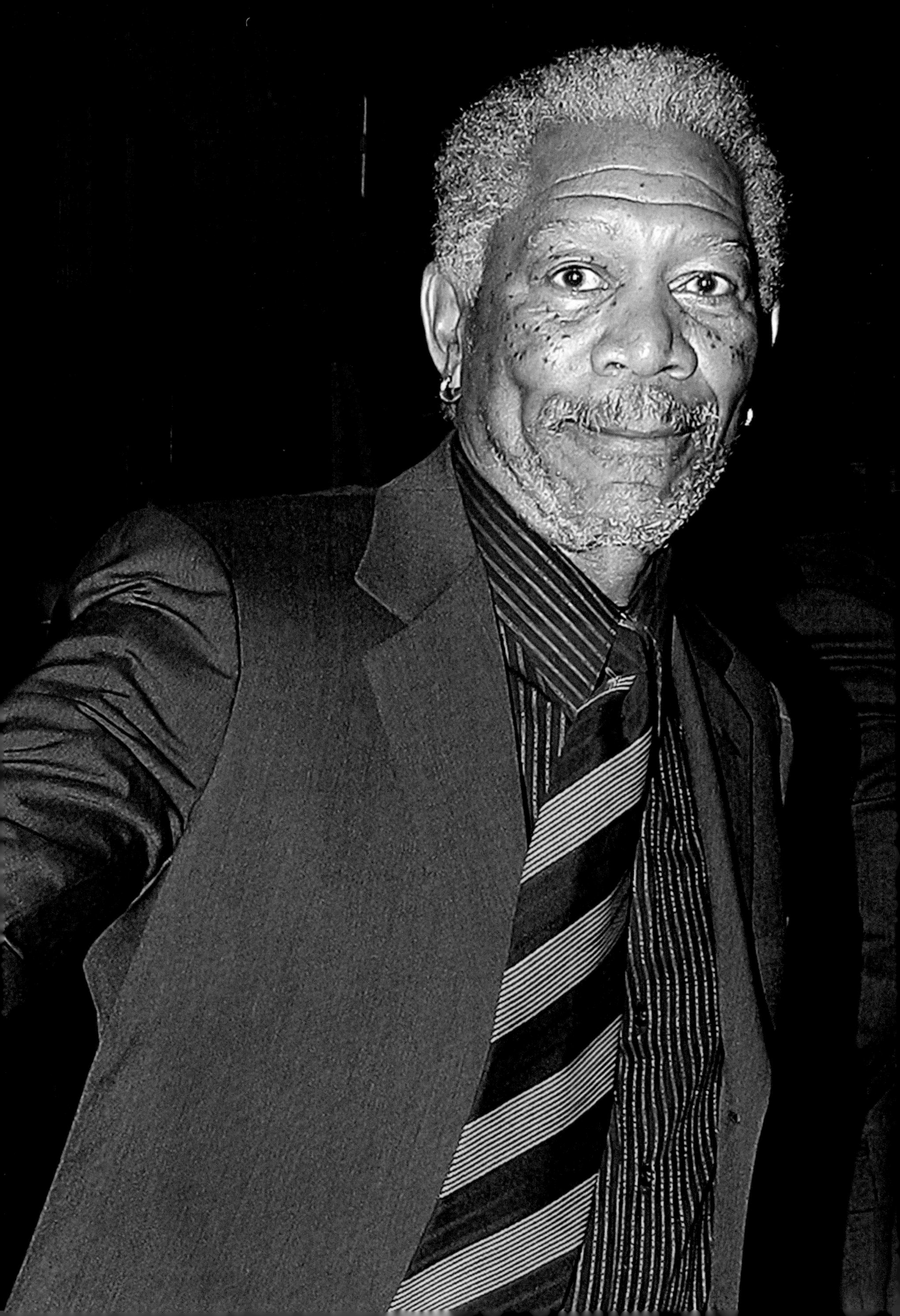

CLINT EASTWOOD
January 2009

Throughout the '90s and 2000s, The Ivy was *the* restaurant – it was London's most exclusive theatre-in-the-round, where the performances happened tableside, and the audience doubled as cast members. It was a glittering culinary beacon where all the world's biggest names gathered. Hollywood royalty, rock gods, literary titans, and even actual crowned heads – The Queen herself had dined there. On that particular January evening, I was outside their Covent Garden restaurant, camera bag slung over my hip as usual, waiting. The night's forecast was uninspiring – "a slow one", I remember being told. But the beauty of this job is that the night can turn in an instant. And then, like a scene from one of his Westerns, he arrived.

Clint Eastwood. A name that reverberated through the annals of cinema. A legend who had carved his place in Hollywood with his stoicism, steely eyes, and general embodiment of rugged, old-school cool. I didn't have to wait long for him to arrive. As I lifted the camera to my eye, there he was – just as I remembered him. A tall, slim man, softly spoken yet never needing to raise his voice to fill a room. Clint was a relic of Old Hollywood, but timeless in his way. As a kid, I'd absorbed his Westerns through osmosis until Eastwood's particular brand of tough, taciturn heroism became part of my visual vocabulary. He was Hollywood's quintessential hard man, the kind of icon whose image could stop you in your tracks. That was the image I wanted to capture: the grit, the toughness, the unmistakable Eastwood swagger. But as soon as I raised my camera, he was gone, vanishing inside before I could get the perfect frame.

A few minutes later, a black cab pulled up. Out stepped Elvis Costello – yes, the bespectacled troubadour of New Wave – and his partner, jazz legend Diana Krall. Completely unknown to me at the time – as close friends of Clint, they joined him inside. Most photographers would have considered the night finished, but intuition – that inexplicable, gorgeous sixth sense that tells you not yet – kept me rooted to my spot. An hour later I returned to my post, drawn by some unshakable certainty that the story had not yet finished.

My patience bore fruit as the restaurant's door swung open and the unmistakable silhouette of Eastwood emerged first. This was my chance. I took a few shots as he strode towards his waiting car. Then, just as he reached for the passenger-side door, he turned to Elvis with a dry grin. "Hey, Elvis, get in the back and don't start singing," he quipped, jabbing a thumb towards the backseat. In that millisecond, I saw my shot. Clint, mid-gesture, a flicker of humour in his eyes; the tough guy and the joker all at once. It was the Clint Eastwood I had always envisioned – the man who could deliver a line with a wry smirk and still radiate that untouchable cool. A split second of magic, exactly what I'd been waiting for.

"Hey, Elvis, get in the back and don't start singing."

Whenever I show people this photograph, they automatically assume (quite reasonably) that Clint is yelling at me in the picture; that I'd somehow provoked the legendary Eastwood wrath. I can't help but laugh when they do. "No, not at all," I tell them. "He was just shouting at Elvis!"

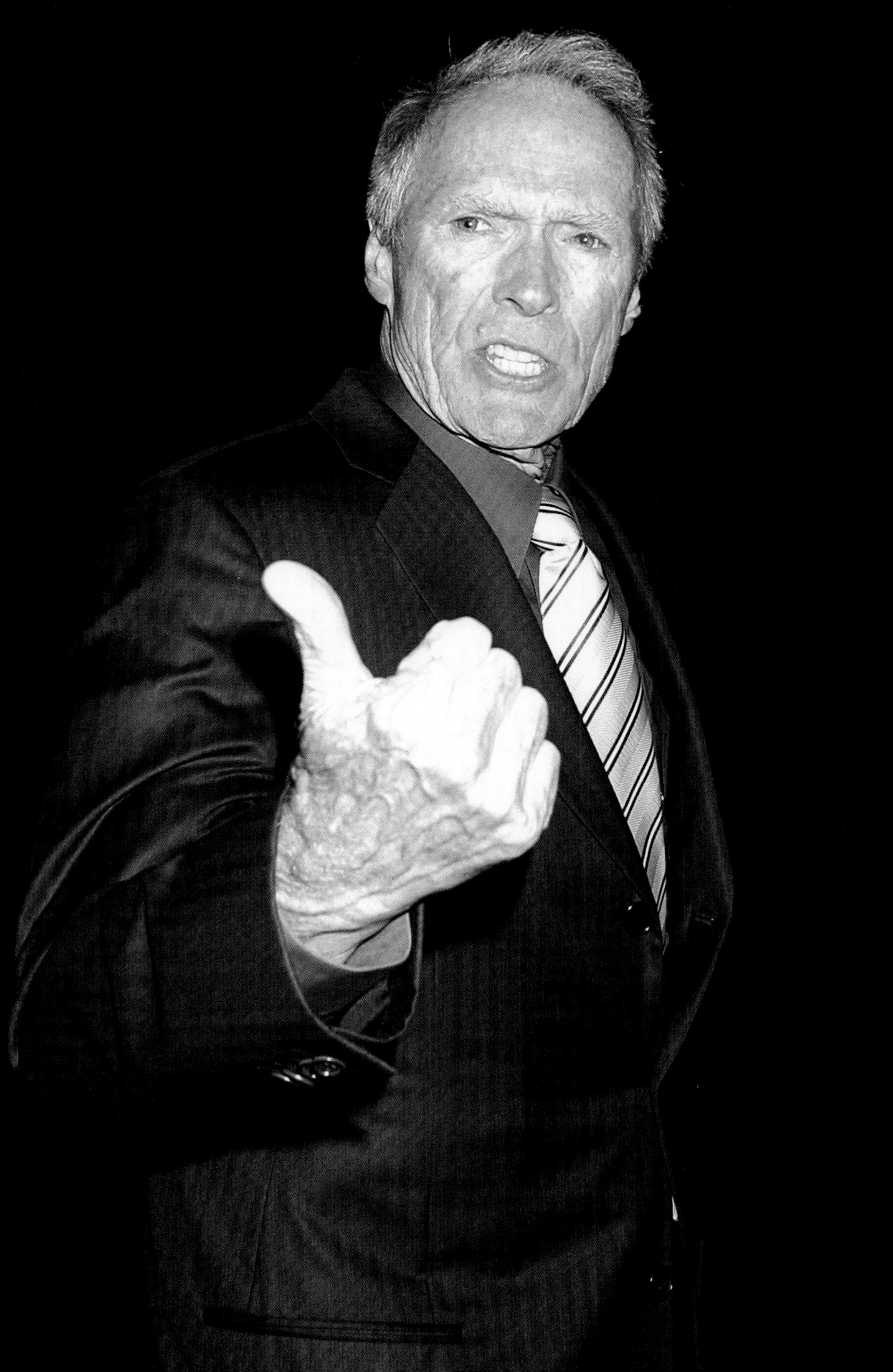

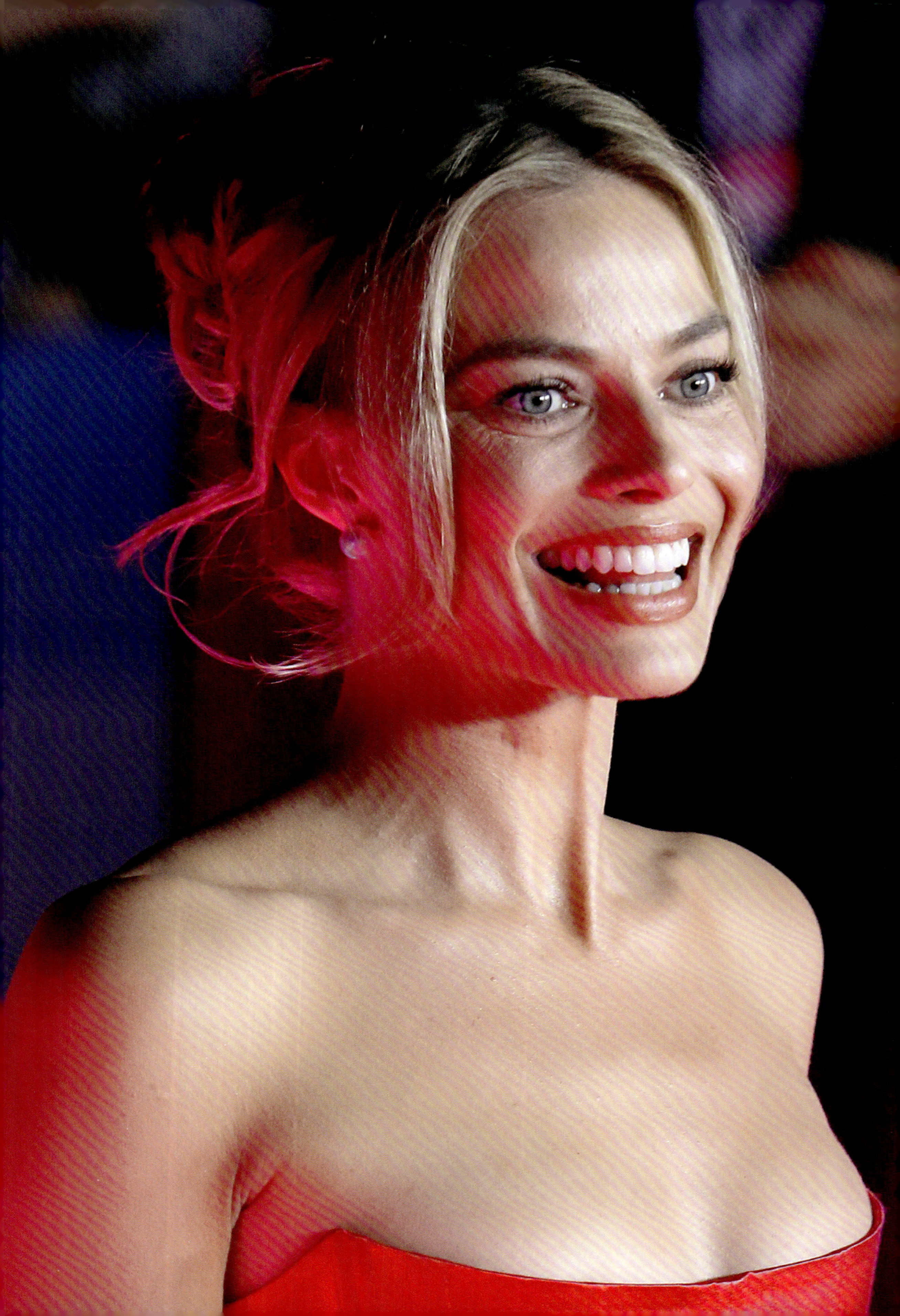

Margot Robbie
London Eye
July 2023
Attending a photo call for 'Barbie'

Following pages:
Joan Collins
The Dorchester, Mayfair
July 2009

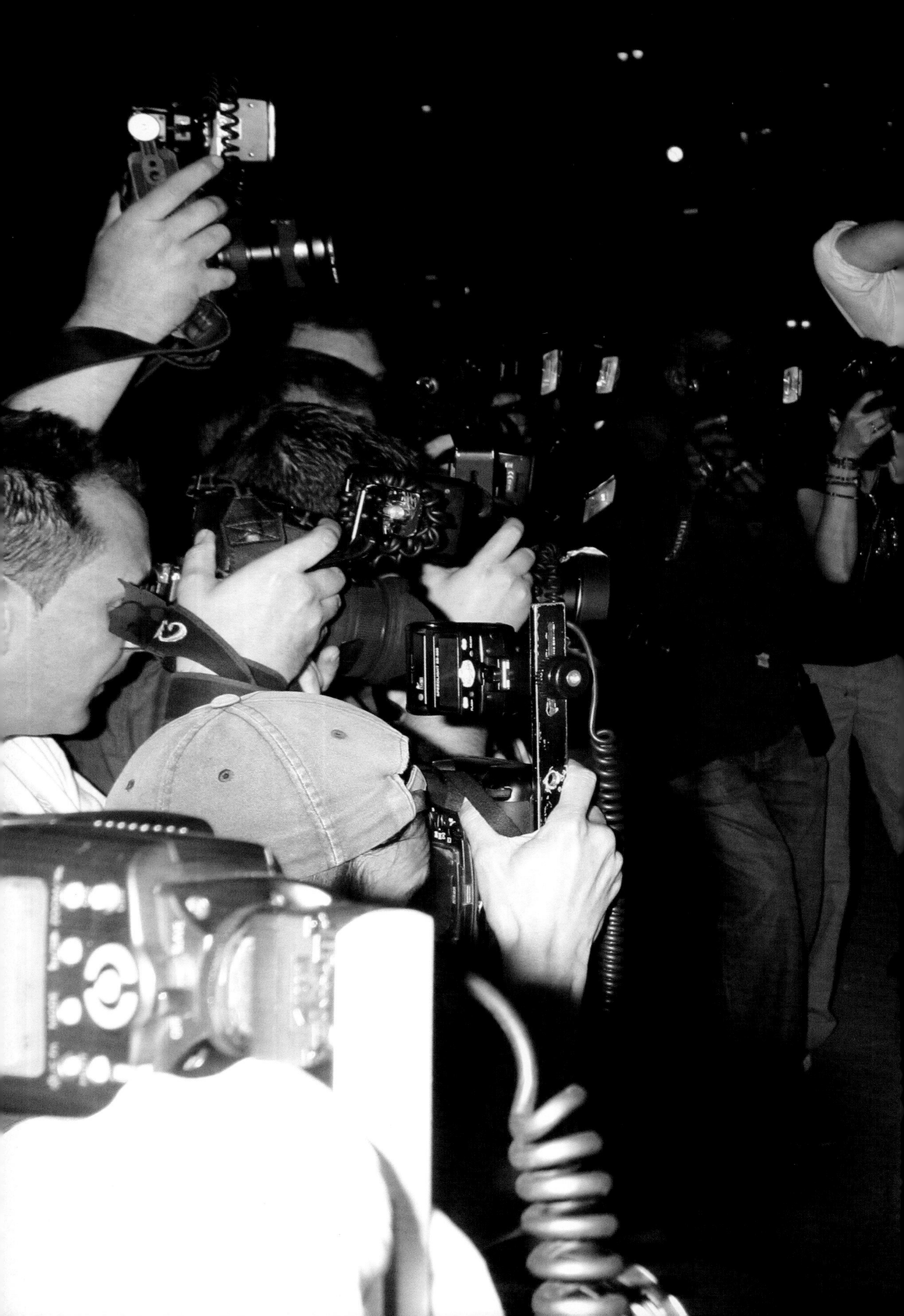

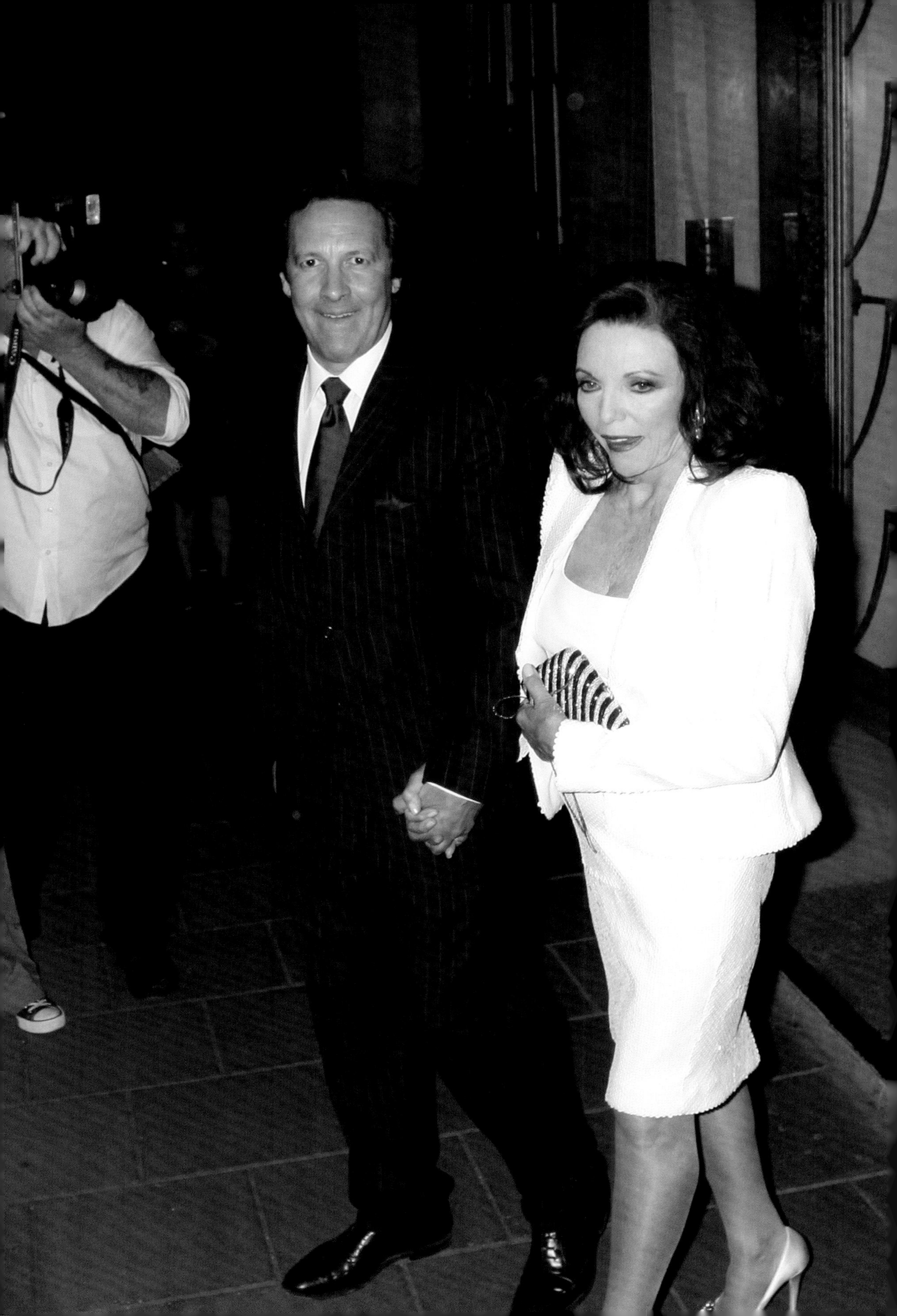

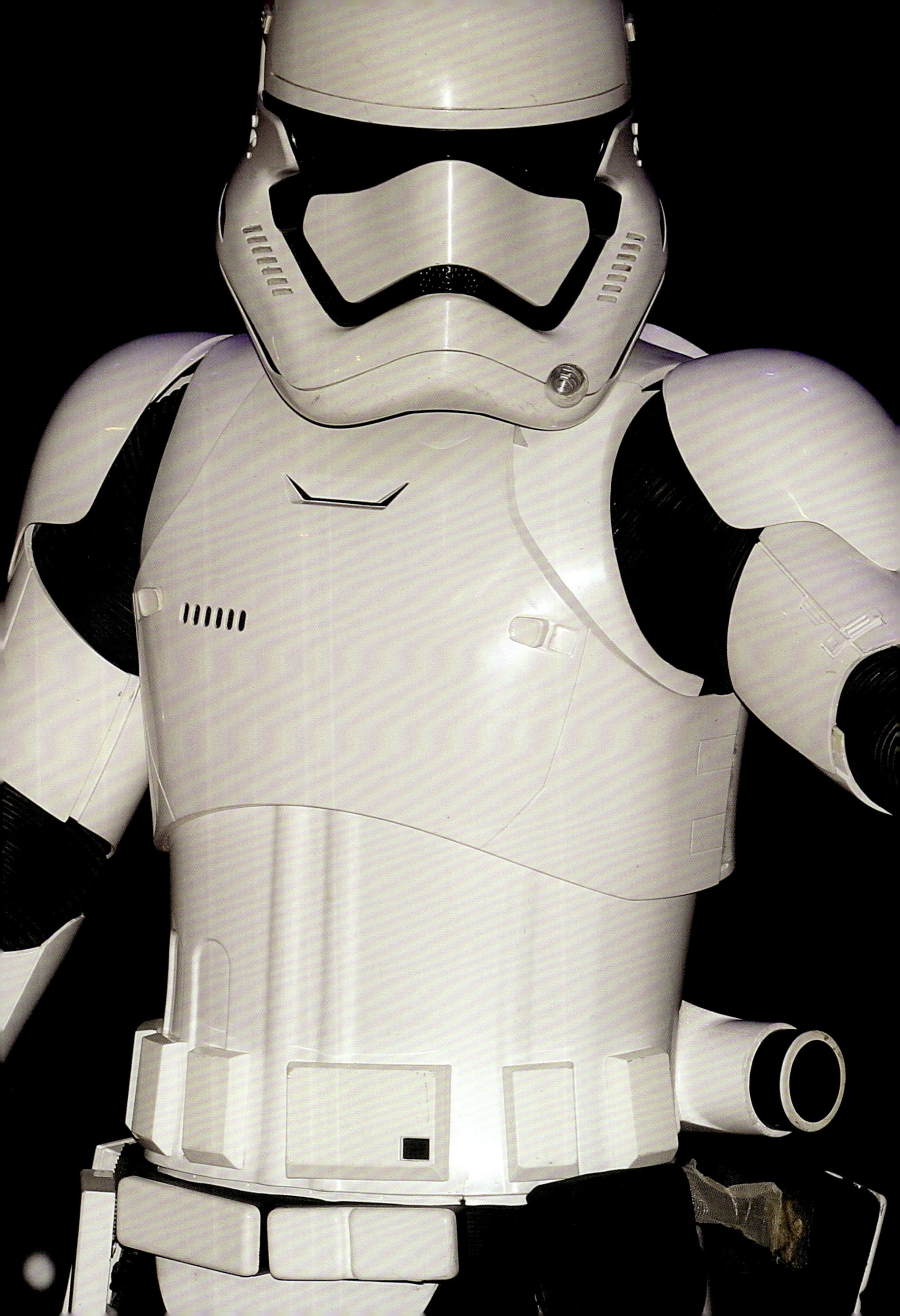

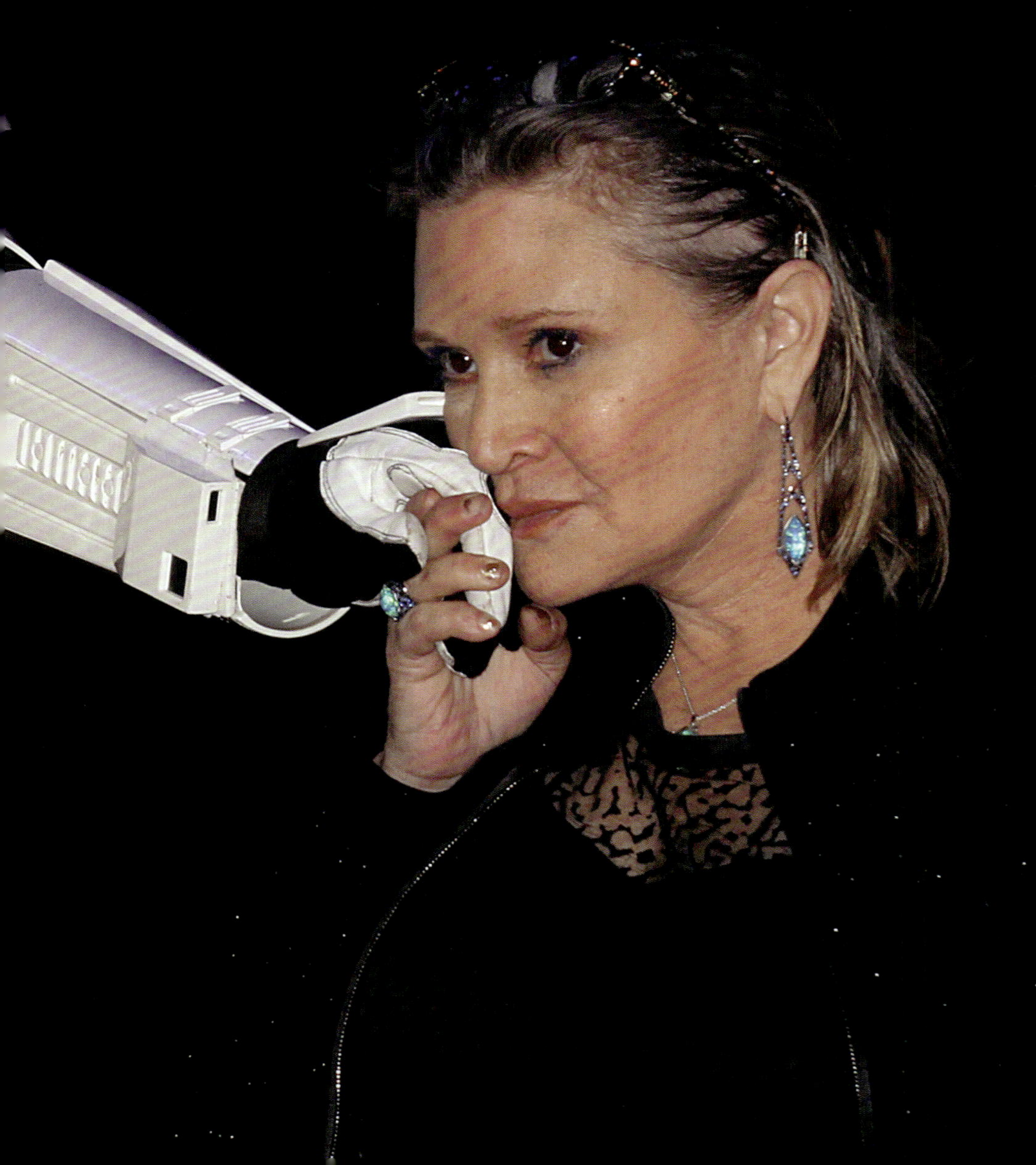

Carrie Fisher
Leicester Square
December 2015
Premiere for 'Star Wars: The Force Awakens'

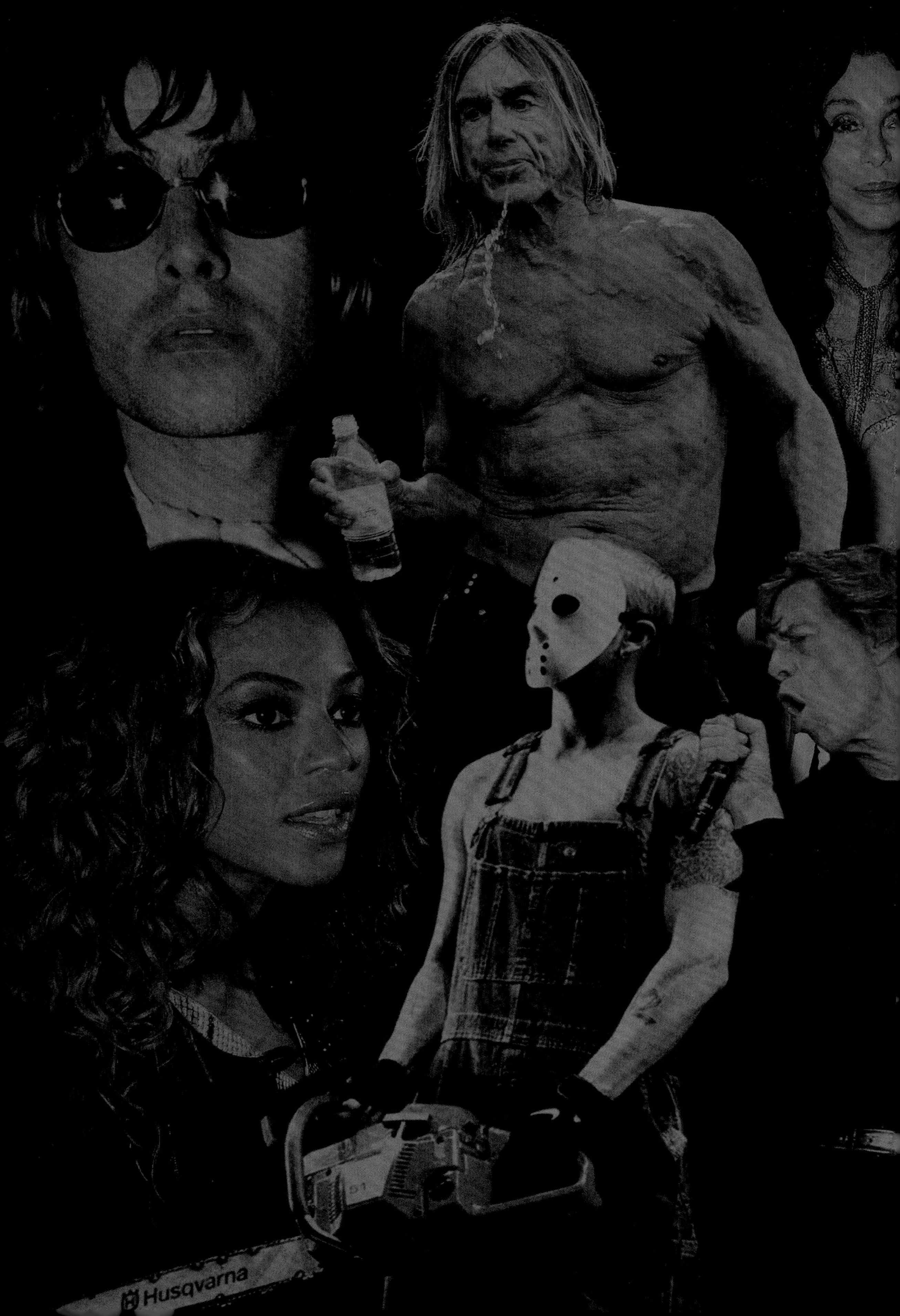
Husqvarna

MUSIC

LADY GAGA
May 2011

"As she prepared to leave, she climbed onto the roof of her car and struck a playful pose for the screaming crowd."

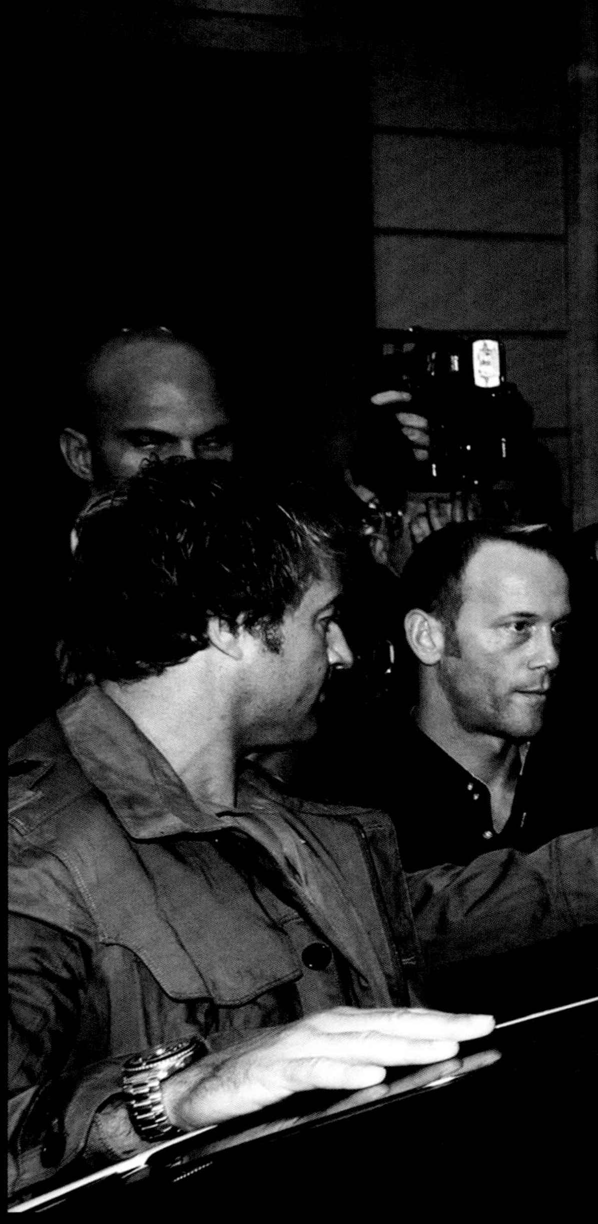

I had been waiting for Lady Gaga to arrive in London for a string of promotional events surrounding the release of her new album *Born This Way* (2011). After what felt like an eternity, she finally arrived at her hotel around 2am. At that hour there were only two die-hard fans and me there to greet her – a rare, intimate moment for someone of her level of fame.

When her car pulled up, she stepped out and posed graciously with the two fans. Seizing the opportunity, I approached and asked if I could take a few shots, but she politely declined, explaining that she had just come off a long flight and needed some time to freshen up and do her makeup. It would've been easy to get frustrated – I had waited for hours – but I chose to respect her wishes. Gaga was genuinely appreciative of my understanding. I assured her that it was no problem, noting how kind she had always been to her fans and the press. As I was leaving, she told me to come back tomorrow, and that she would make sure I'd get my shots.

The following morning, I arrived to find a swarm of around a hundred fans and photographers, all fighting for position. It was chaos, and I thought to myself that getting a good shot would be near

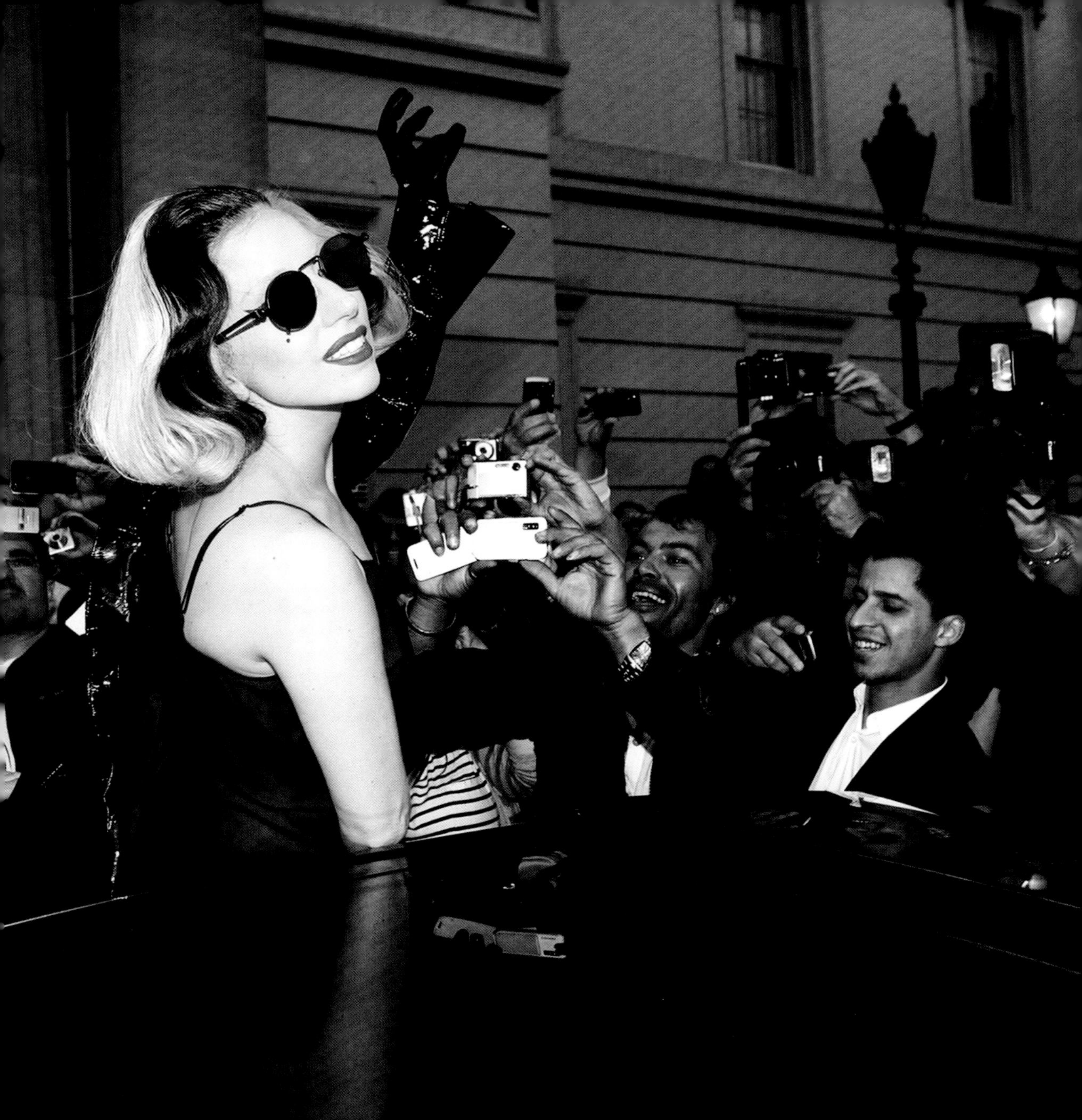

impossible. Just then, a man approached me from behind, tapped me on the shoulder, and asked if I was Greg. When I nodded, he told me to follow him, saying that Gaga wanted to speak with me. I was guided to the back of the hotel, through a door, down a corridor, and into an elevator, and we ascended to the top floor where she was waiting. She thanked me once again for my patience and fulfilled her promise: "Let's shoot." For the next half an hour I had the pleasure of working with her one-on-one, capturing her as she struck pose after pose, fully in her element.

Once we wrapped up the shoot, I escorted her downstairs to her waiting car and heaps of enthusiastic fans. One thing that truly stood out to me about Gaga was how genuine her connection with her fans was. As she prepared to leave, she climbed onto the roof of her car and struck a playful pose for the screaming crowd. I managed to capture that moment and sent a copy of the photo to her security guard the following day.

That night, as Gaga departed London, it was announced she had become the first celebrity to reach 10 million followers on Twitter. To celebrate, she tweeted this image, that final shot I took of her posing on the car.

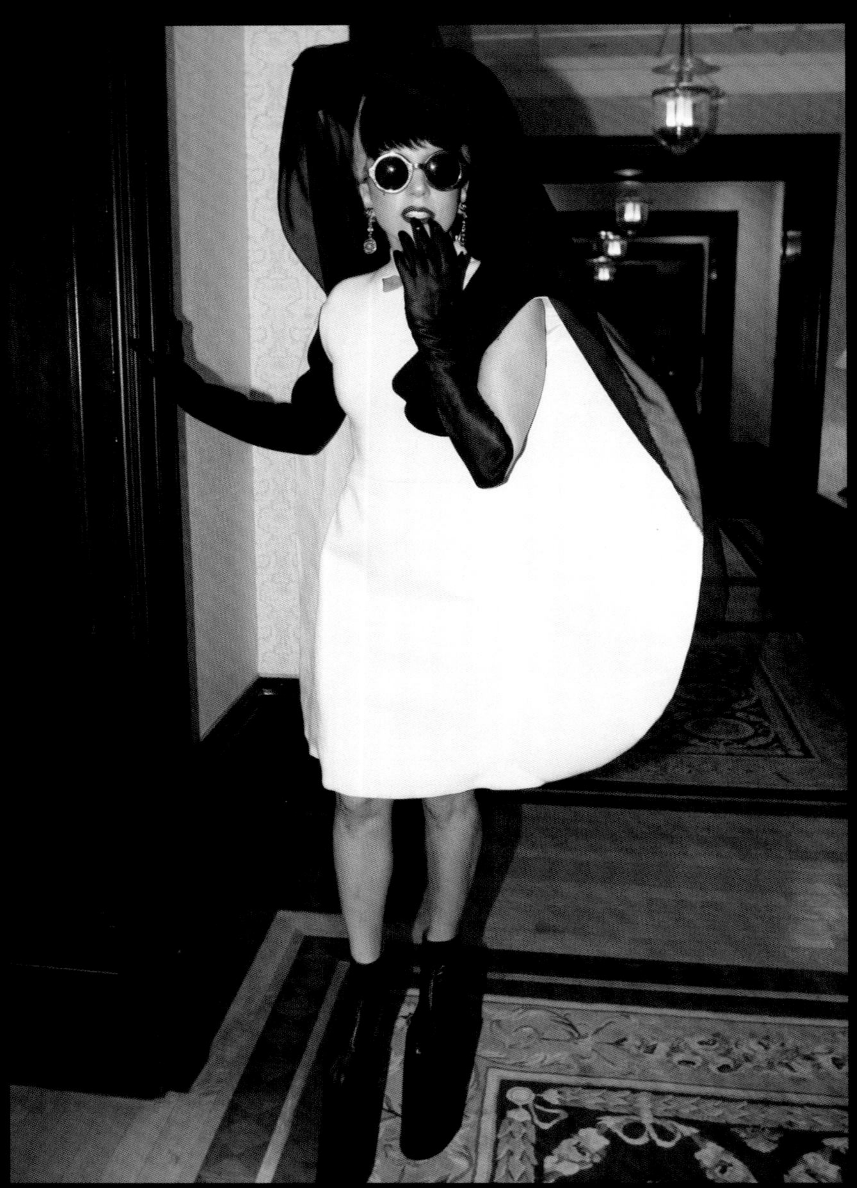

Lady Gaga
The Lanesborough, Knightsbridge
May 2011

Lady Gaga
Annabel's, Mayfair
December 2013

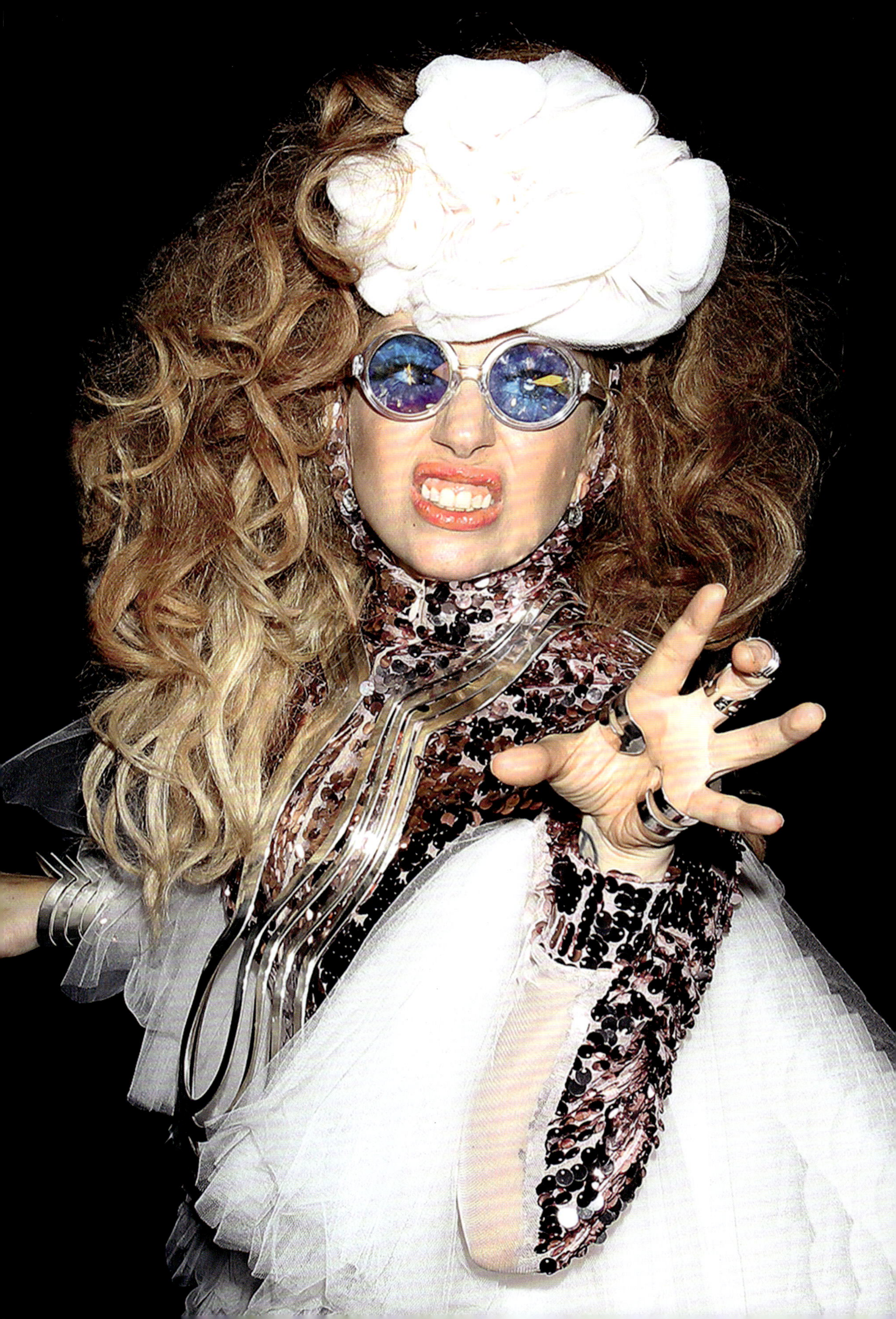

Paul McCartney
Stella McCartney, Conduit Street, Mayfair
November 2008
Leaving his daughter's Christmas party

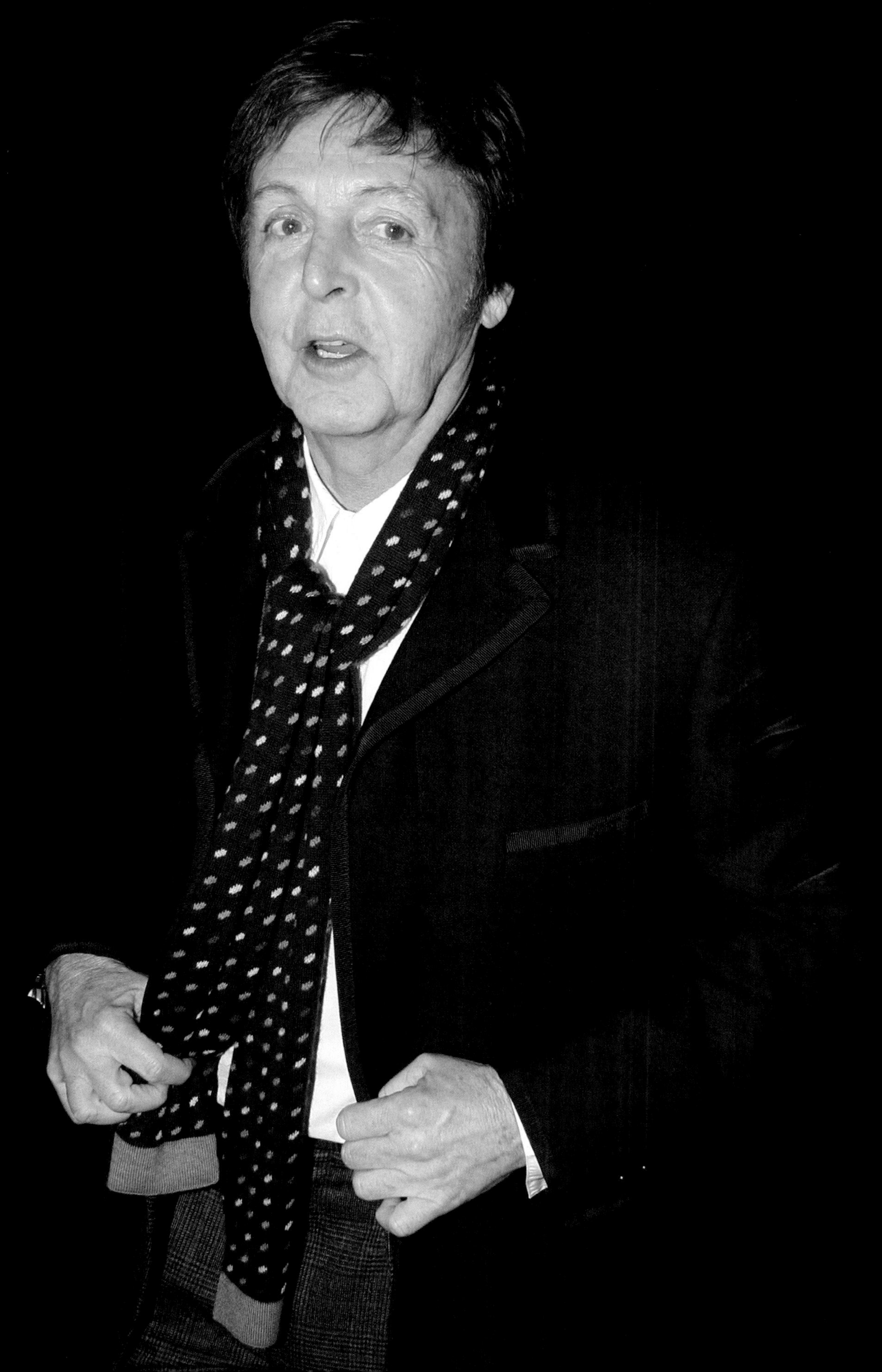

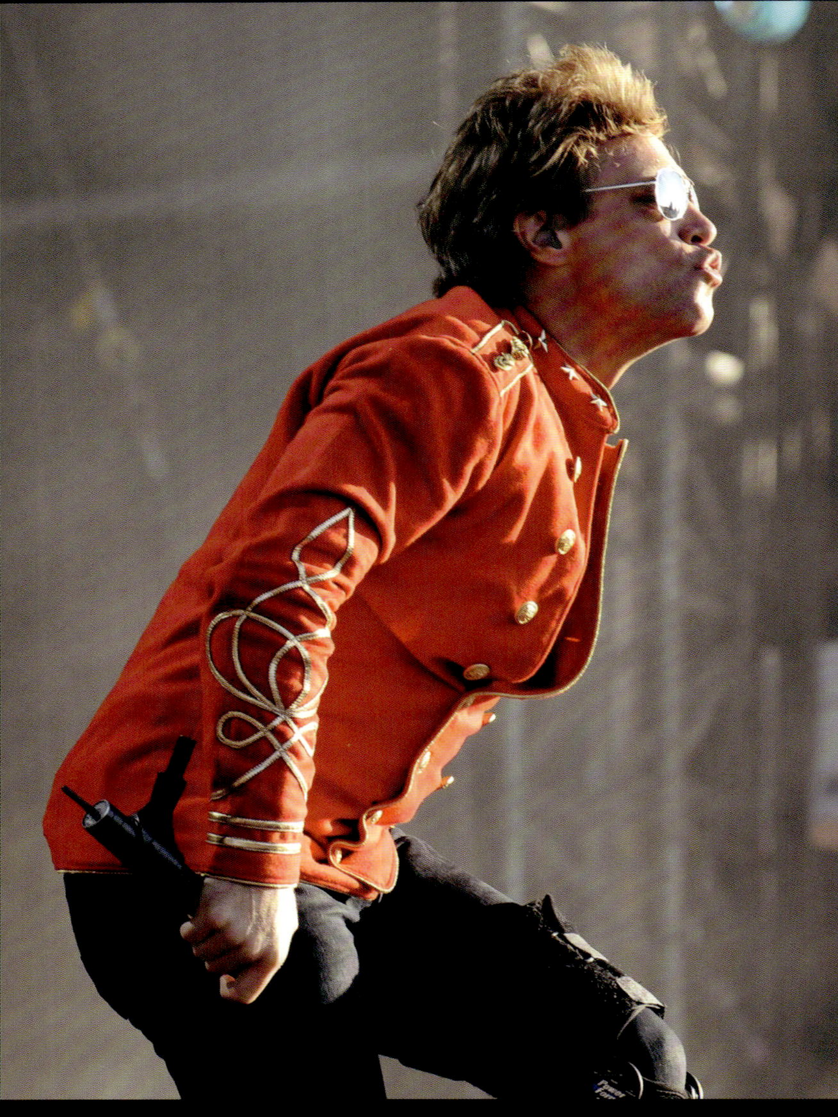

Jon Bon Jovi
Hyde Park, June 2011
Performing at the Hard Rock Calling Festival

Amy Winehouse
Hyde Park, June 2008
Performing at Nelson Mandela's 90th birthday concert

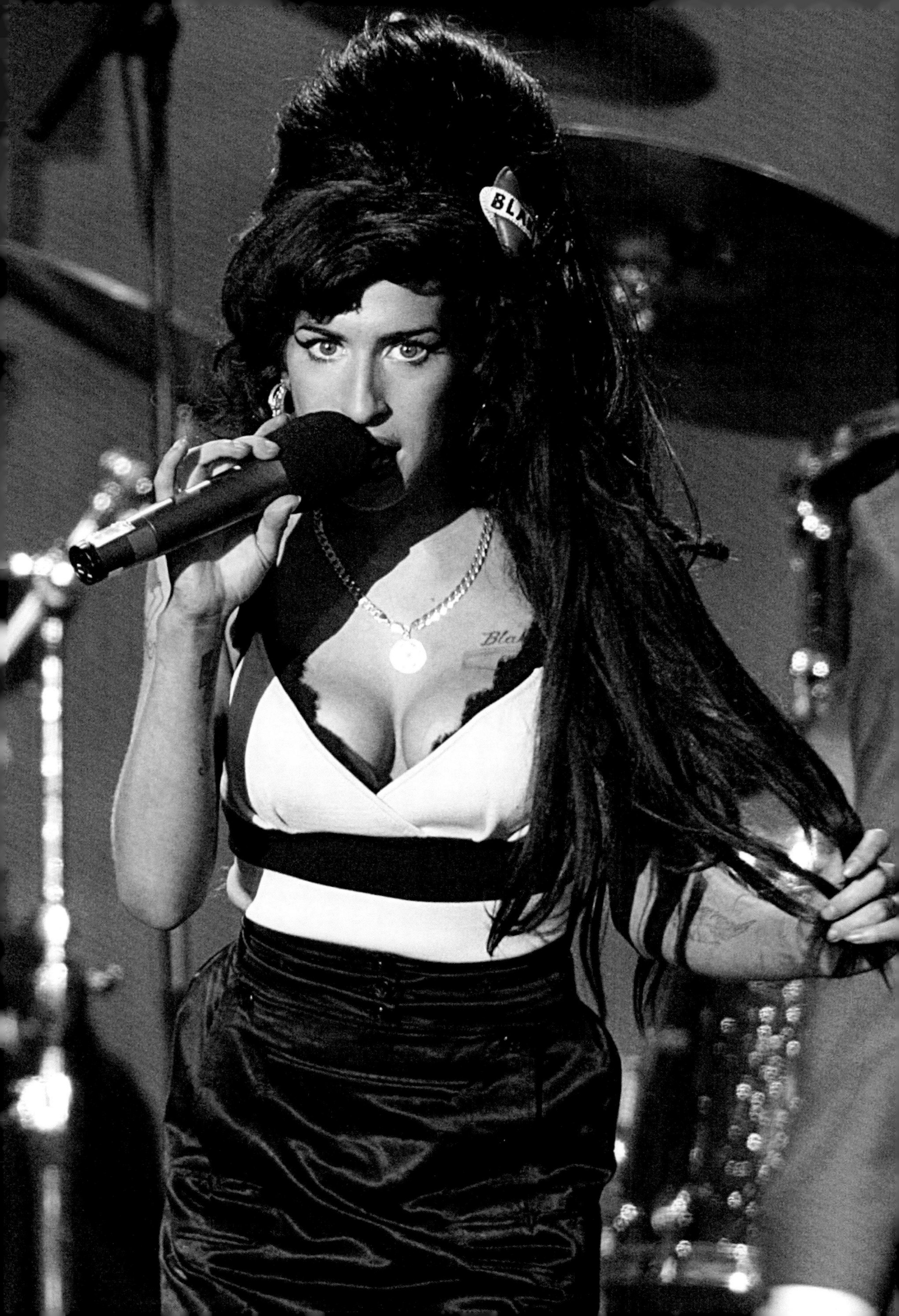

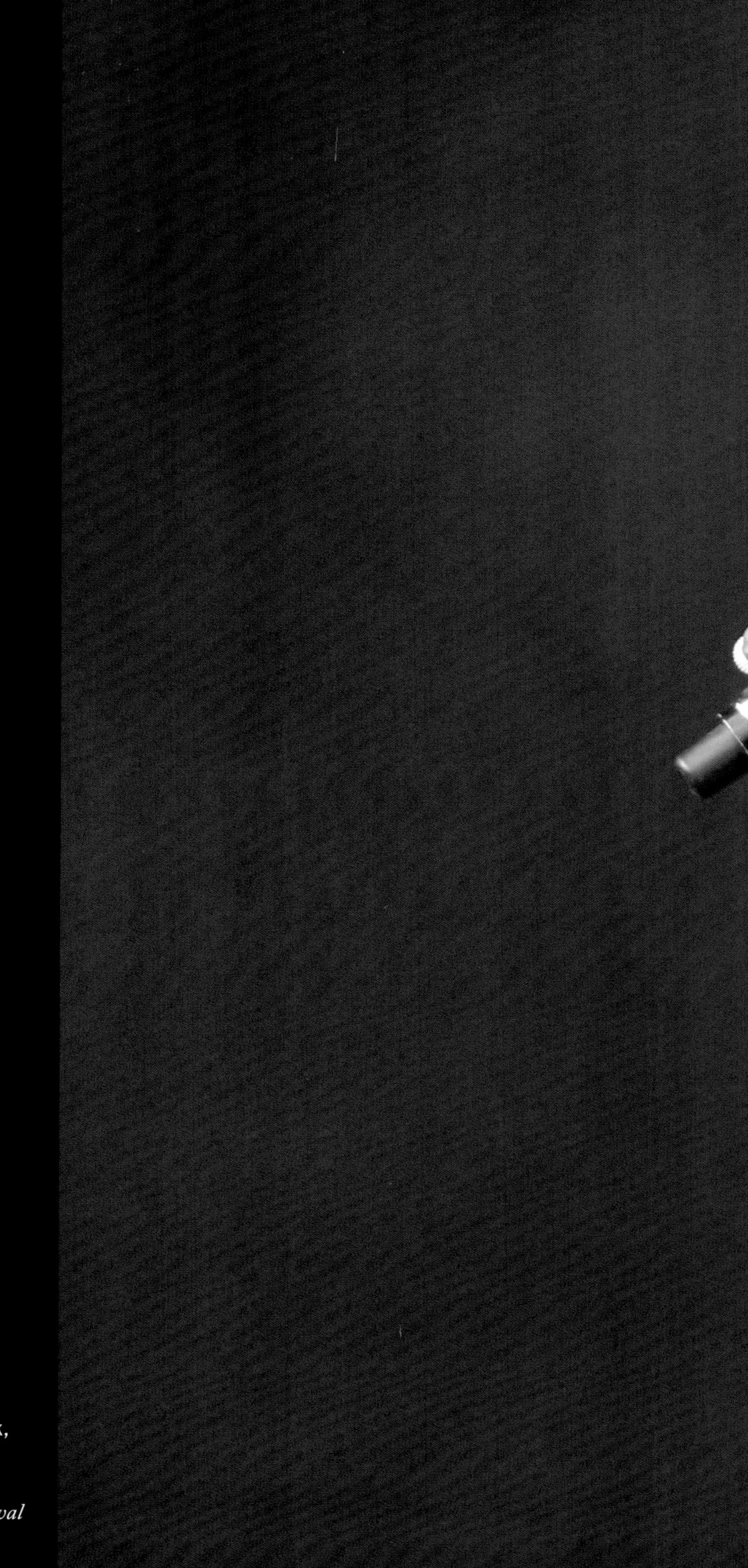

Snoop Dogg
Queen Elizabeth Olympic Park,
Stratford
July 2013
Performing at the Wireless Festival

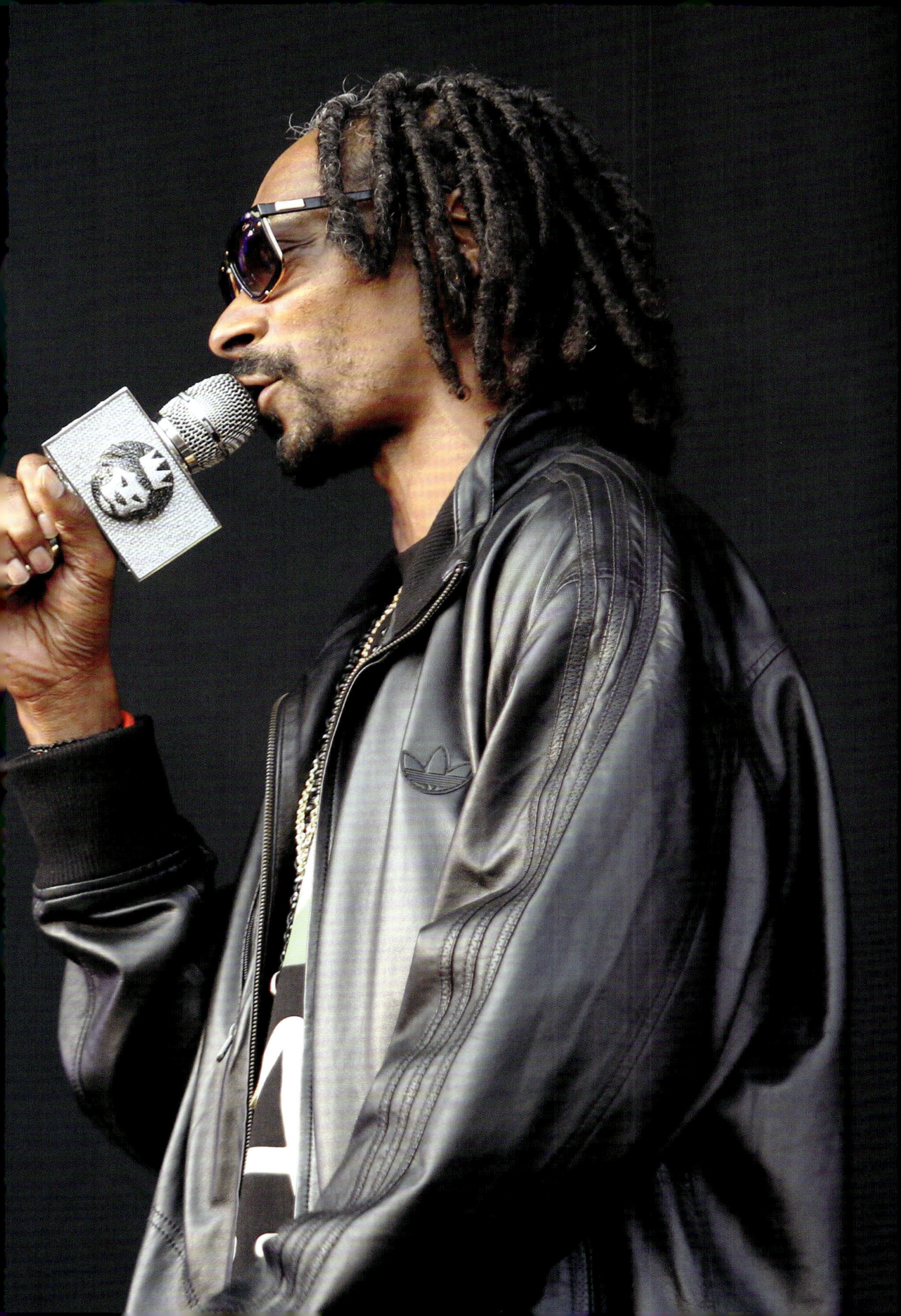

EMINEM
July 2013

The London Arena was buzzing with the kind of electric tension only 15,000 voices bellowing excitedly at once can spew. This was the Anger Management Tour, and at its heart was a man who set fire to the rulebook of rap and threw the ashes in the industry's face. He had never been an easy subject to capture because his fame was so stratospheric. But this night, I was ready. Or so I thought.

Before I even stepped foot inside, the streets surrounding the arena set the tone. Protesters had gathered at the entrance; their signs and shouts directed at the man whose lyrics had become synonymous with controversy. They rallied against his words – misogynistic, violent, incendiary, they claimed. And yet, as I watched, I knew these protests were the very oxygen to his flame, the kind of backlash that only elevated his status as the anti-hero of rap. If anything, their presence was helping him evolve into something even harder to ignore.

Inside, the lights dimmed, and the real show began as our focus was diverted to a small house on stage. But then, amidst the sudden hush, a chainsaw came shrieking through the air, deafening, frenzied. The crowd went wild, and then he was there, stepping into the chaos like a nightmare made flesh – Eminem, wearing a Jason Voorhees mask and blue dungarees, brandishing the chainsaw as if it were an extension of himself. It might just be the most memorable stage entrance I've ever seen. So, business as usual, I snapped away at the rapper, roaring his truth into a sea of willing worshippers. It was rebellion with a backing track.

Years later, my time with him would take an entirely different turn. Rather than seeing him dressed like a demented slasher film icon, I found myself in the early hours of the morning shooting him as he perused the aisles of Forbidden Planet, hunting for toys and comics. Gone was the masked madman commanding an arena; here was a quiet, almost contemplative man, dodging fans and photographers as he indulged in his love for rare collectibles.

I felt like I had captured the secret side of him,

"But then, amidst the sudden hush, a chainsaw came shrieking through the air, deafening, frenzied."

one that every celebrity has, as if I had pulled the curtain back just a little bit. And then, somehow, we ended up at Jonathan Ross's house, where Em was flipping through box after box of the presenter's stash of vintage comics like a kid on Christmas morning. I was supposed to be somewhere else entirely by then, but once he was in motion, there wasn't really any getting off the ride.

Whether he's exploding onto stage with a chainsaw or quietly flicking through a comic book, one thing is always certain: with Eminem, you're never quite sure what's coming next, just that you will never shoot the same man twice. And that's exactly what makes photographing him such a ride.

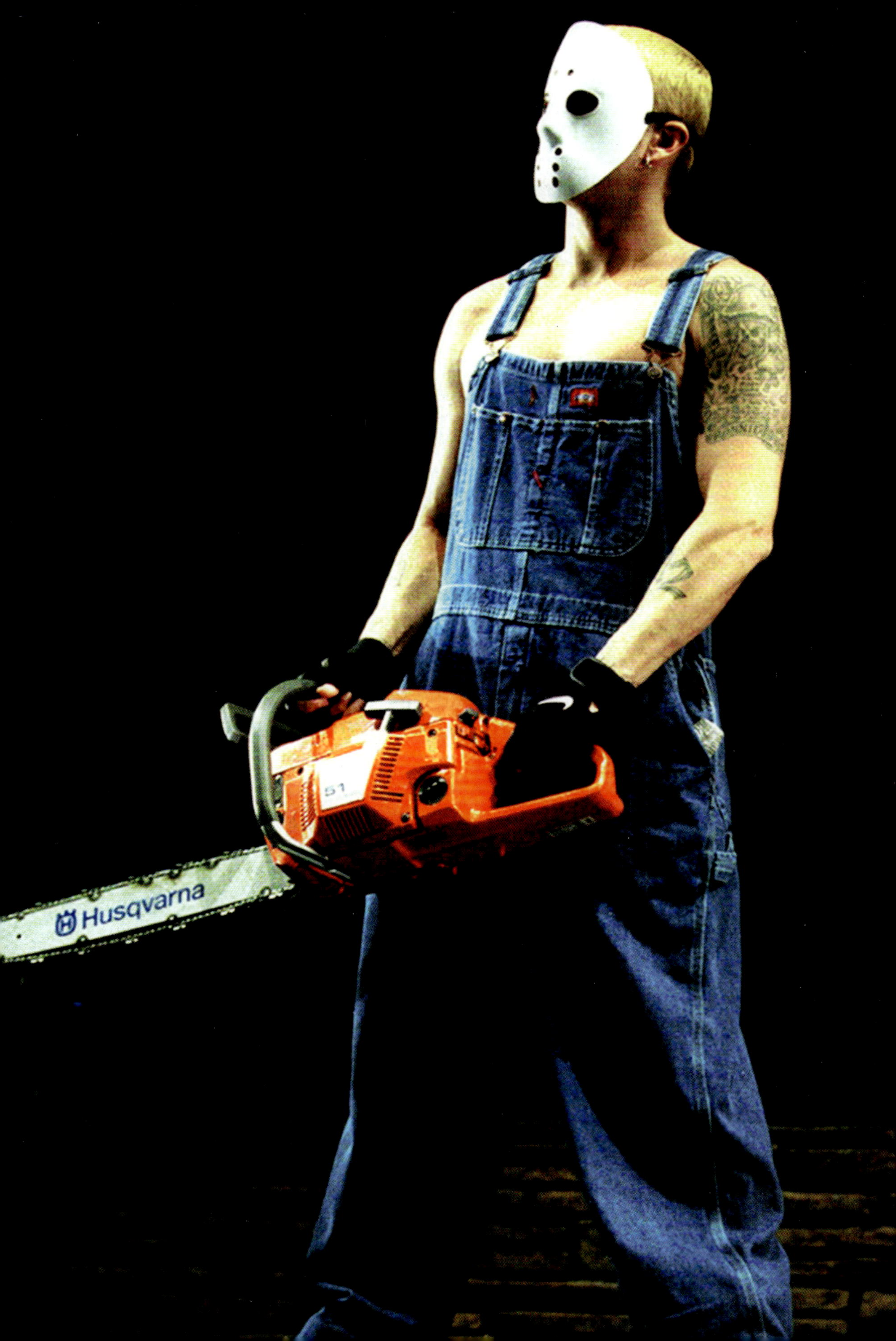
Husqvarna
51

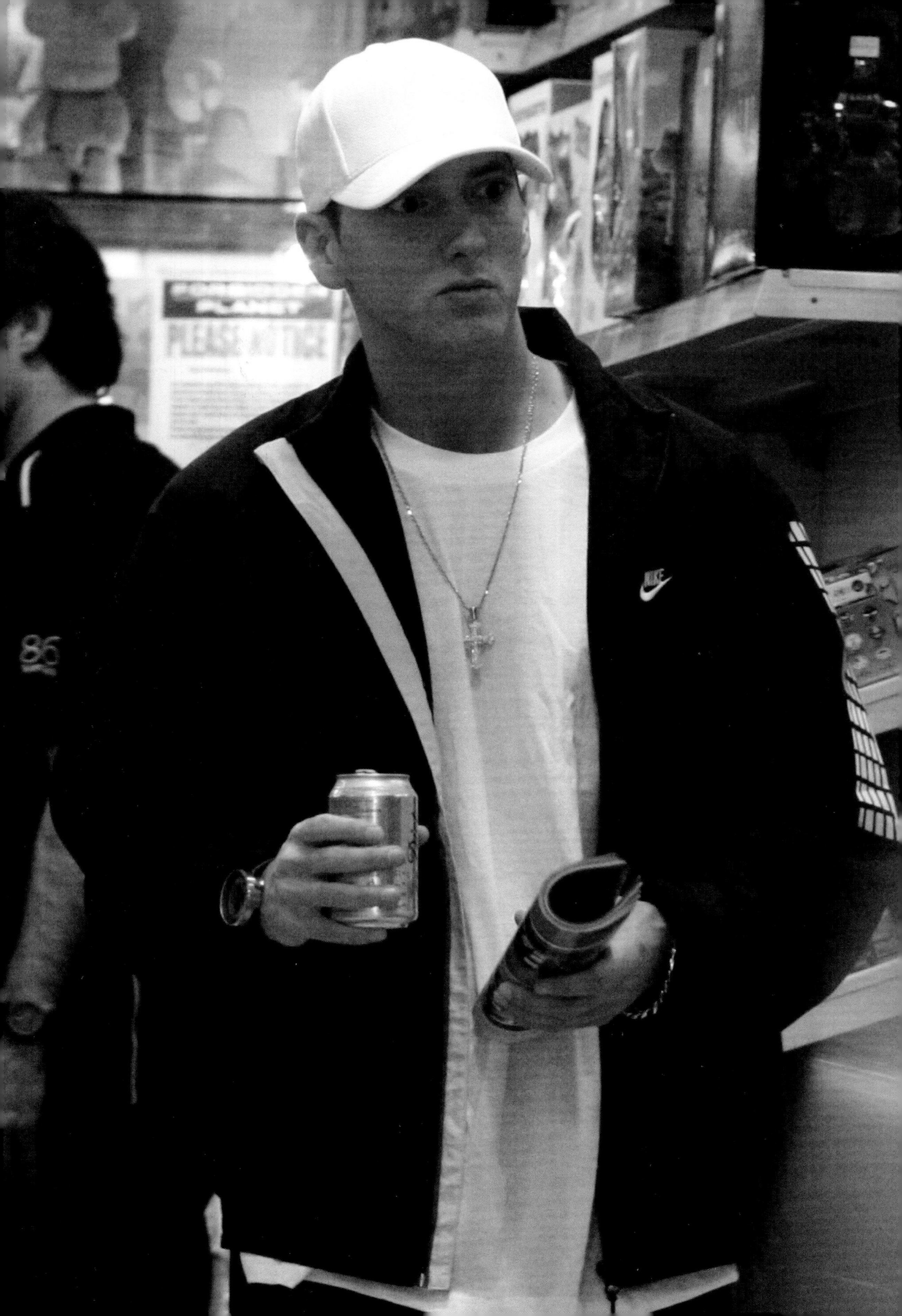
NIKE
86

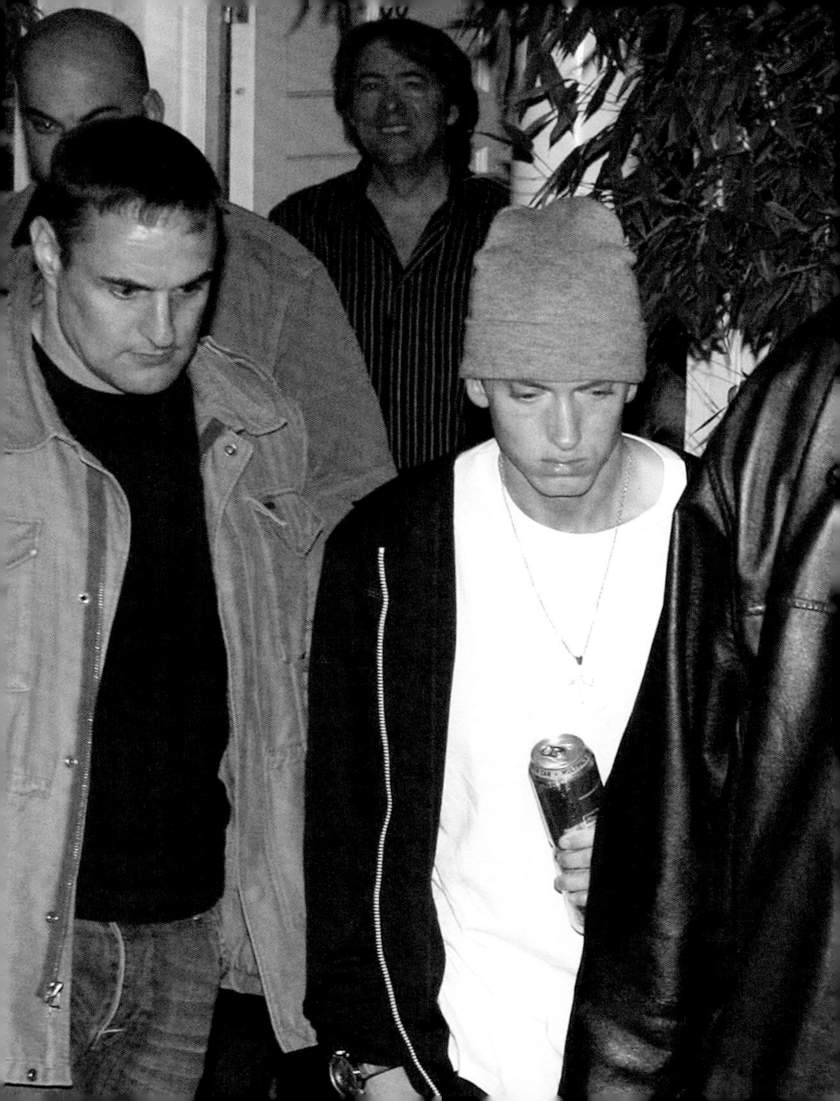

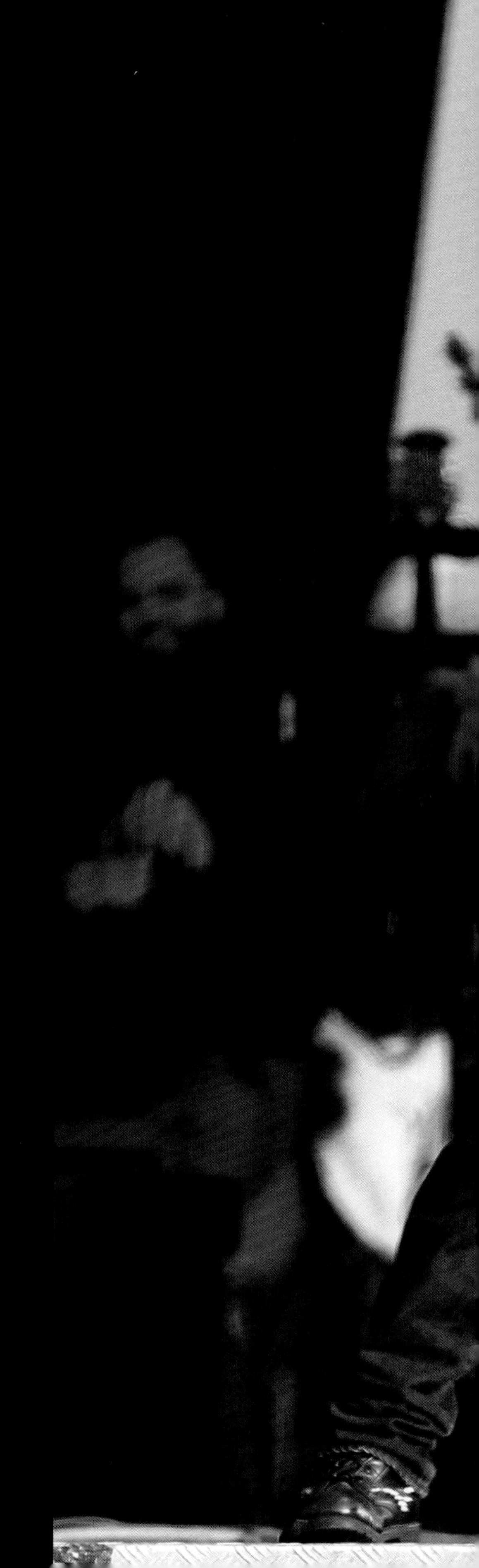

Bruce Springsteen
Hyde Park
July 2012
Performing at the Hard Rock Calling Festival

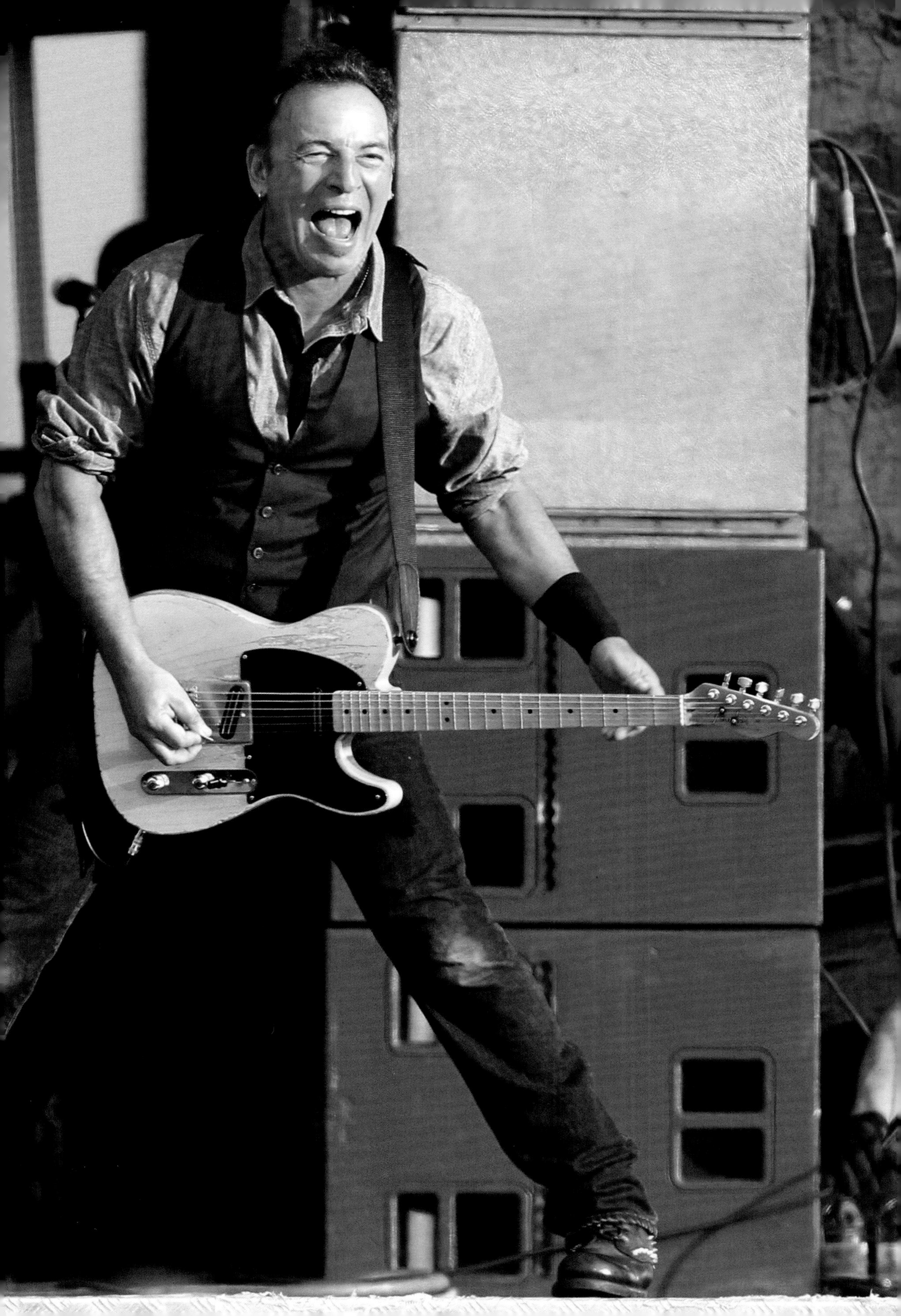

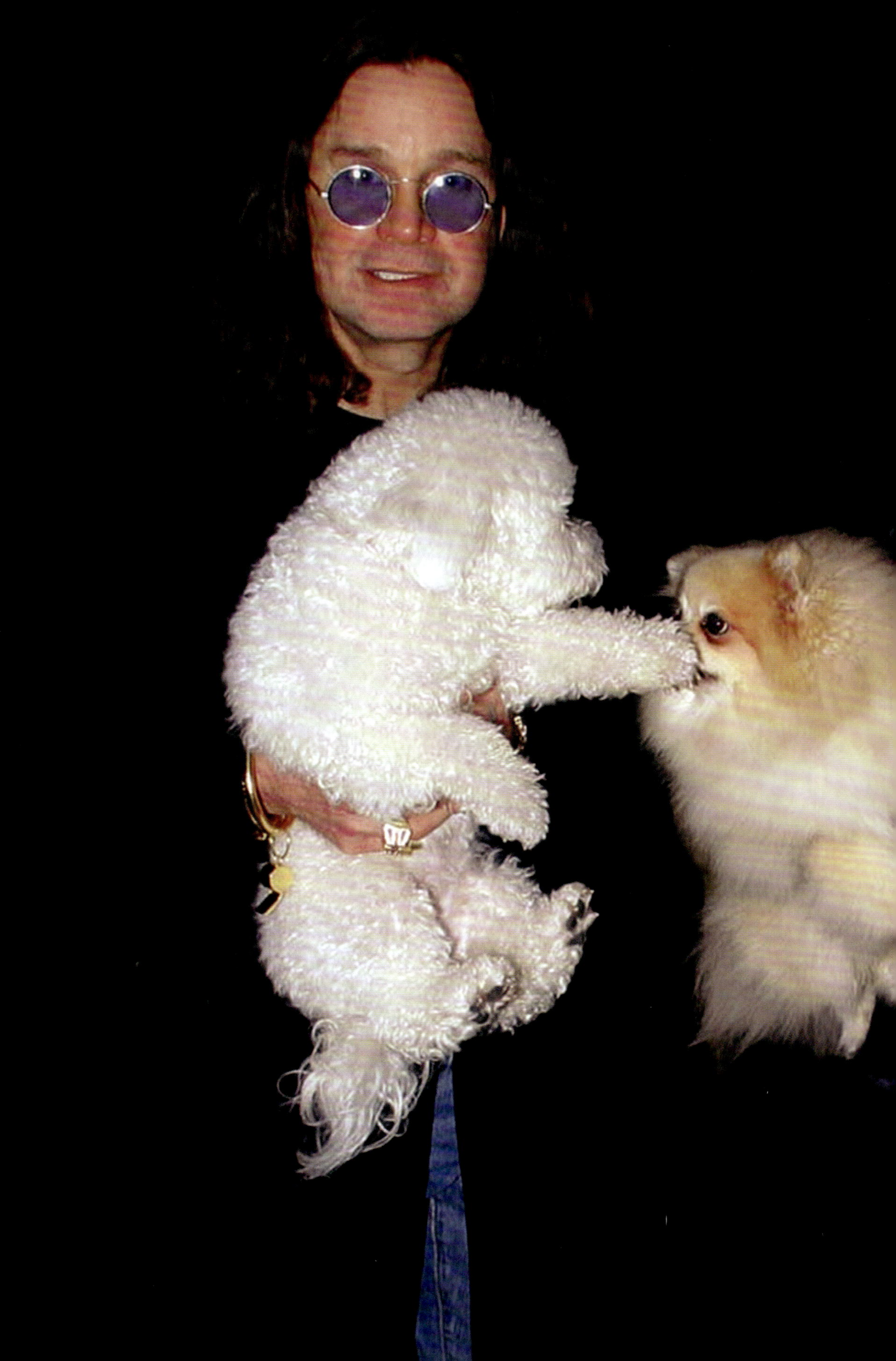

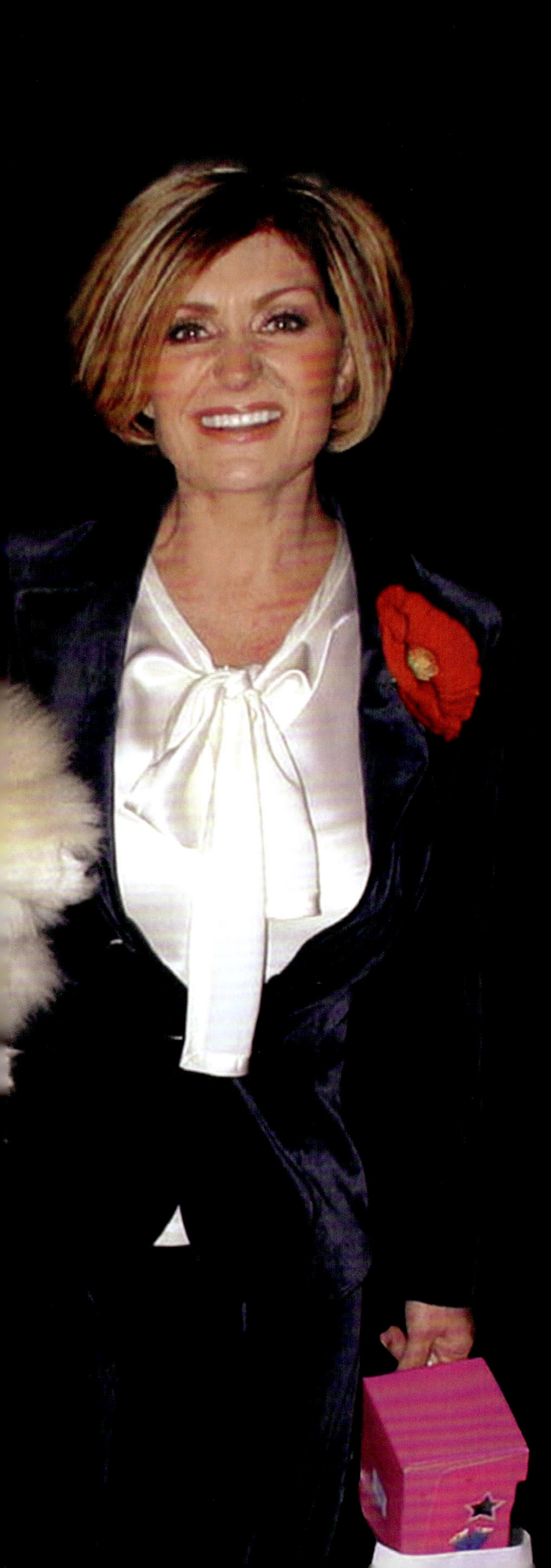

Ozzy and Sharon Osbourne
Fountain Studios, Wembley
November 2005
Ozzy is trying to kidnap my dog, Missy

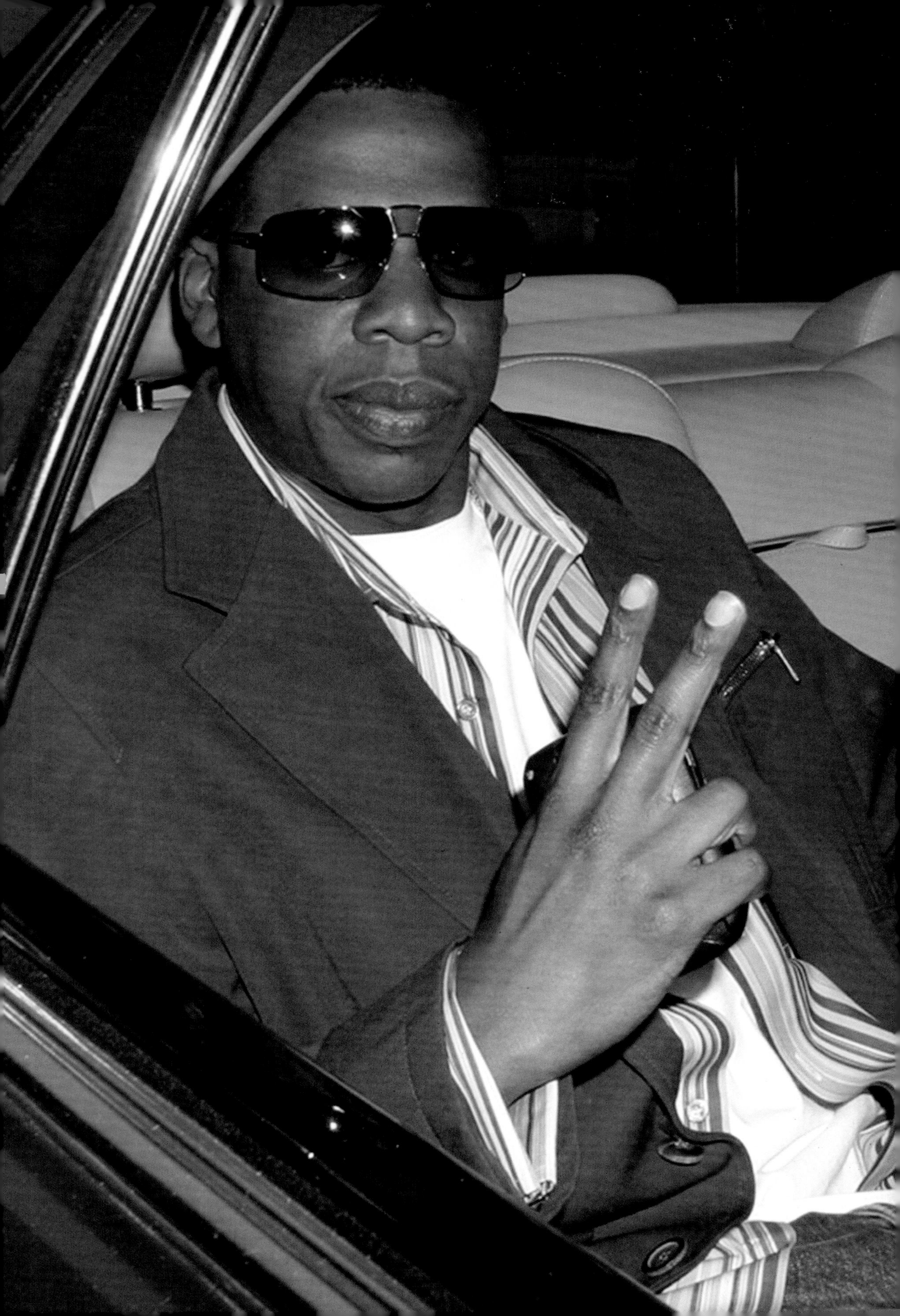

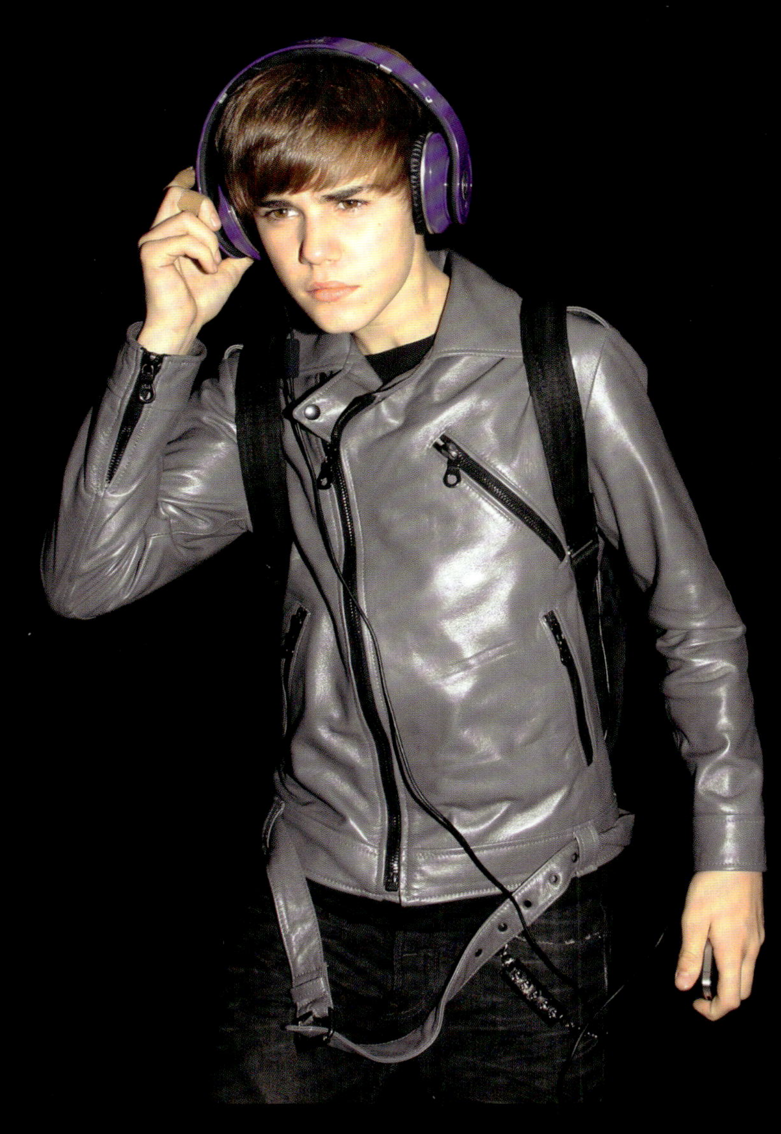

Jay-Z
The Lanesborough, Knightsbridge
March 2008

Justin Bieber
Heathrow
November 2010

Following pages:
Grace Jones
Hyde Park, July 2011
Performing at the Wireless Festival

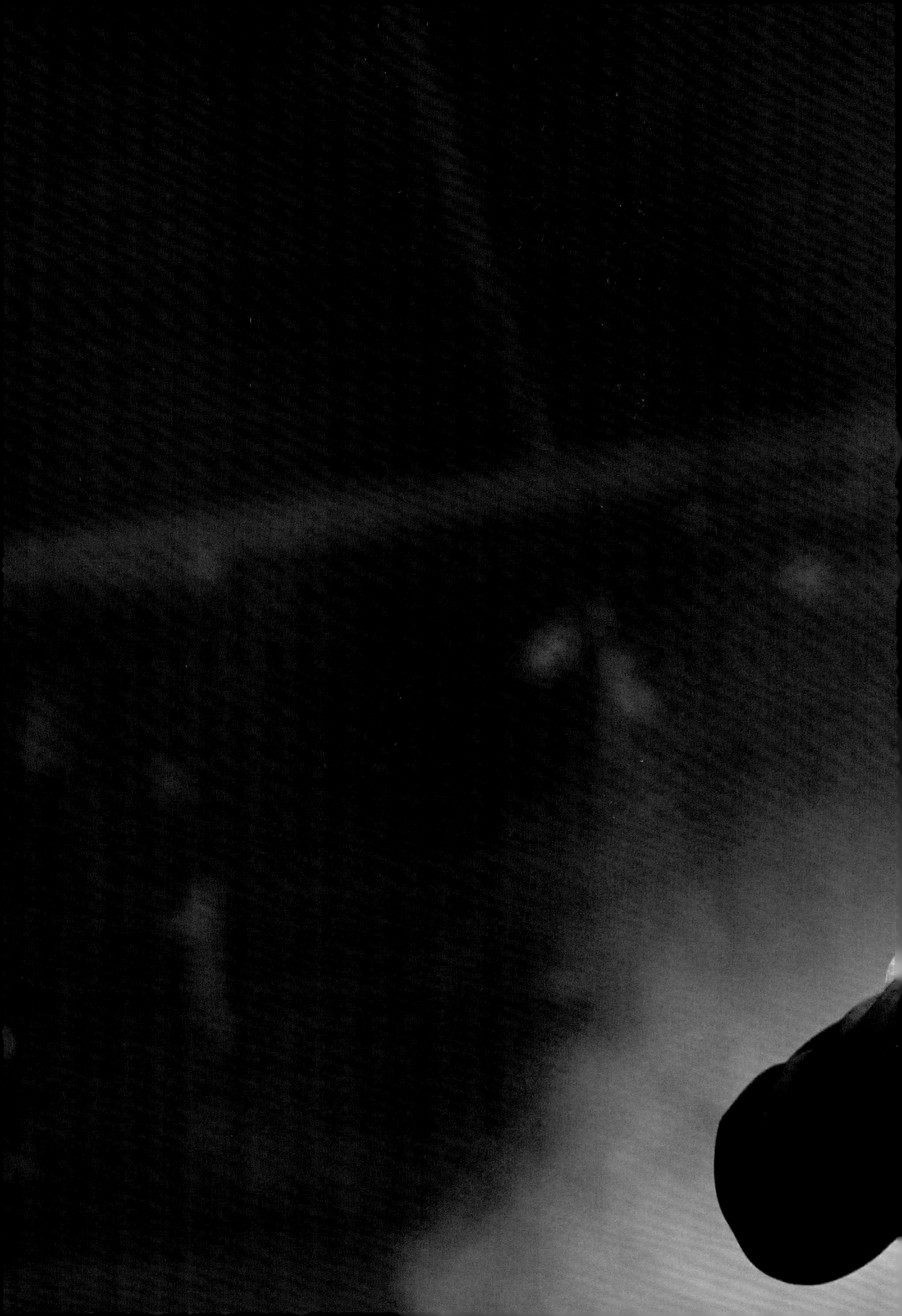

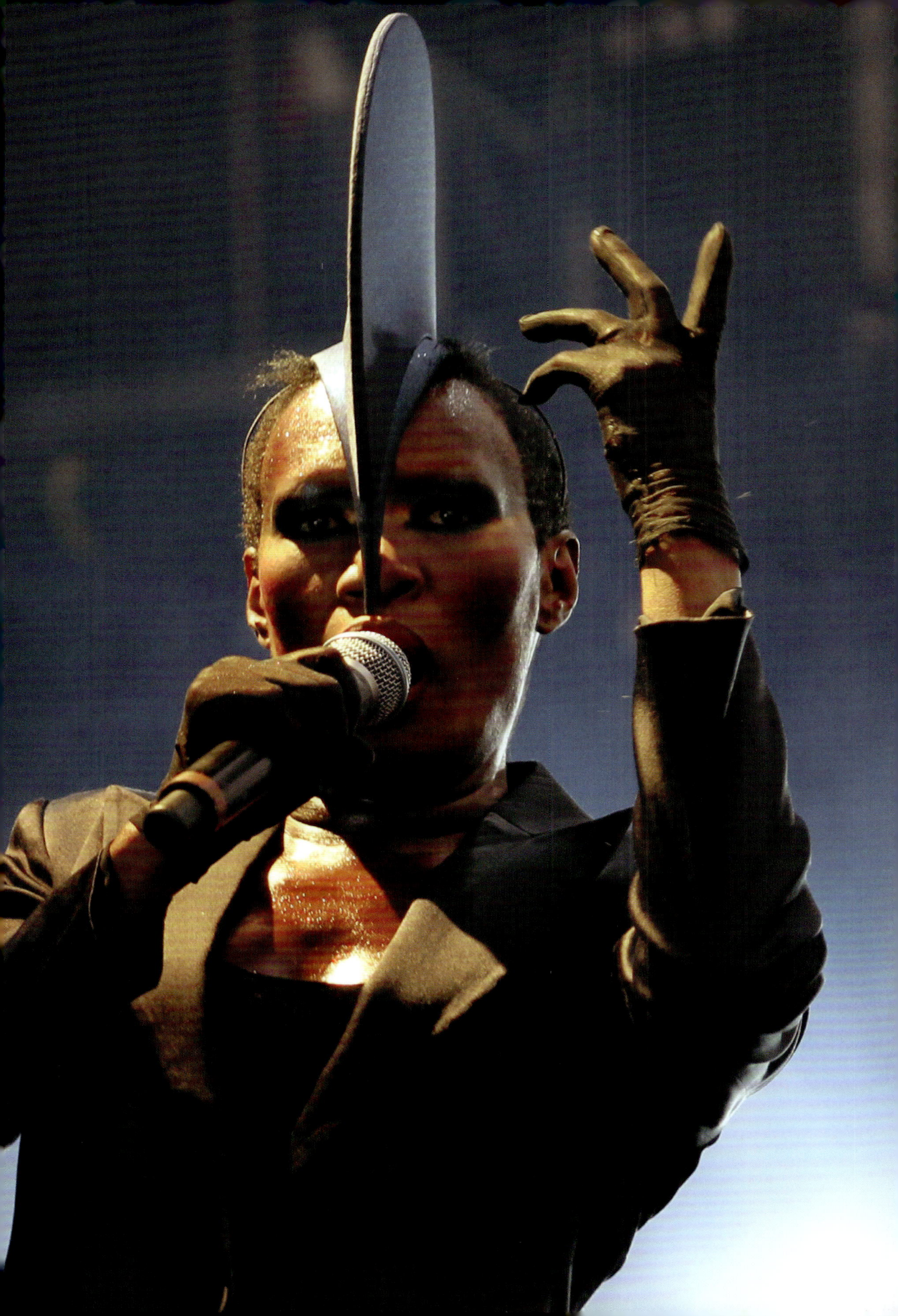

JAMES BROWN

June 2004

"The moves? They had slowed down a bit, sure, but the magic was still there. And that voice?It shook its head at any notion of age."

Growing up in America, I was lucky enough to witness the living legend that was James Brown, on TV. His music, combined with those enthralling dance moves, absolutely captivated me when I was young. The way he could shuffle across the stage like he was floating was just unreal to watch, and I spent many afternoons trying (and failing) to copy him. I still can't fully describe the thrill I felt every time I saw him on-screen. There was something about him that was simply untouchable, utterly unique. But as much as I idolised him, I'd never seen him in person, let alone had the chance to shoot him. Unfortunately, life didn't go too smoothly for James, and after a rough turn he ended up in prison, which I thought had crushed any hope I had of ever capturing the Godfather of Soul with my camera.

Then, out of the blue, an opportunity landed in my lap. James was released from jail, and not long after he went back on tour. Eventually, the Red Hot Chili Peppers announced a gig at Hyde Park, with James Brown as the opening act. I couldn't believe my luck. I felt like the universe was giving me a second chance. I absolutely adore the Chili Peppers but, as great as they are, forget them this time – my heart was absolutely set on James. I applied for accreditation immediately, fuelled by the idea that I was finally going to photograph the Motown legend I had grown up idolising. Would he still be the same electric performer I remembered? Could he still pull off those moves after everything he'd been through? Prison has a way of breaking people, and I wondered if it had changed him. Plus, he was much older now. Could he still bring that same energy to the stage?

When the day finally came, I watched in awe as he took to the stage. The moves? They had slowed down a bit, sure, but the magic was still there. And that voice? It shook its head at any notion of age. Hearing him belt out the classics live, even at this stage in his life, almost made my camera an afterthought since I was seeing a musical legend from my youth defy expectations. It was everything I'd hoped for and more.

A few days after the gig, I was walking down the street when, out of nowhere, I spotted James and his wife. I couldn't believe it. I just happened to have some prints from the concert in the back of my car – call it fate. I quickly grabbed a few and nervously approached him. To my surprise, he was warm and gracious, and after chatting for a bit, I gave him a couple of the prints. He even signed one for me, scribbling "Get Down, James Brown" across the bottom. That signed print still hangs in my office to this day, a reminder of when I got a piece of my childhood dream written into my reality.

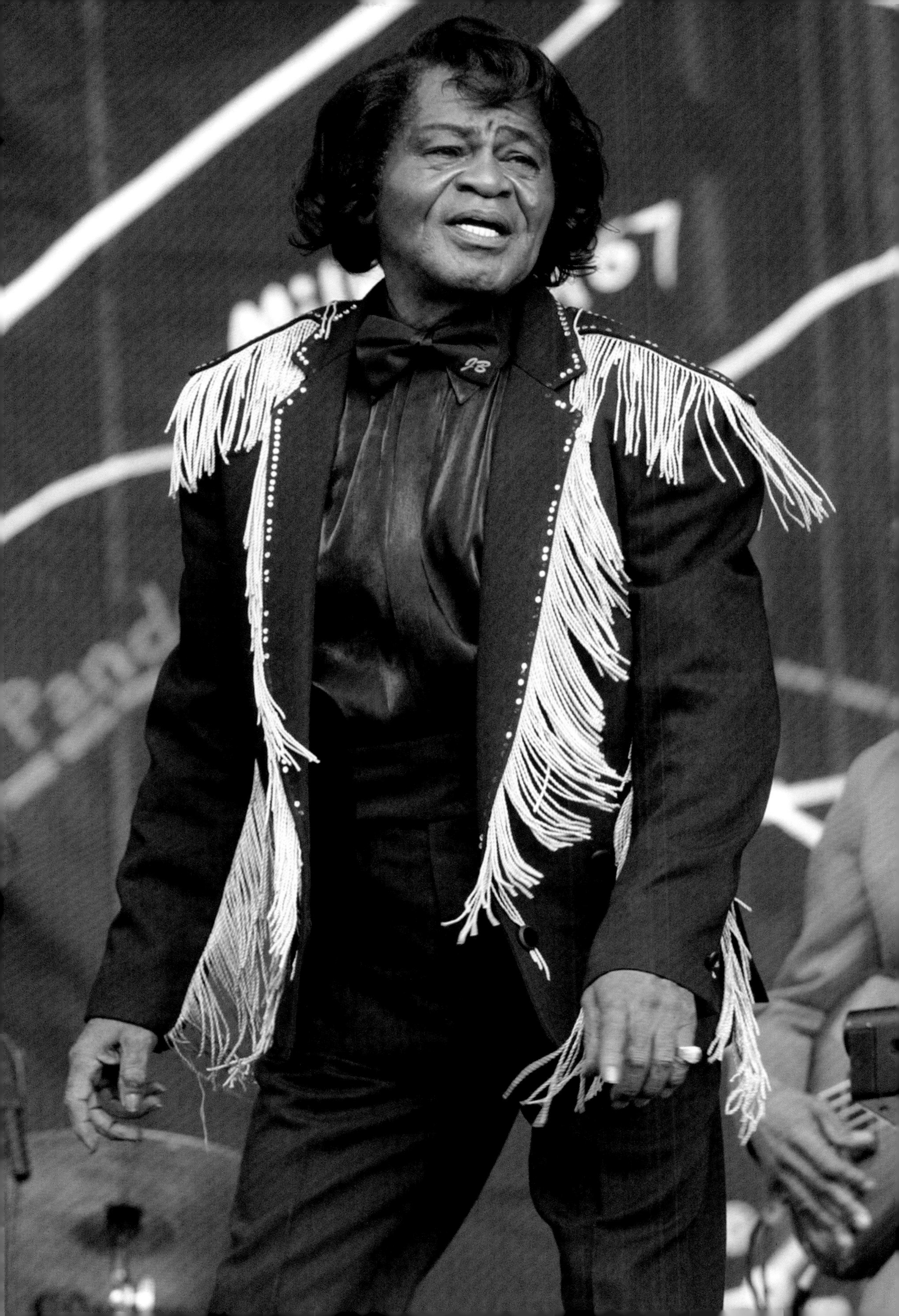

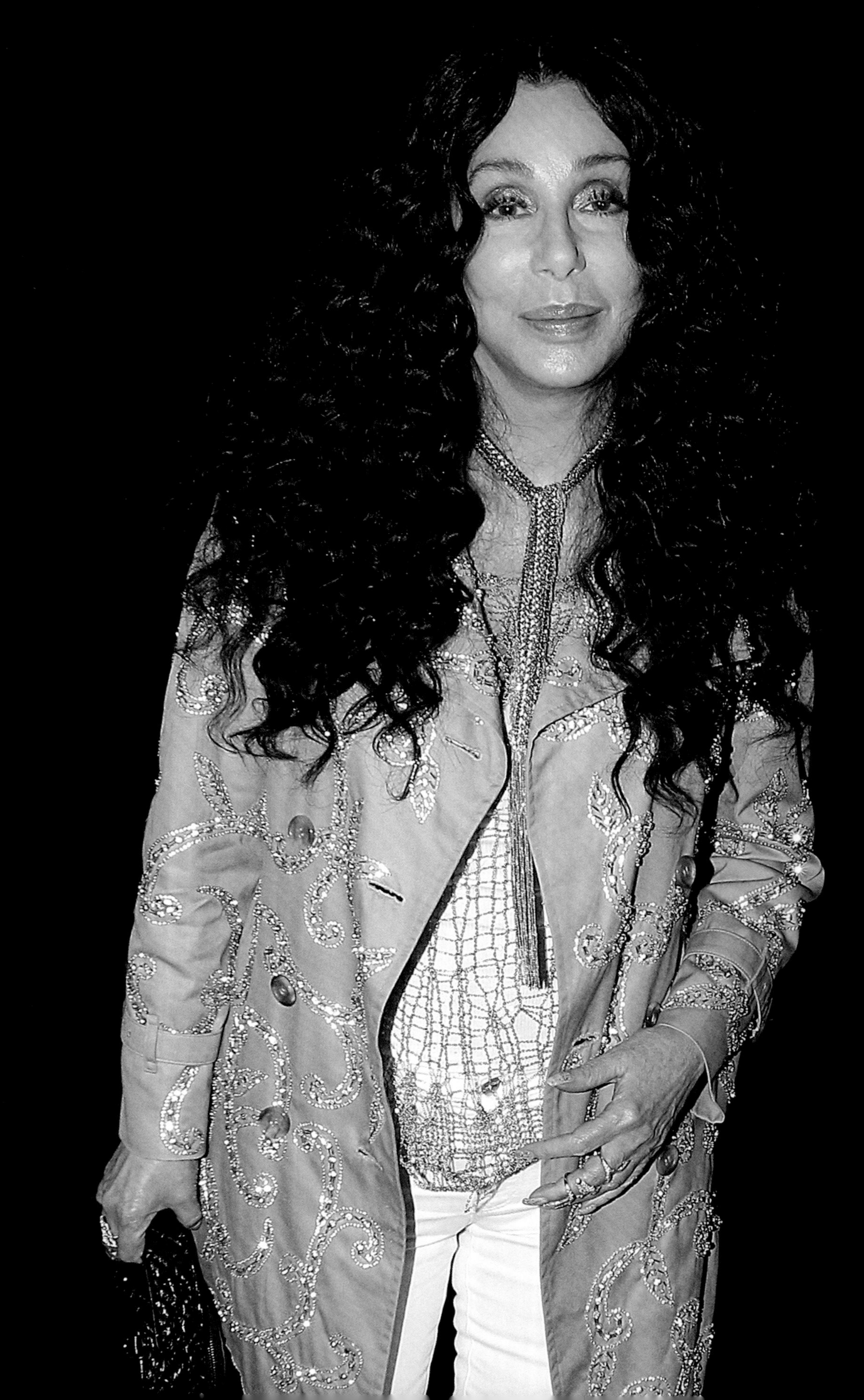

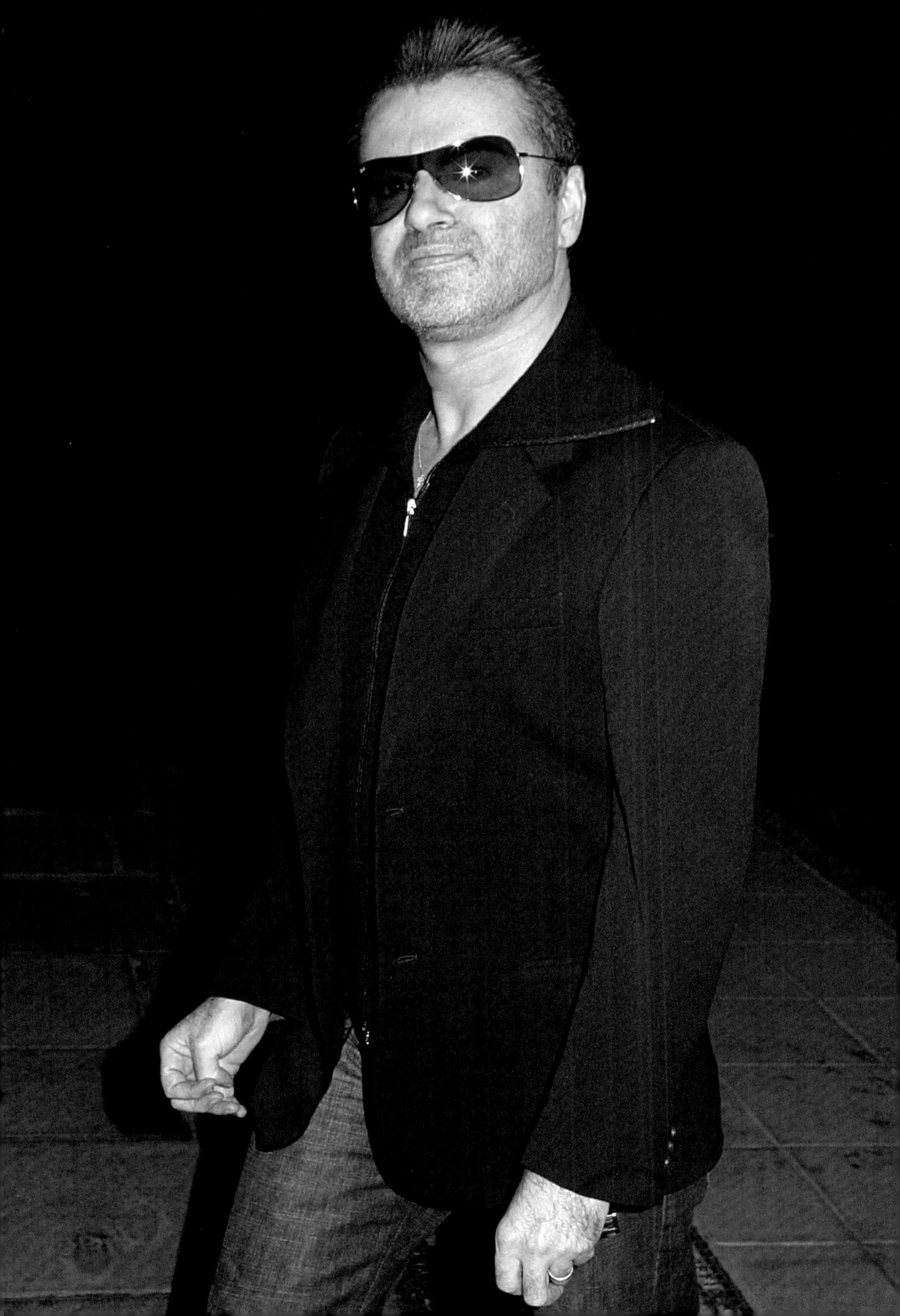

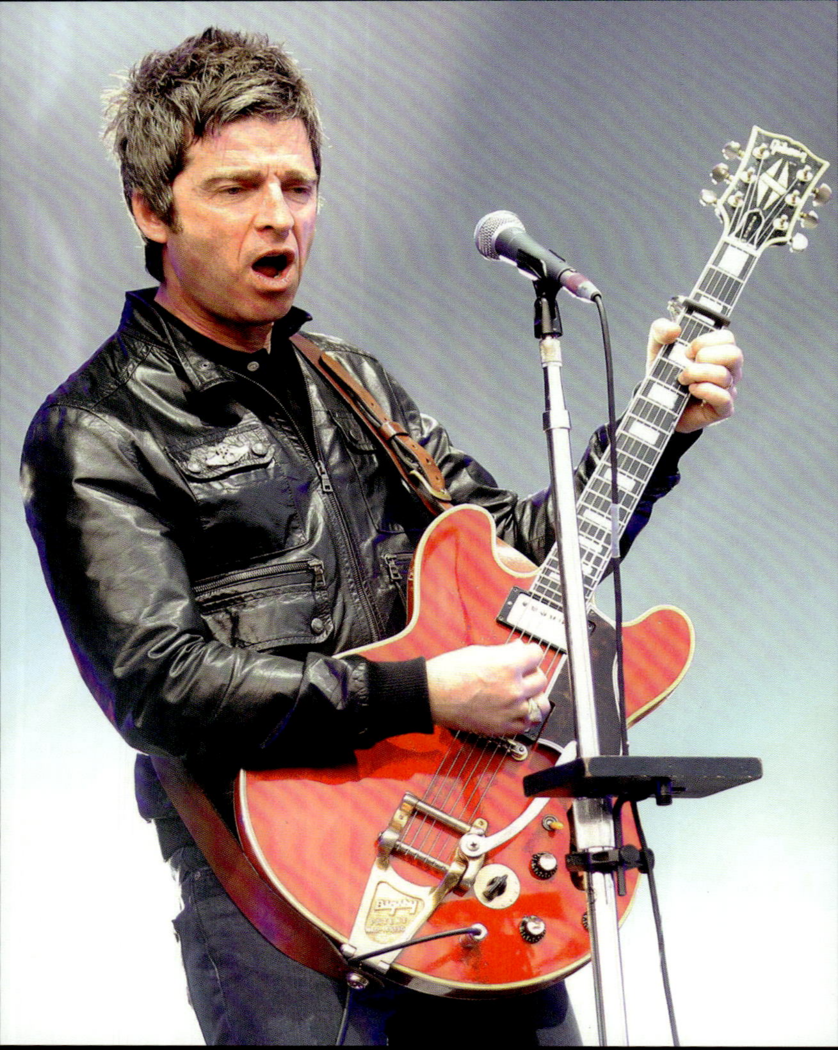

Noel Gallagher
Clapham Common
July 2015
Performing at the Calling Festival

Liam Gallagher
The Forum, Kentish Town
May 1999
Kosovo Aid Benefit Party

Previous pages:
Cher
Quilon, St James's
June 2018

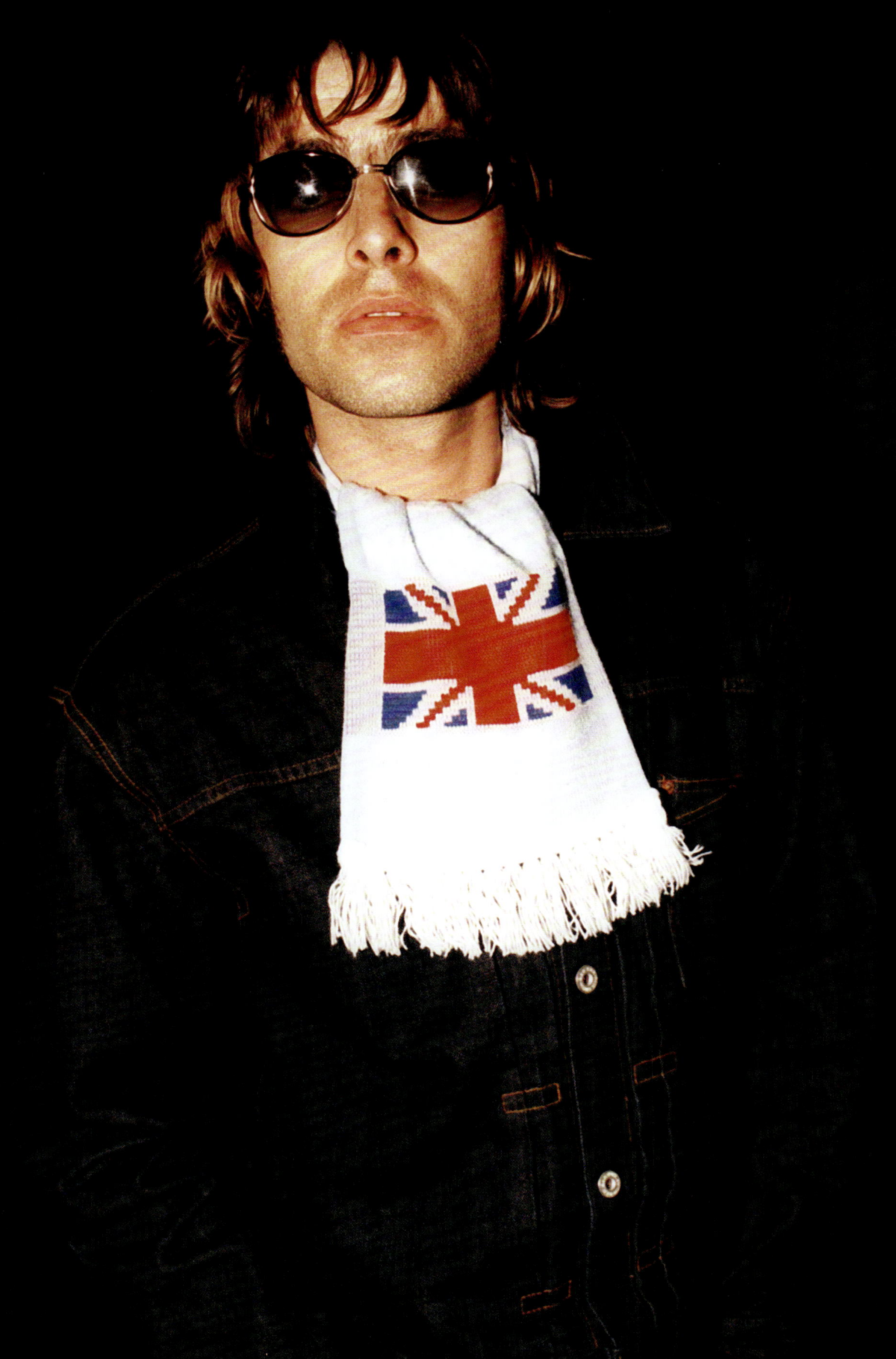

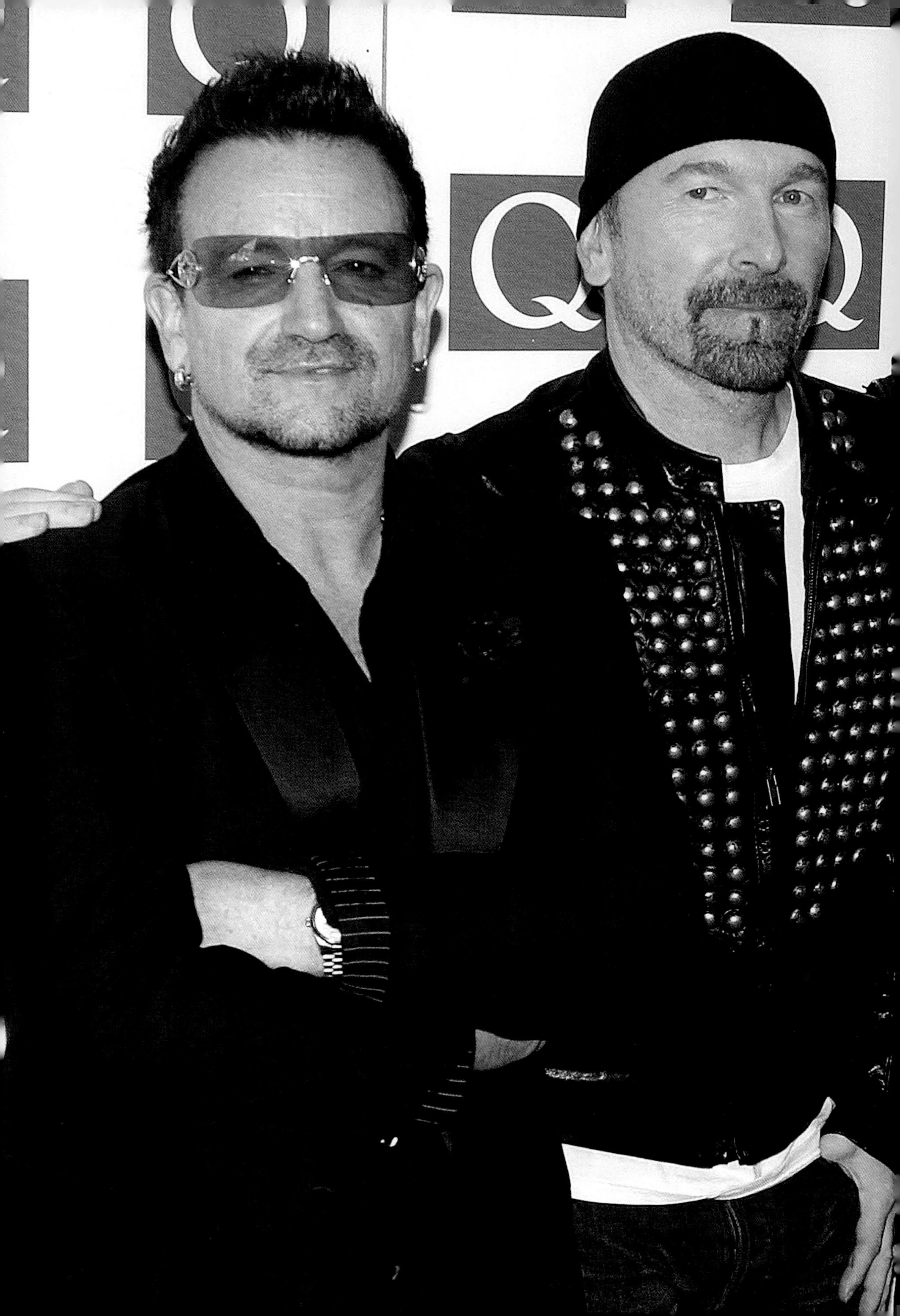
Q
Q

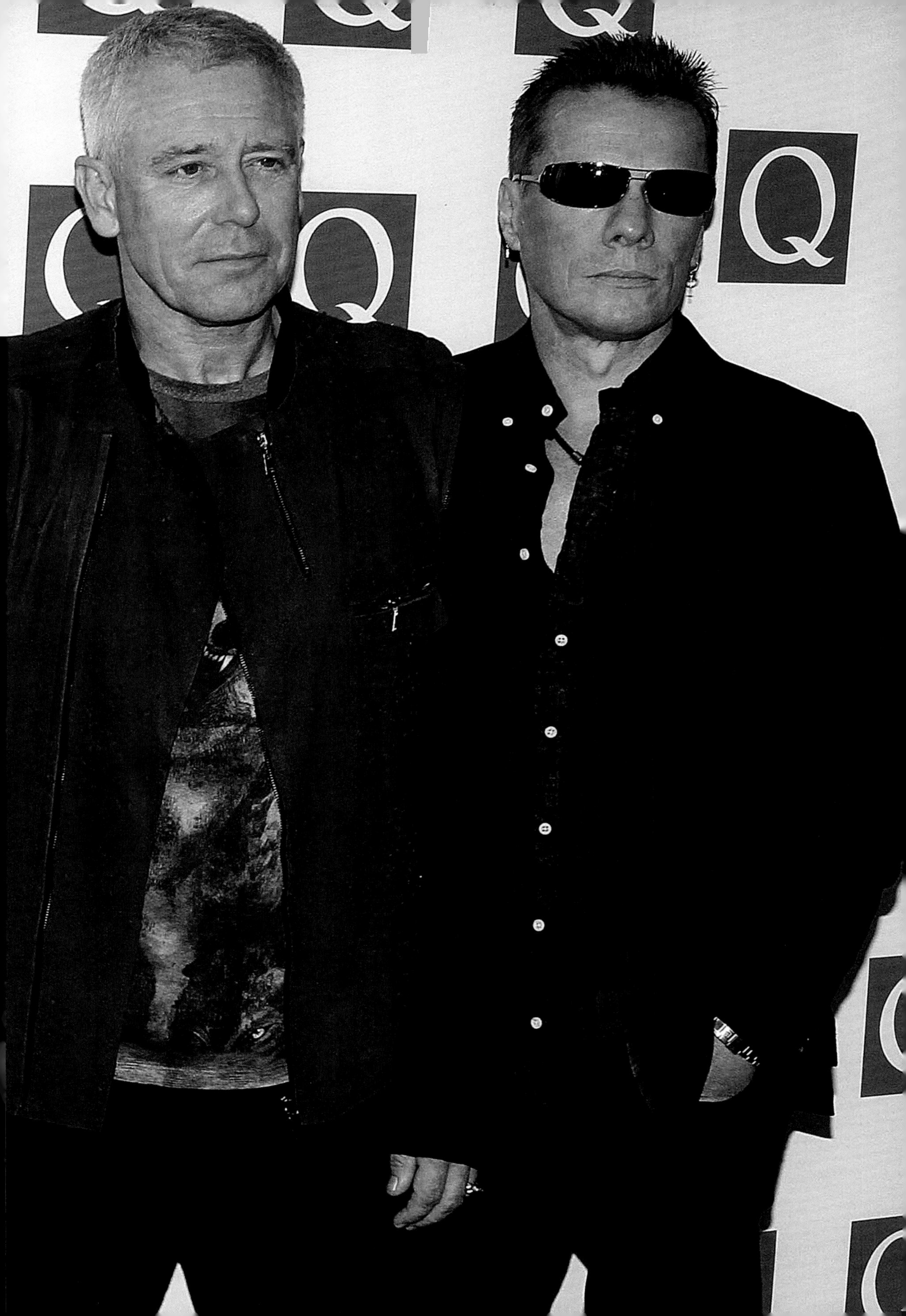
Q

Iggy Pop
Hyde Park, July 2012
Performing at the Hard Rock Calling Festival

Previous pages:
U2
Grosvenor House Hotel, Mayfair
October 2011
Q Awards

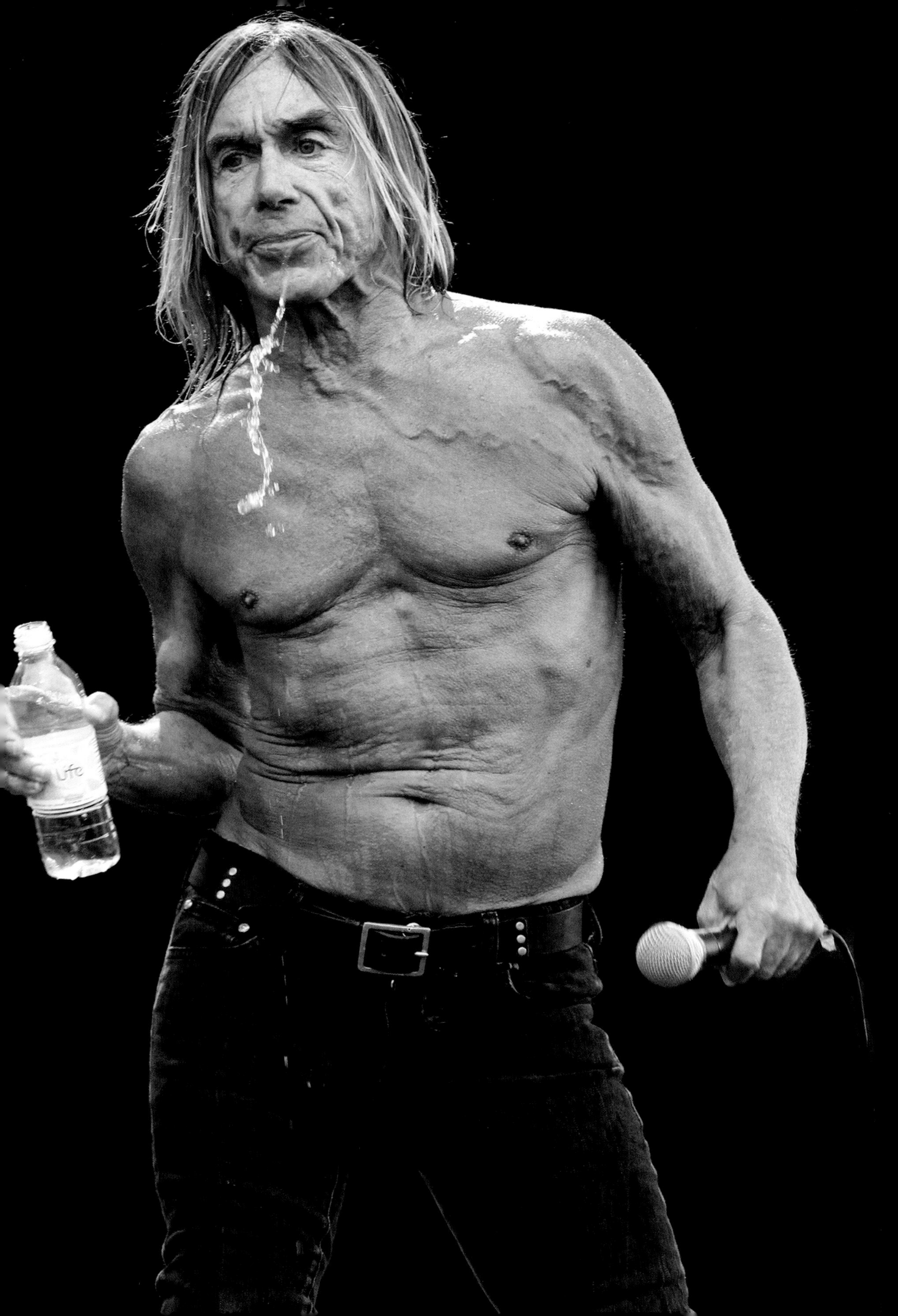
Life

BRITNEY SPEARS
September 2011

"As the crew murmured about 'one last shot' before they wrapped, she emerged, gun in hand."

Over the years, I had the chance to shoot Britney countless times, both onstage, under the dazzling glare of the spotlight, and offstage, amidst the mundane rhythms of life. But none come close to the day she stormed through the streets of Hackney with a gun gripped tightly in her hand.

It was 2011, and Britney had just arrived in London with her then-boyfriend, Jason Trawick, to record the music video for 'Criminal'. Stoke Newington Town Hall had been chosen as the backdrop for a Bonnie-and-Clyde-style robbery scene in the video. I had settled into my usual spot, camera poised, watching as Britney, sporting a balaclava, burst out of the building with Jason, their escape punctuated by the roar of a sleek silver Mini Cooper. Take after take of that same sequence, each one carefully choreographed.

Then came the final take, when the sense of routine began to shift. As the crew murmured about "one last shot" before they wrapped, she emerged, gun in hand – not the harmless, replica kind you'd see in a stage play, but a shockingly realistic prop, so eerily lifelike it might have still been warm from its last shot. Click.

A few days later, I would learn that this was something far bigger than I had imagined. The scene had ignited a firestorm, with Hackney Council blindsided by the use of the weapon, fake or not. Only a month had passed since the explosive London riots that followed the killing of Mark Duggan by police, which saw mass looting and arson from gangs all over England. As a result, the government was very sensitive to any acts that could be seen as glamourising the gang lifestyle. Labour MP Diane Abbott and Councillor Ian Rathbone quickly stepped in, demanding explanations. The controversy was swift and unapologetic, forcing Britney's production crew to scramble to issue a public apology, insisting it had all been a terrible misunderstanding. But the damage had been done.

That wasn't my first time photographing Britney. A few years earlier in 2007, I attended her Circus Tour. I remember the lights, the designed chaos, the way she moved so fluidly, hypnotically, like a magician spinning an illusion before an audience too enchanted to question what lay beyond the glittering image. Her world has been just like that, caught between the intoxicating fantasy of the stage and the sourer truths lurking just beneath. And I, camera in hand, have captured plenty of both.

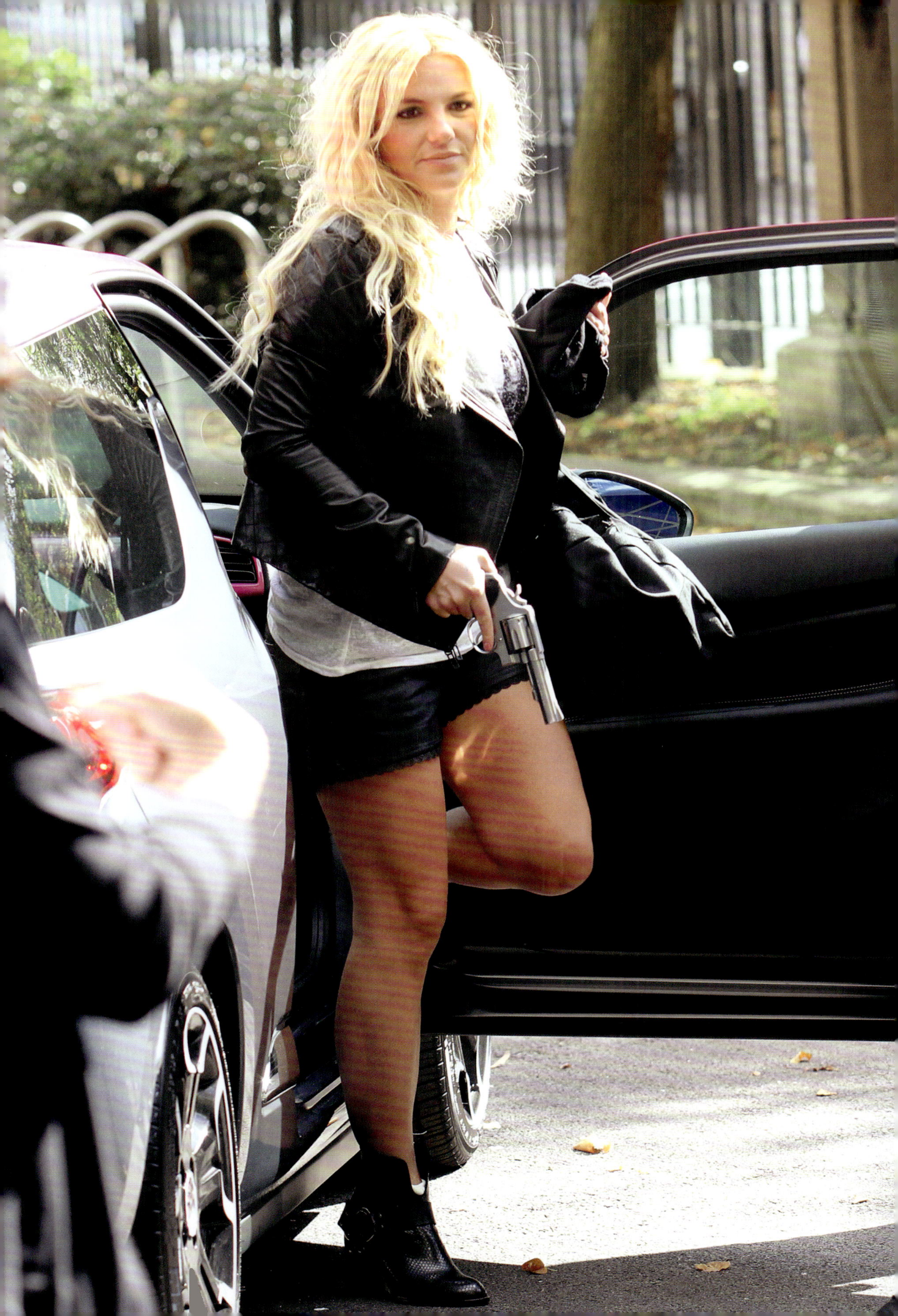

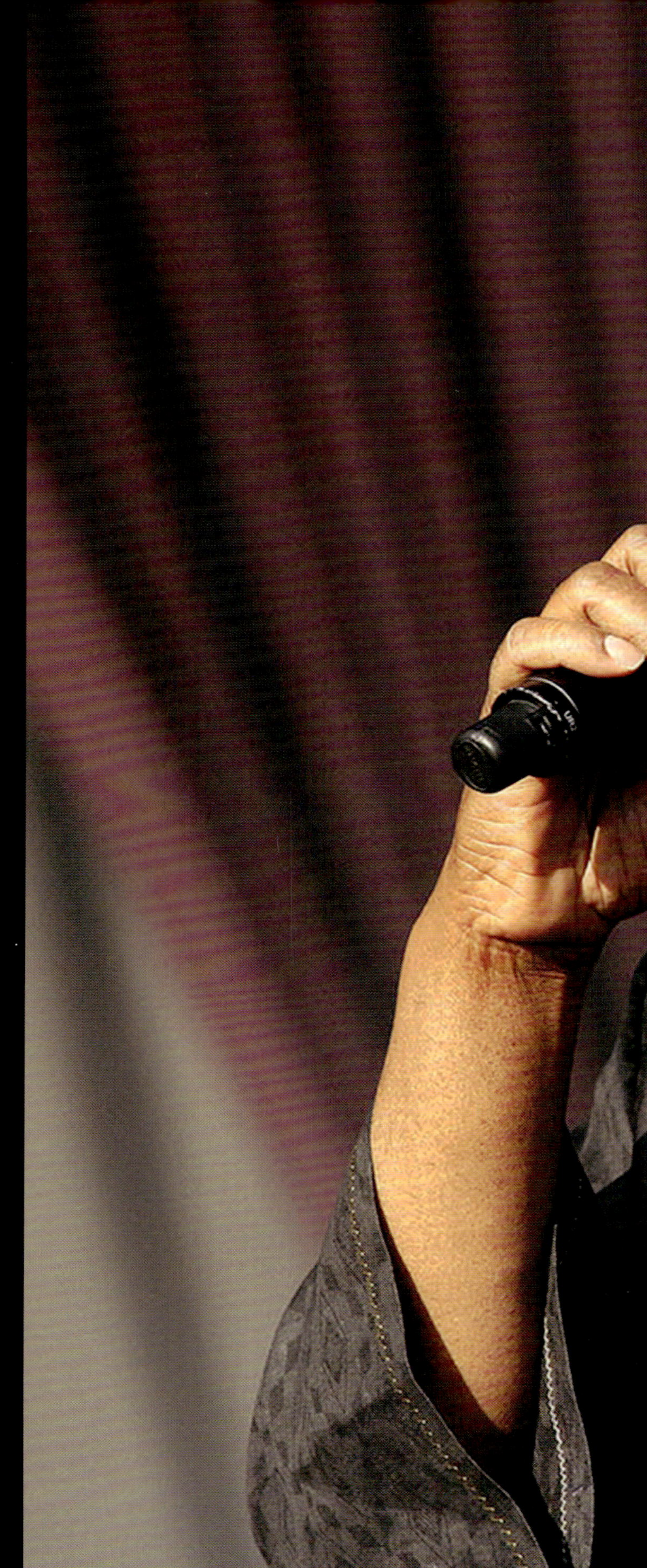

Stevie Wonder
Clapham Common
June 2014
Performing at the Calling Festival

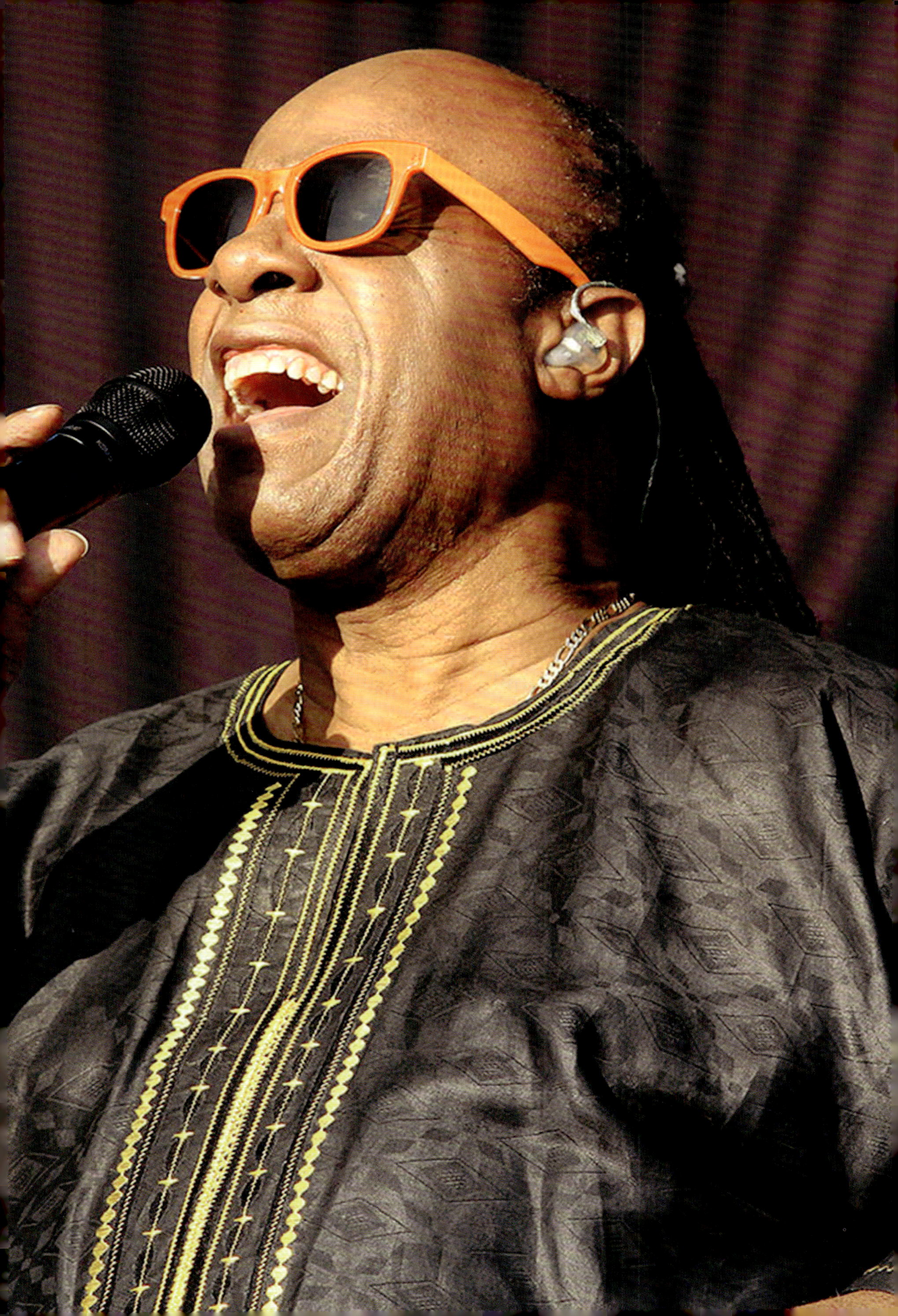

MICHAEL JACKSON
April 1999

On a cold April night in London, I received a call that instantly spiked my adrenaline: "Are you interested in Michael Jackson?" What kind of question was that? Who wouldn't be? My friend on the other end explained that Michael had just walked into Harrods for some private late-night shopping. Without hesitation, I grabbed my gear and raced to Hans Place, a side street that ran alongside the iconic department store.

When I arrived, I was greeted by the sight of a light-blue classic Mercedes, with discreet curtains in the back, parked nearby – the sort of car usually reserved for VIP guests of the store. I'd seen that exact car around London before, always associated with high-profile clients. The presence of several other vehicles suggested Michael was already inside, and if they weren't evidence enough, a crowd of about 50 eager fans had gathered, craning their necks for even the briefest glimpse of the King of Pop. It struck me then, as it had many times before, that no one – not even the biggest A-listers – could pull a crowd like Michael Jackson. I had photographed a lot of big stars in my time, but Michael was in a league of his own. A true megastar.

I weaved my way through the throng, angling for a clear view through the door. Sure enough, there he was, descending the stairs. My heart raced as I adjusted my camera settings, firing off a quick test shot to make sure everything was primed. The door swung open, and the sea of people rushed forward. A wave of security flooded out, unnecessarily pushing and shoving, making the scene far messier than it needed to be. Michael followed behind and I stood my ground, camera ready, waiting for that perfect moment. I had been preparing for this shot for years. I still remembered vividly how, during my first attempt to photograph Michael, someone had shoved me, ruining my shot. I was just a kid back then and I hadn't expected it. But this time, I was ready. As Michael walked past, I called out his name. He turned, and I managed to raise my camera just enough to fire off a series of shots. Click, click, click. Eight in total. Michael looked straight into my lens, and I knew I had what I needed. A second later, it was over – Michael slipped into the car, and it sped off into the night.

A couple of years later, I got another call from the picture desk: Michael was back in town and they wanted me to cover him again. I wasn't expecting anything too different from the last encounter, but things took an unexpected turn. When I arrived, security opened the door and, to my shock, waved me inside.

"More than a star – he was an era unto himself."

For the next half-hour, I had the rare opportunity to photograph Michael as he browsed through Harrods in private. It was a dream come true. We cracked jokes, complimented the extravagant displays – just a regular hangout, except one of us happened to be the most famous musician on the planet.

Unfortunately, I only saw Michael a few more times in London before his untimely death, but these encounters with him, especially that second night at Harrods, remain etched in my memory. MJ was more than a star – he was an era unto himself.

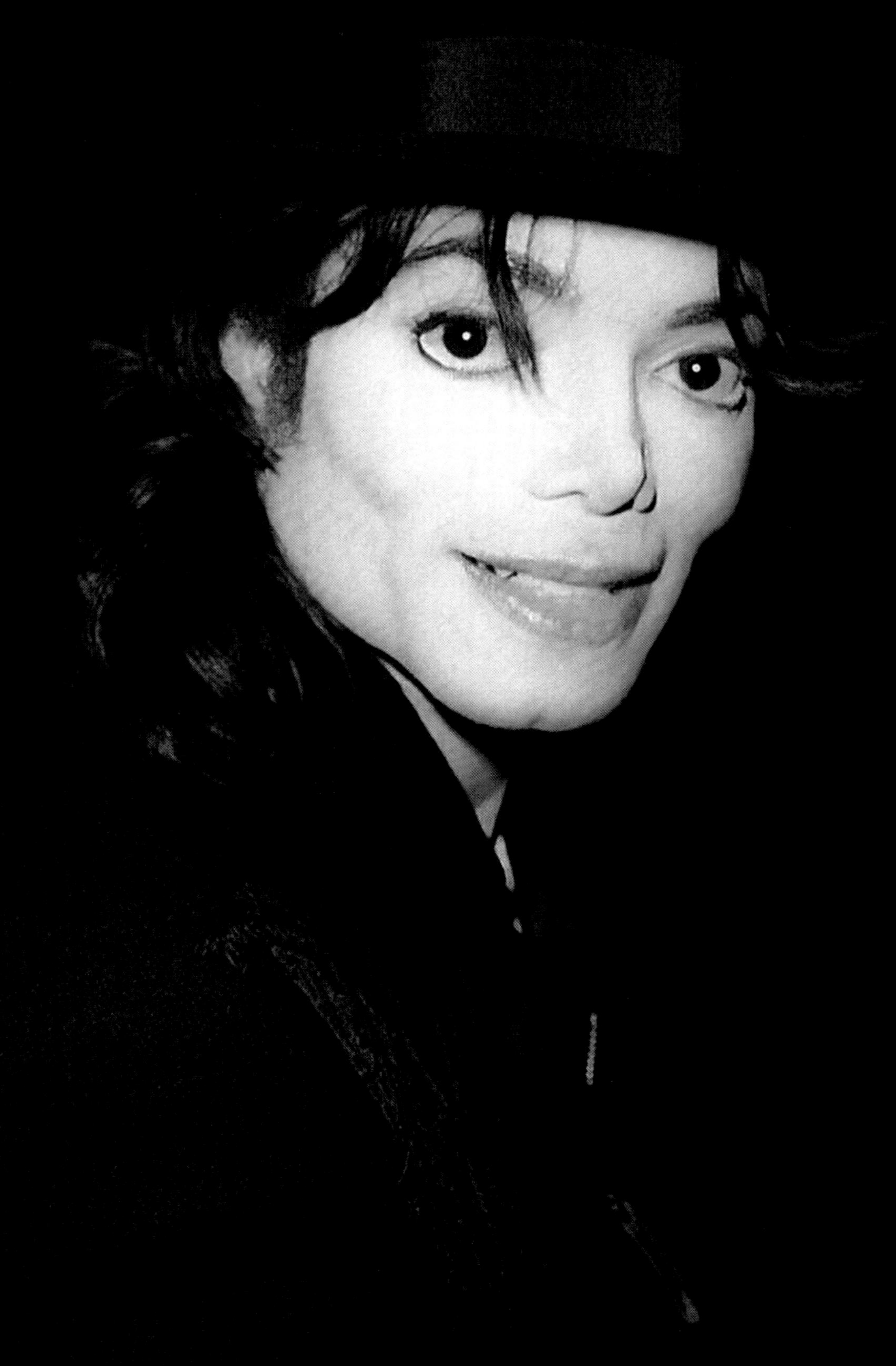

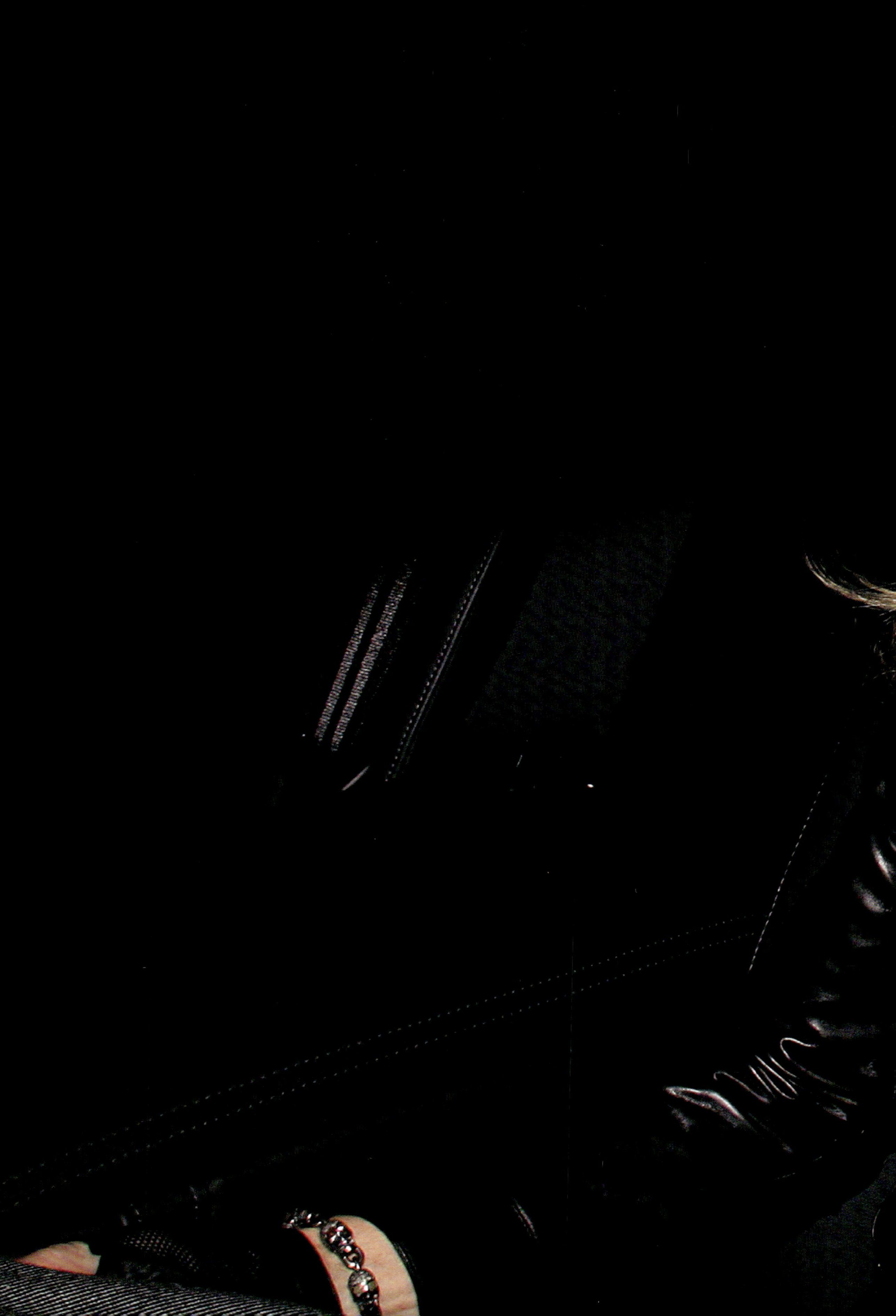

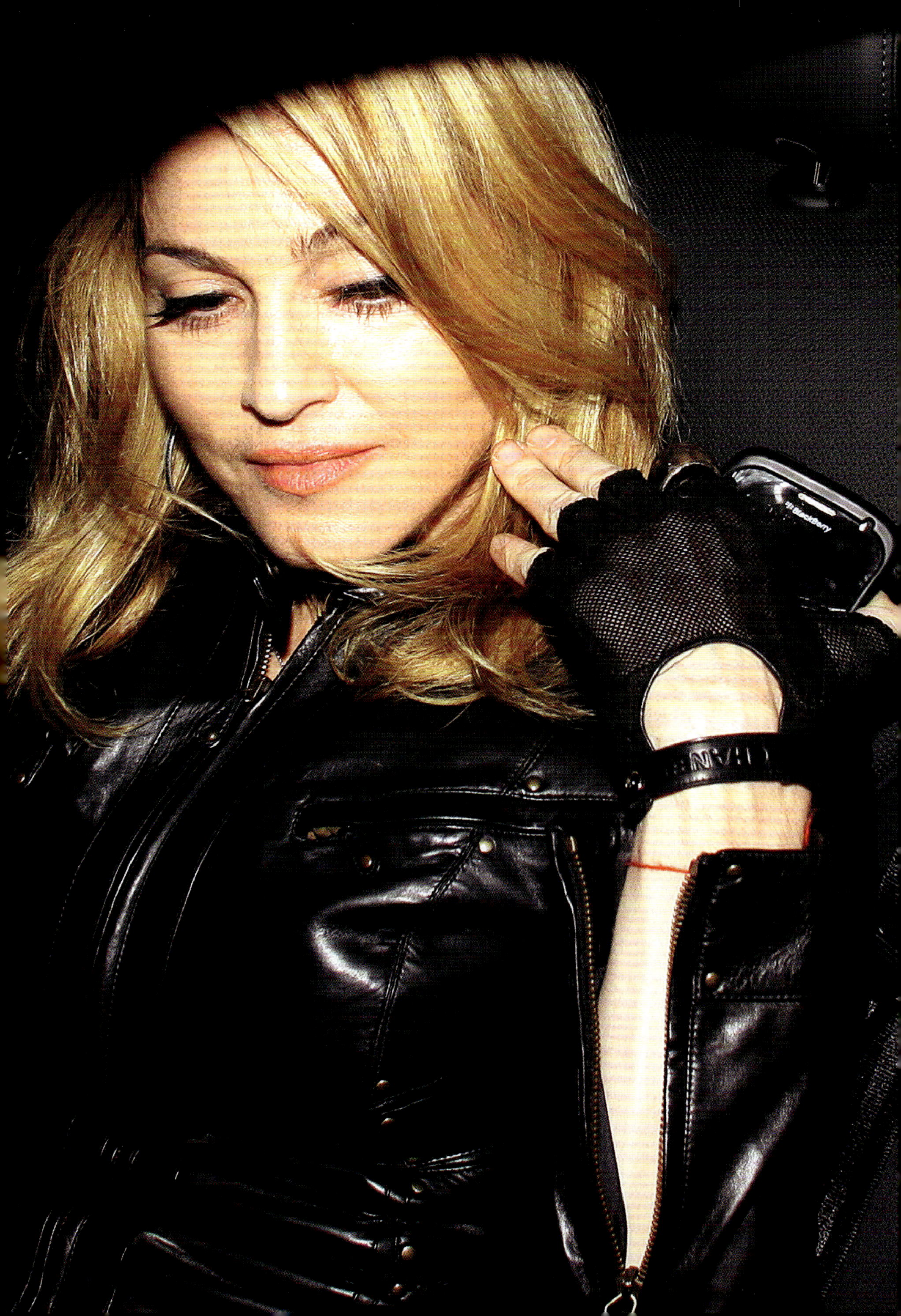
BlackBerry

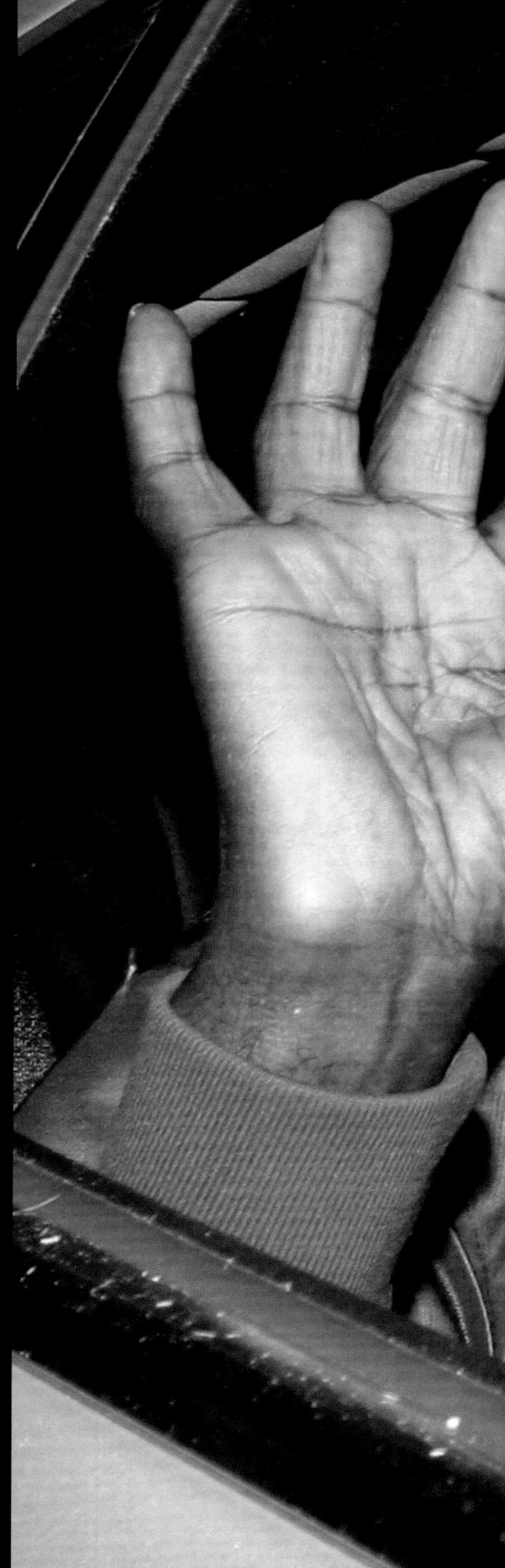

Chuck Berry
Jazz Café, Camden
November 2008

Previous Pages:
Madonna
Locanda Locatelli, Marylebone
October 2009

Following Pages:
Red Hot Chili Peppers
Roundhouse, Camden
January 2005

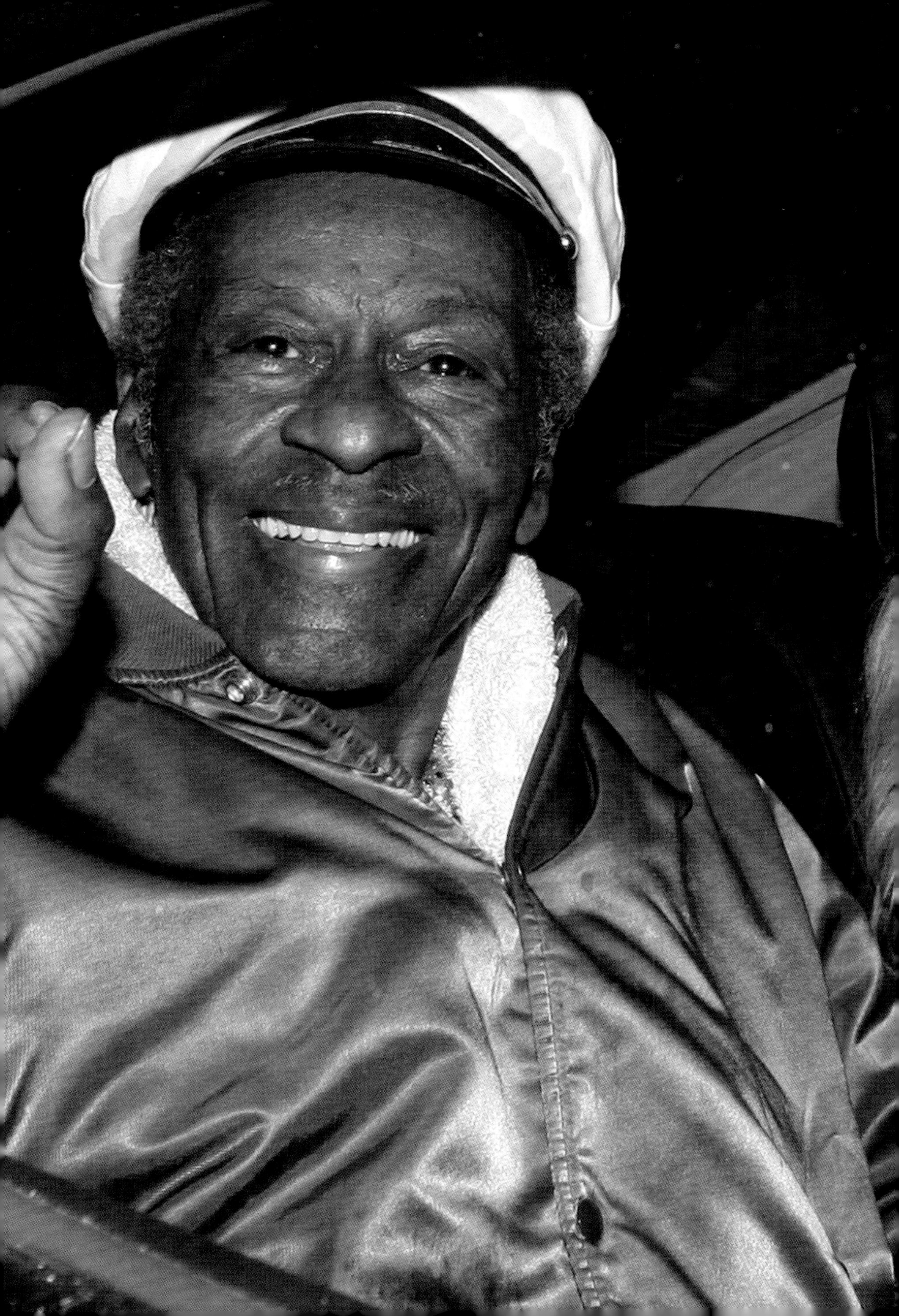

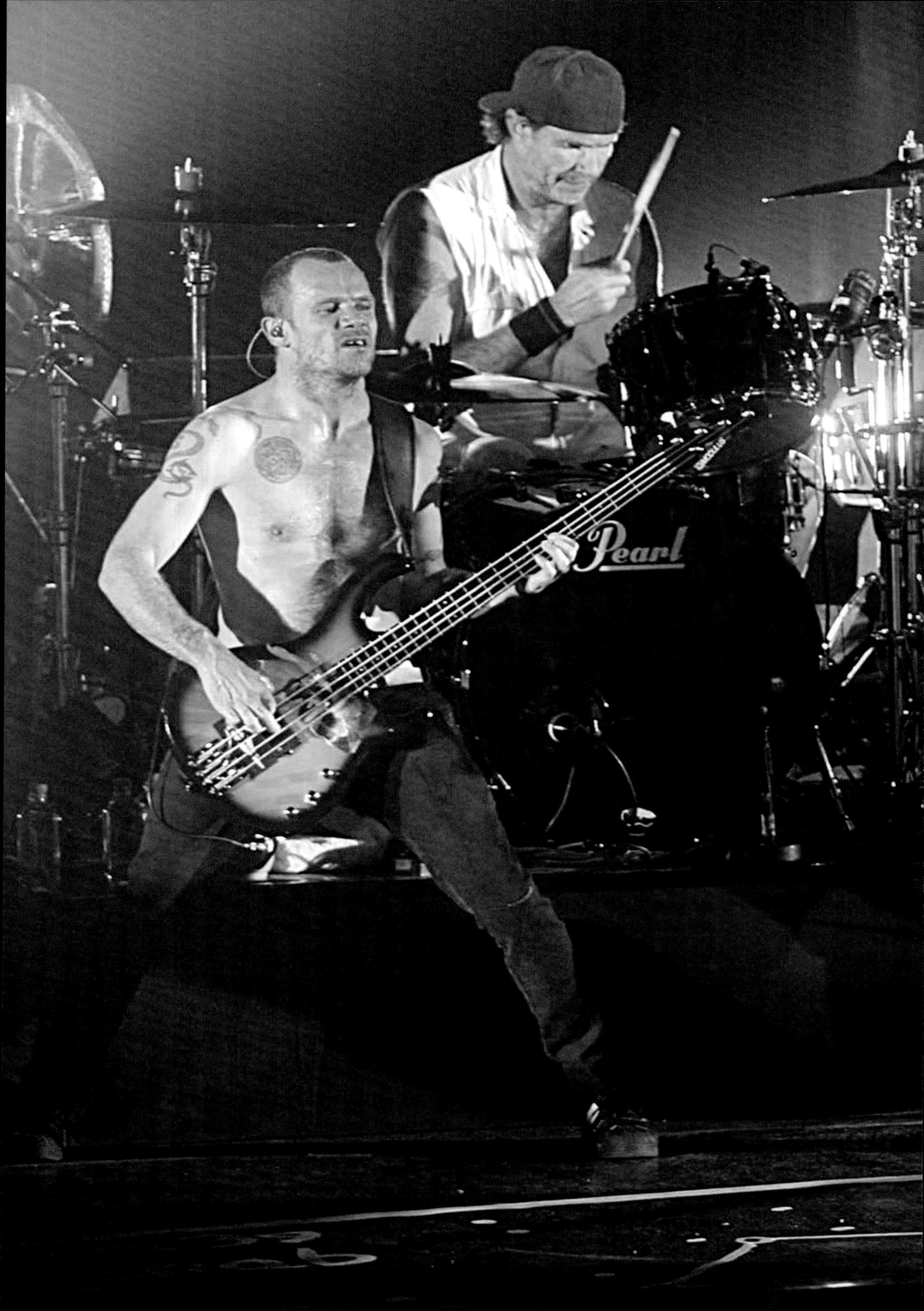
Pearl

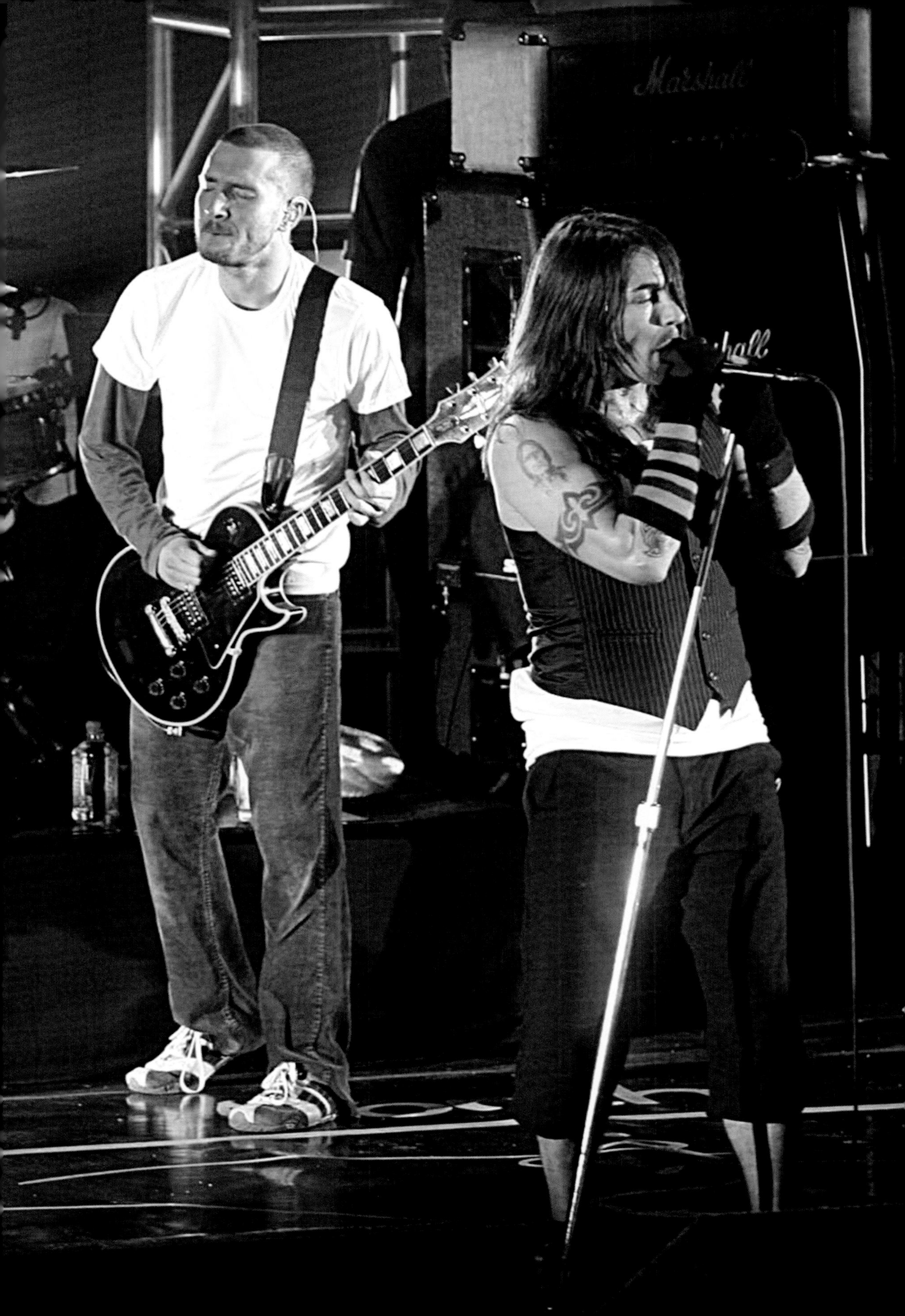
Marshall

THE ROLLING STONES

July 2013

My first brush with The Rolling Stones wasn't seeing them onstage or from behind a velvet rope. Rather, it was at a party, buried somewhere in the early '90s. I was still an untested photographer, fumbling through assignments for a local paper, when suddenly he walked in. Mick Jagger, whose voice had once poured through my childhood living room like molten gold, spinning on a turntable.

Time folded in on itself. As Jagger stood just a few feet away, memories of my father came rushing back. He loves rock and roll, and I used to stand with him by the record player, the crackle of vinyl filling the air as classics like *Hot Rocks* (1971) and *Exile on Main St.* (1972) ran on all night. Those smooth melodies had wrapped themselves around my formative years, and now, standing in front of one of the men who shaped that soundtrack, it all felt cyclical.

The Stones, to me, represented the unadulterated, unpolished soul of rock and roll – the primal pulse of a generation that had refused to sit quietly. But getting close to them, especially in those early days, felt as distant as the Moon. Publicists, PR reps and gatekeepers surrounded them, making access to their gigs a near-mythical quest for an up-and-coming photographer like me. But rock and roll, like all wild things, rewards the stubborn. And eventually, the door cracked open.

I was invited to shoot a live Rolling Stones concert in Hyde Park, a venue that embodied the grandeur of their music. It was a night of history – The Stones back in front of 100,000 roaring fans. When Jagger took the stage, it was as if the crowd inhaled all at once, a collective gasp of awe and anticipation. Then: eruption. Jagger ripped through the stage like a man half his age and twice as alive. The band was relentless, their energy volcanic, and I was right in the eye of the storm, snapping frame after frame like I was trying to trap lightning.

Over 2,000 frames later, I felt like I had done it – preserved every scream, every chord, every instance of pure, untamed electricity that had surged through Hyde Park. The next morning, my photographs were everywhere – papers around the world had chosen those shots to tell the story of the night. The Stones, immortalised again. And the kid who used to sit by the record player finally telling the story from the other side.

"I was right in the eye of the storm, snapping frame after frame like I was trying to trap lightning."

To anyone who's ever doubted the staying power of rock and roll, I say: look to The Rolling Stones. Look at the way their music has lived through generations, how it has ignited the passions of millions, from my father's era to my own son's. Jagger, Keith, Ronnie – and of course, the late, great Charlie – they are legends, the embodiment of what it means to endure. Their untamed spirit, their relentless pursuit of the music, has united us across time, reminding us that rock and roll isn't just a genre. It's a lifeblood. Long may they rock!

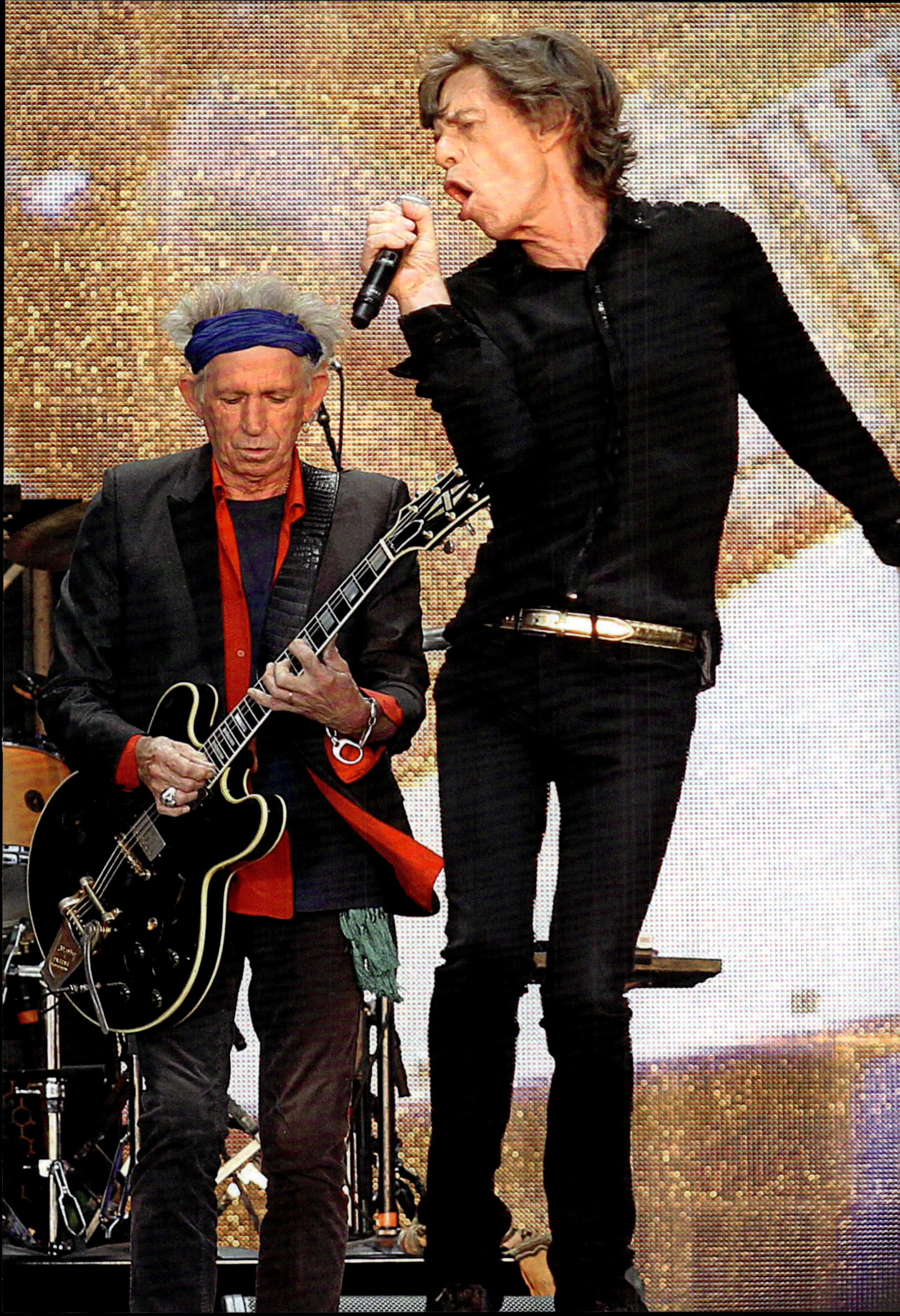

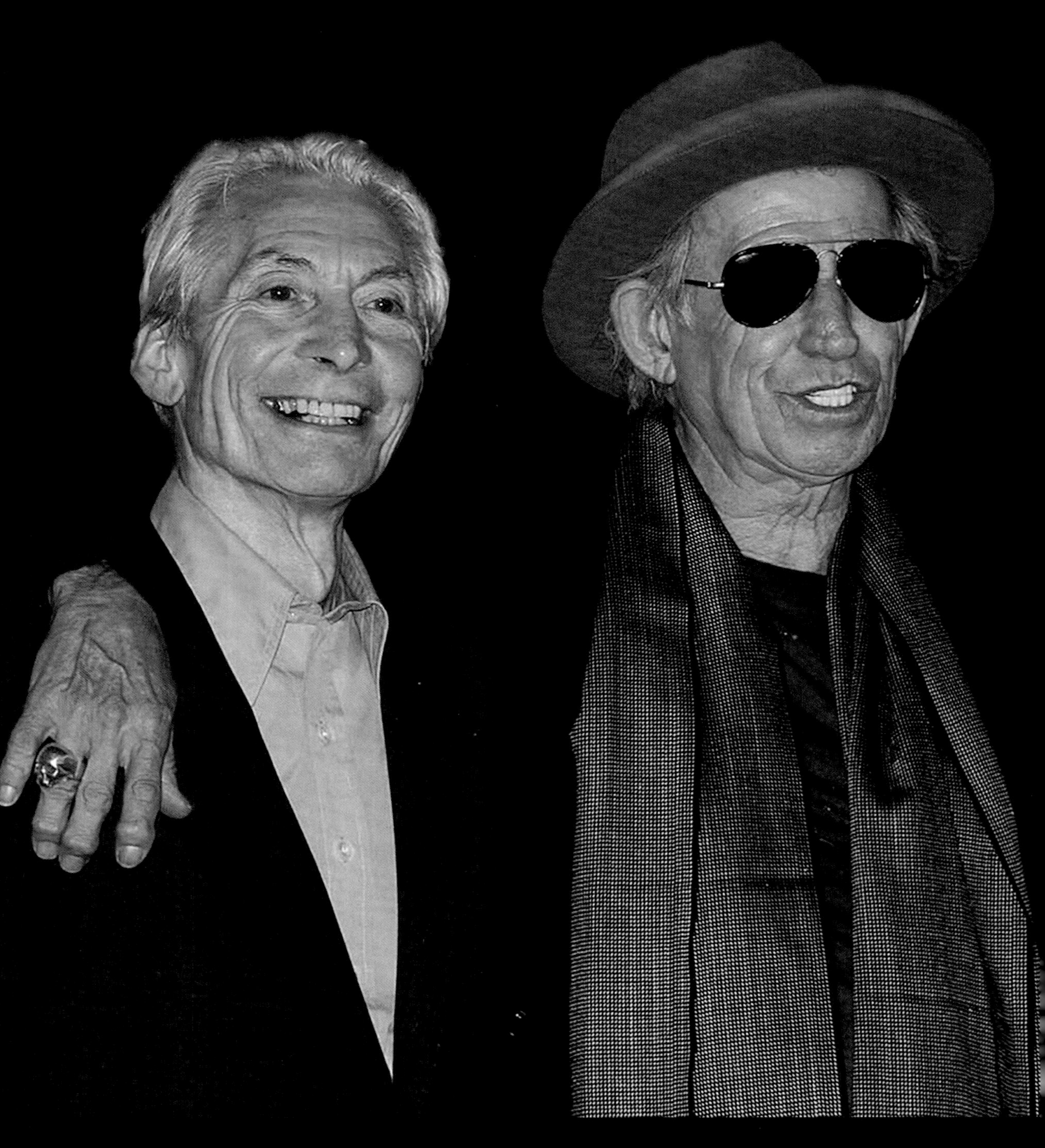

The Rolling Stones
Somerset House, Strand
July 2012
Arriving for their 50th-anniversary party

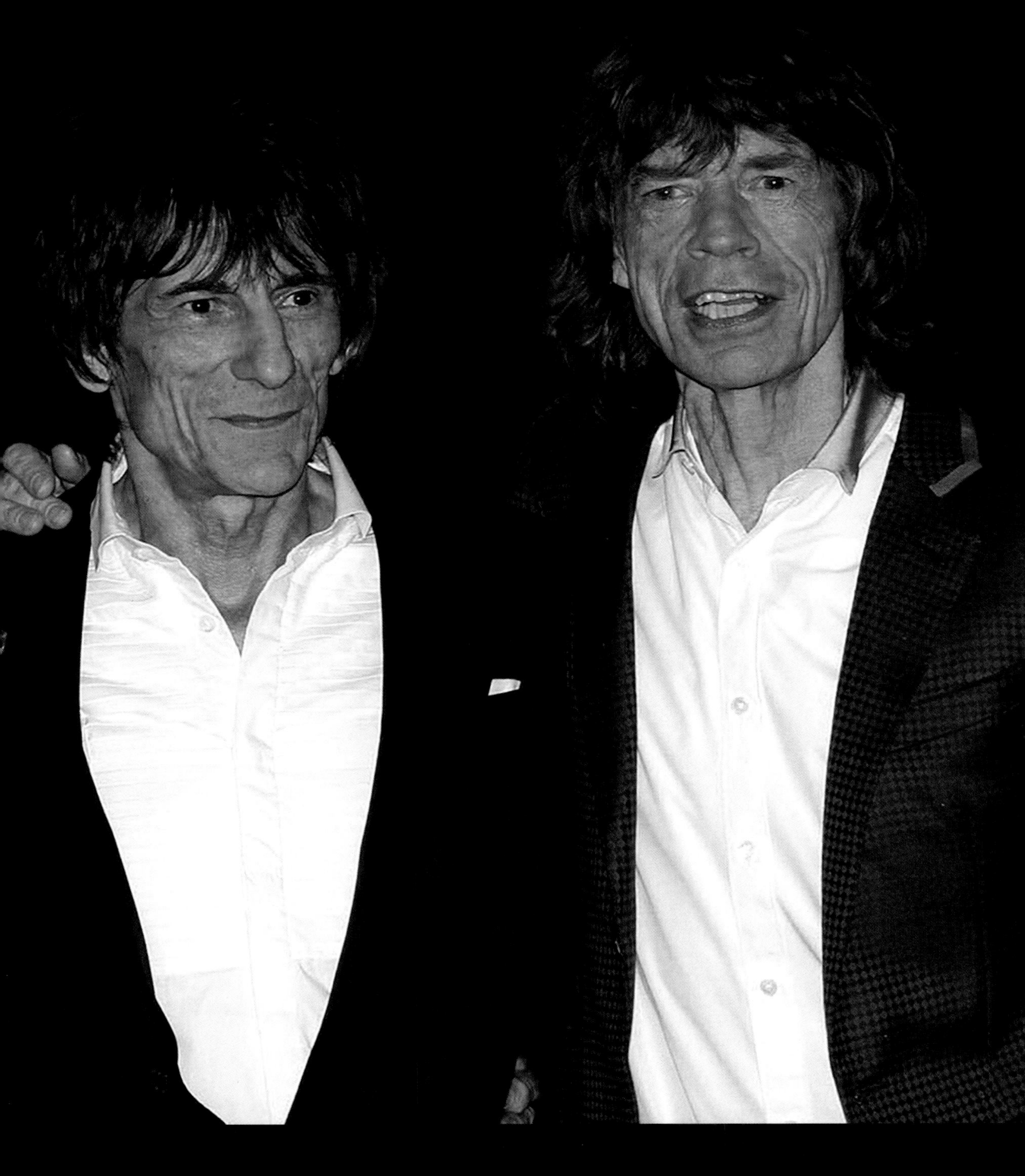

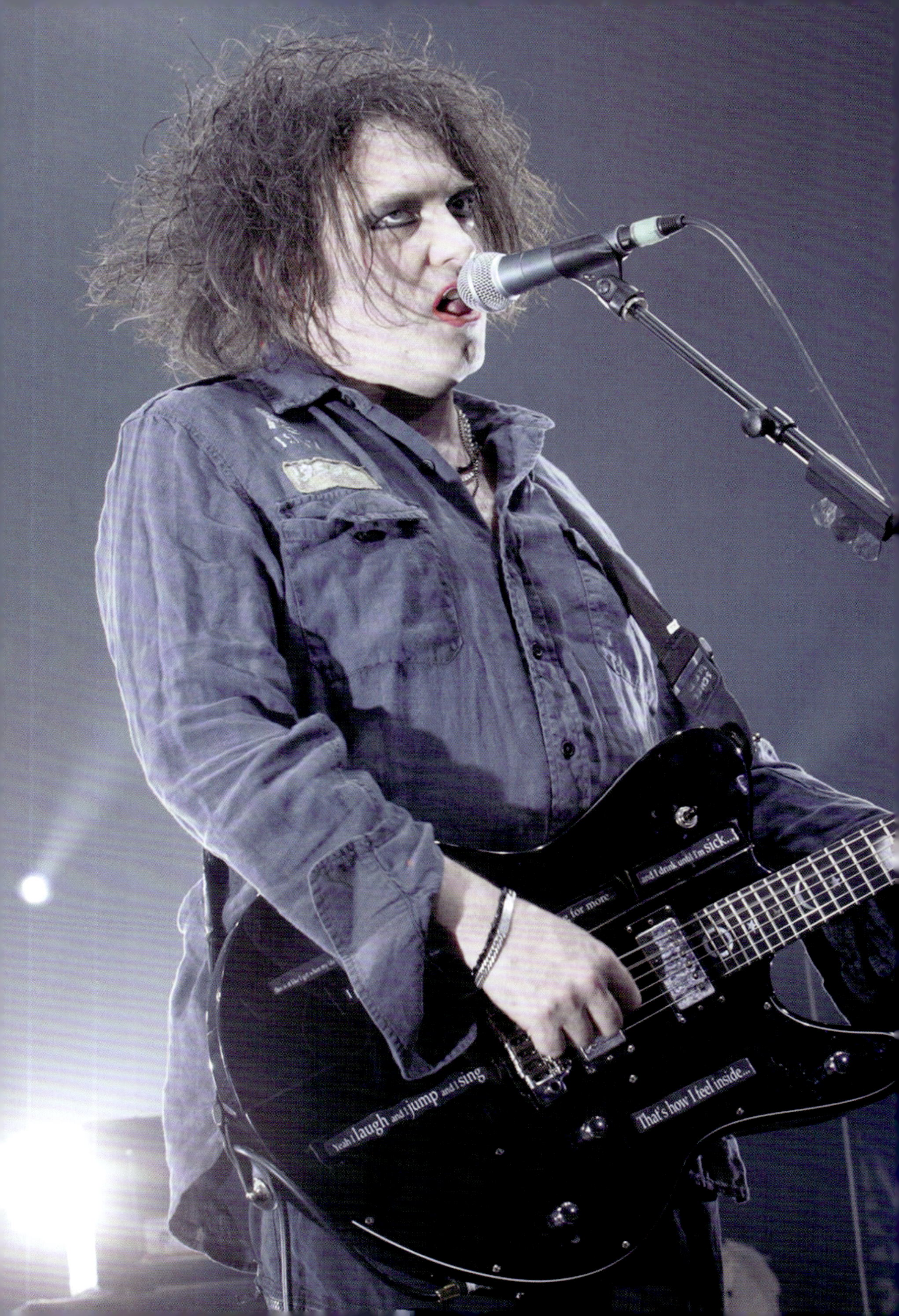
and I drink until I'm sick...
for more.
Yeah I laugh and I jump and I sing
That's how I feel inside...

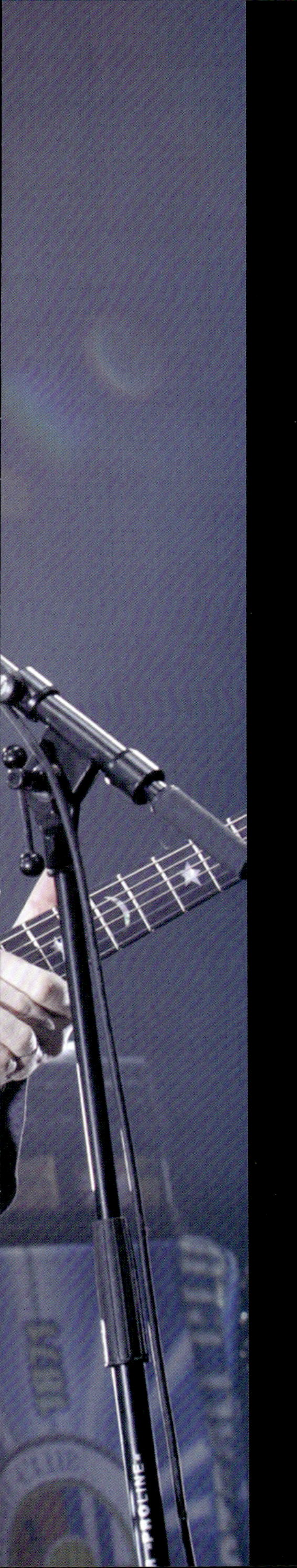

Robert Smith
Royal Albert Hall
April 2006
Performing for the Teenage Cancer Trust

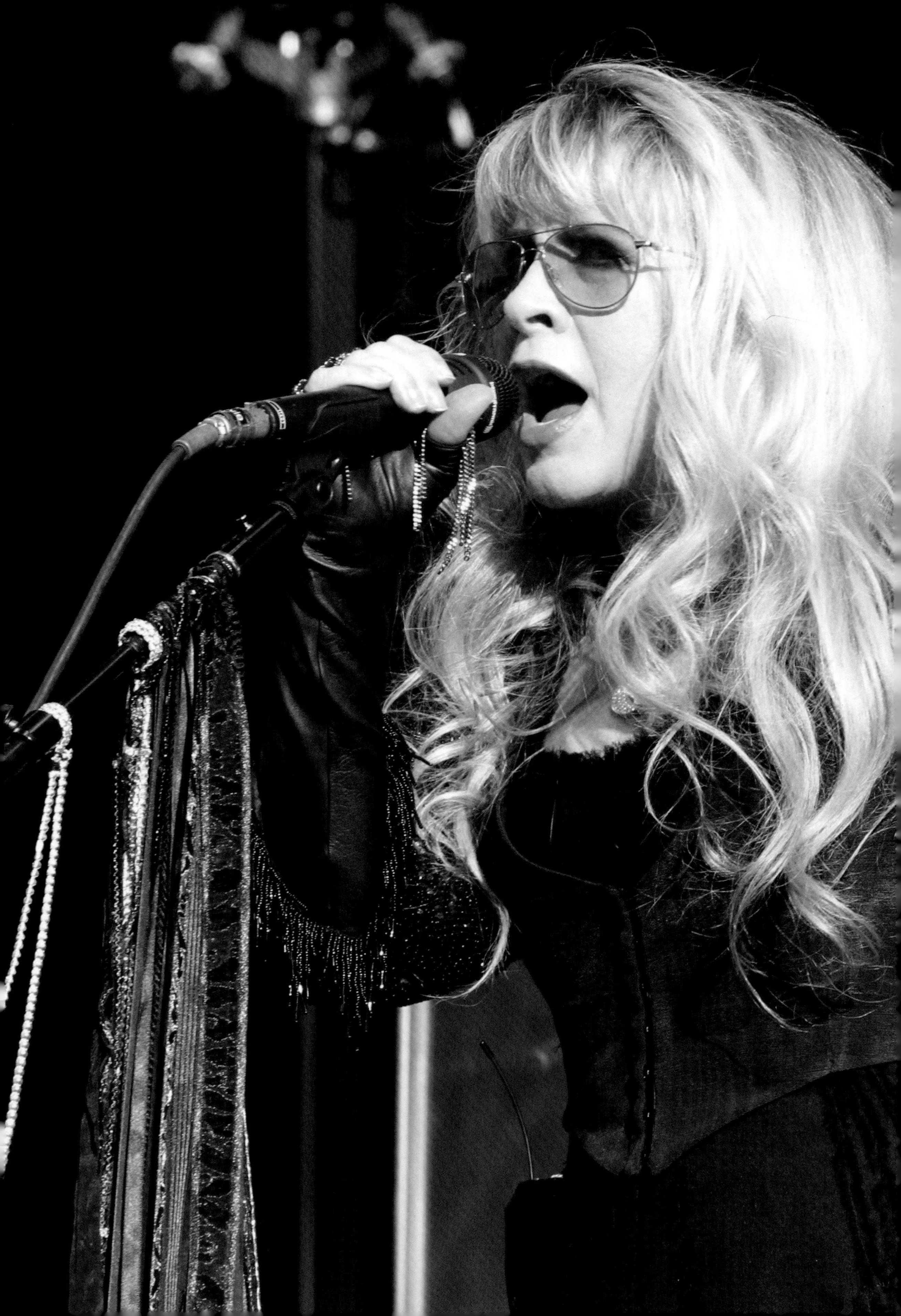

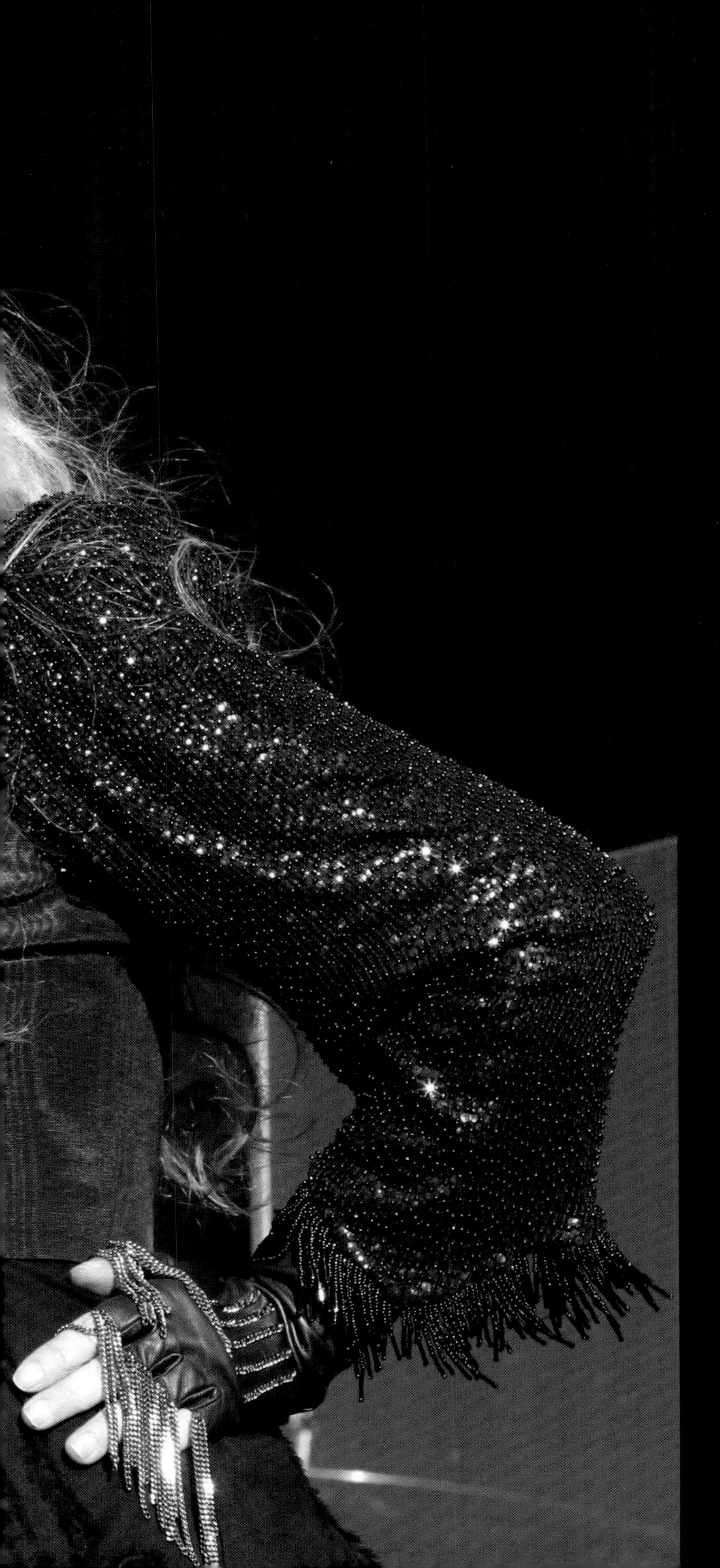

Stevie Nicks
Hyde Park
June 2011
Performing at the Hard Rock Calling Festival

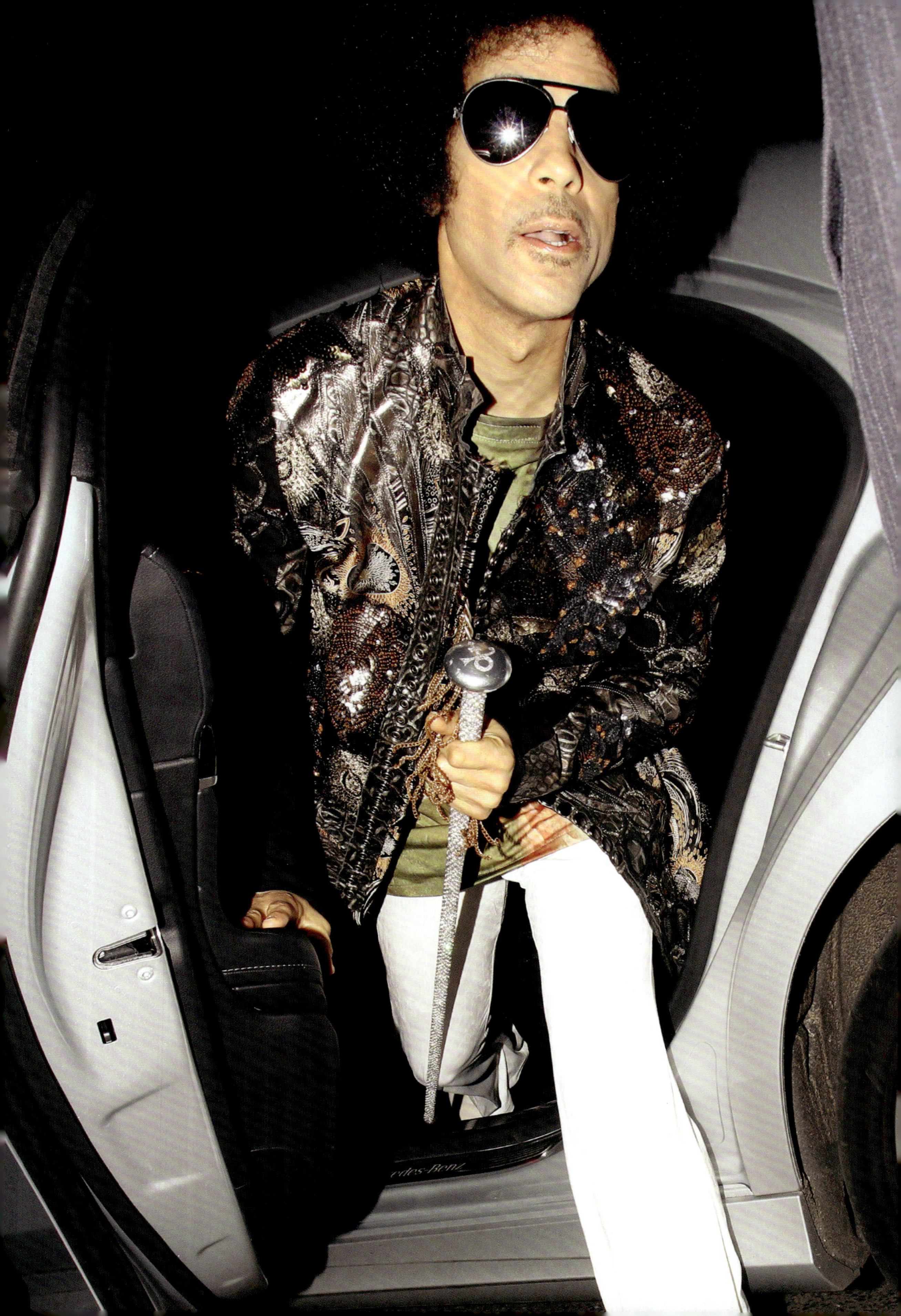

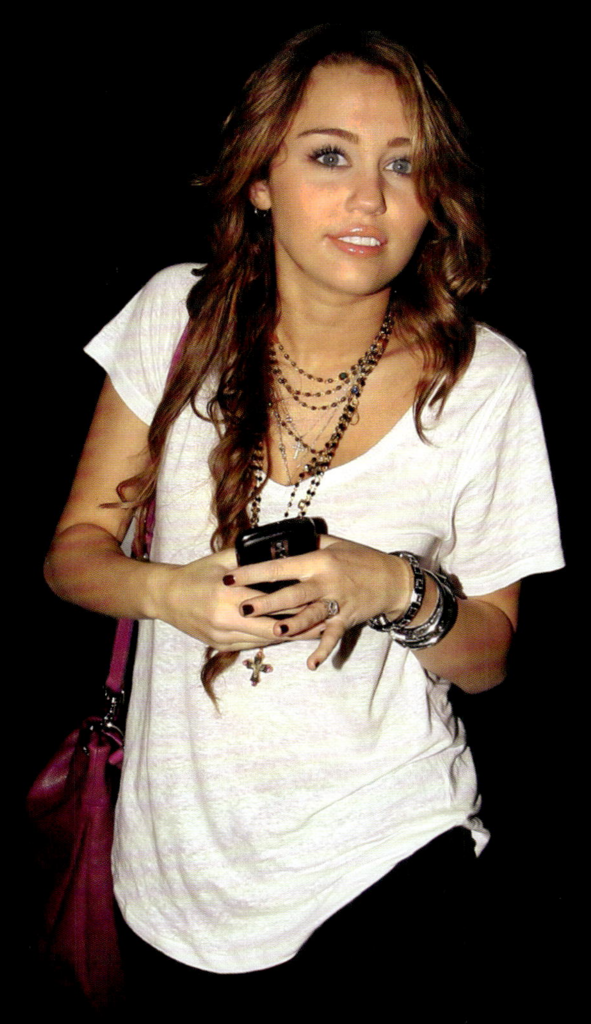

Prince
London Hippodrome
June 2014

Miley Cyrus
Nobu, Mayfair
April 2009

Following pages:
Spice Girls
The O2 Arena, Wembley
June 2007
At a press conference, announcing The Return of the Spice Girls Tour

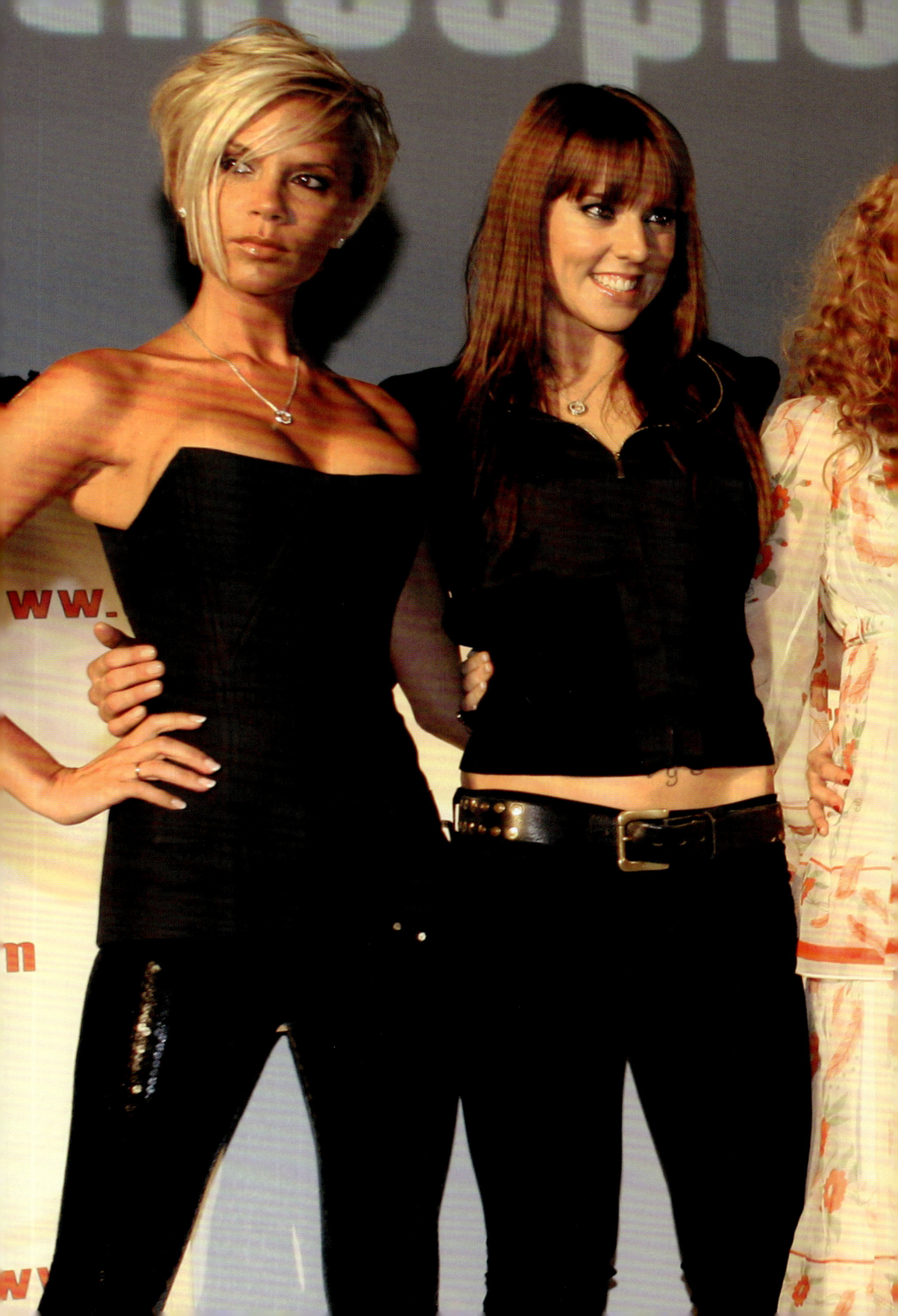

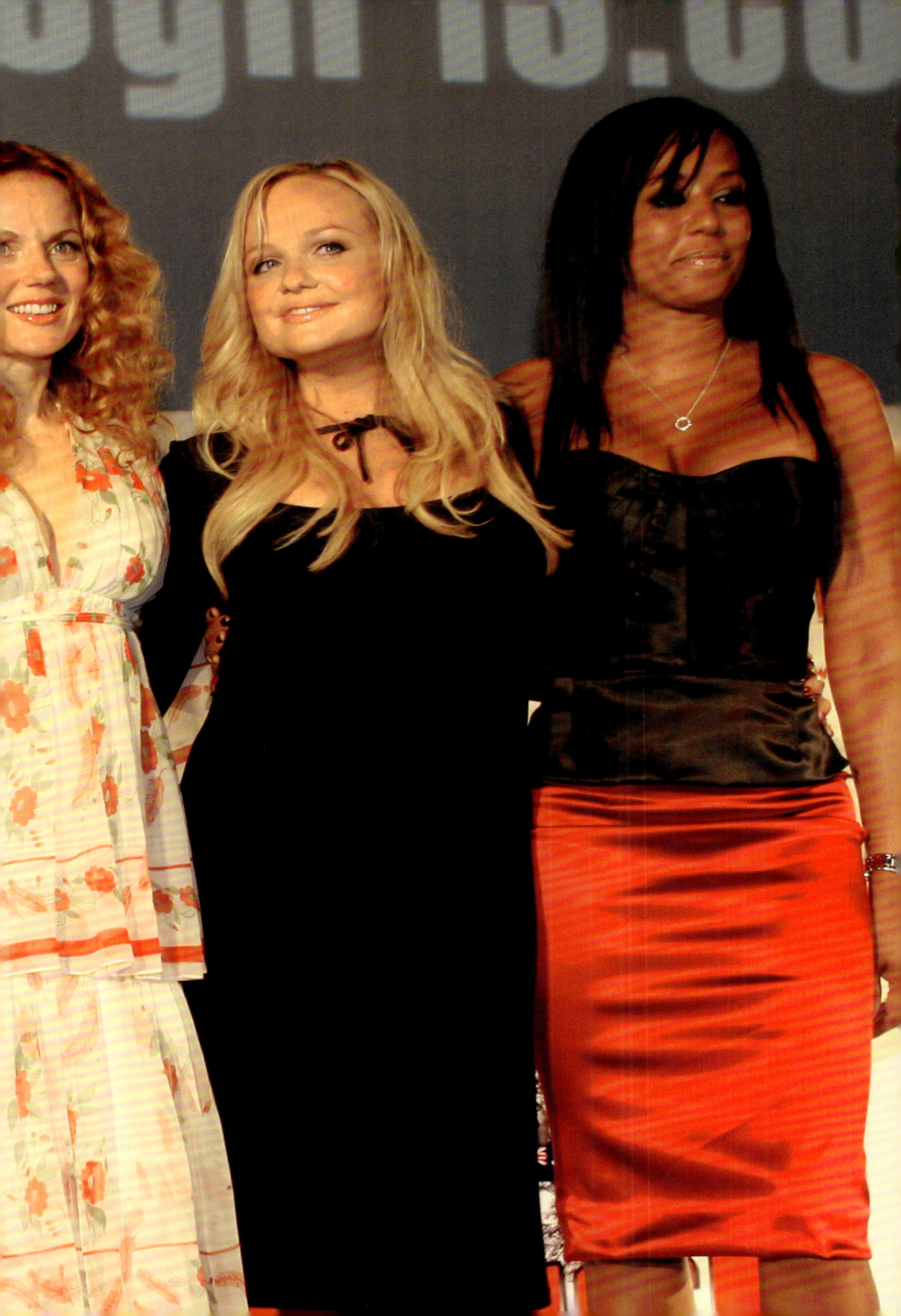

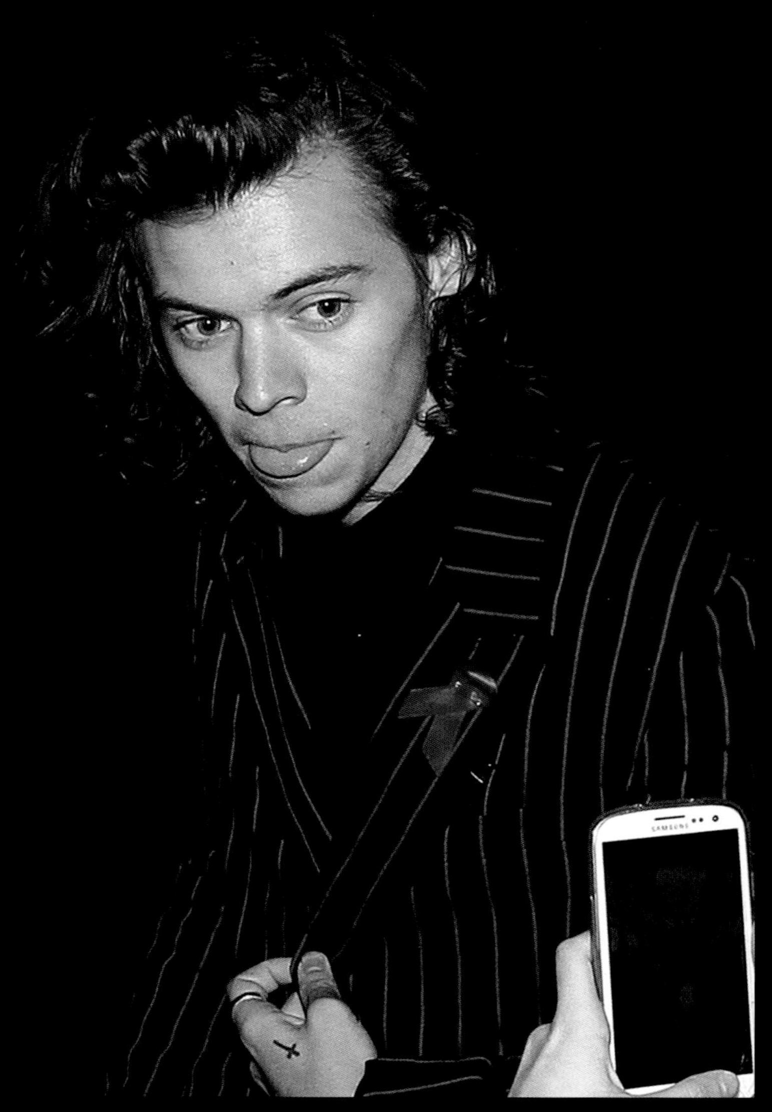

Harry Styles
St Martins Lane hotel, Soho
December 2014
Leaving the British Fashion Awards

Dolly Parton
The Ivy, Covent Garden
June 1998

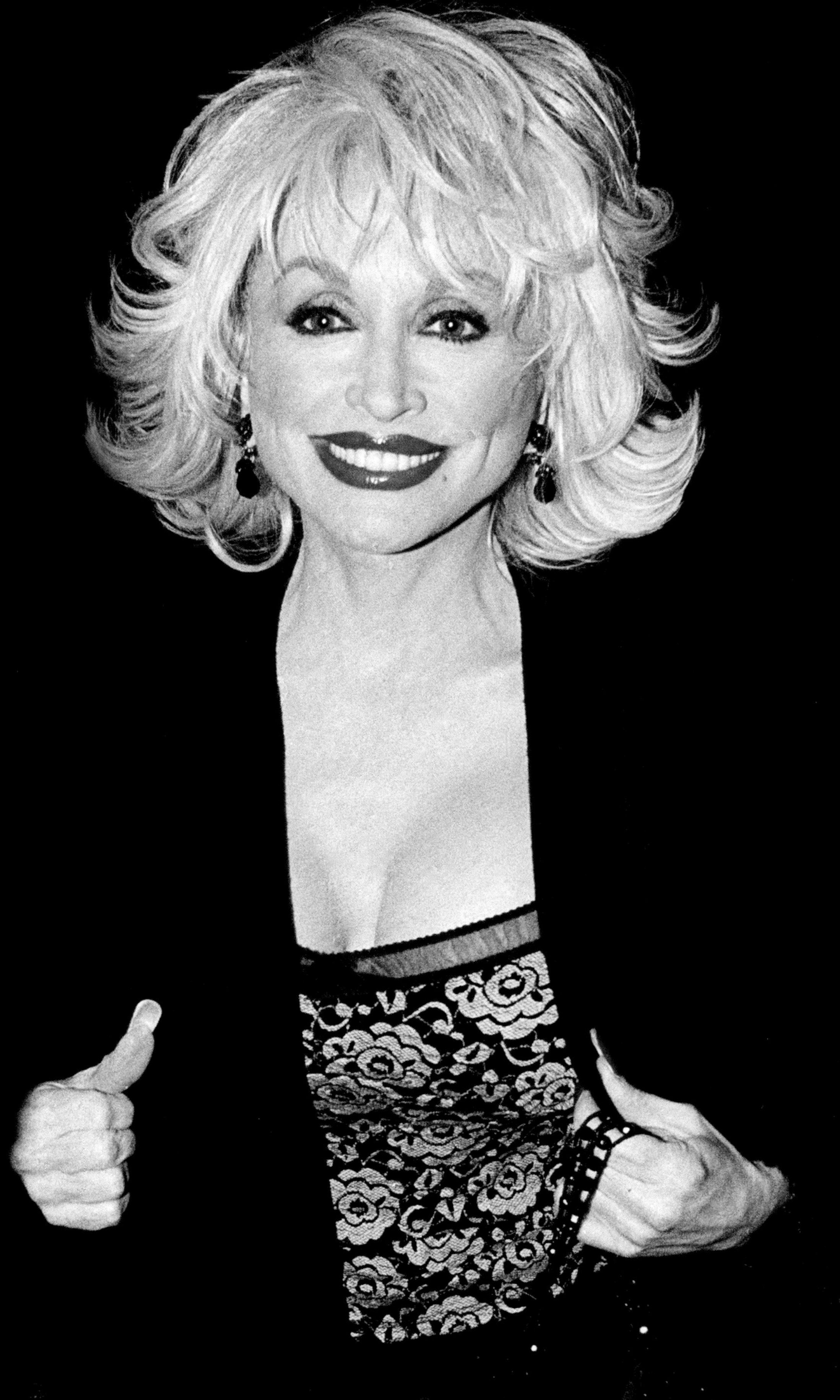

TAYLOR SWIFT
May 2009

I was covering an awards show at The Connaught hotel in London one evening, ready to pack it in for the night when, on my way out, I bumped into an old PR friend who looked as if he was waiting for someone. I asked him what he was up to, and he explained that he was waiting for an American country singer who had been out enjoying a dinner in Mayfair. Naturally, I asked who it was, and with a knowing smirk he said, "Taylor Swift". Now, at that point, the name meant absolutely nothing to me. I hadn't heard of her, but he assured me she was going to be the next big thing – one of those bold predictions you hear in this line of work all the time. He suggested I hang around and take some pictures of her. So, with nothing better to do, I decided to stick around.

A few minutes later, a car pulls up and out steps Taylor, no more than 19 at the time. My PR friend darted over to her, had a quick word and then came back, giving me the green light to take some photos. I introduced myself and, despite being at the start of her career and likely exhausted from a long day, she couldn't have been more polite. She had a charming, thick American accent and radiated genuine enthusiasm – none of the diva behaviour you sometimes get from young artists with big ambitions. As she posed for some pictures, I had no idea that I was capturing the early stages of what would become one of the biggest pop careers on the planet. The shoot didn't take long and as I thanked her, I wished her the best of luck, not realising just how much luck she really wouldn't need.

Looking back, I love those images because they capture something truly special: a superstar before the entire world knew their name. I've always had a soft spot for catching musicians when they're still starting out, as it's when they're most open, most ambitious, and still wide-eyed about the possibilities ahead. In those early days they're more eager to make an impression, unlike the guarded, highly choreographed interactions that come later when their fame explodes. I've photographed Taylor a few times since then, but as her fame skyrocketed, the dynamics changed. You can't just casually bump into her anymore; the entire operation is on another level.

"I had no idea that I was capturing the early stages of one of the biggest pop careers on the planet."

Years later, I met that same PR friend again. We reminisced about that night, laughing about how casual it all seemed back then. I jokingly told him, "That was a good call on your part," and with a grin, he replied: "It's Taylor's world now, and we simply exist in it." And he wasn't wrong. Watching her go from that wide-eyed country singer to the global sensation she is today has been surreal. Funny how a random night outside a hotel turned into a moment I'll never forget.

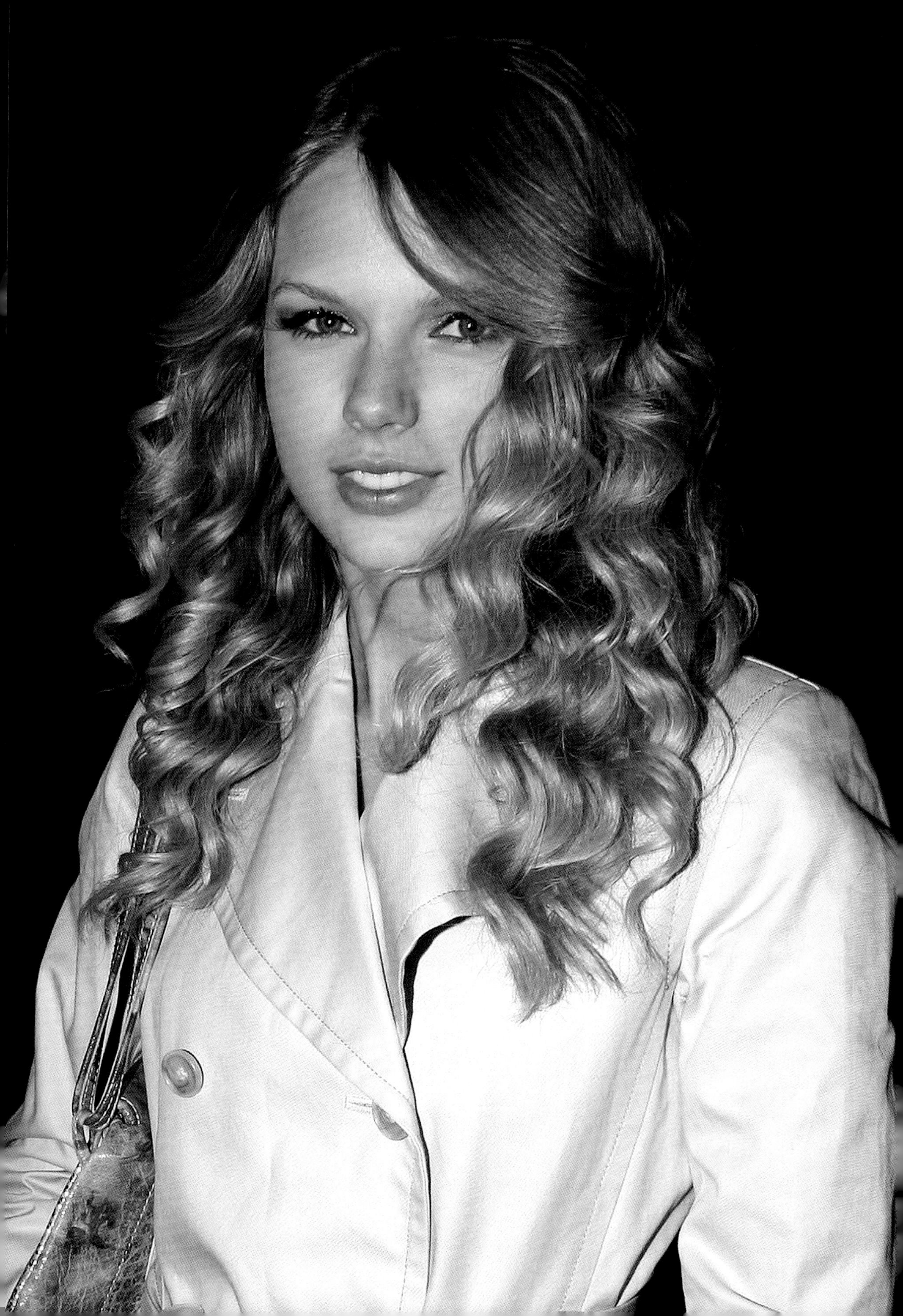

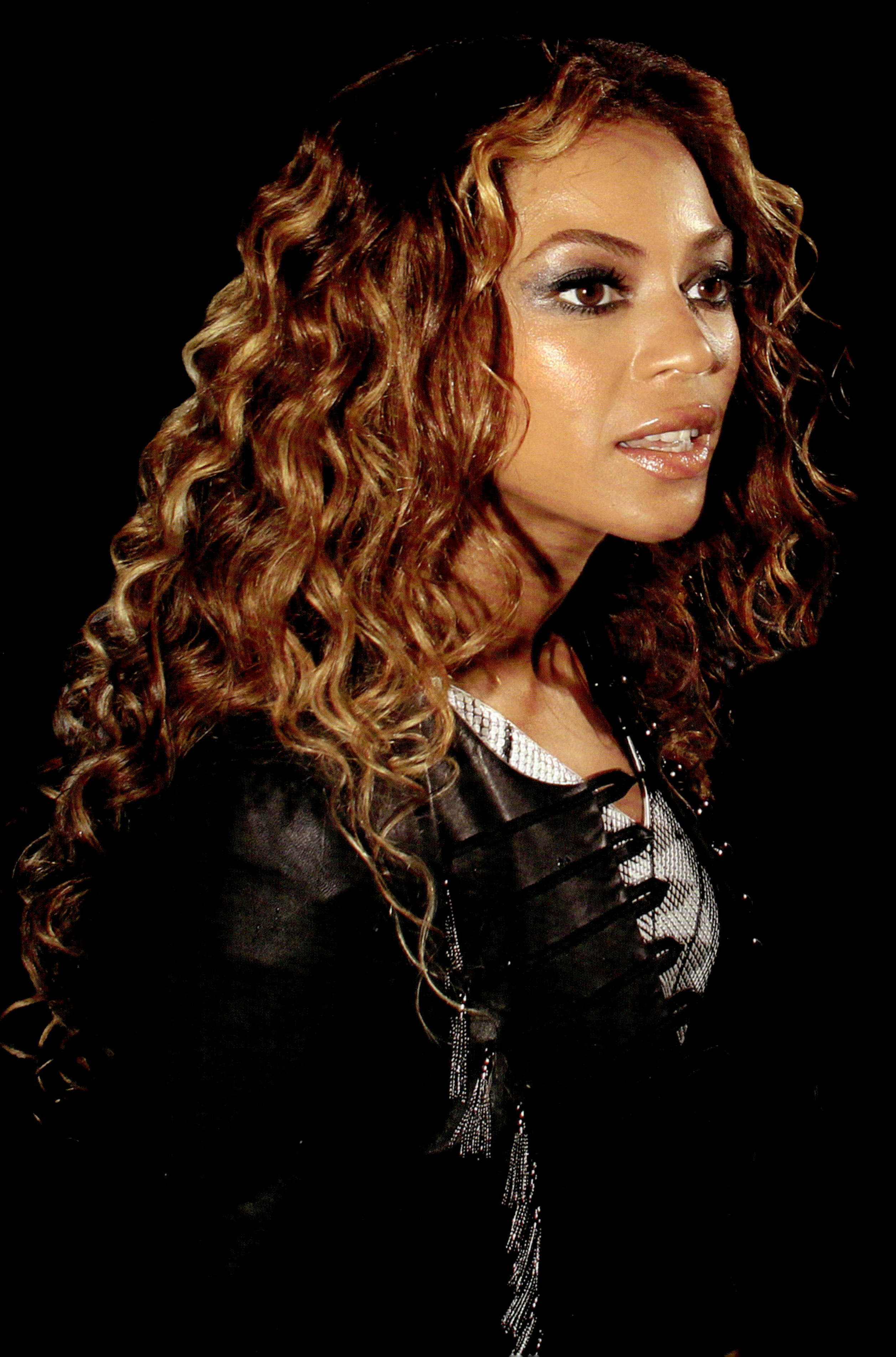

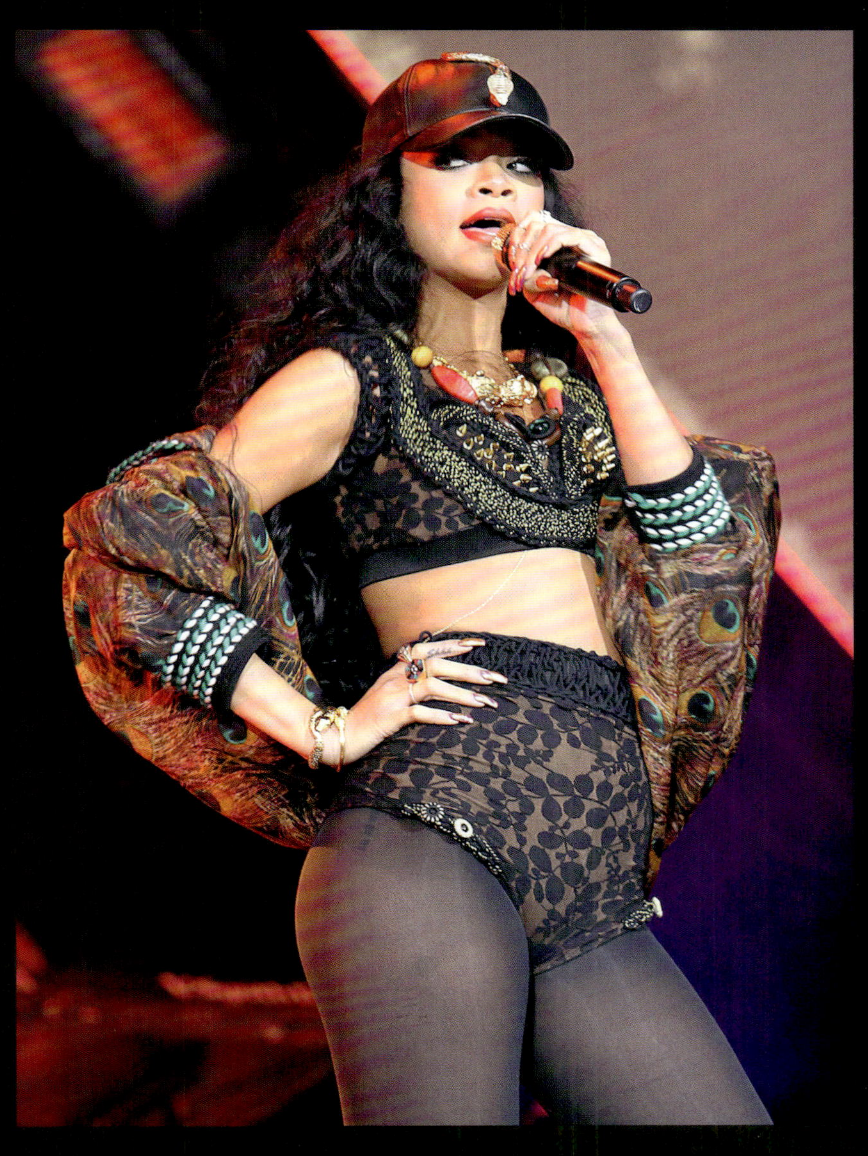

Beyoncé
Mandarin Oriental Hotel,
Knightsbridge
November 2008

Rihanna
Hyde Park
July 2012
Performing at the Wireless Festival

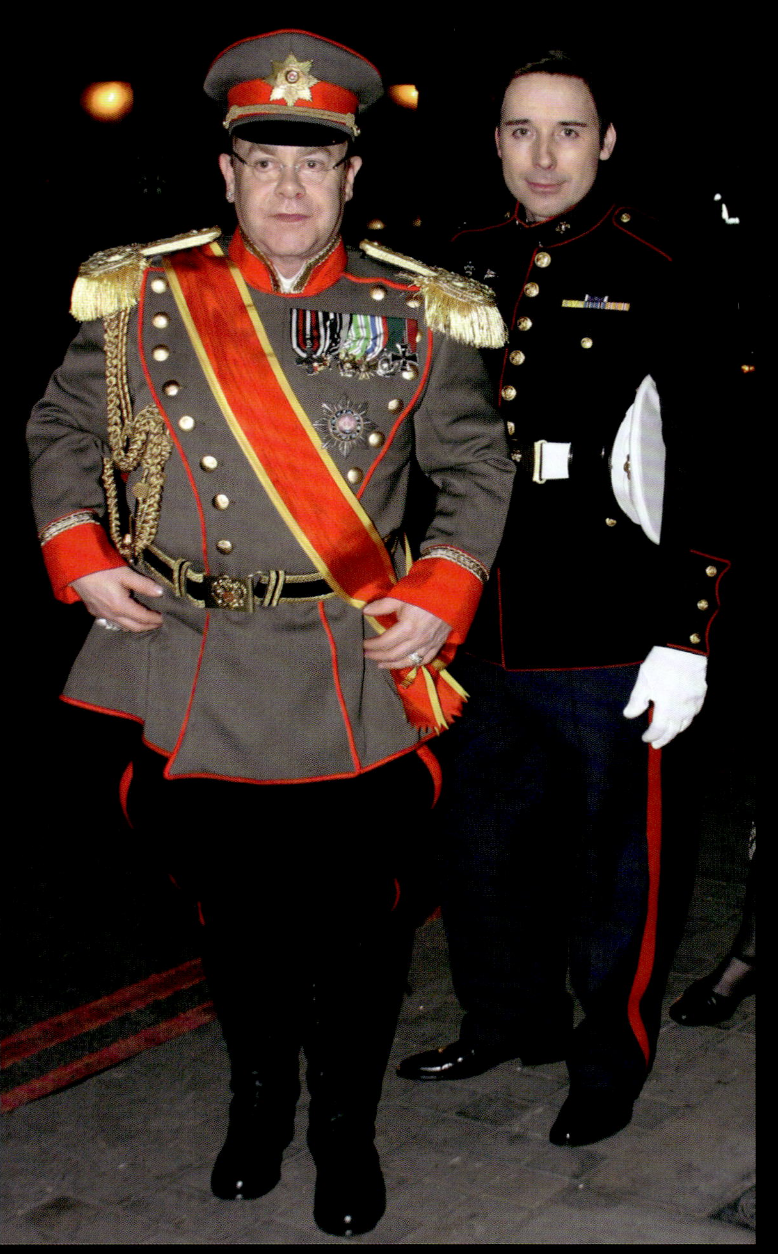

Elton John and David Furnish
Shoreditch Town Hall
March 2007
Arriving for Elton's 60th birthday party

David Bowie and Iman
The Ivy, Covent Garden
May 2001

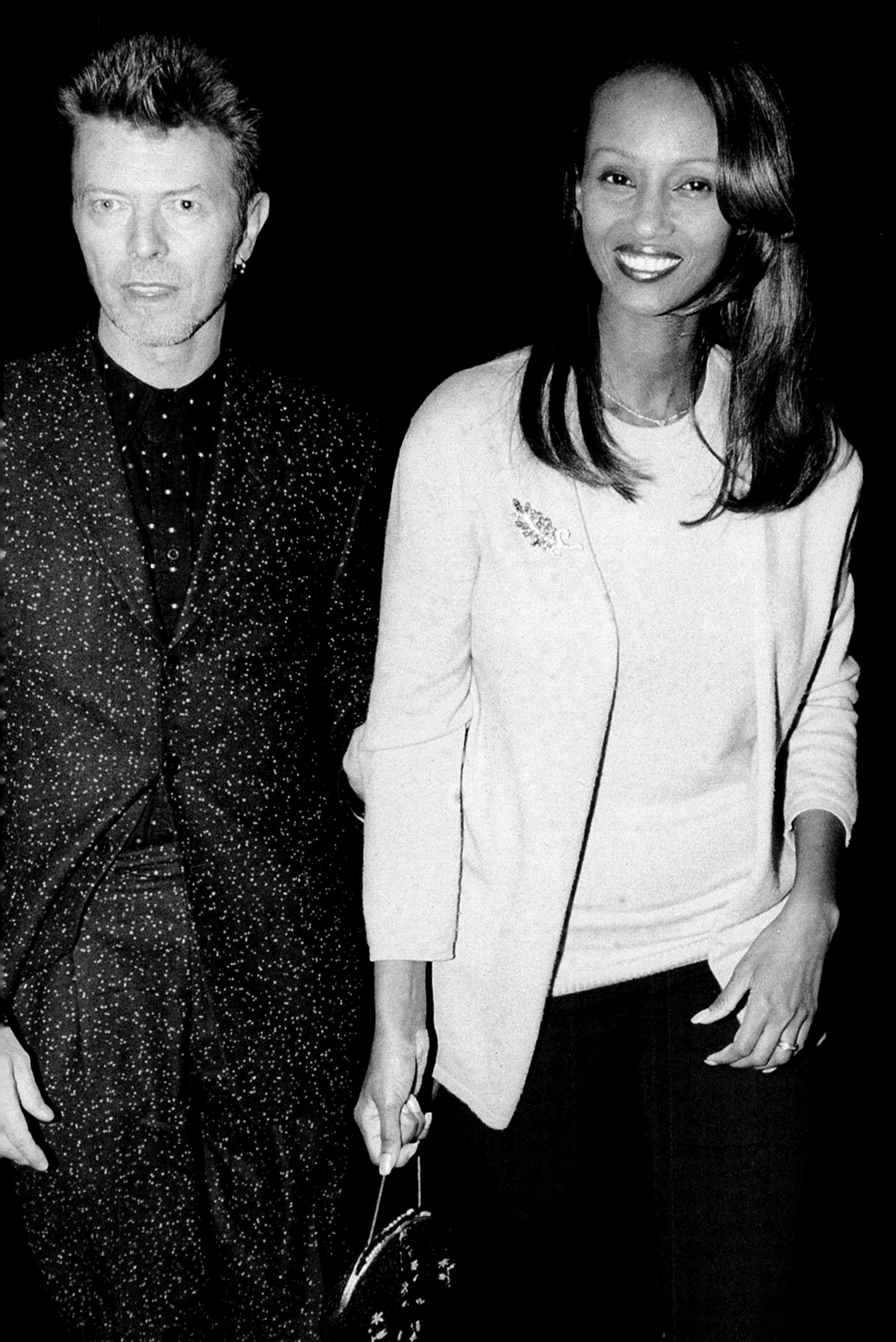

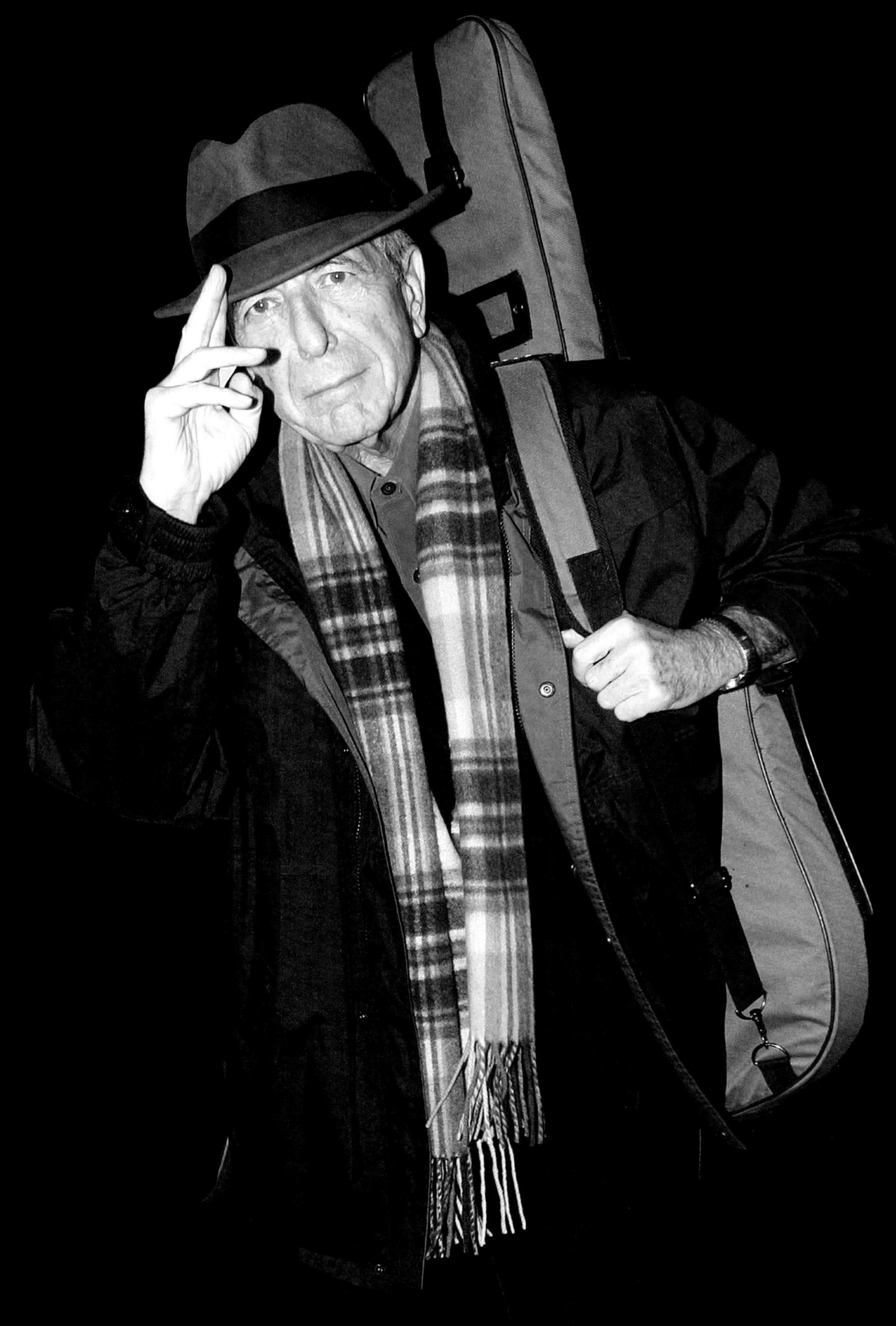

Leonard Cohen
Royal Albert Hall
November 2008

FASHION

KATE MOSS
January 2007

It was the day of Kate Moss's 33rd birthday, and I was on assignment, covering the arrivals for her party at The Dorchester hotel. However, word spread quickly: she wasn't at the hotel at all. Rather, she was across town at the Donmar Warehouse, attending an afternoon play, *Don Juan in Soho*, starring Rhys Ifans, with her then-boyfriend Pete Doherty. The place was already swarming by the time I arrived – an absolute frenzy of photographers clogging the front door, lenses raised like bayonets, along with theatre patrons who were just making it worse. There must have been 100 cameras, all pointed in the same direction, waiting for the perfect shot.

As I glanced at the pack, I realised my flash batteries were nearly dead. There was no way I could afford to miss the moment, so I dashed back to my car, only a few streets away, to grab fresh ones. On my way back, I remembered something – a secret back door, a fire exit on the next street over, just off Seven Dials. Years ago, I had seen Nicole Kidman use that same door after her performances. A back door to the stage and, maybe, to gold.

As I approached, I couldn't believe my luck. The door was slightly ajar and, as I walked past fiddling with my batteries, I spotted her – Kate Moss, perched on the stairs like a scene from a lost French film, cigarette delicately balanced between her fingers as if she had all the time in the world. She was waiting for her car, completely unaware of my presence. I couldn't waste the moment. I walked over and began taking shots. It was a rare, candid moment, no flashing lights, no bodyguards, no screaming fans. Just Kate, sitting quietly, waiting to make her next move. As I snapped away, I heard the unmistakable sound of a car engine roaring, fast. It swerved into view from around the corner, the getaway already underway, clearly trying to avoid the mass of photographers at the front entrance. I knew I had mere seconds. Footsteps pounded in the distance – the sound of two other photographers who had figured out the back-door strategy too. But by then, it was too late. Kate, cool as ever, stood, slipped through the door, and jumped into her car. She was gone before they even had a chance to get a decent shot. Most of the pack, camped out at the front, missed her entirely.

This shot I had taken would prove to be one of the most iconic pictures ever taken of Kate, far more valuable than any staged red-carpet appearance. I headed home, confident that I had something special. The next morning, I found out

> *"Kate Moss, perched on the stairs like a scene from a lost French film, cigarette delicately balanced between her fingers."*

that the rest of the photographers, who had staked out The Dorchester, stayed until 5am waiting for her to leave. But Kate, always one step ahead, had outwitted them once again. She slipped out a side door and jumped into a black cab while her chauffeur created a diversion at the main entrance. The whole crowd was duped. Brilliantly.

By the time the papers hit the stands the next day, my photos had taken every front page. Kate, in her stunning dress and vintage Halston fur coat, had outsmarted the pack at every turn. But not me! This image has gone on to be, without a doubt, one of my most famous. Kate is my all-time favourite model, no question. A true English rose: beautiful, elusive, and far cleverer than people give her credit for.

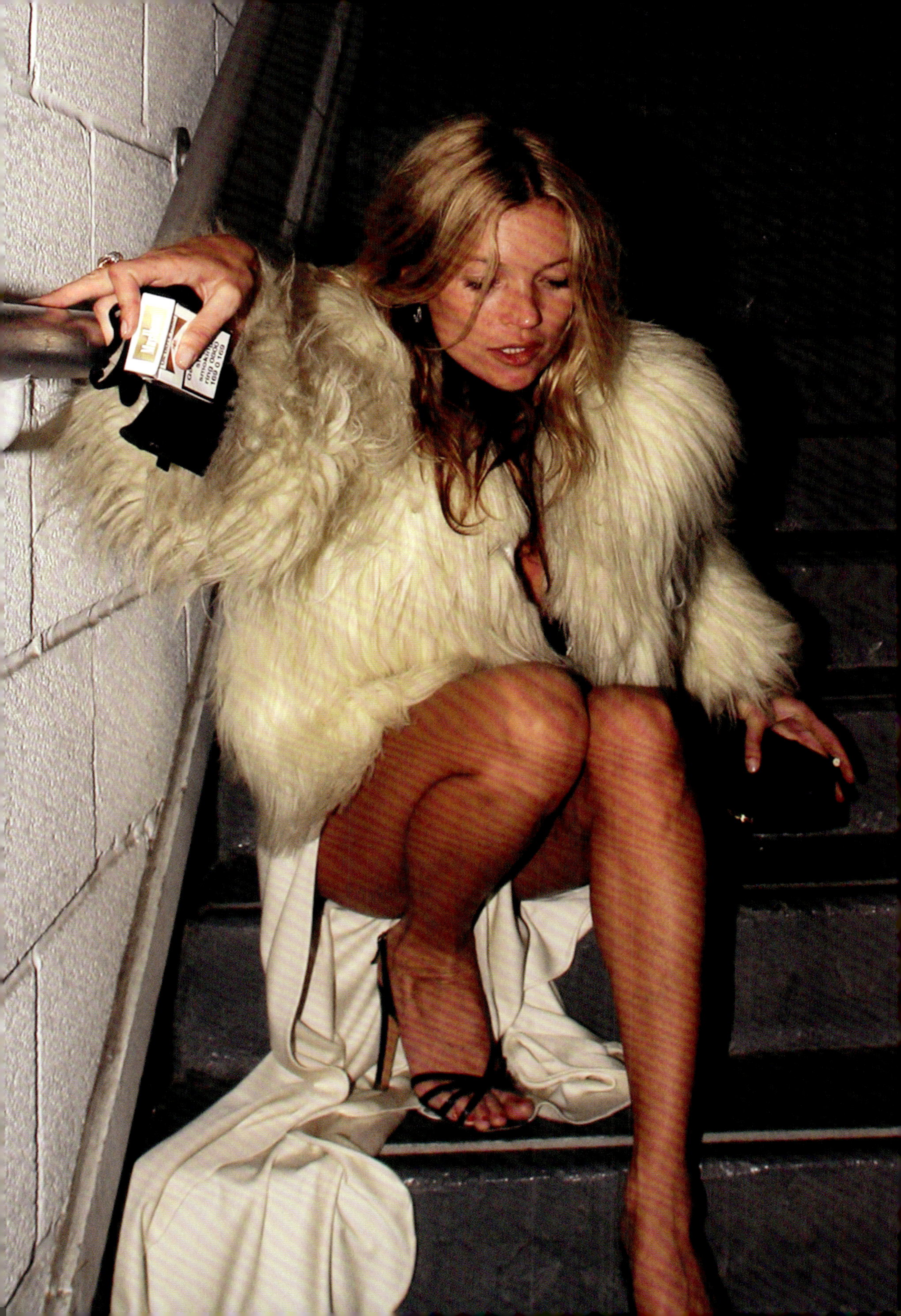

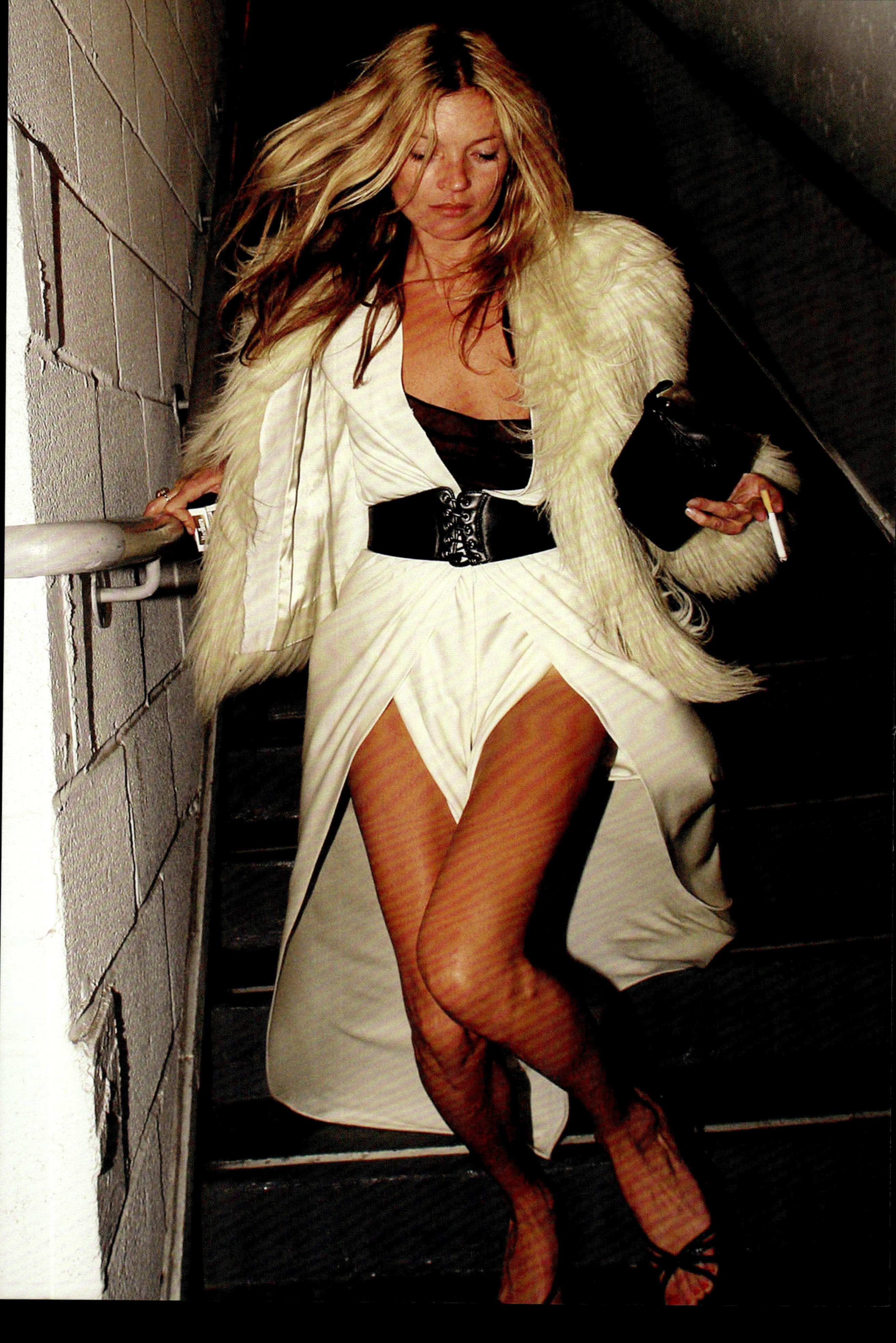

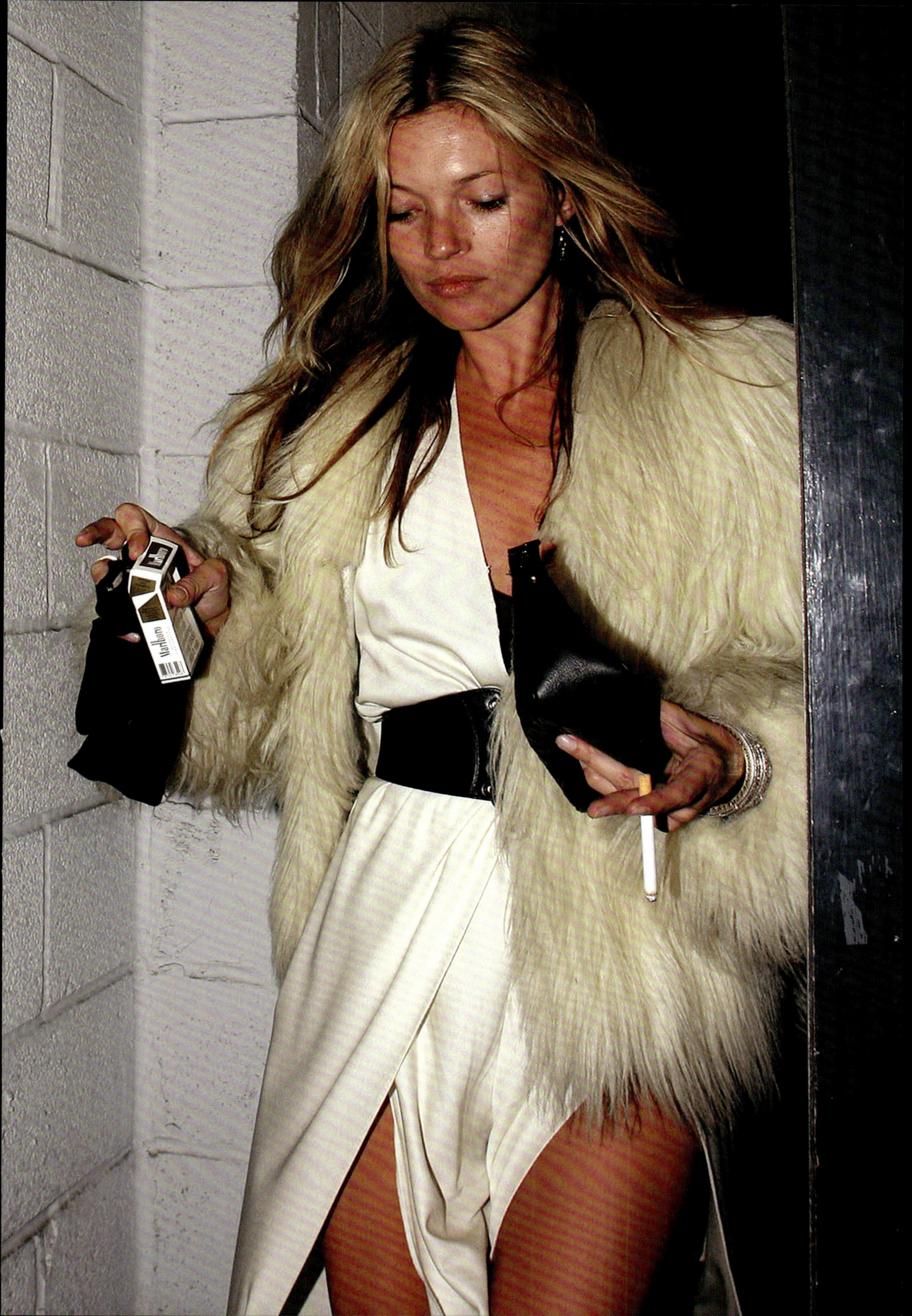
Marlboro

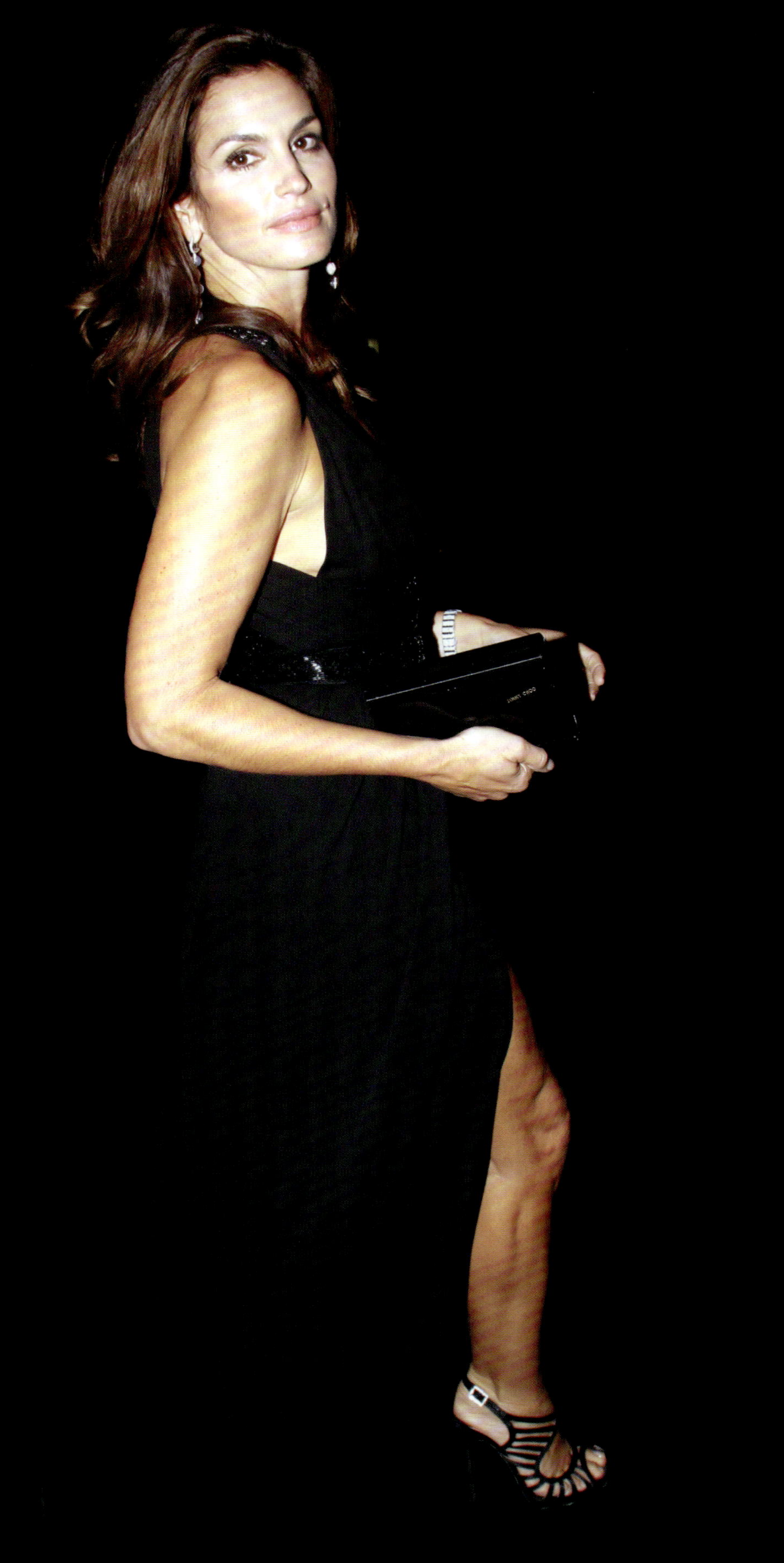

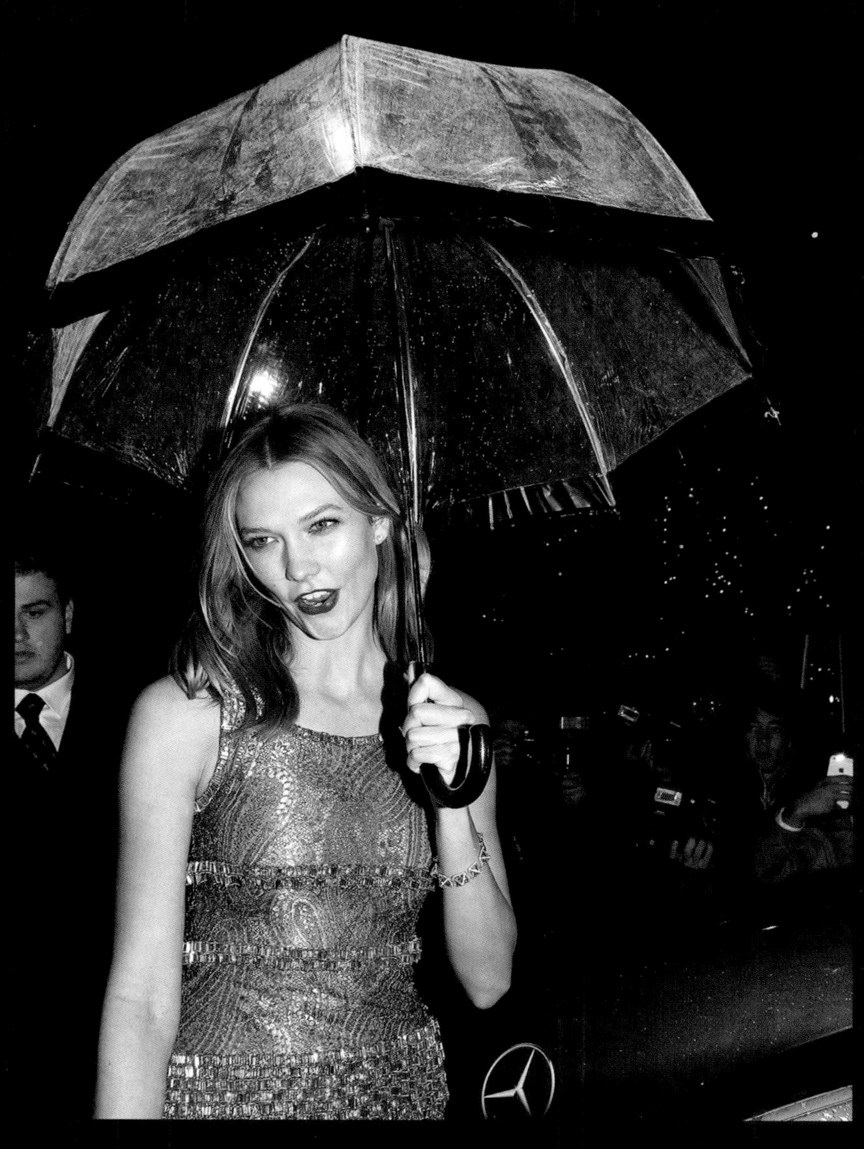

Cindy Crawford
Mayfair
October 2009
Leaving a party at banker Roger Jenkins's home

Karlie Kloss
Mark's Club, Mayfair
September 2015
Arriving for a London Fashion Week party

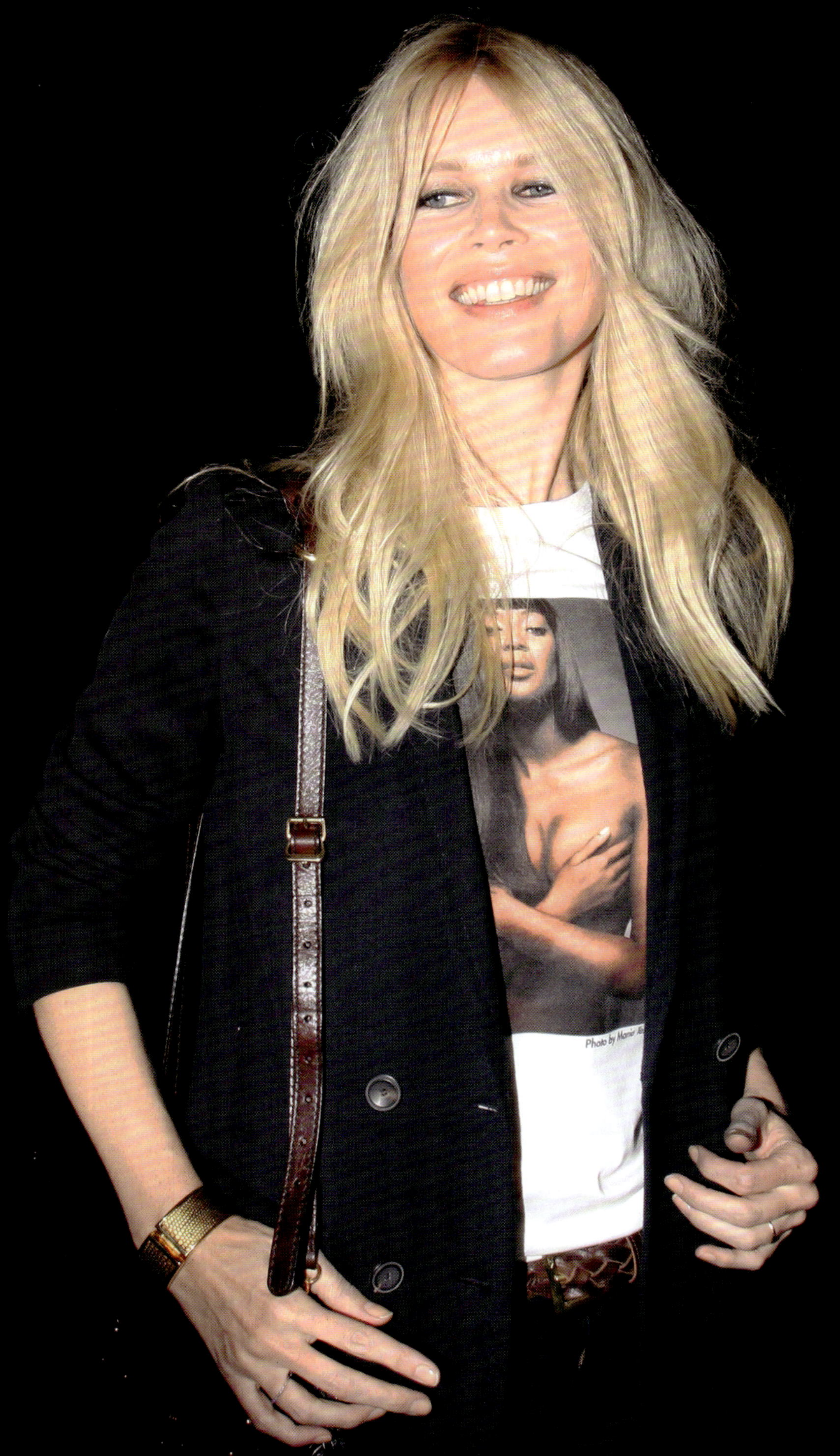
Photo by Mario

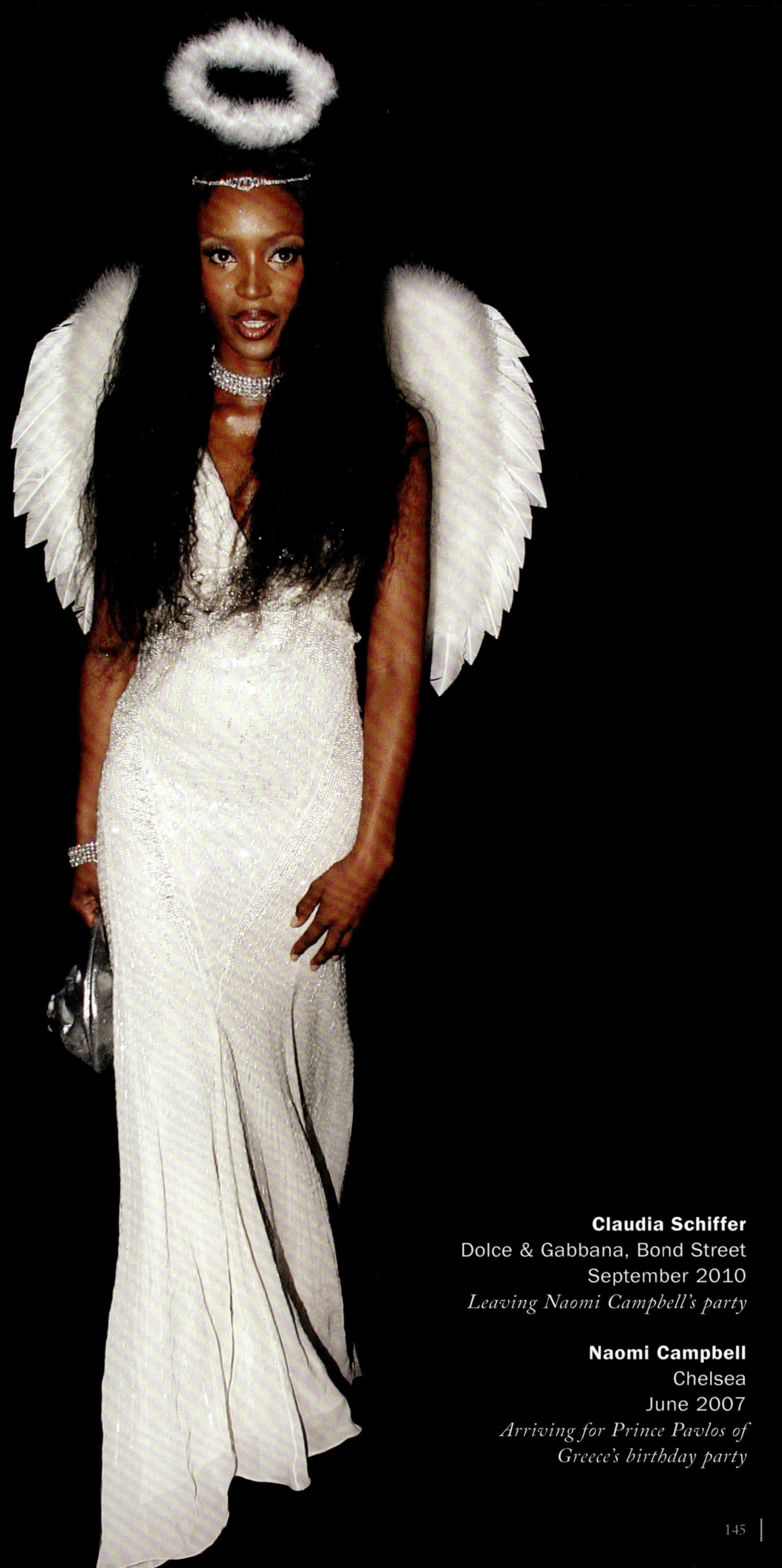

Claudia Schiffer
Dolce & Gabbana, Bond Street
September 2010
Leaving Naomi Campbell's party

Naomi Campbell
Chelsea
June 2007
Arriving for Prince Pavlos of Greece's birthday party

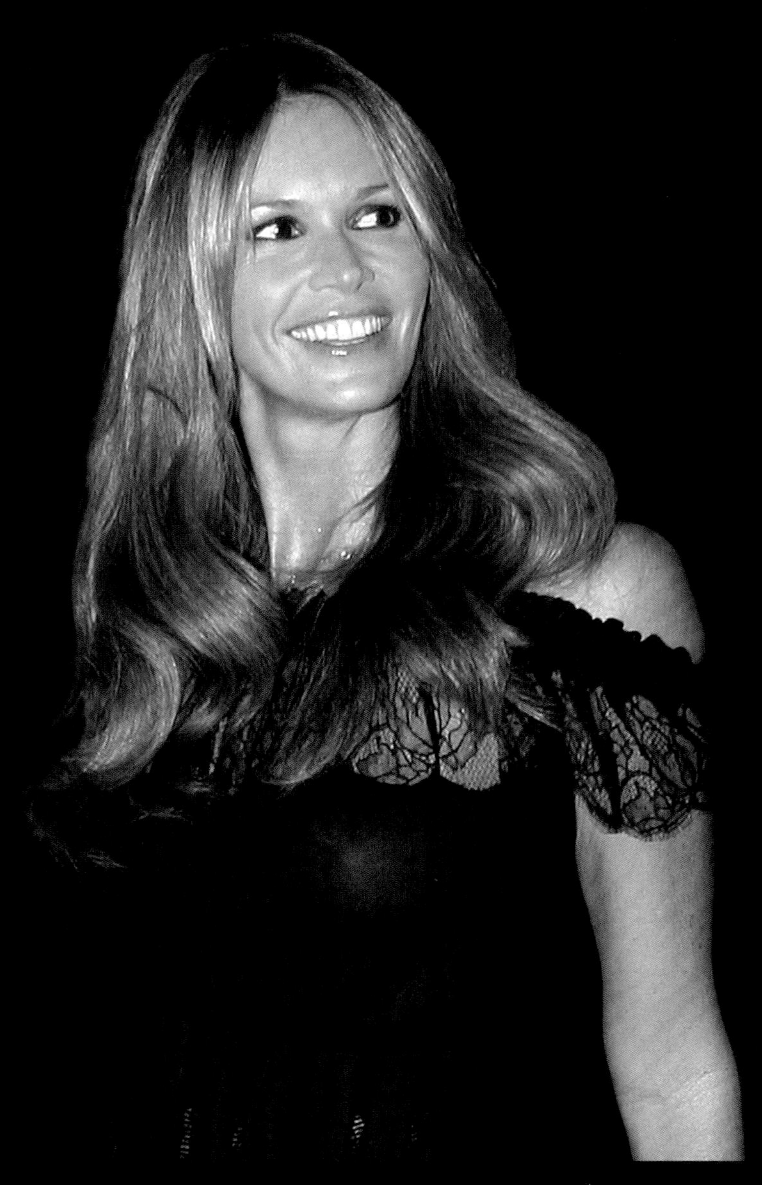

Elle Macpherson
Hampton Court Palace
June 2007
Arriving for a charity event on behalf of Mikhail Gorbachev

Victoria Beckham
Claridge's, Mayfair
December 2005
Heading to Elton John's civil partnership afterparty

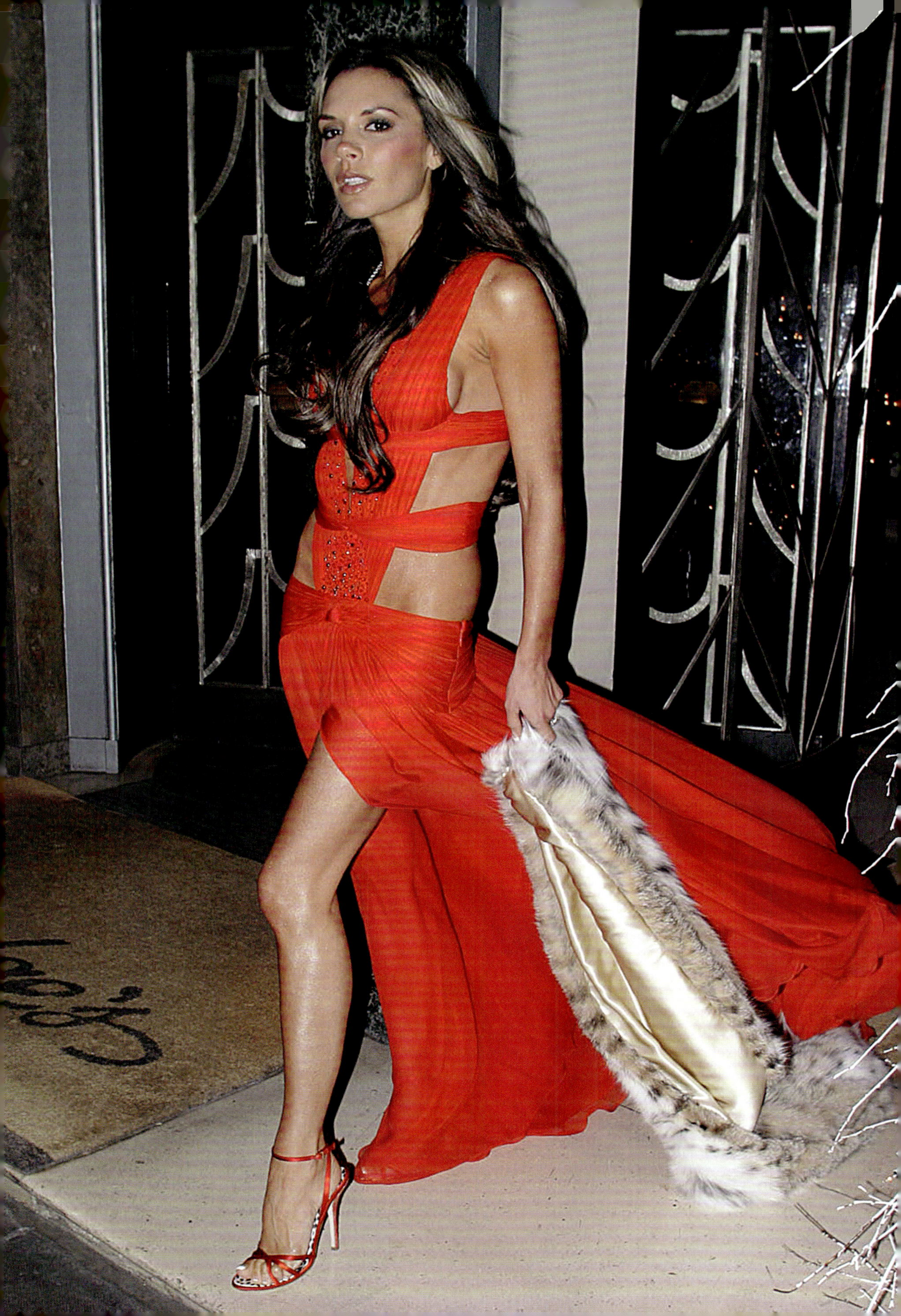

HELENA CHRISTENSEN

September 1998

The '90s were dominated by a rare breed of public figure: the supermodel. They were everywhere – on the covers of magazines, in fashion campaigns, on runways, and even in music videos. Names like Cindy Crawford, Naomi Campbell, Christy Turlington and Claudia Schiffer became household icons. Behind them, rising stars like Kate Moss were quickly joining the ranks. And while fashion wasn't my main focus as a photographer, the cultural force of these women meant I couldn't help but find myself in their orbit occasionally, snapping shots at award shows and parties.

Among them was Helena Christensen, whose face already lived in the cultural subconscious by this point, thanks in no small part to her unforgettable role in Chris Isaak's 'Wicked Game' music video from 1991. That video alone immortalised her hypnotic eyes, of a colour you only find in Nordic folklore, which seemed to look straight into your soul. So, when I found myself outside the Swiss Centre in Leicester Square in 1998 at the Elle Style Awards and she suddenly appeared, I was both surprised and awestruck. There she was, as stunning in person as she was on screen – perhaps more so. As she walked out, she seemed to know the effect she had on those around her, but not in a conceited way. She was poised and confident, but approachable.

As we photographed her, she unexpectedly started talking, not some rehearsed lines for the press but rather asking about our cameras. For a moment, I wasn't sure if I'd heard her right. Here we were, focused on the world-famous supermodel, and she was turning the conversation around, curious about *us*. It turned out Helena wasn't just a model; she was a photographer herself, and a proper one, which immediately explained her interest. It was not idle chatter. She was genuinely curious.

Intrigued by her enthusiasm, I handed her my camera. She took it naturally, like it belonged in her hands, and took a few shots herself, eyes lighting up like a child with a new toy. She wasn't just another pretty face in front of the camera – she understood what it meant to be behind it. For the next 15 minutes, we chatted about photography, the ins and outs of different cameras, and the artistry behind the craft. Rather than celebrity worship, in my eyes this night was simply a late-night chat with a fellow artist. The supermodel mystique gave way to something far more compelling: shared passion.

"I handed her my camera. She took it naturally, like it belonged in her hands, and took a few shots herself."

At the end of the night, there was no entourage, no private car waiting to whisk her away. She didn't have a ride back to her hotel, so we stood with her on the pavement until a cab arrived. I couldn't help but be reminded of something I had learned through my years of working with celebrities: many of them, no matter their fame, are far more grounded than the public perceives them to be. Helena embodied that. Here was a woman who had graced the covers of every major magazine, yet she stood there chatting with a couple of photographers about cameras, just like anyone else. For a supermodel, she was remarkably real. And, after all, why wouldn't she be? Models may be used to being in front of the camera, but sometimes they enjoy being behind it just as much.

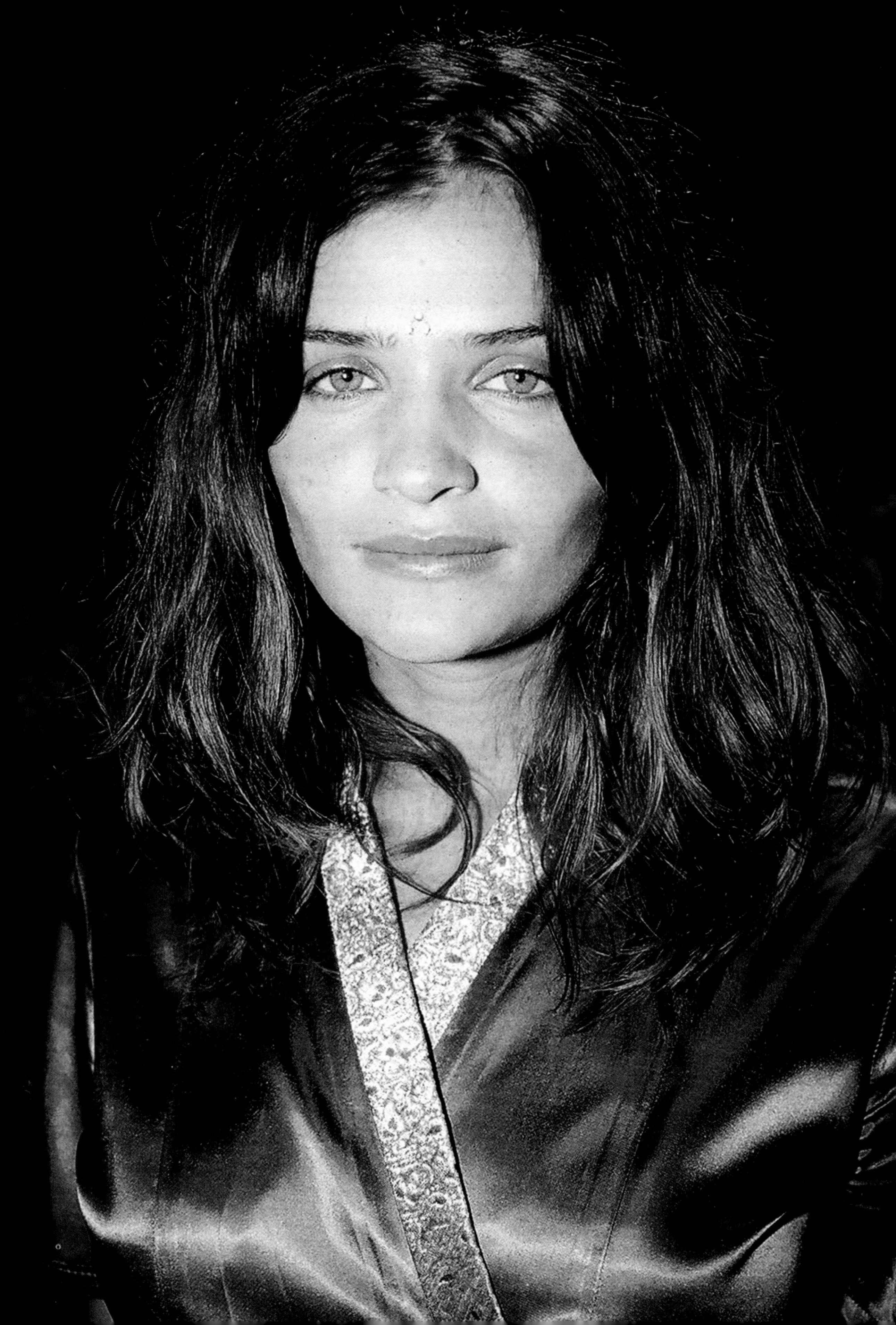

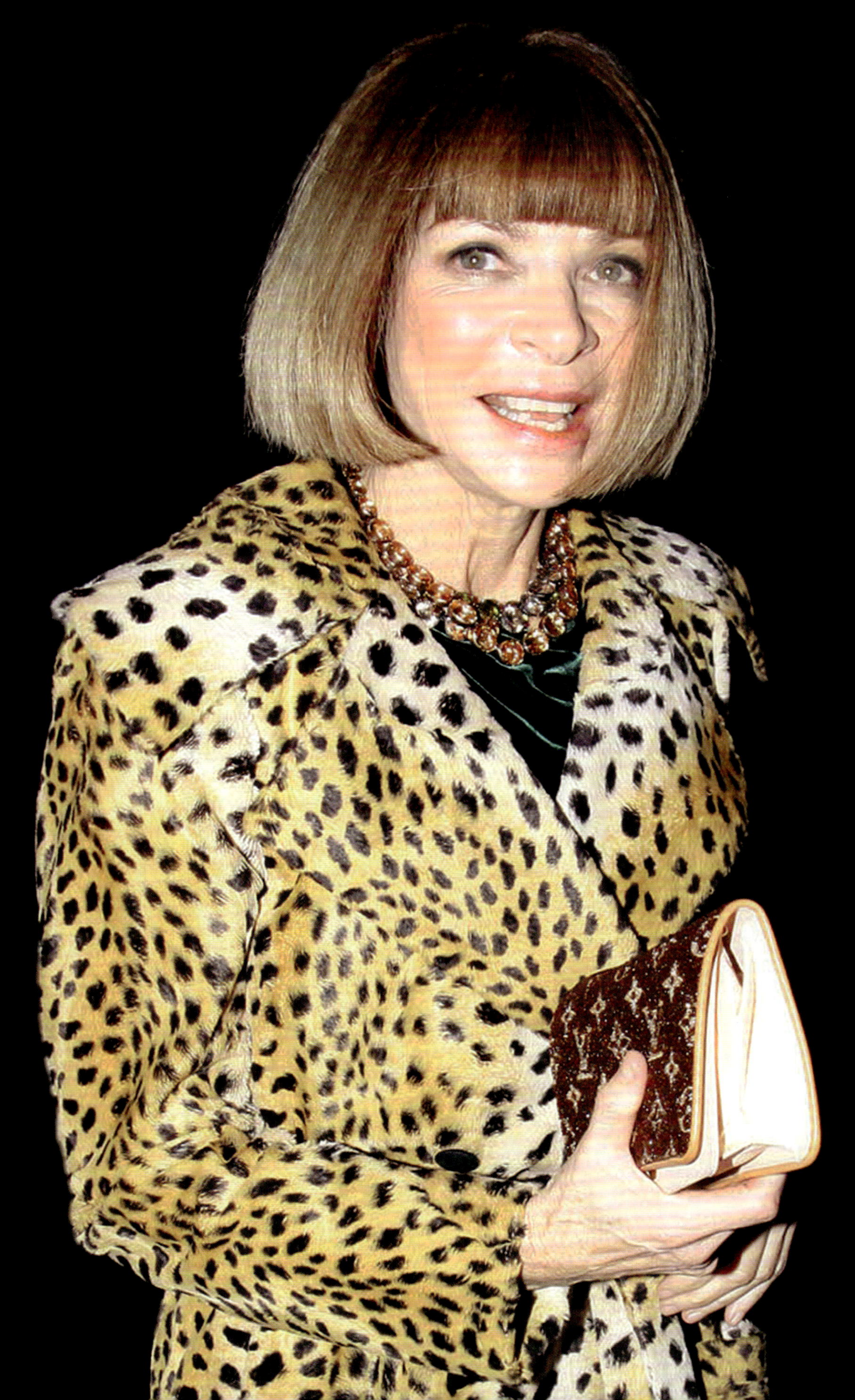

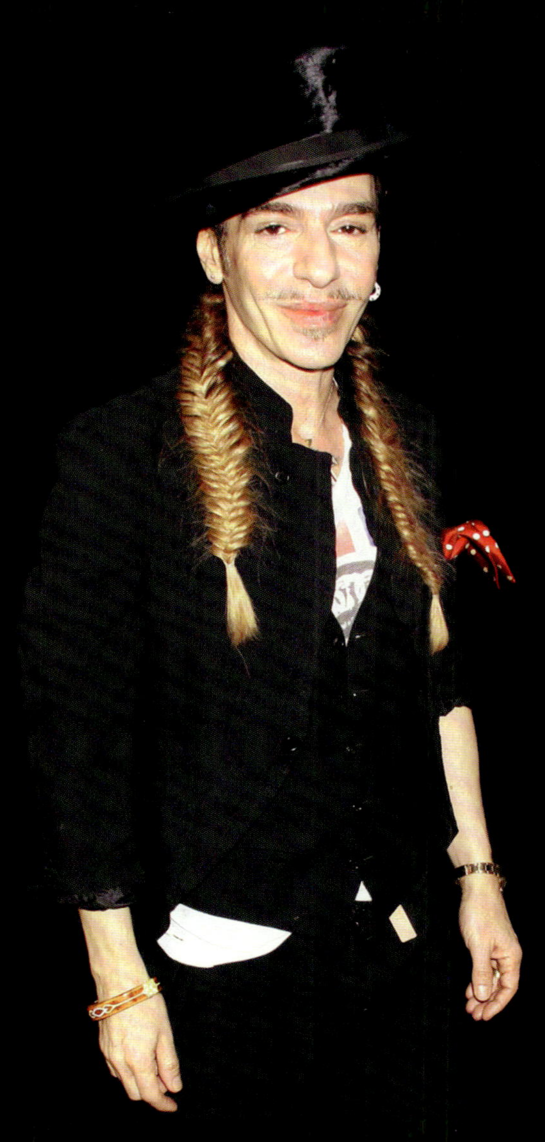

Anna Wintour
Harry's Bar, Mayfair
February 2011
After having dinner with Simon Cowell and friends

John Galliano
The Ivy, Covent Garden
March 2011

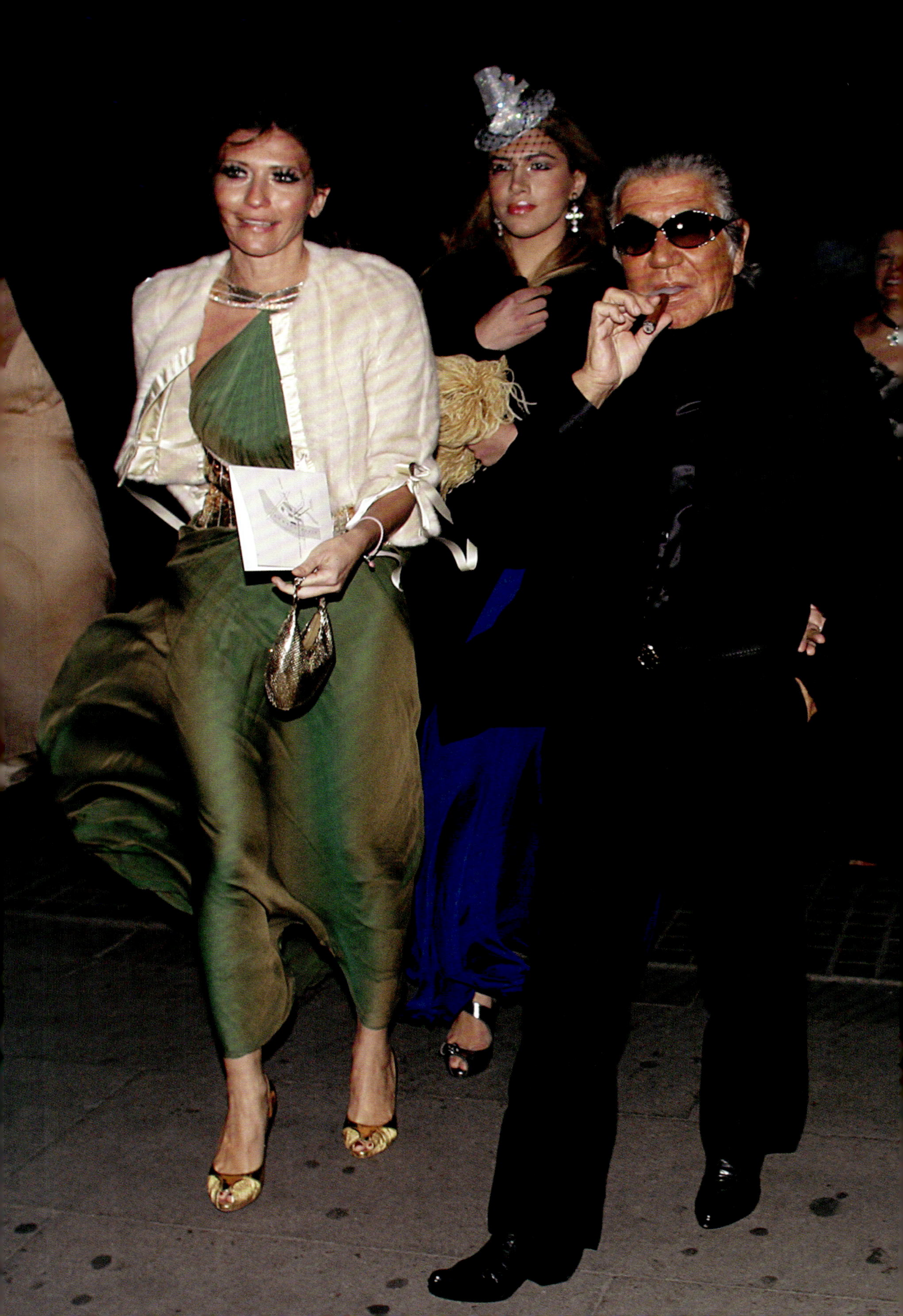

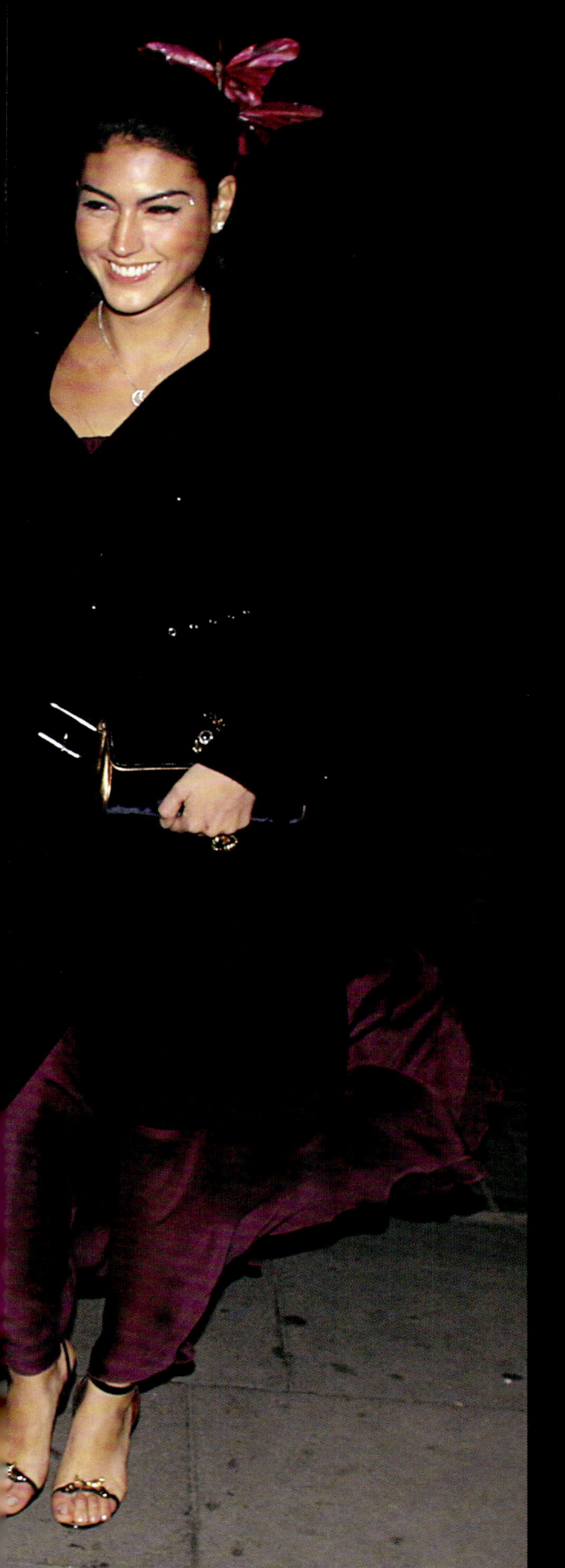

Roberto Cavalli
Chelsea
February 2008
On his way to a London Fashion Week party at the Saatchi Gallery

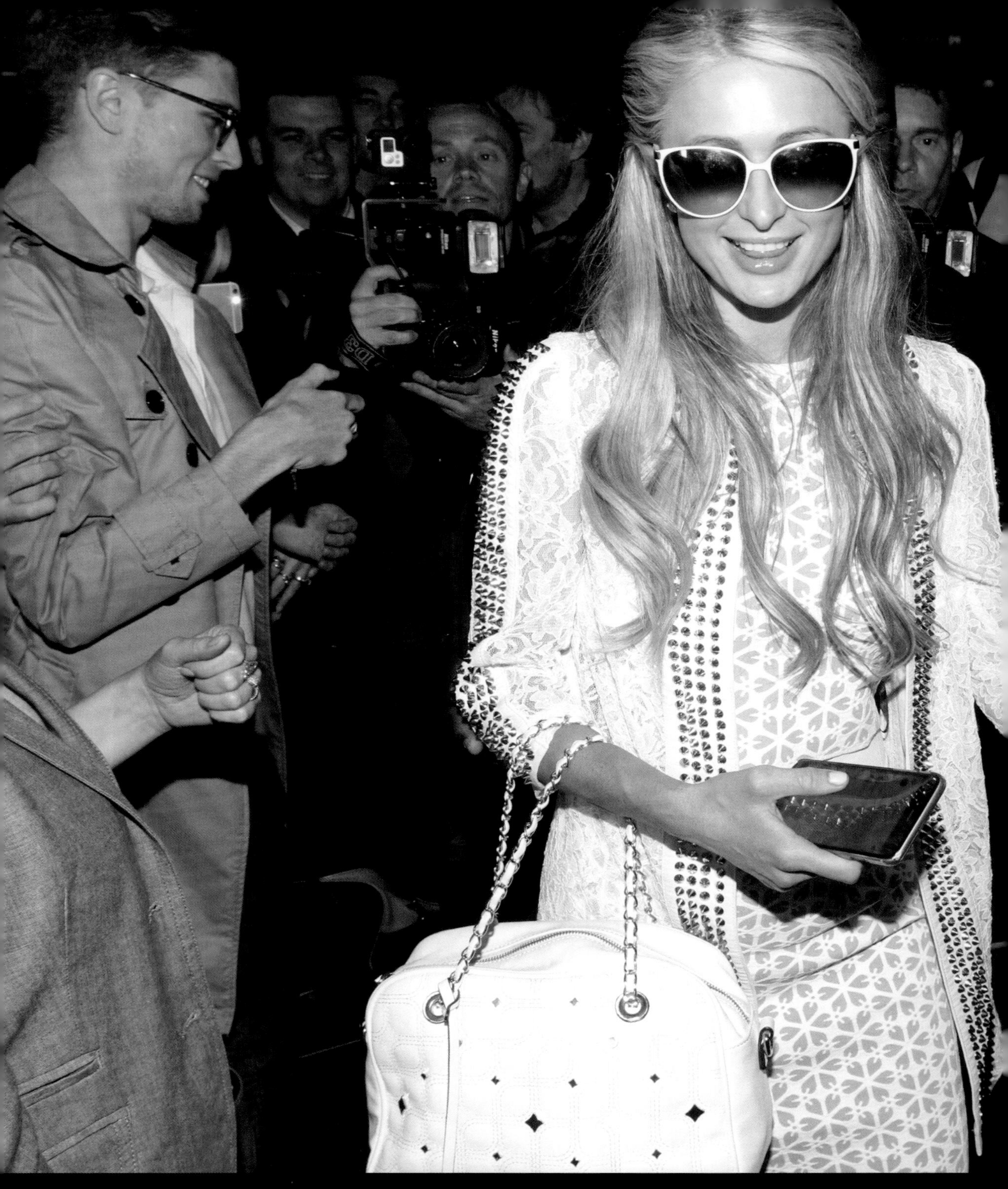

Paris Hilton
Covent Garden
May 2015

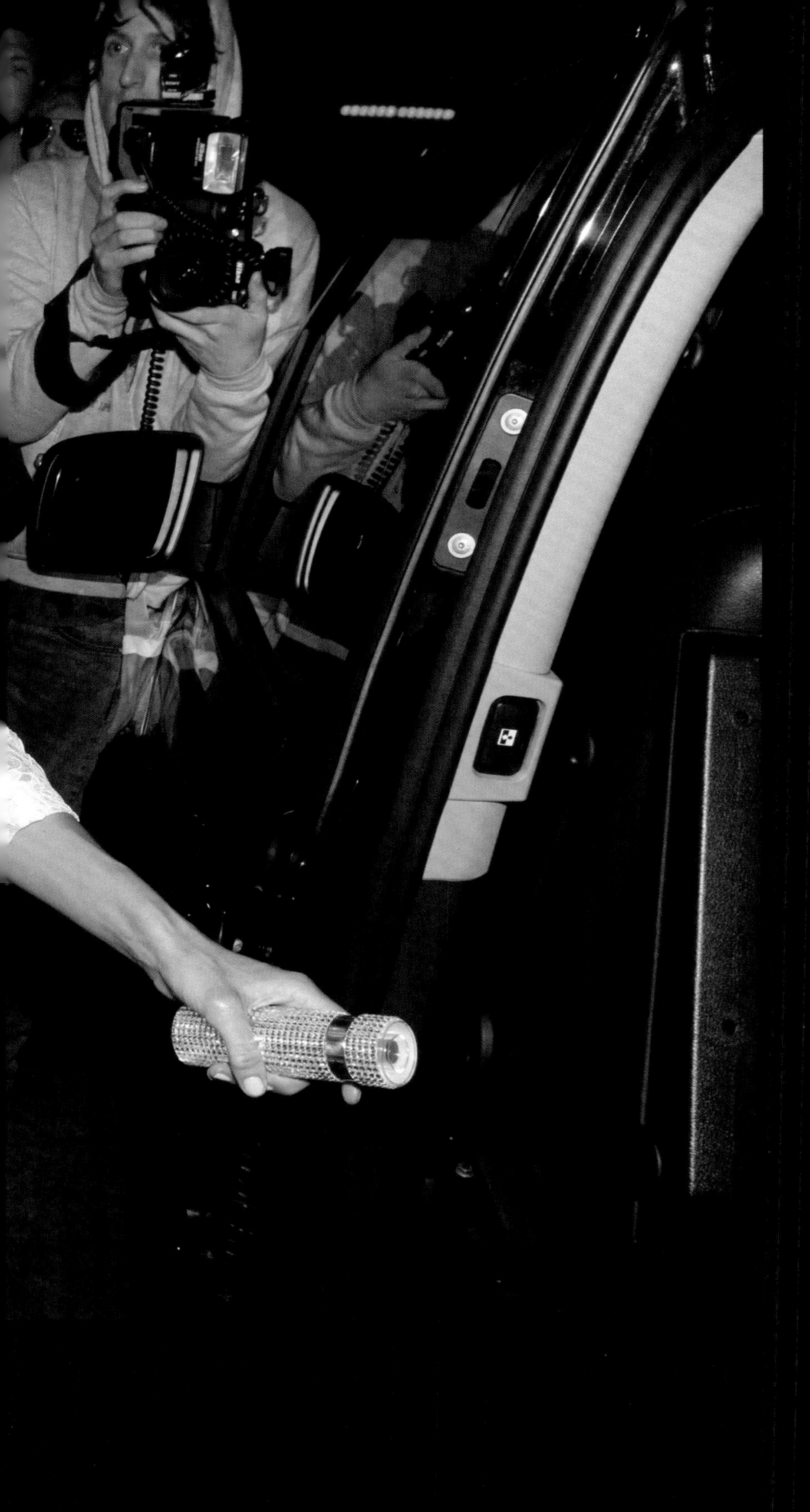

KARL LAGERFELD

November 2015

There are few in the world of fashion whose presence eclipses the runway, the campaigns, the labels; whose very image becomes a kind of mythology. Karl Lagerfeld was one such figure. For years, I had quietly harboured a hope of photographing him. Not just to check off a box or be able to say I'd done it – but because, for me, Karl wasn't only a titan of fashion. He was a kindred eye. A fellow photographer. A few years earlier, a friend had gifted me a copy of *Off the Record* (1994), a book of Karl's photography. I particularly loved his black-and-white portraits, which (as you have seen by now) have become a staple of my work as well. He could weave a story visually, making his models into characters in a silent film. His work mirrored the kind of storytelling I aspired to. I'd long been eager to shoot him, but as fate would have it, the opportunity never seemed to arise. Until one night in 2015.

By then, I had resigned myself to the idea that I might never cross paths with the man himself. It was the night of the Fashion Awards afterparty, and I had been running late – another assignment had pulled me to the other side of town, so I arrived at Loulou's in Mayfair long after the party had reached its fever pitch, without any real expectations. It was bedlam when I got there. Photographers packed like sardines, fans pressing forward with phones aloft, flashes ricocheting off car doors, and engines idling as their passengers prepared to melt into the night.

Amidst the chaos, I spotted a cluster of photographers huddled around someone, cameras flashing in a frenzy, mouths shouting. My instincts kicked in. Whoever it was had to be someone big. I edged closer, squeezing through the crowd to catch a glimpse, and there was Lagerfeld in his signature black suit, immaculate leather gloves, and sunglasses catching the flash like a mirror to the Moon. The universe had granted me my moment. Despite the crowd, Karl was moving in my direction, cutting through the madness with his own kind of elegant calm. I didn't have much time to think – just enough to ask him to stop for a photograph. And to my surprise, he did. He paused, turning to me with a graciousness that I hadn't expected but should have known was inherent to his character. He didn't just pose; he gave me that knowing look,

> *"He didn't just pose; he gave me that knowing look, a quiet acknowledgement between two photographers meeting in a flash of mutual understanding."*

a quiet acknowledgement between two photographers meeting in a flash of mutual understanding. He recognised the pursuit in my eyes. The reverence. The shared addiction to freezing time.

I had longed for this photo for years, only for it to come together in the most perfect of ways. Karl was, in every sense, larger than life – yet there he was, just a few feet away, obliging a fan with the kind of ease that reminded me why I had admired him for so long. And then, just as quickly as he had appeared, he was gone, swallowed back into the chaos of Mayfair's buzzing streets. But I had my shot. One shutter click. And in it, a lifetime of admiration.

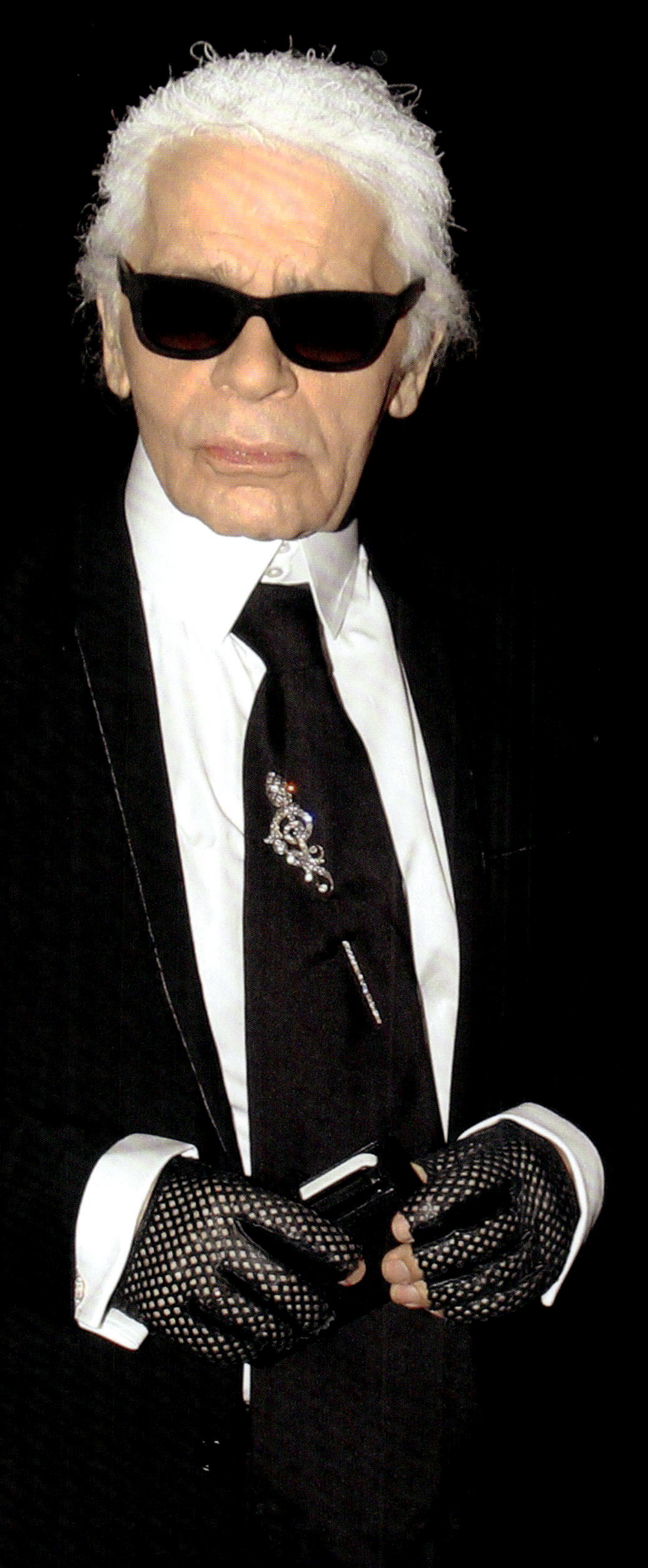

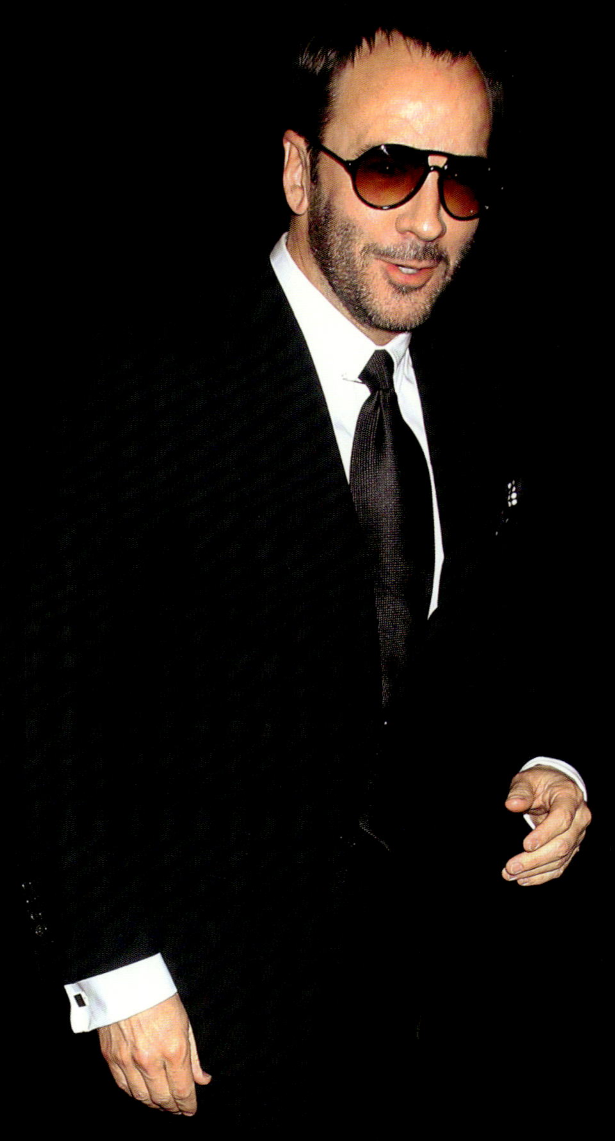

Tom Ford
Loulou's, Mayfair
December 2013
Leaving the British Fashion Awards

Dita Von Teese
Royal Horticultural Halls
November 2007
At the British Fashion Awards

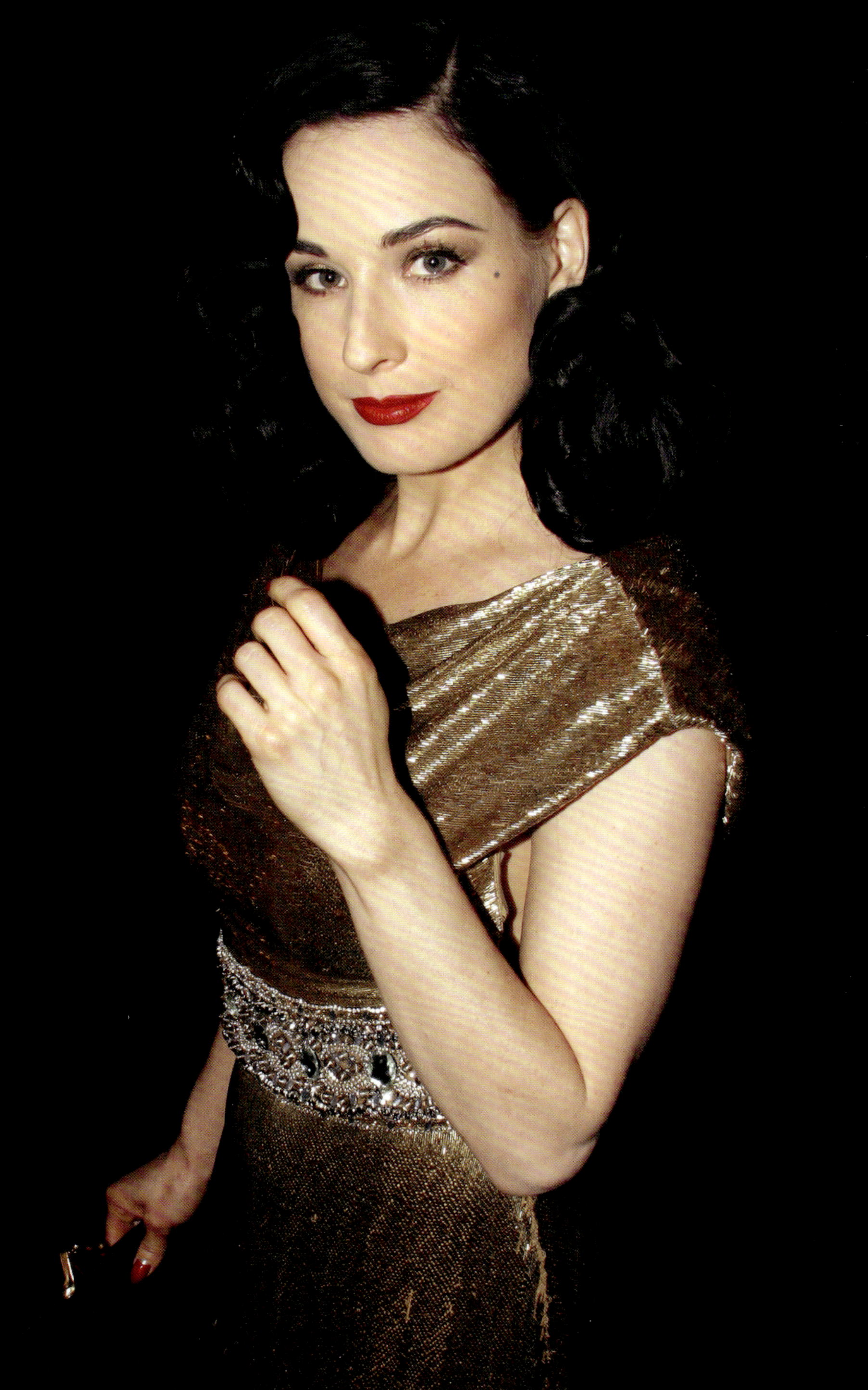

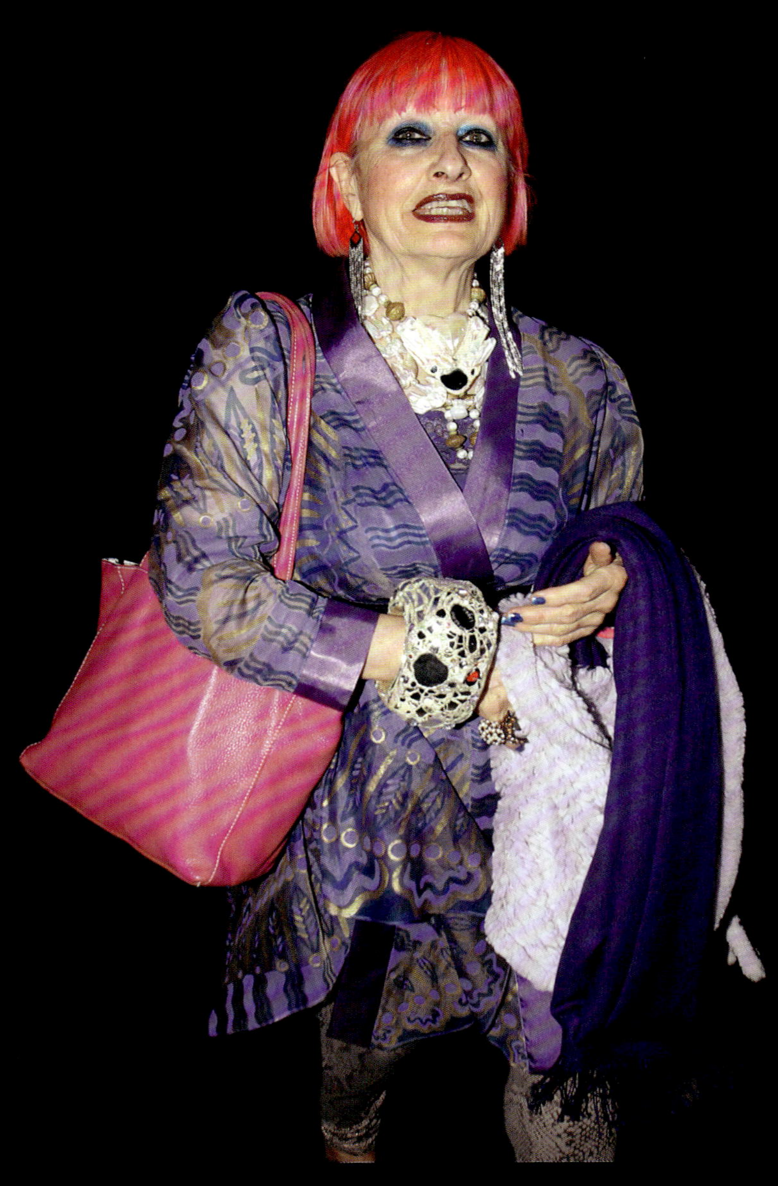

Dame Zandra Rhodes
Somerset House, Strand
September 2012
Leaving London Fashion Week

Vivienne Westwood
Serpentine Gallery, Hyde Park
February 2008

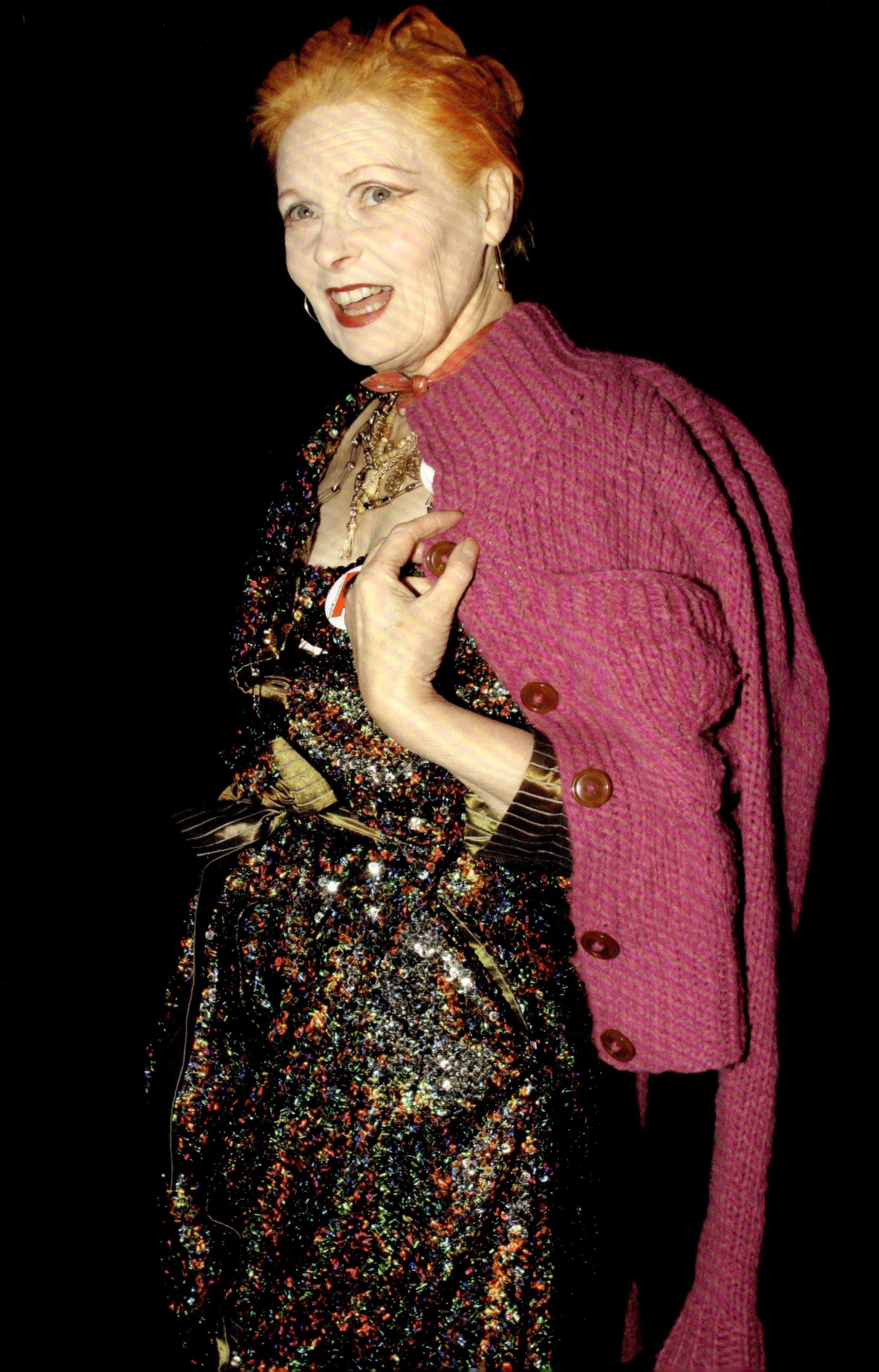

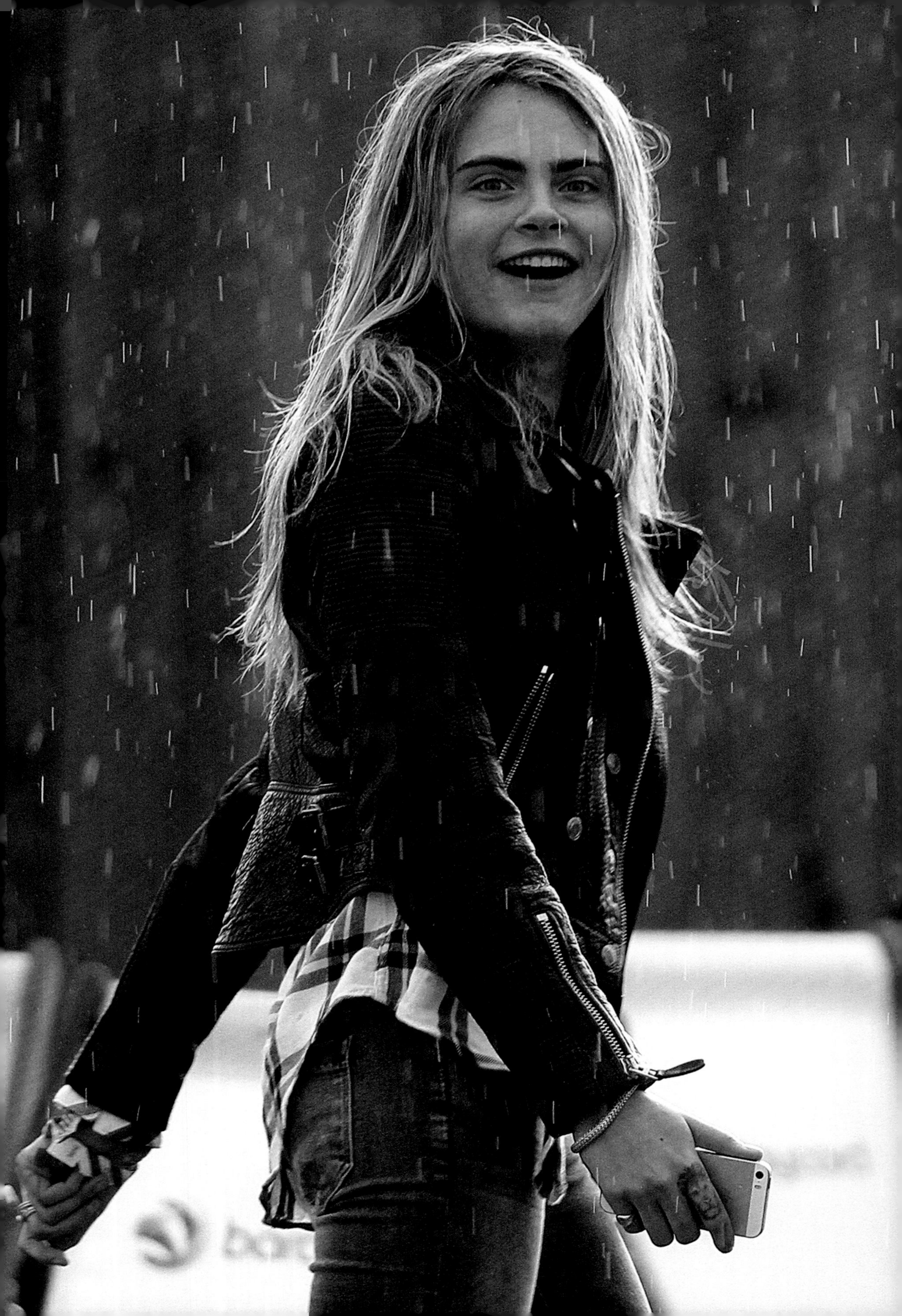

Cara Delevingne
Hyde Park
July 2014
Backstage watching McBusted
at BST Hyde Park

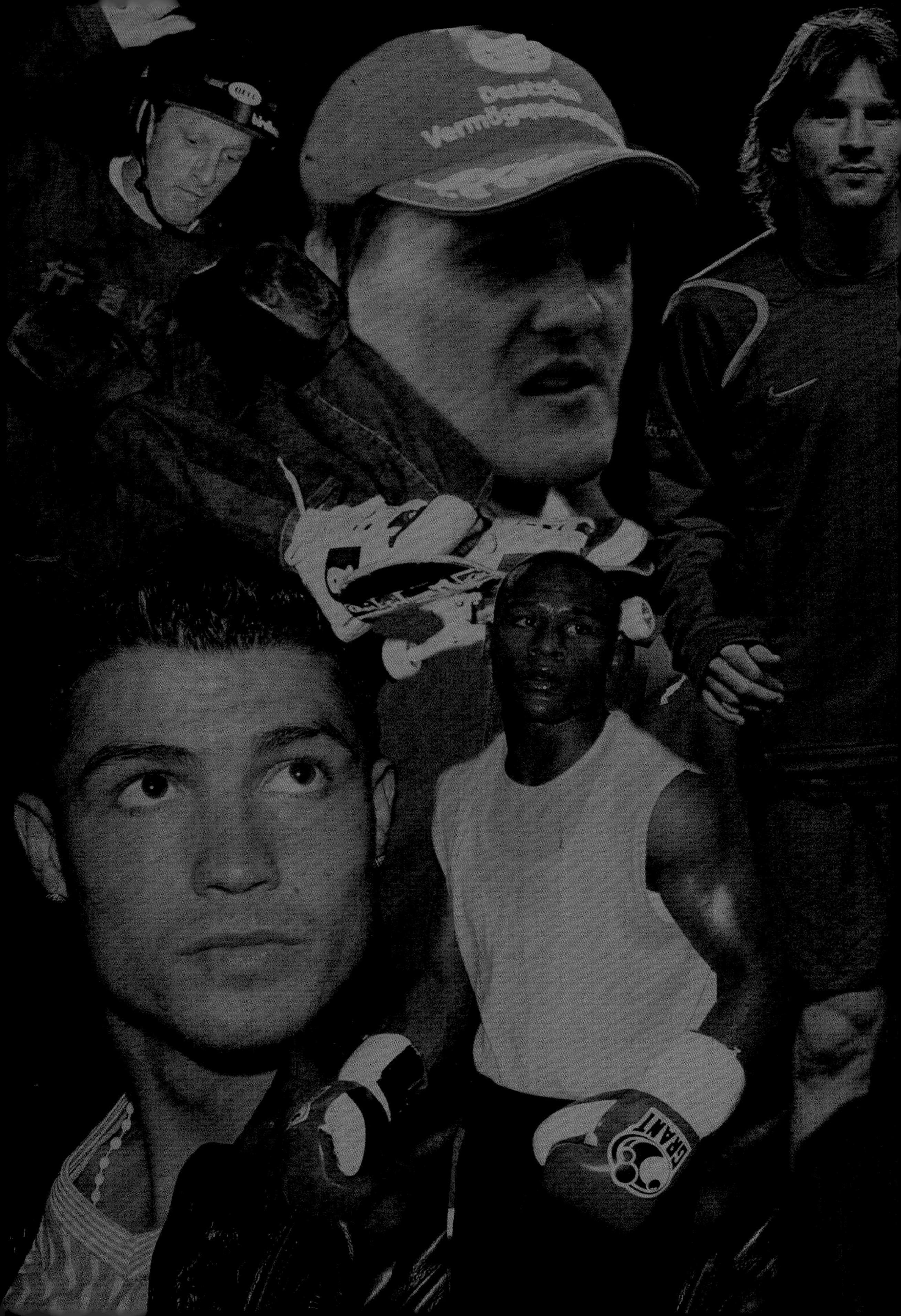
Deutsche
GRANT

SPORT

LIONEL MESSI

February 2006

"I knew he would be eternal, someone that might one day be spoken of in the same breath as Pelé or Maradona."

It was an unseasonably cold evening In London, and the football world was buzzing with excitement. Lionel Messi, the 18-year-old Argentinian wonderkid, had finally arrived. I had been following Messi's rise for some time – he was already putting the fear of God into defenders with every touch of the ball, and he was simply amazing to watch play. Even as a lifelong Chelsea fan, I felt no rivalry towards him. He was different. No one could deny his utter brilliance on the pitch.

FC Barcelona were in town for a Champions League clash against Chelsea, and I knew where the team were staying. On my way to Stamford Bridge for the evening's training session, I decided to stop by the hotel, hoping for a chance to catch Messi and the team before they headed to the ground. The scene outside was typical: fans lingering, cameras ready, and a big team bus parked out front. As the players began to emerge, I readied my gear. When Messi finally appeared, I was struck by how small he looked in person, far more diminutive than he seemed on the pitch; a boy amongst titans. But he carried himself with a quiet confidence, and as he gave me a smile and a wave, I pressed the shutter. The other players followed, including some of the big names like Eto'o and Puyol, but it was Messi that had my focus.

I left the hotel and made my way to Stamford Bridge, though I ended up missing most of José Mourinho's press conference – no big loss, Messi was what mattered to me. Once I arrived at the ground, we were led out to the lower terrace, and I was pleased to find that Chelsea had granted us a good amount of freedom to move around. It allowed for excellent vantage points for the photos. For this shoot, you needed at least a 300mm lens and, luckily, I was well-prepared. I knew I'd need every bit of reach to capture the magic of Messi and Barcelona's other big star, Ronaldinho.

When the players finally came out, I spent the next 40 minutes shooting the session. My lens rarely left Messi, though I couldn't help but snap a few shots of Ronaldinho – the two were the crown jewels of football at the time. Messi, with his long, slightly unbrushed hair, looked every bit his young age. But as soon as the ball was at his feet, the youthfulness melted away and all you saw was brilliance, even just in training.

I shot through the chill until the light gave out. I knew he would be eternal, someone that might one day be spoken of in the same breath as Pelé or Maradona. That training session I photographed was a prelude to a legend. Not the birth of greatness, but its revelation.

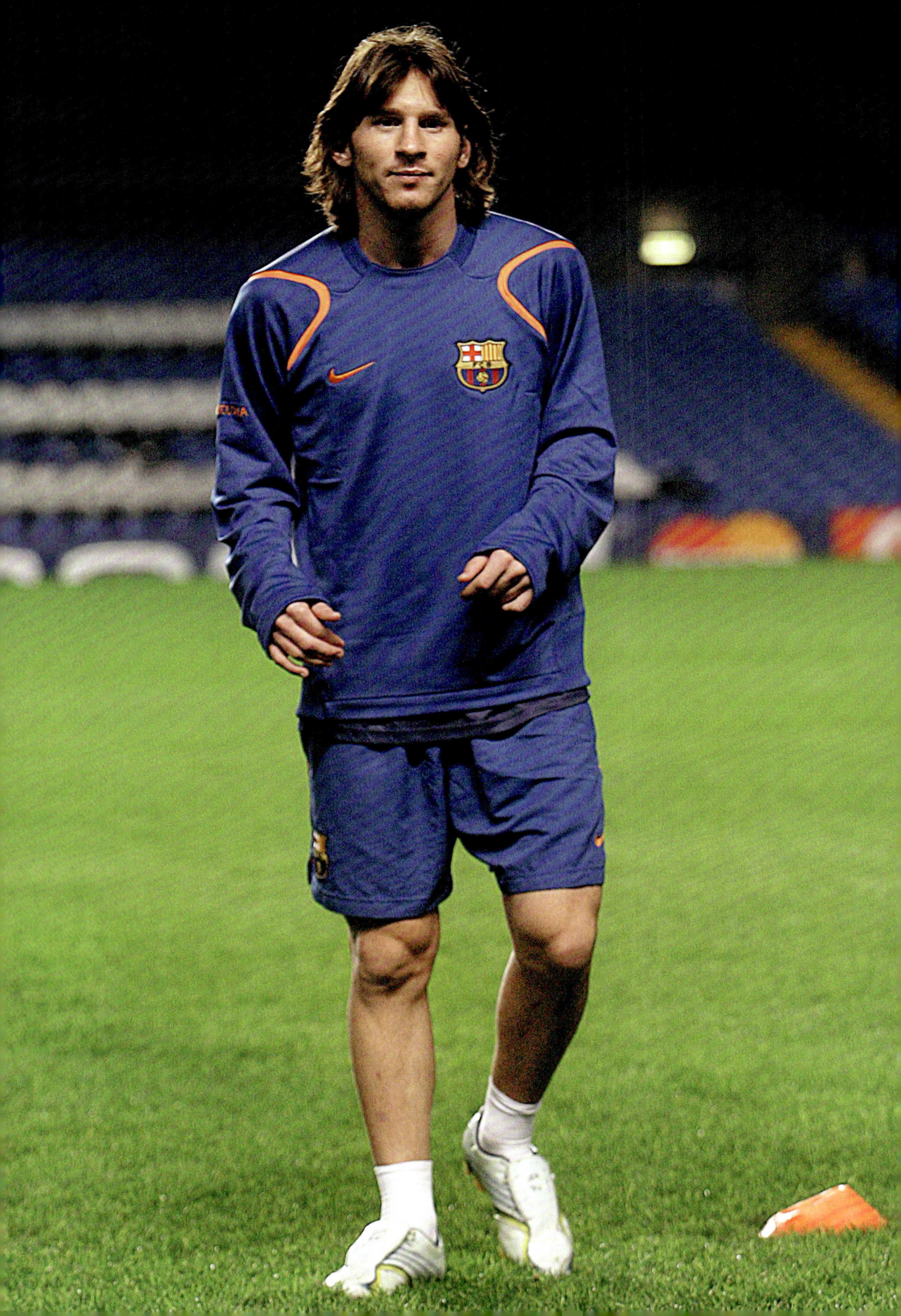

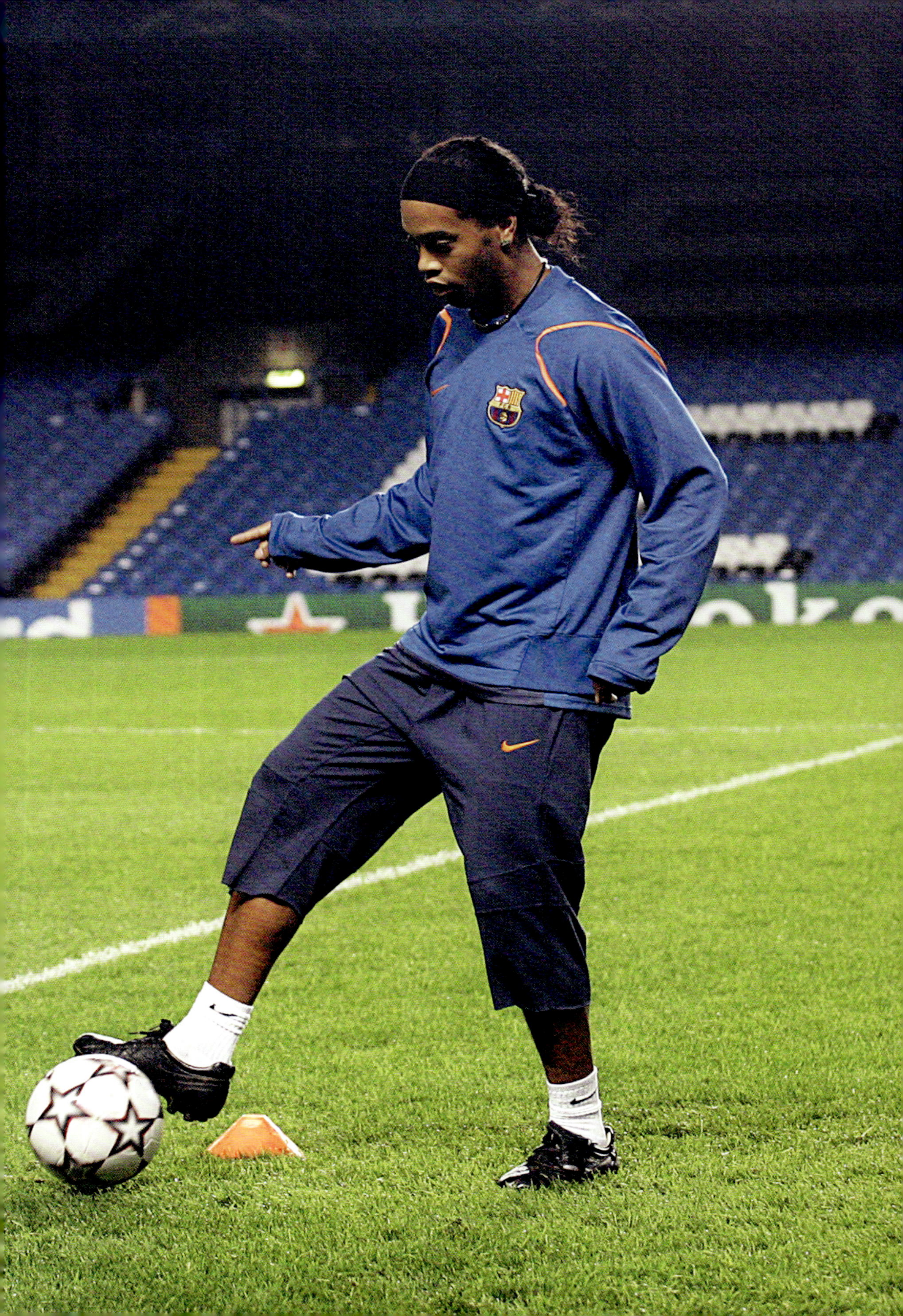

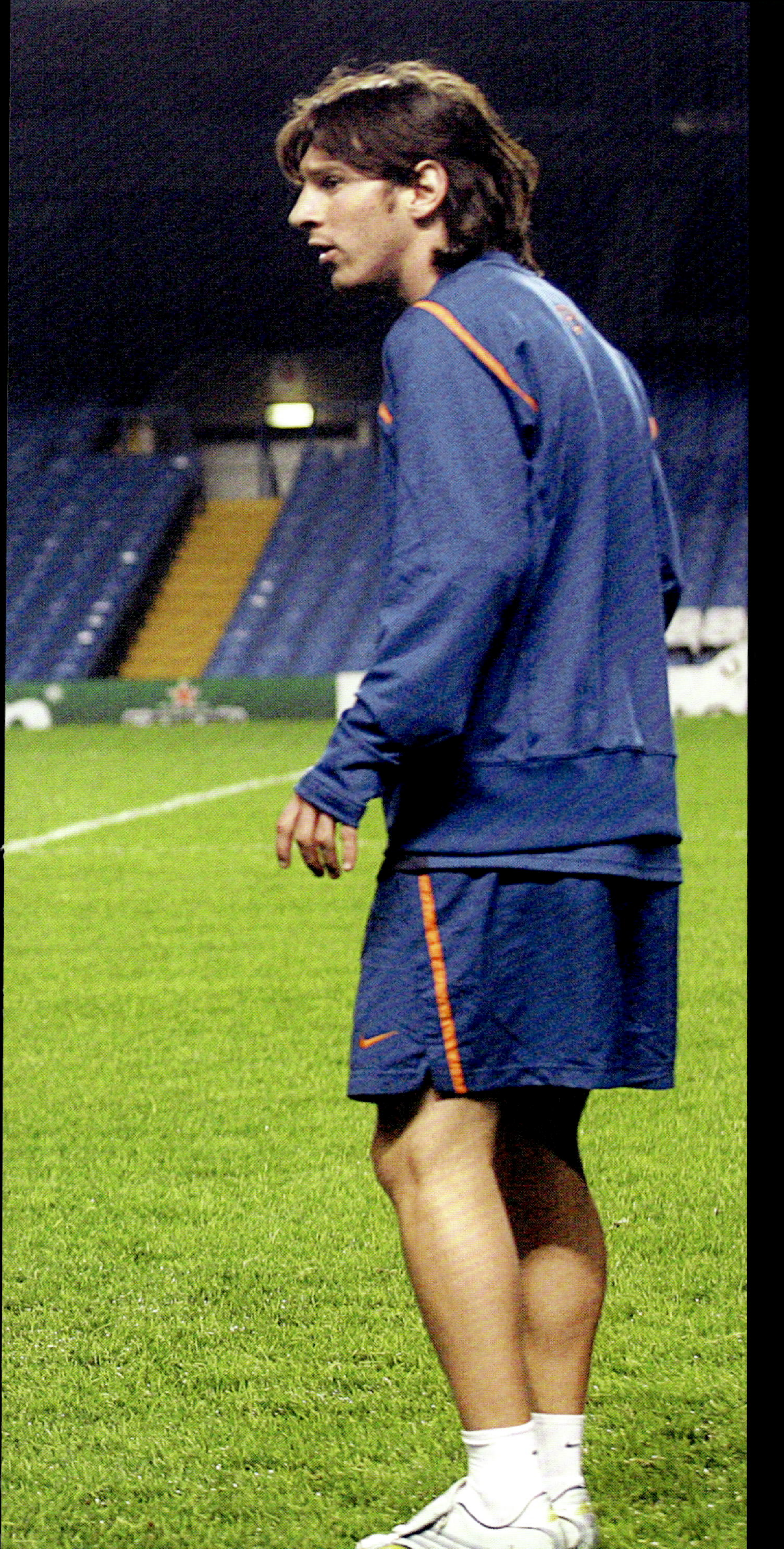

Lionel Messi and Ronaldinho
Stamford Bridge
February 2006

CRISTIANO RONALDO
May 2008

Some of the best moments in photography aren't at all planned; they just happen. You think you're done for the night and the job's wrapped; then, out of nowhere, something extraordinary lands in your lap. That's exactly how it was the first time I crossed paths with Cristiano Ronaldo.

I was at the Royal Lancaster Hotel, which had become something of a footballers' den over the years. The place was steeped in sporting history, with the FA's offices just a stone's throw away. On that particular evening, I had been covering a fairly low-key football event, nothing too glamorous – just a few random players. No one you'd write home about. My night was winding down and I was sitting in the lobby wiring my photos, ready to call it a day.

Suddenly the ding of the lift echoed through the lobby and a group of well-dressed men spilled out. They were deep in conversation, speaking in rapid Spanish. I watched them for a moment, intrigued, and listened in – Spanish is a language I speak well. Lawyers, I deduced. Football lawyers. Just another part of the machine that keeps the sport ticking.

But before I could return to my work, the second lift opened. Out stepped someone taller than expected, dressed impeccably with an unmistakable aura about him. Cristiano Ronaldo.

I'd never seen him before in person, and the effect was immediate. He was magnetic, not just because he was one of the most famous footballers in the world at that moment, but because there's something about Ronaldo that commands a room. I didn't react right away – no rushing over or shoving a camera in his face. There's a dance to moments like these, and timing is everything.

I watched as Ronaldo, cool and collected, strolled out of the lift, still deep in conversation with his entourage. I wasn't there to photograph him but when the opportunity presents itself, you don't say no. Especially not when it's Ronaldo.

I chose my moment carefully. No interruptions, no fuss. I made my way outside, casually positioning myself near the hotel entrance. When he emerged, he was relaxed, smiling, clearly at ease. He spotted me as he walked towards a waiting cab, and without a word, he acknowledged me – just a small nod, but one imbued with that unspoken understanding between photographer and subject.

"He acknowledged me – just a small nod, that unspoken understanding between photographer and subject."

He flashed a grin and gave a playful thumbs-up as he slid into the cab. I snapped a series of frames. It was effortless, like Ronaldo himself – confident, poised and in control of the moment. Little did I know then, but that grin likely had a lot more to do with what was happening behind the scenes. He had just come from what was probably the final conversation confirming his world-record transfer from Manchester United to Real Madrid, a deal worth £80 million. No wonder he was smiling!

He slipped into the cab and vanished into the night. The whole encounter lasted seconds. But in those seconds, something timeless lived: the face of a man who knew he was going to permanently redraw the borders of his beloved sport.

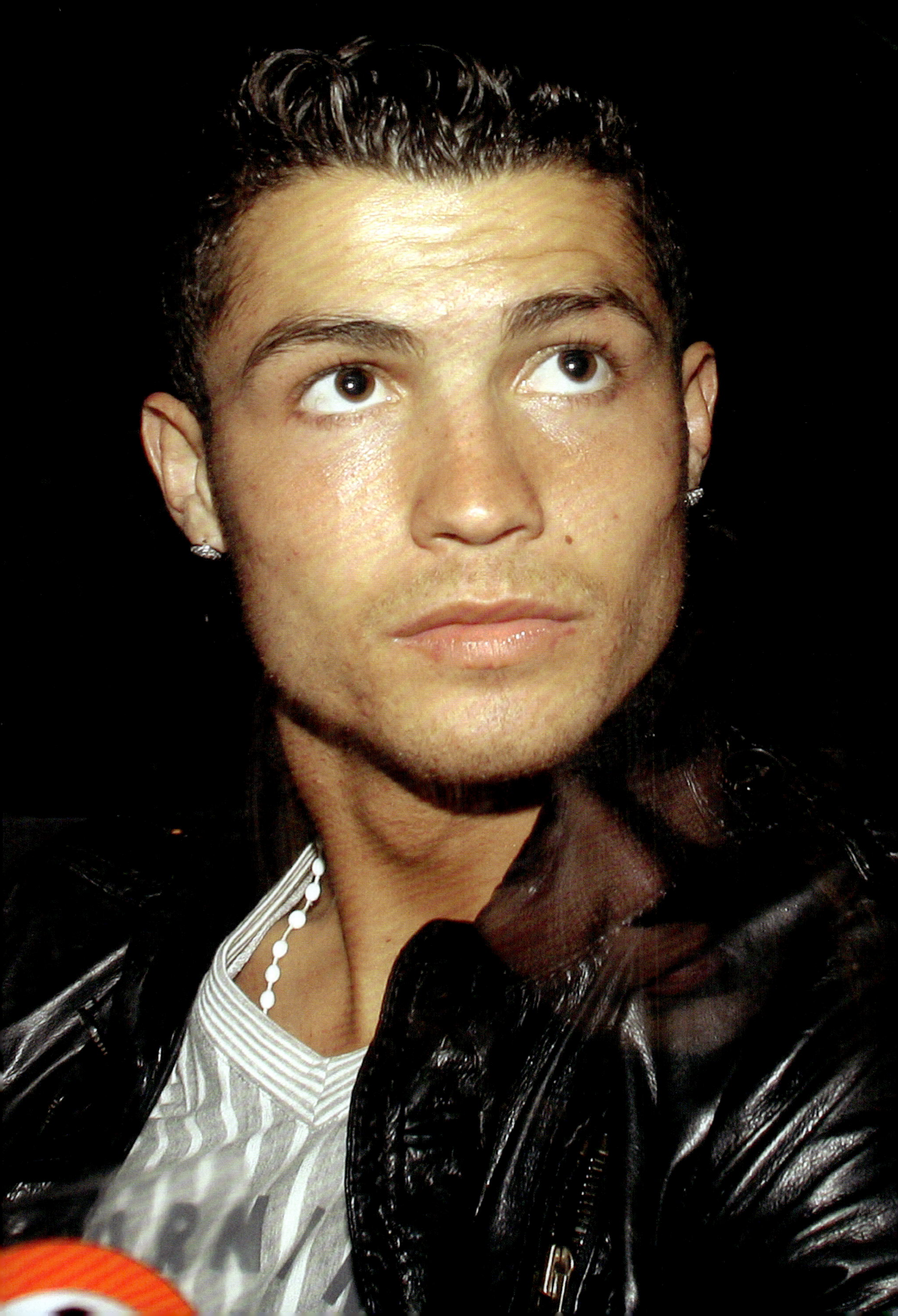

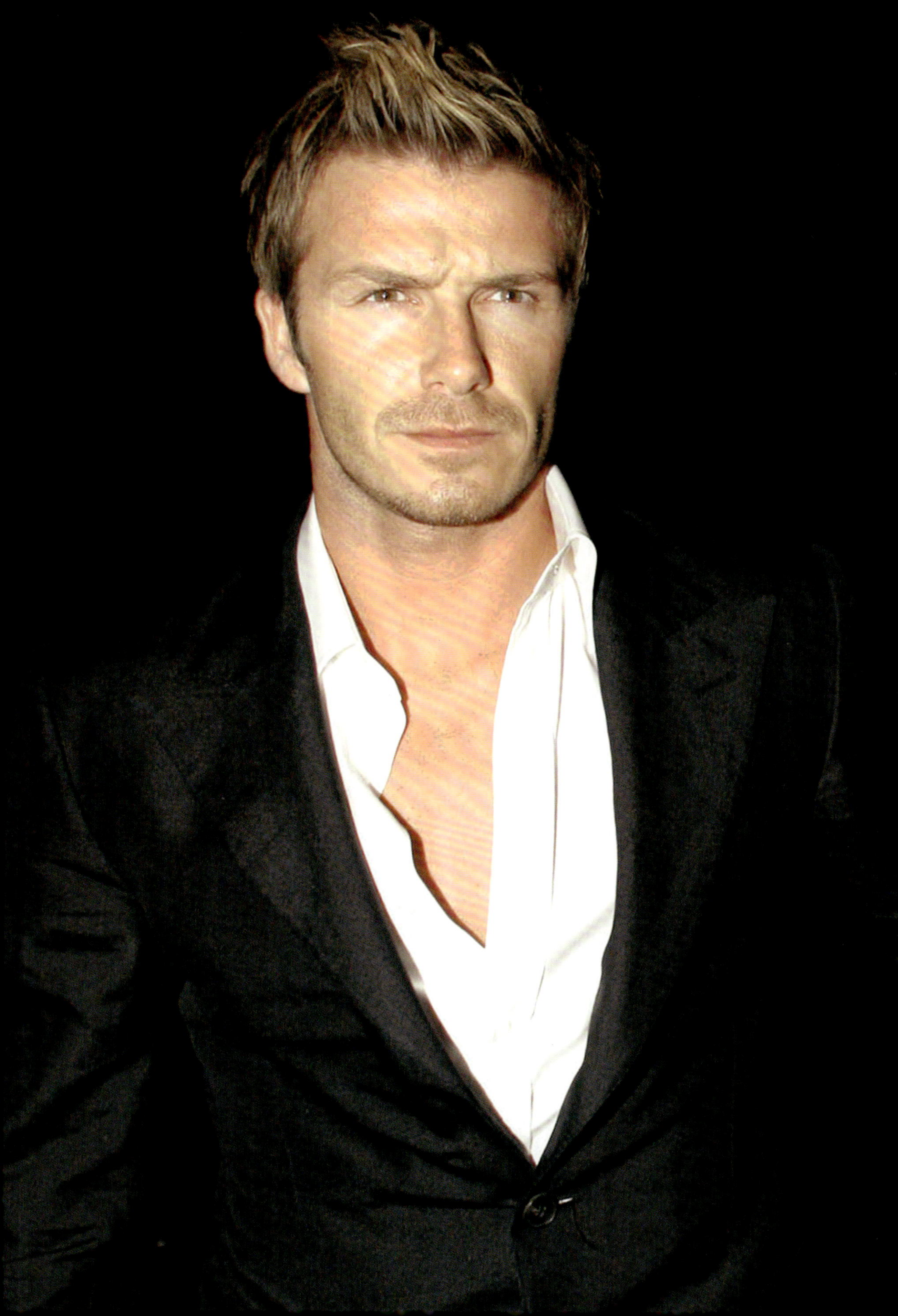

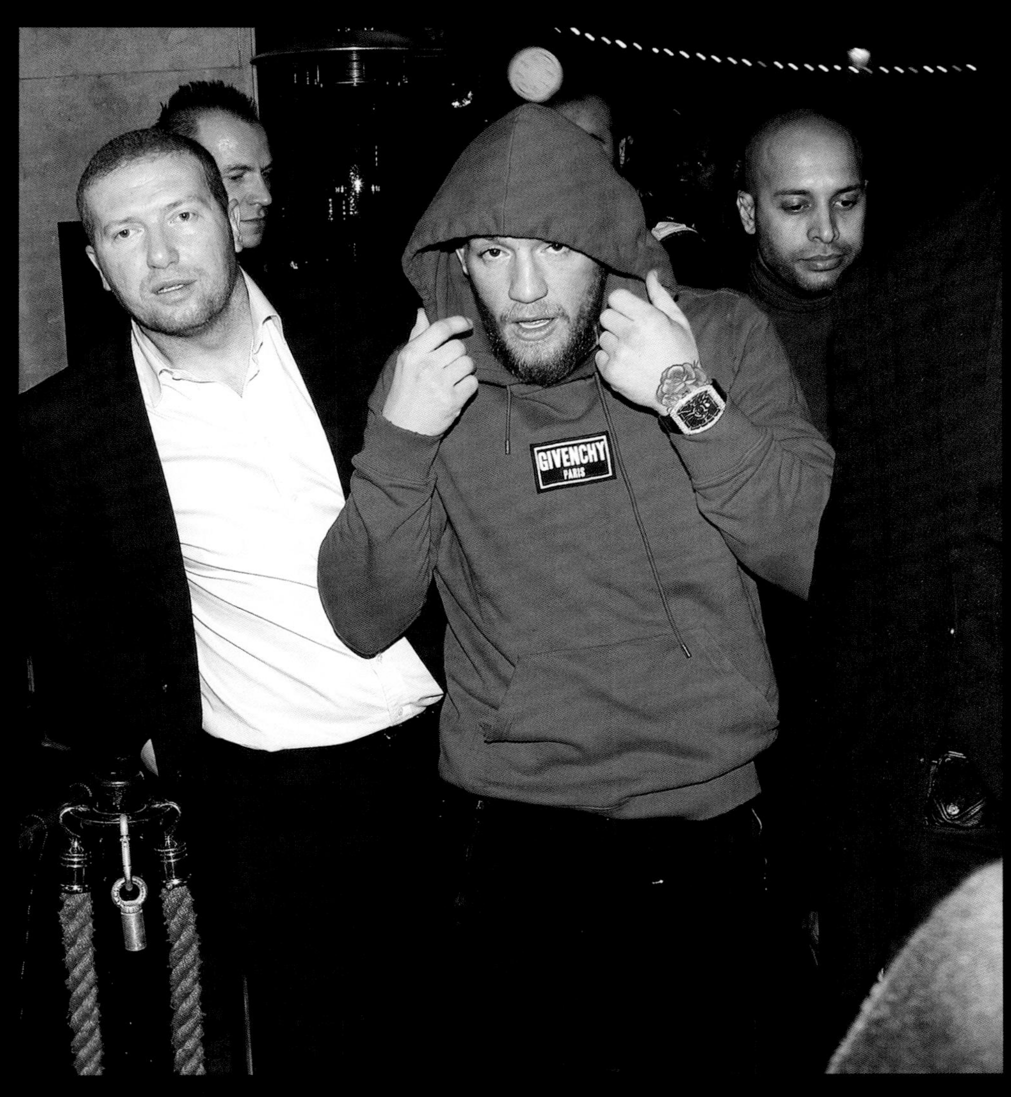

Sir David Beckham
Scott's, Mayfair
May 2005
Dinner with Gordon Ramsay

Conor McGregor
Cirque Le Soir, Soho
December 2017

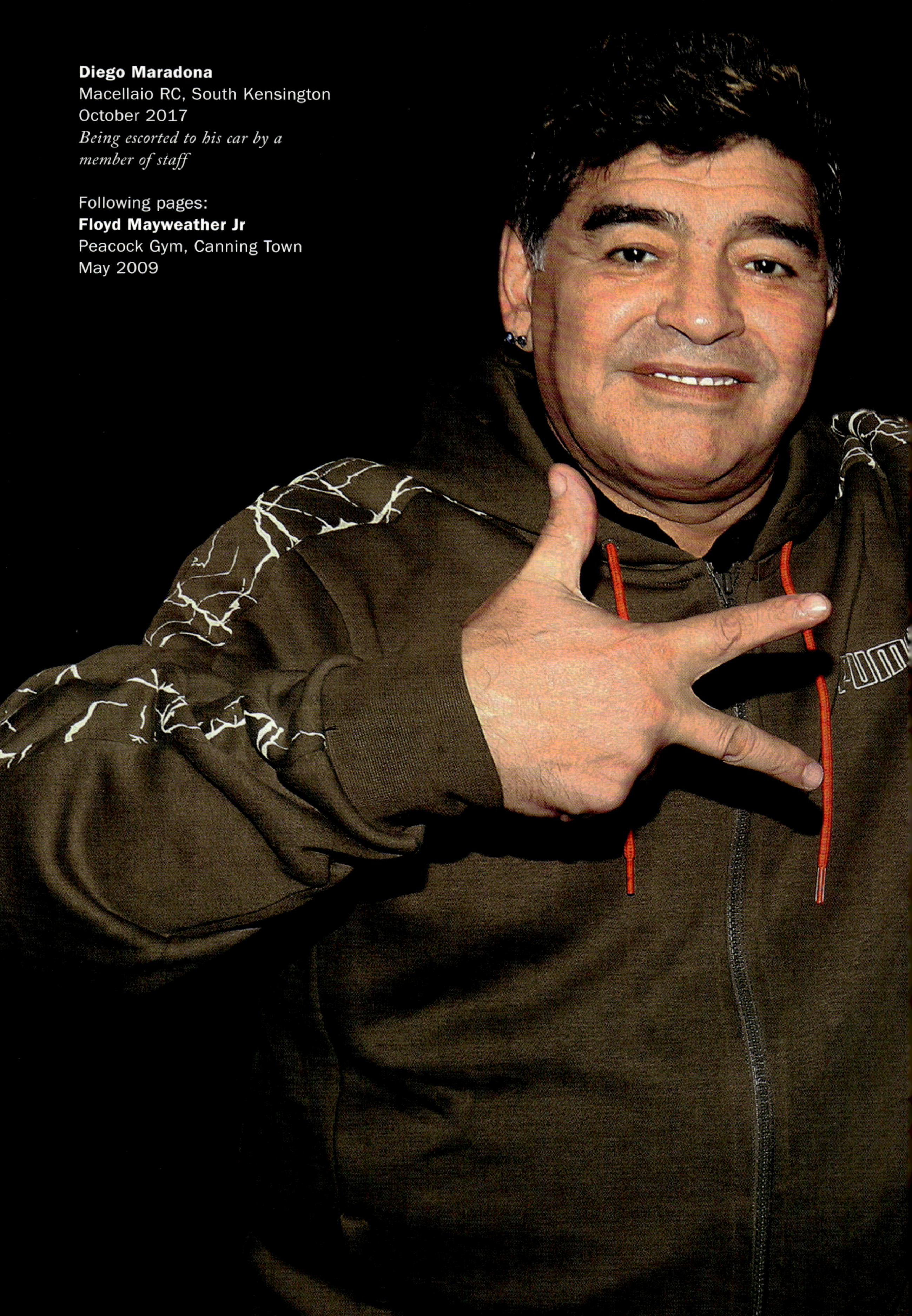

Diego Maradona
Macellaio RC, South Kensington
October 2017
Being escorted to his car by a member of staff

Following pages:
Floyd Mayweather Jr
Peacock Gym, Canning Town
May 2009

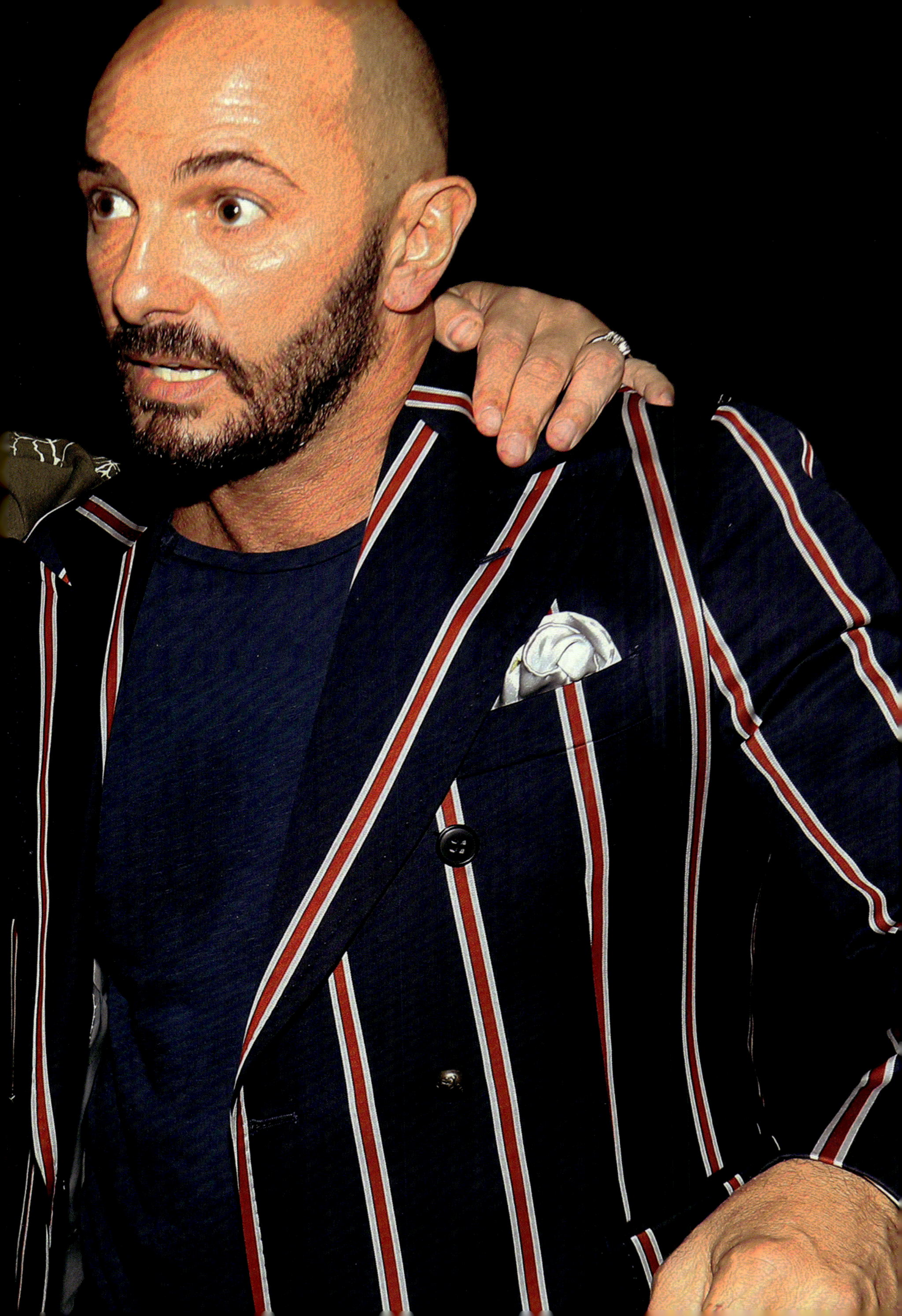

Brian

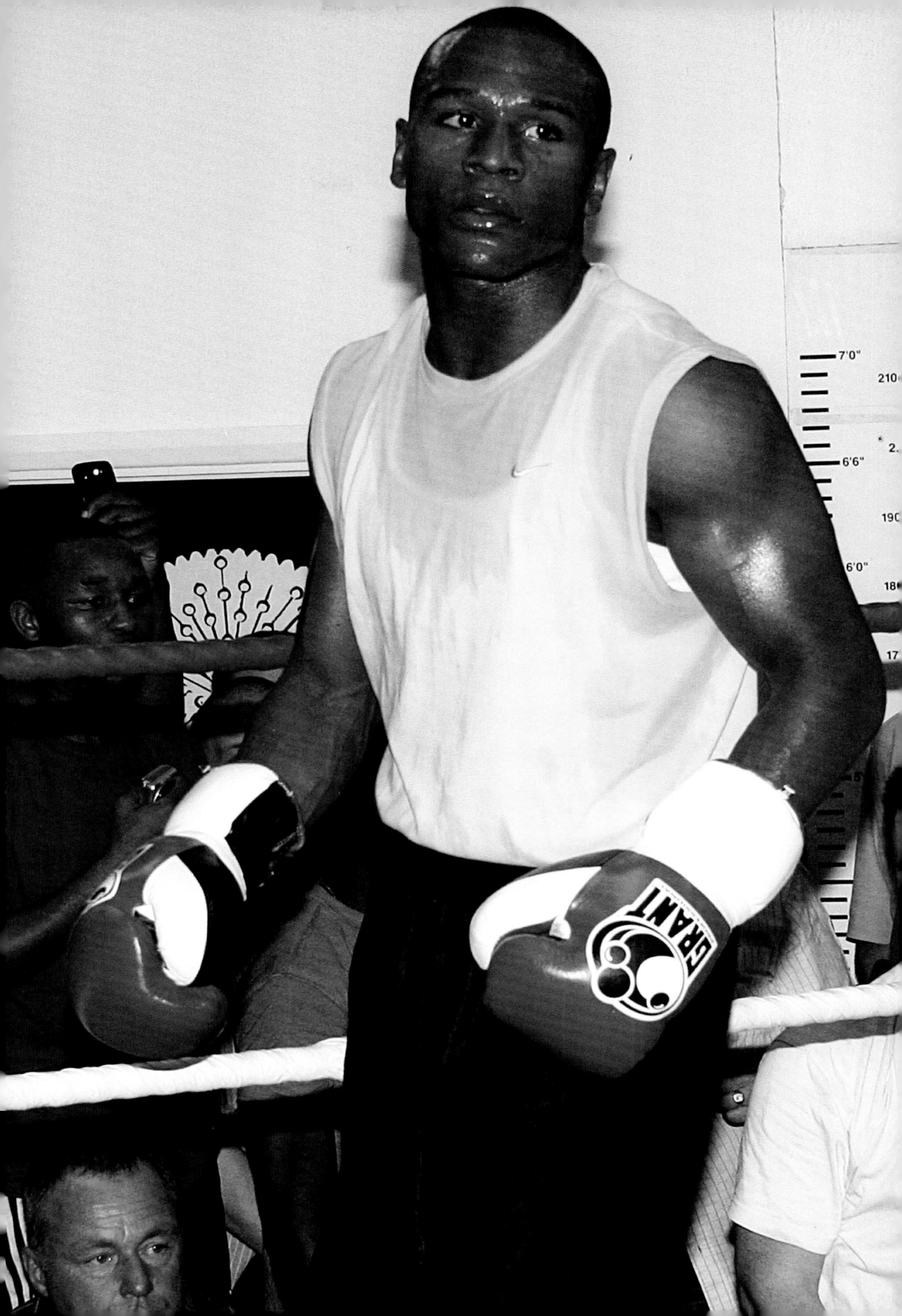
7'0"
6'6"
6'0"
GRANT

MIKE TYSON
January 2000

The Baddest Man on the Planet was in town, and wherever he walked, magic followed. Tyson had arrived in London to prepare for his fight against British heavyweight Julius Francis, and his entourage made sure everyone knew it. Outside the Grosvenor House Hotel, photographers, fans and media were all jockeying for a glimpse of the man himself. But thanks to an old friend of mine, the boxing legend Lloyd Honeyghan, I had the kind of access most could only dream of.

Tyson wasn't just there to train, though. Day one of his stay saw him playing the part of tourist, hitting up London landmarks like Big Ben and Buckingham Palace, even stopping by Madame Tussauds to see his own wax figure. But sightseeing quickly gave way to an extravagant shopping spree, the likes of which I'd never witnessed before. Versace, Gucci, the Aston Martin showroom on Park Lane – Tyson breezed through Bond Street. He hit top-end jewellery stores like Graff, eyeing all the pieces that sparkled most. Money was spent like air.

It was outside Versace when things took a turn for the unexpected. I was lingering by the door, camera in hand, when Tyson's team beckoned me inside. I found myself in an absurdly exclusive scene – just me, Tyson, Lloyd, Tyson's hype man Steve 'Crocodile' Fitch, promoter Frank Warren, and some of his security detail. Tyson wanted a photo – not of himself, but of a mannequin dressed in a suit. "Mike wants you to snap this," his guard explained. I clicked away, wondering what this odd request was all about. As we left, his guard dropped the punchline: Tyson wanted the photo so his tailor back home could replicate the suit – without him actually having to buy it. After a day of watching him drop a small fortune across London, this thrifty moment caught me off guard. Tyson was a man of contradictions, no doubt about it.

That evening, I found myself in a Blockbuster-style video rental shop on Kensington High Street, watching Mike browse VHS tapes like an ordinary guy. Amid rows of films, he pulled out one tape and turned to us. "You all need to watch this," he said, with his soft but commanding lisp. It was the first-ever episode of *The Sopranos*. "Watch it, man. Moms is cold," he muttered, referring to Tony Soprano's mother Livia. "It's about a crime family from New York." This was long before the show became a cultural phenomenon, and I'd forever have the story of how Iron Mike introduced me to TV's greatest crime family.

As the day grew darker, we returned to the hotel, where he held court in his seventh-floor suite. The reception area was like something out of a boxing club: guys hanging around, lounging on couches, while Tyson cast light on his career and the sport he loved. I sat, mostly quiet, as he spoke. What struck me wasn't just his stories, but his encyclopaedic knowledge of boxing history. The man could recall the most obscure details, recounting fights, tactics and legends with the ease of a historian. When it came to the sport, Tyson's intellect was deeply underrated.

> *"He was a finely tuned machine, decades of skill and instinct compressed into each punch."*

The next day, I finally got the chance to photograph him in action at the gym. We were in the company of other boxing greats too, like Jeff Fenech and Joe Calzaghe. After waiting a good while – he was clearly jet-lagged – Tyson arrived, ready to work. And work he did. Watching him train was nothing short of awe-inspiring. His speed, his power, his massive presence, it all came together in the ring. He wasn't just brute strength; he was a finely tuned machine, decades of skill and instinct compressed into each punch, each movement. The week culminated in a trip to Manchester where I sat ringside, thanks to Lloyd, watching Tyson dismantle Julius Francis.

It was the contradictions that made Tyson. All at once he could be wild, generous, intimidating and soft-spoken, a hurricane with a poet's memory. One moment he was flexing on Bond Street, the next he was geeking out over a TV drama in a video shop. That's Tyson. A force you could never quite predict, but would never, ever forget.

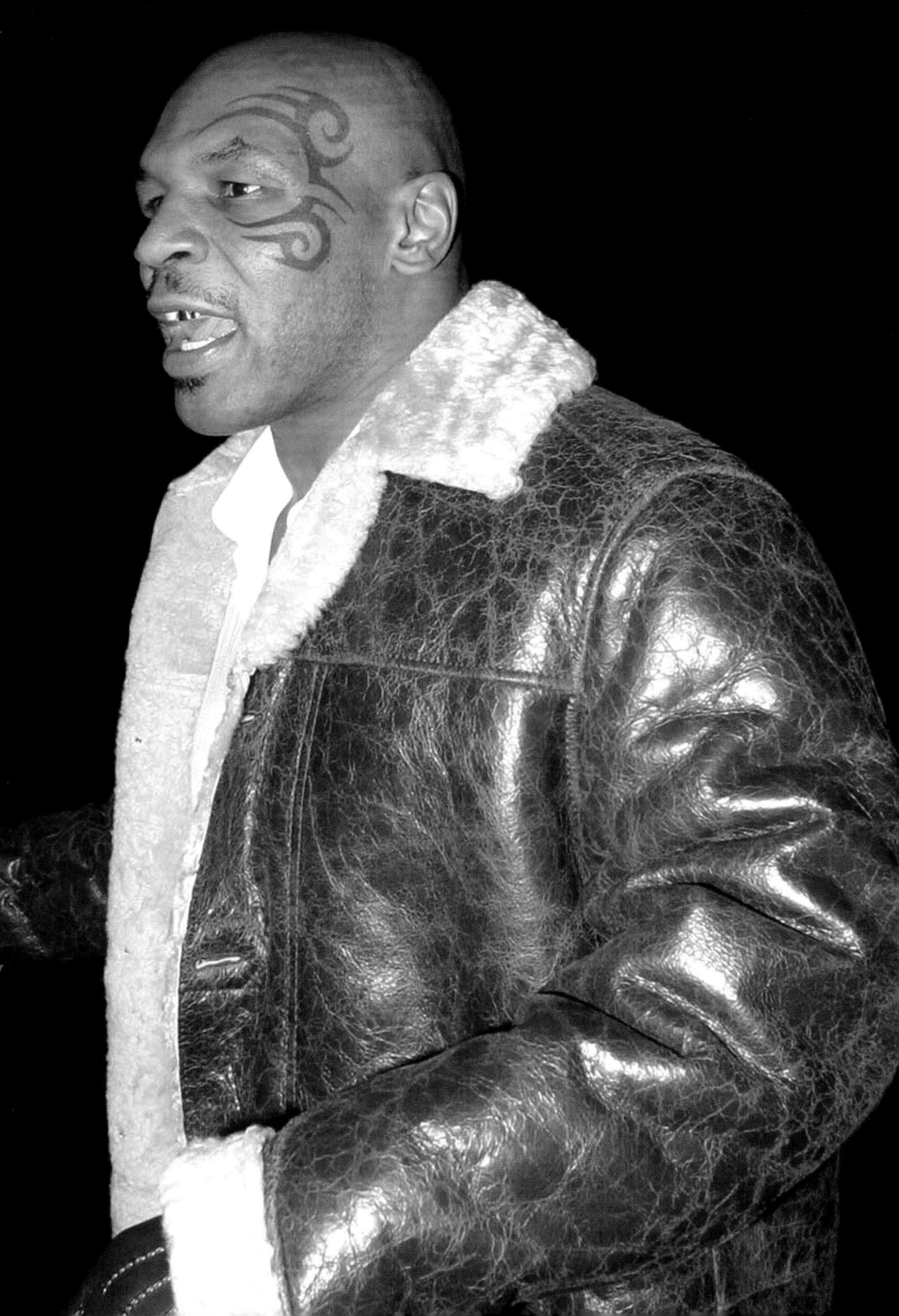

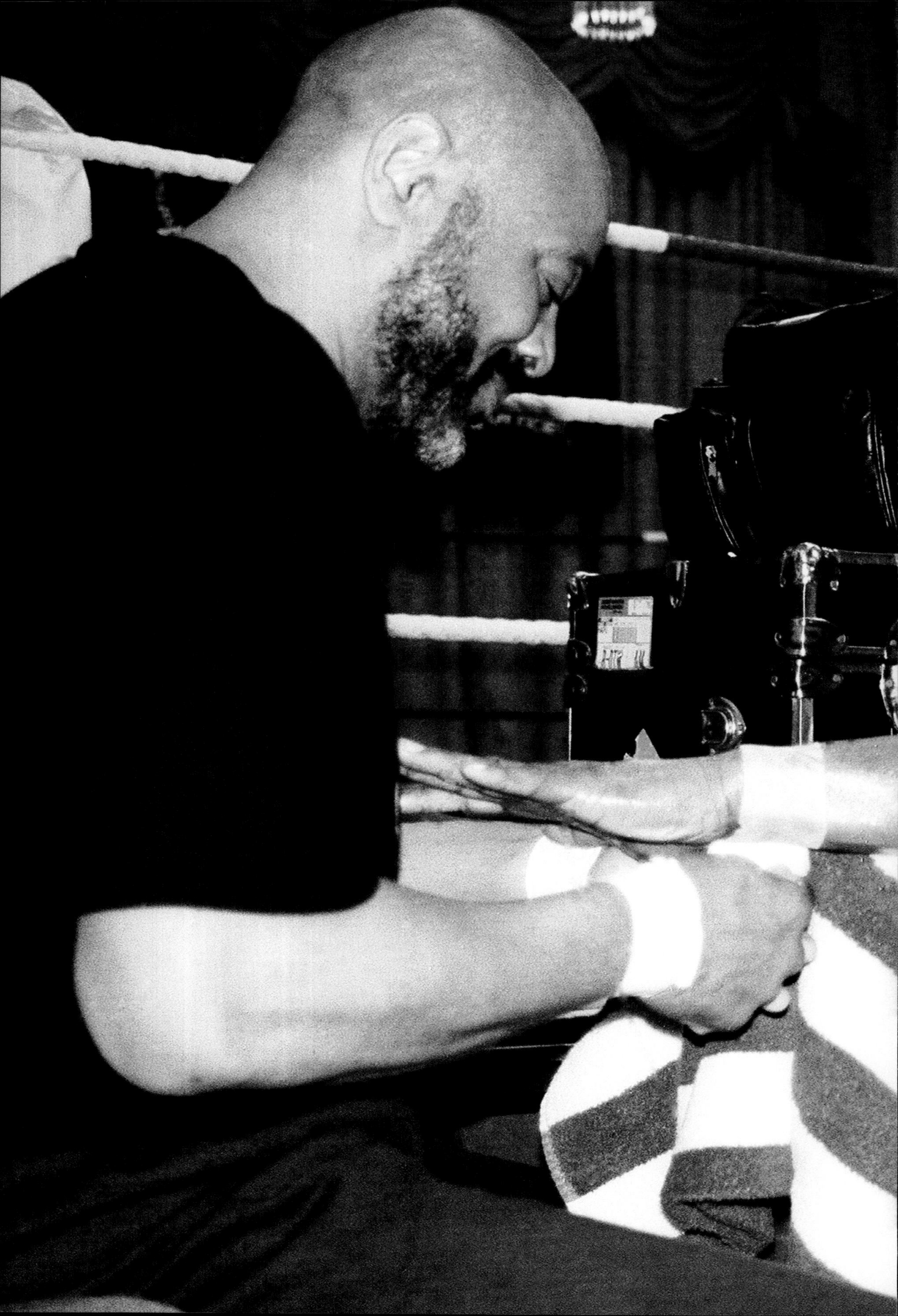

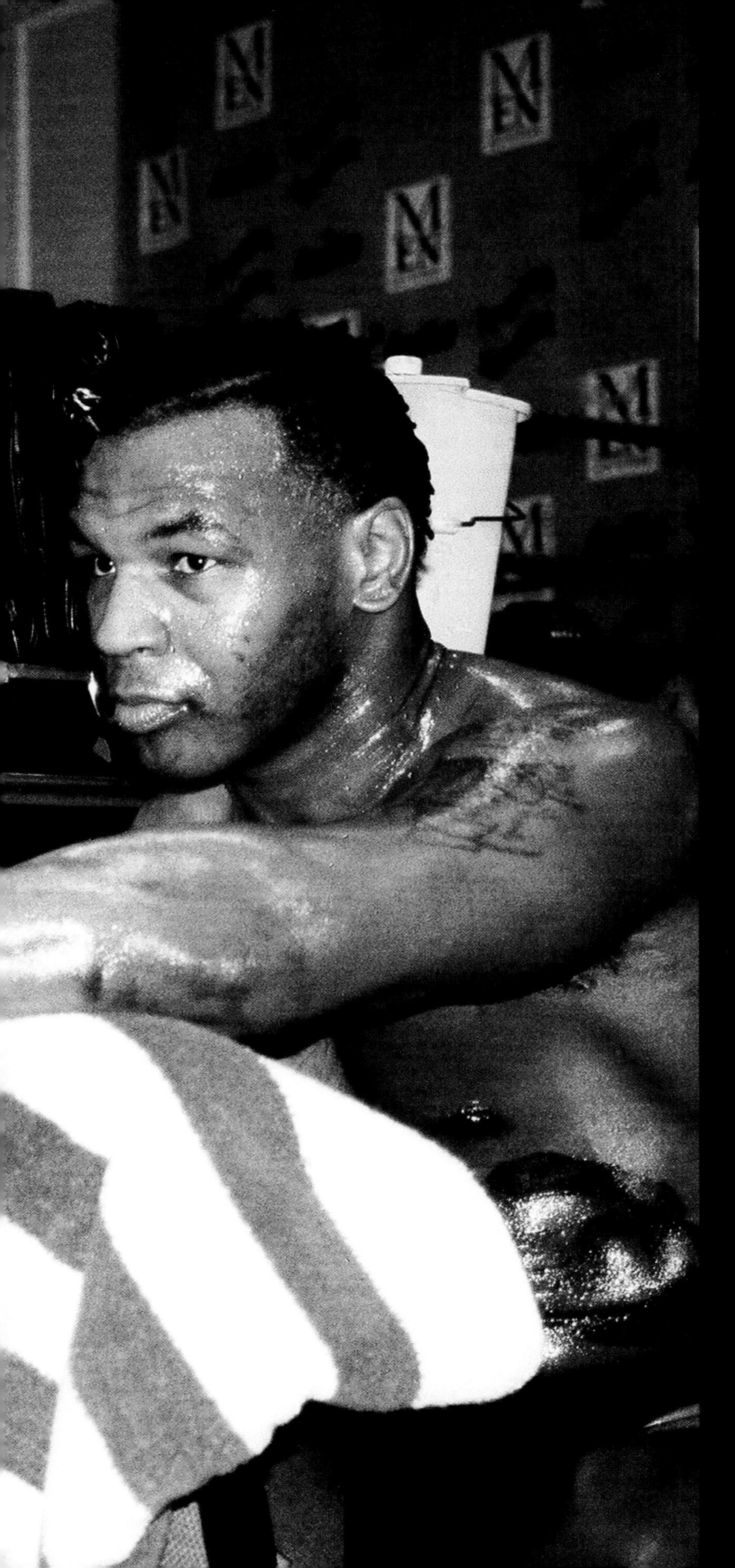

Mike Tyson
Grosvenor House Hotel
January 2000
Training for his fight with Julius Francis

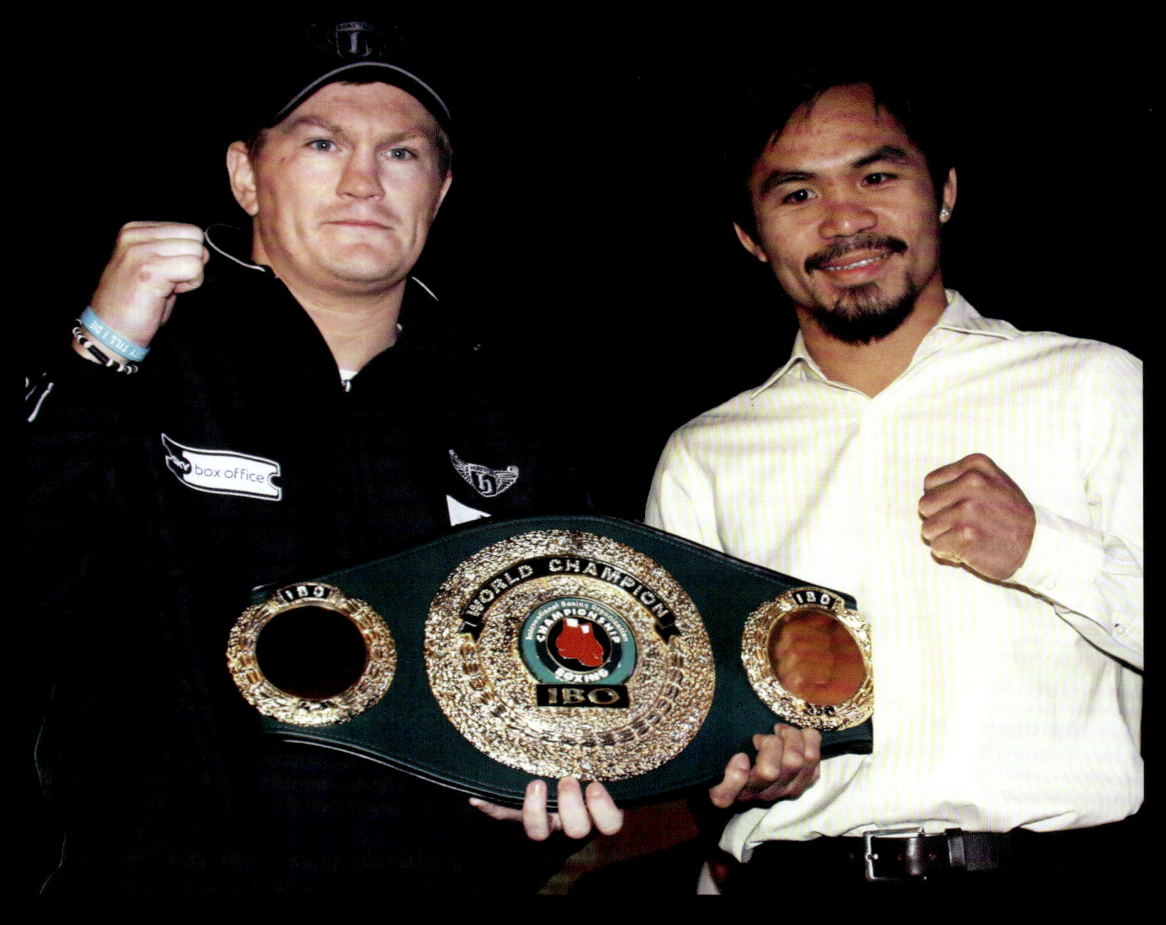

Ricky Hatton and Manny Pacquiao
Imperial War Museum
March 2009
Press conference to promote their upcoming World Junior Welterweight Championship fight

Muhammad Ali and Naseem Hamed
London Hilton, Park Lane
March 2012

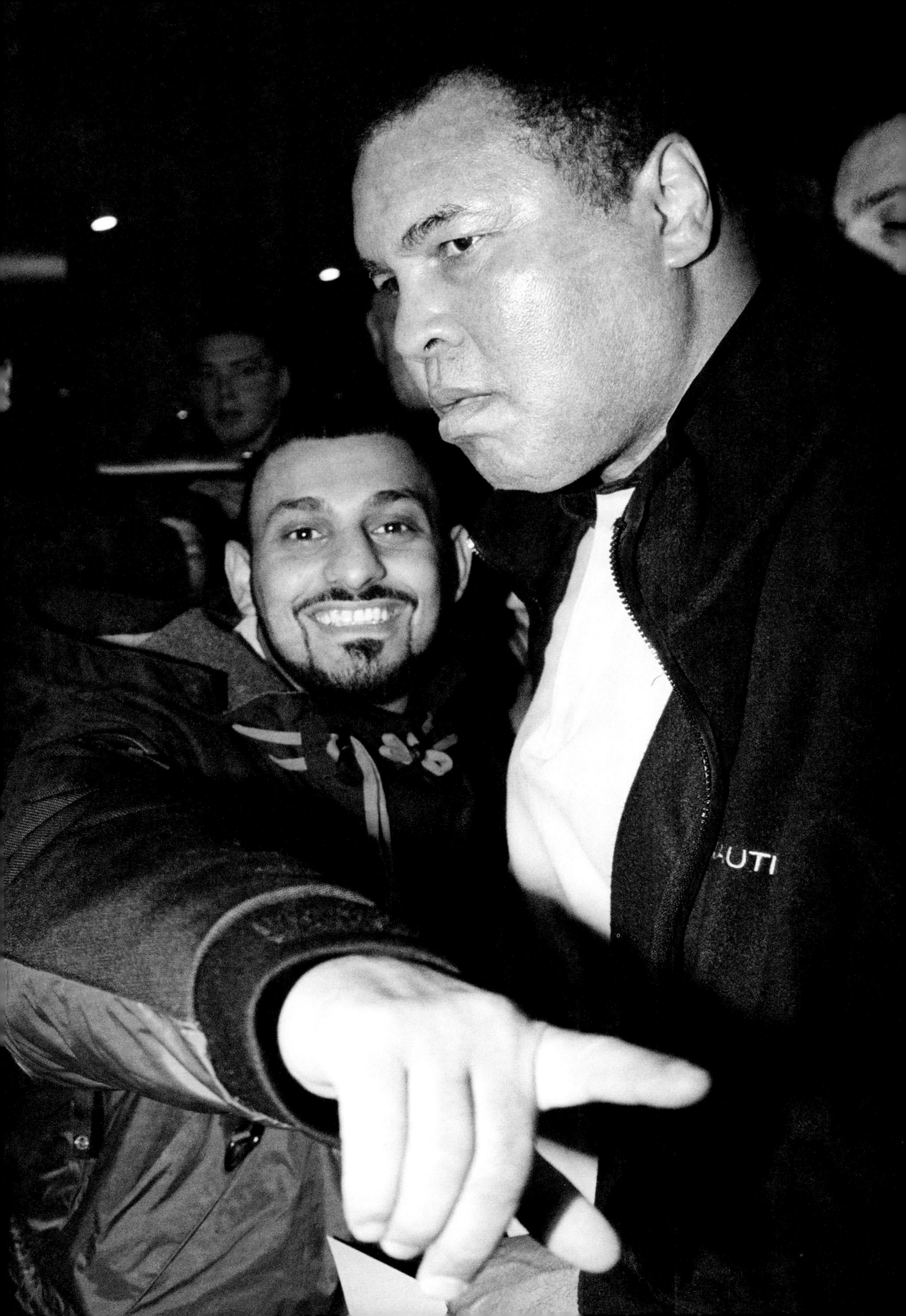

MICHAEL SCHUMACHER

May 2000

It was late on a Wednesday night when my phone rang like a starter pistol. A journalist friend of mine was on the other end, asking if I wanted to cover the upcoming F1 race in Barcelona with Jaguar Racing. Needless to say, I jumped at the chance. The next day, we all met at the airport and were off to Spain. We landed in Barcelona at around 10am and headed straight to our hotel, which was conveniently located at the top of the famous Las Ramblas. It was my first time in the city, and the heat slapped me the moment we stepped off the plane. But there was no time for sightseeing yet – after a quick check-in, we were straight off to the Circuit de Barcelona-Catalunya, about a 30-minute drive from the city.

As soon as we arrived at the track, the first thing that hit me was the noise. You never forget your first F1 engine scream – it vibrates your chest, rattles your bones, rewires your expectations. The deafening roar of the engines was unlike anything I'd ever heard. They handed out ear protector headphones, which I quickly understood were an absolute necessity. We were then taken on a tour of the paddock, where I got my first glimpse behind the scenes of F1 – a world I had only ever seen on TV before.

The team paddocks were buzzing with activity. Cars were nothing more than skeletal shells, balanced on trellises with mechanics swarming around them, piecing together engines and preparing for practice. It was a brilliant hive of precise engineering, something you never fully grasp when you're just watching the race. As much as I wanted to shoot the action in the garages, we weren't allowed to. I had to wait for the practice laps, so I did. And when the cars finally howled back onto the tarmac, I was ready.

Watching the cars whip around the circuit, hearing the engines shriek with each lap, I felt the adrenaline of it all. For the next few hours, I snapped photos of the Jaguar team as they prepared, practised, and fine-tuned their machines: sleek metal bullets dancing across the blazing Spanish afternoon. It was an entirely different world from the football pitches and boxing rings I was used to shooting. We eventually headed back to the hotel for lunch, with the rest of the day left for a bit of sightseeing before the evening's events.

Later that night, Jaguar Racing hosted a pre-race party at Casa Batlló. While I was supposed to be focusing on the drivers and celebrities in attendance, I found myself more captivated by the building itself. Being a fan of Antoni Gaudí, I couldn't help but take a moment to explore the architecture inside and out. I wandered the bones of the building, marvelling at the curved windows, the sea-blue tiles, the iron spine of the staircase. I forgot the roar of the track for a while and became just a man in love with beauty.

The days leading up to the race were more of the same – practice shooting and capturing the precision and intensity of the team. And then, finally, race day came. I was making my way through the paddock, grabbing some lunch before the action started, when suddenly I saw him – Michael Schumacher, that force of nature in Ferrari red. He was walking right towards me, the best driver in the world, a living legend. I wasn't supposed to shoot him; I was there for Team Jaguar, after all, and I was supposed to be focusing on their drivers, their story. But some instincts run deeper than contracts. How could I pass up the chance to capture a few shots of Schumacher?

> *"But some instincts run deeper than contracts. How could I pass up the chance to capture a few shots of Schumacher?"*

I went for it. A few photos as he passed by, trying to be as discreet as possible. I knew it wasn't what I was there for, but the opportunity was too good to resist. After all, how often do you get the chance to photograph a seven-time World Champion up close?

I returned to my assigned position and spent the rest of the race shooting Jaguar's efforts on the track. Eddie Irvine finished 11th that day. Mika Häkkinen took the win, with Schumacher ending up in 5th. Despite Jaguar's lacklustre result, the week had been one of the most thrilling assignments I'd ever covered. I'd spent a week behind the curtain of F1's greatest theatre. I'd seen the sweat beneath the carbon fibre, the grease behind the glory. And I'd captured, if only for a heartbeat, the face of speed itself.

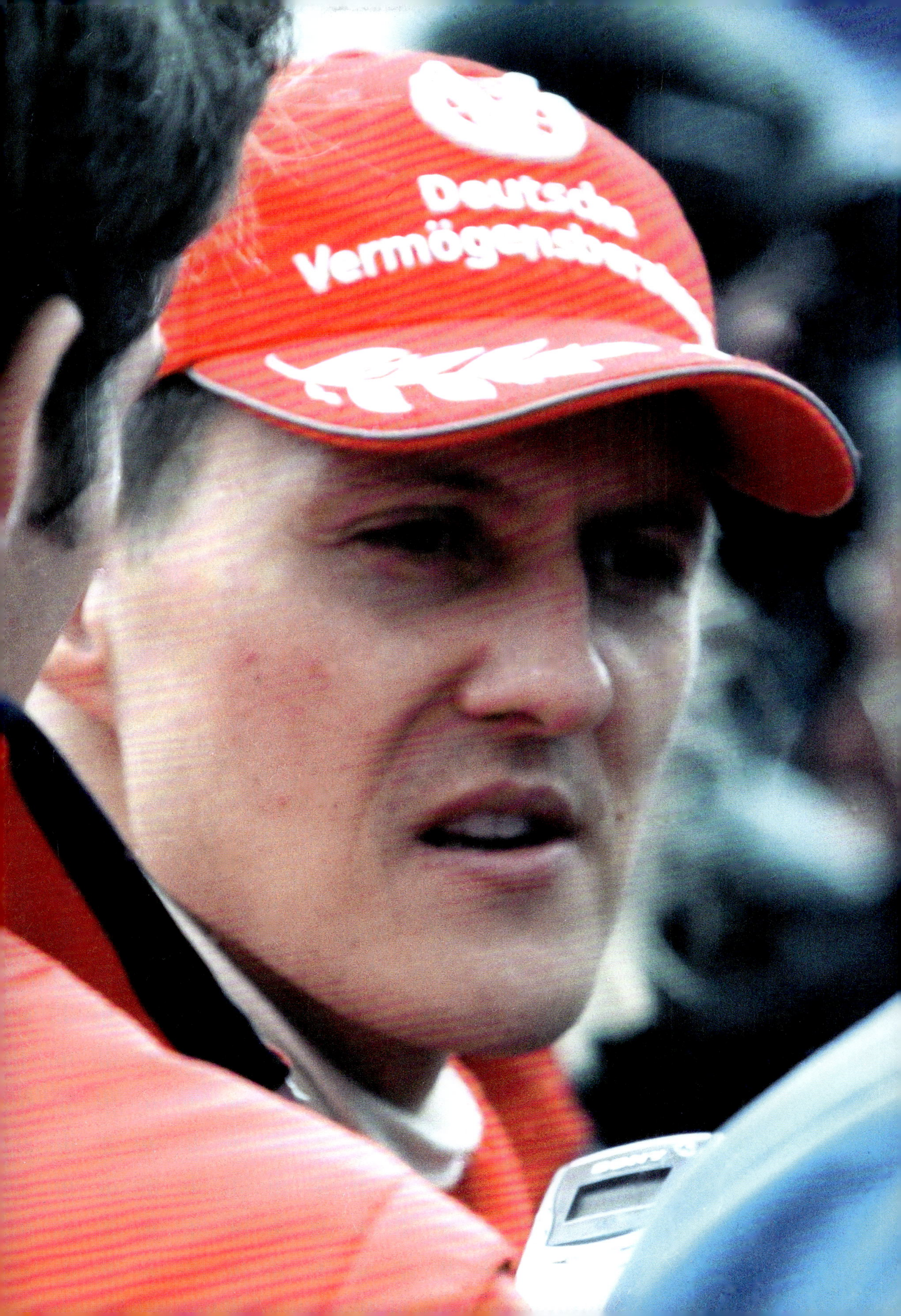

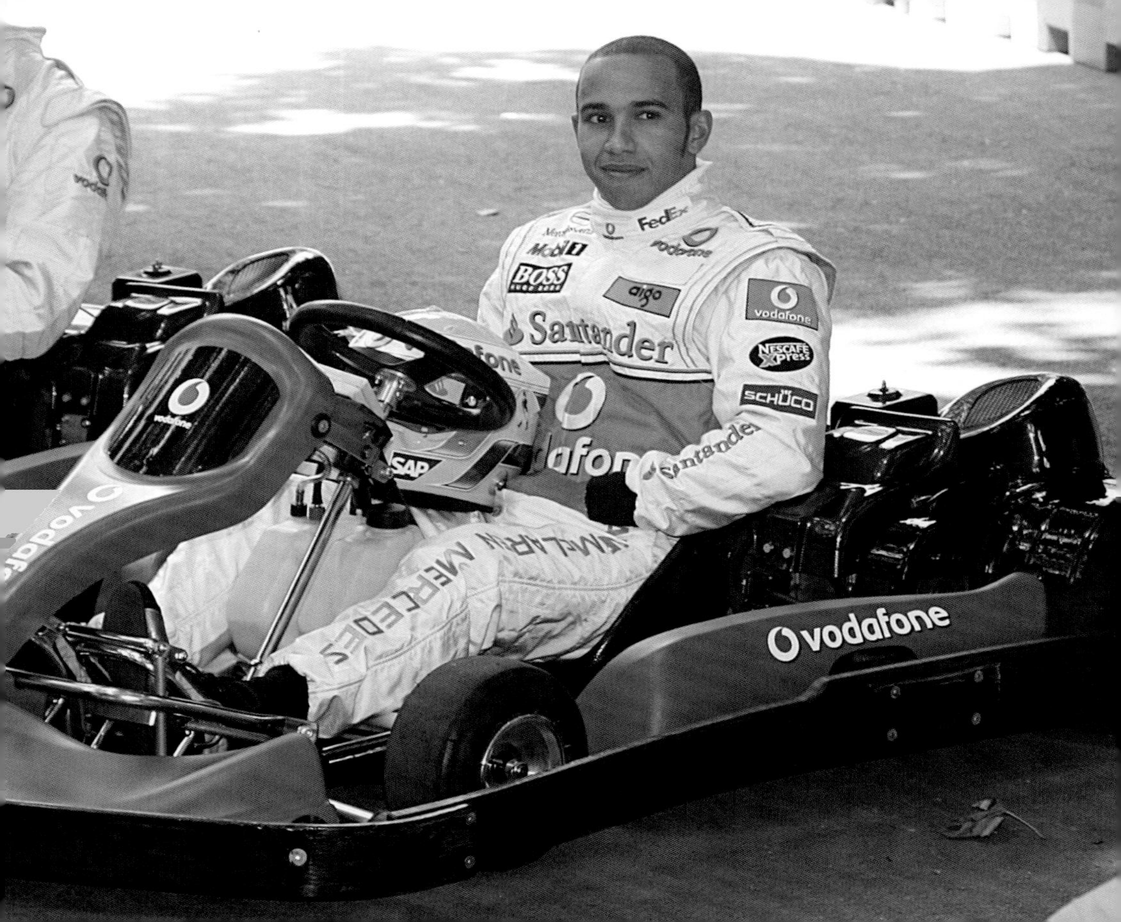
FedEx
Mobil 1
BOSS
aigo
vodafone
Santander
NESCAFÉ Xpress
SCHÜCO
vodafone
SAP
vodafone

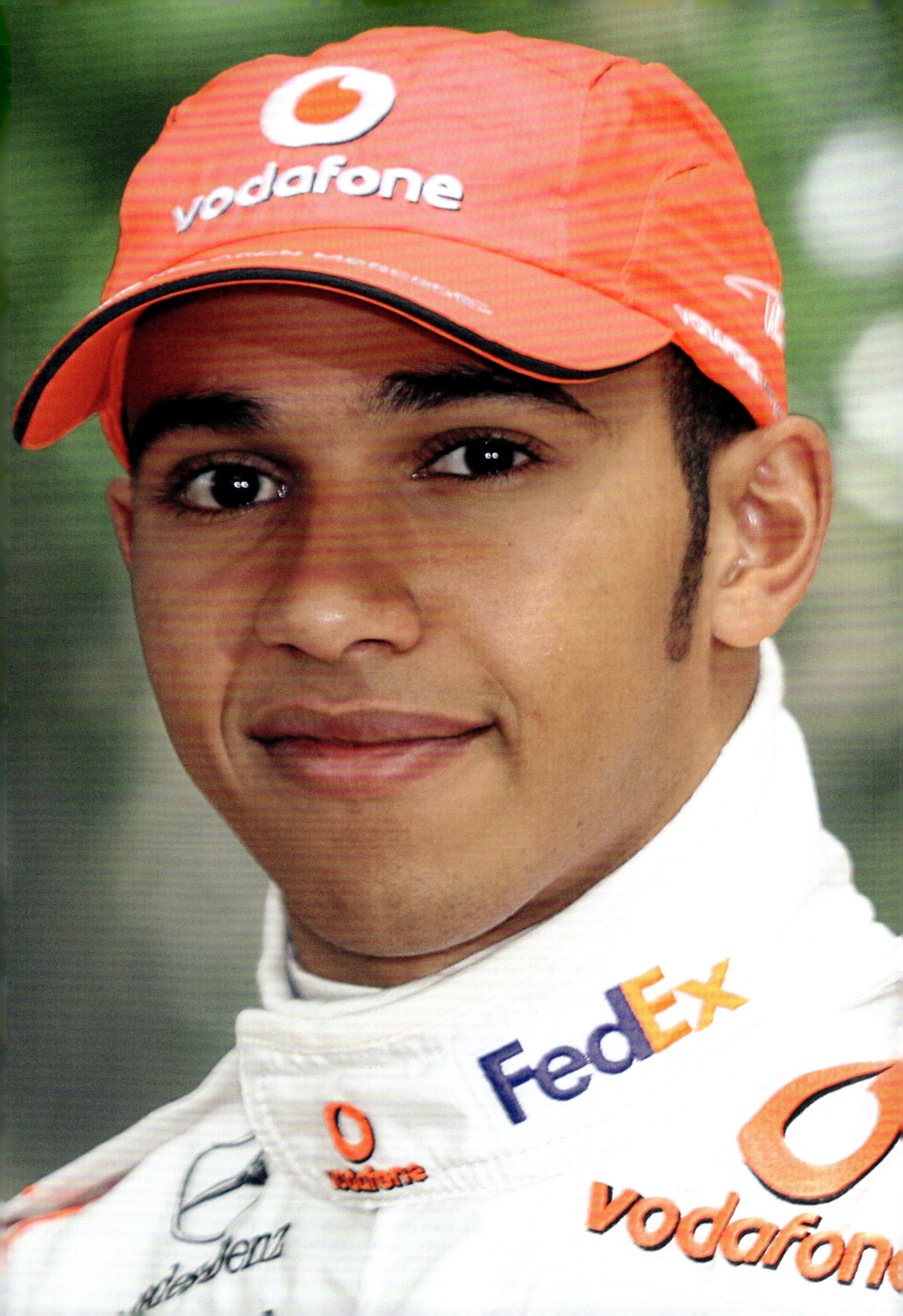
vodafone
FedEx

TONY HAWK

November 2006

"Skating was the language of my youth – scraped knees, warped decks, and the distant echo of polyurethane wheels."

I was working for the picture desk at a newspaper when I got a call that seemed pretty standard at first. They asked if I knew anything about skateboarders. I nearly laughed. Do I? Skating was the language of my youth – scraped knees, warped decks, and the distant echo of polyurethane wheels spinning across cracked concrete. So I said yes, unaware of the golden ticket I was being offered. They needed a photographer to accompany a group of skateboarders and a BMX rider during their trip around London. Without thinking much of it, I agreed. Beyond their occupations, I didn't have any details about who the athletes were, as I hadn't bothered to ask more. I headed to their hotel in the West End – St Martins Lane, a recently opened spot. After meeting my contact and chatting with someone from management, I sat in the lobby, waiting for the group to come down.

When the elevator doors opened, I was in for a huge surprise. Walking out with their boards in hand were none other than Tony Hawk, Bam Margera, Mike Vallely, and Mike 'Rooftop' Escamilla with his BMX bike. I couldn't believe it – some of the biggest legends of the sport standing right in front of me. When I saw Tony, I was suddenly 15 again, wondering how any human could move like that on a board. After introductions, we left and headed across town to Ladbroke Grove, to a skate park under the Westway tattooed with graffiti and decades of youthful sweat. The reactions when the group walked in were priceless – every skater knows Tony Hawk, Bam was at the height of his fame due to starring in MTV's *Jackass*, Mike Vallely was a beast of a skater and Rooftop was a BMX legend. Jaws were dropping all over the floor.

Tony was the first to hit the halfpipe. The sky seemed to bend to him as he climbed into the air effortlessly. Then Bam took over, wild and raw, grinding and pulling off the most insane tricks, his signature style dashed all over them. Vallely followed up with a bike and skateboard, rippling through every line he carved, while Rooftop's BMX traced arcs of impossible geometry against the grey London sky. After the impromptu show, the guys took some time to sign autographs, pose for pictures, and just chat with the wide-eyed skater kids who would never forget this day.

From there, we decided to do some sightseeing around central London. Imagine walking around the London Eye, Buckingham Palace and Trafalgar Square with Tony Hawk and the crew. It's incredible how, in this line of work, icons from your childhood can end up standing right next to you.

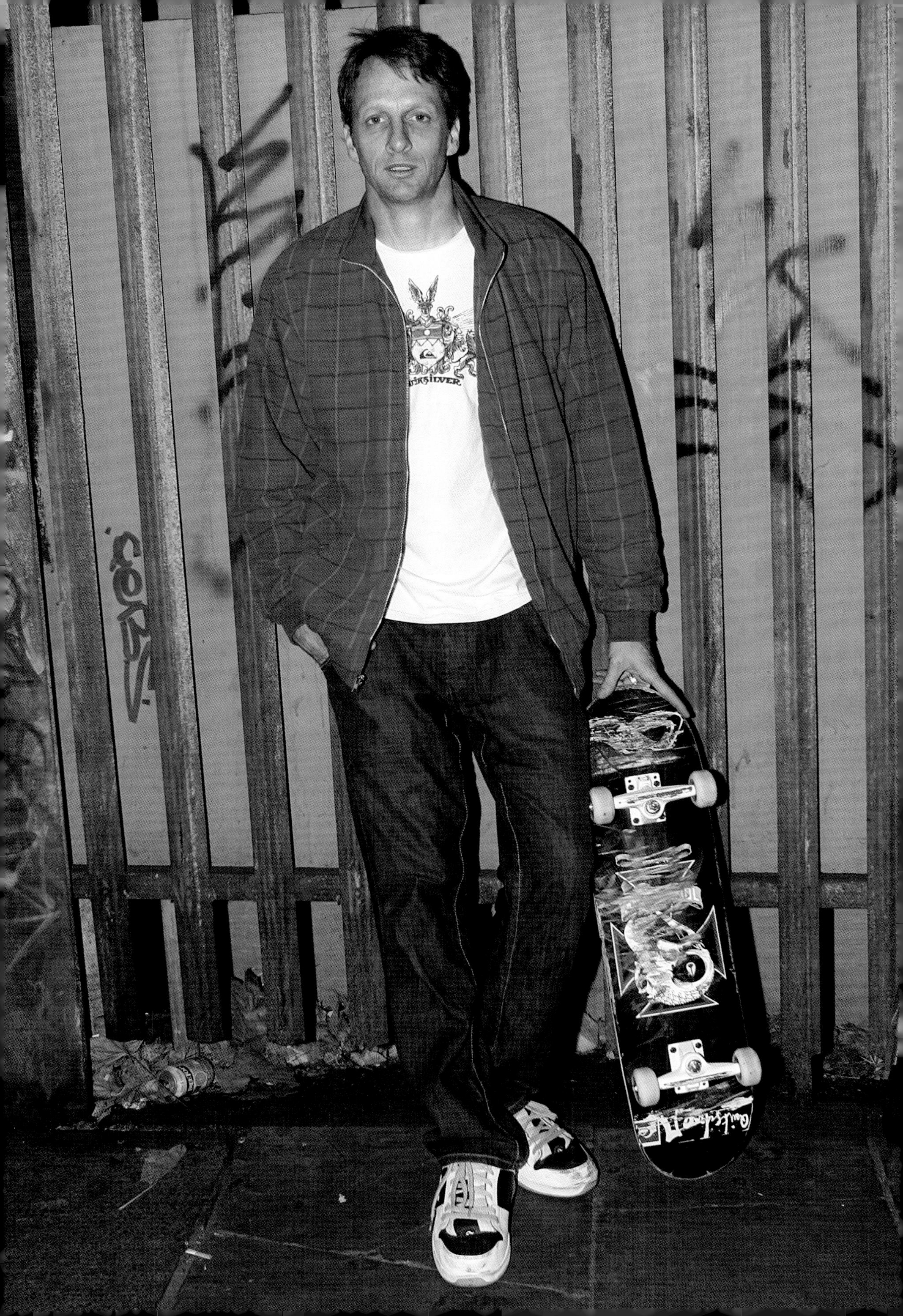

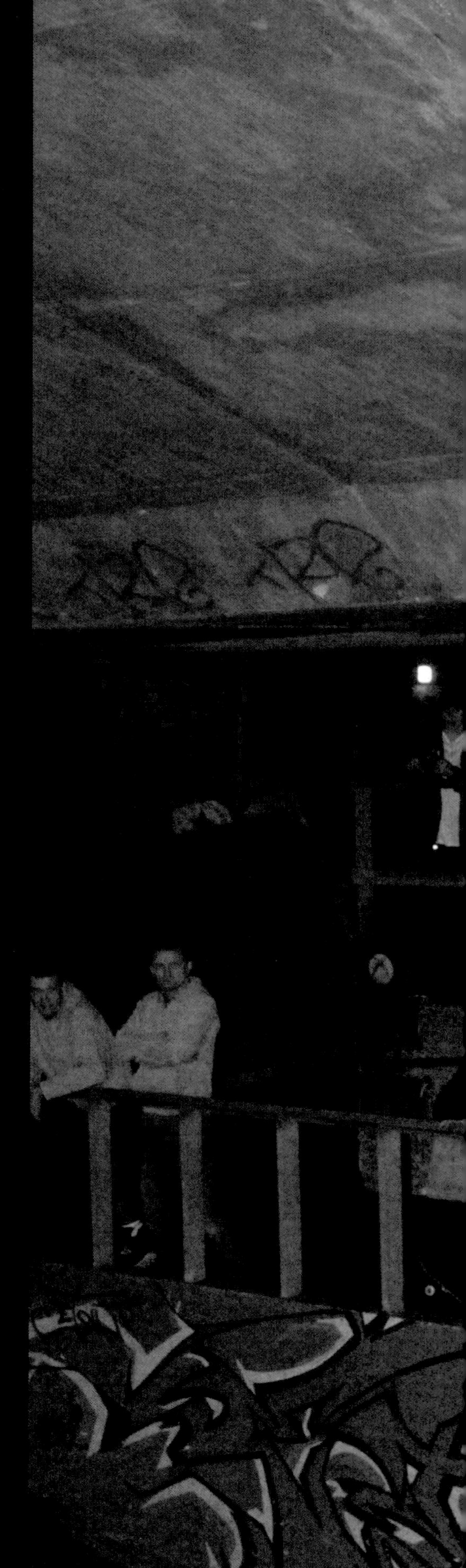

Tony Hawk
Ladbroke Grove
November 2006

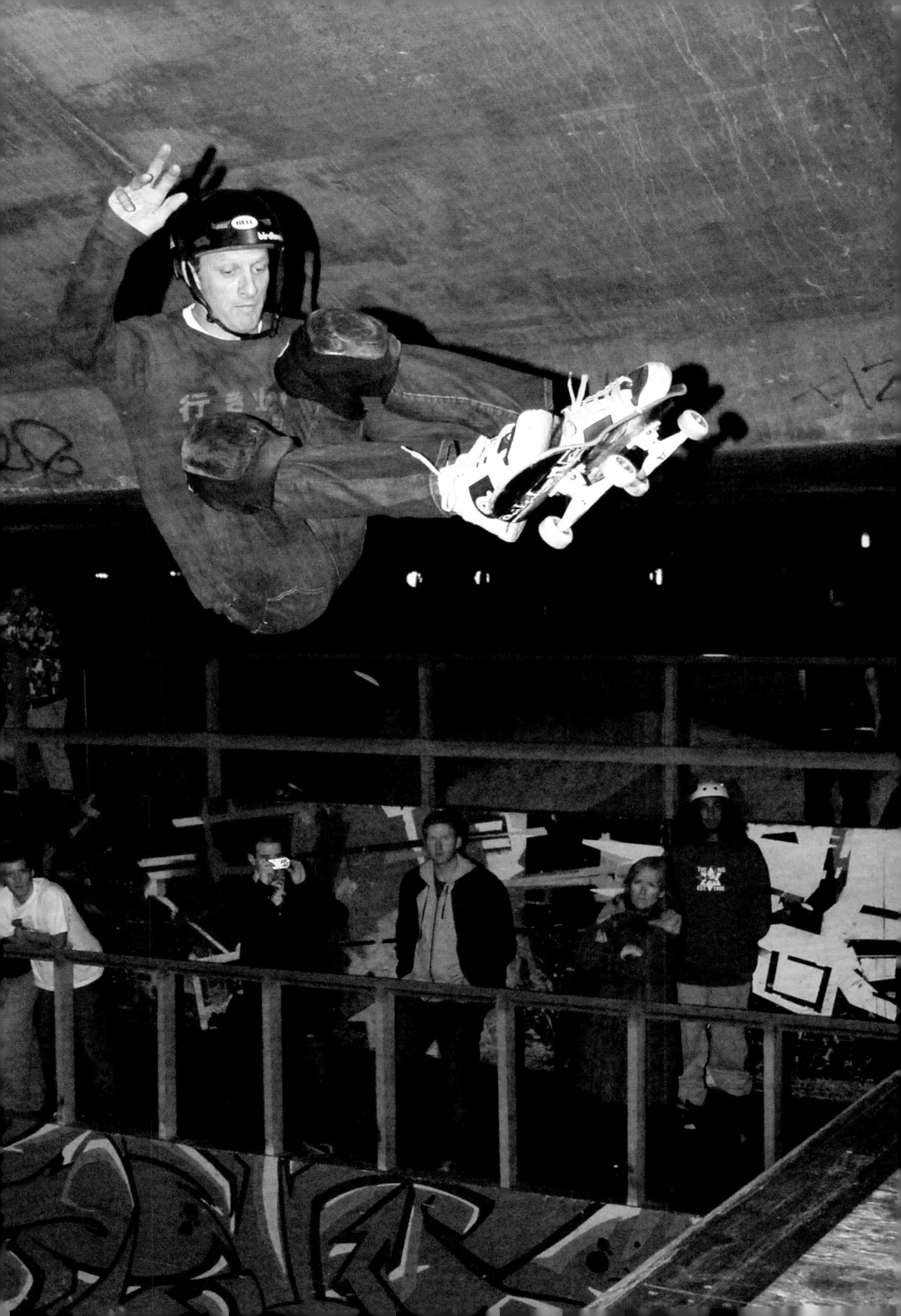

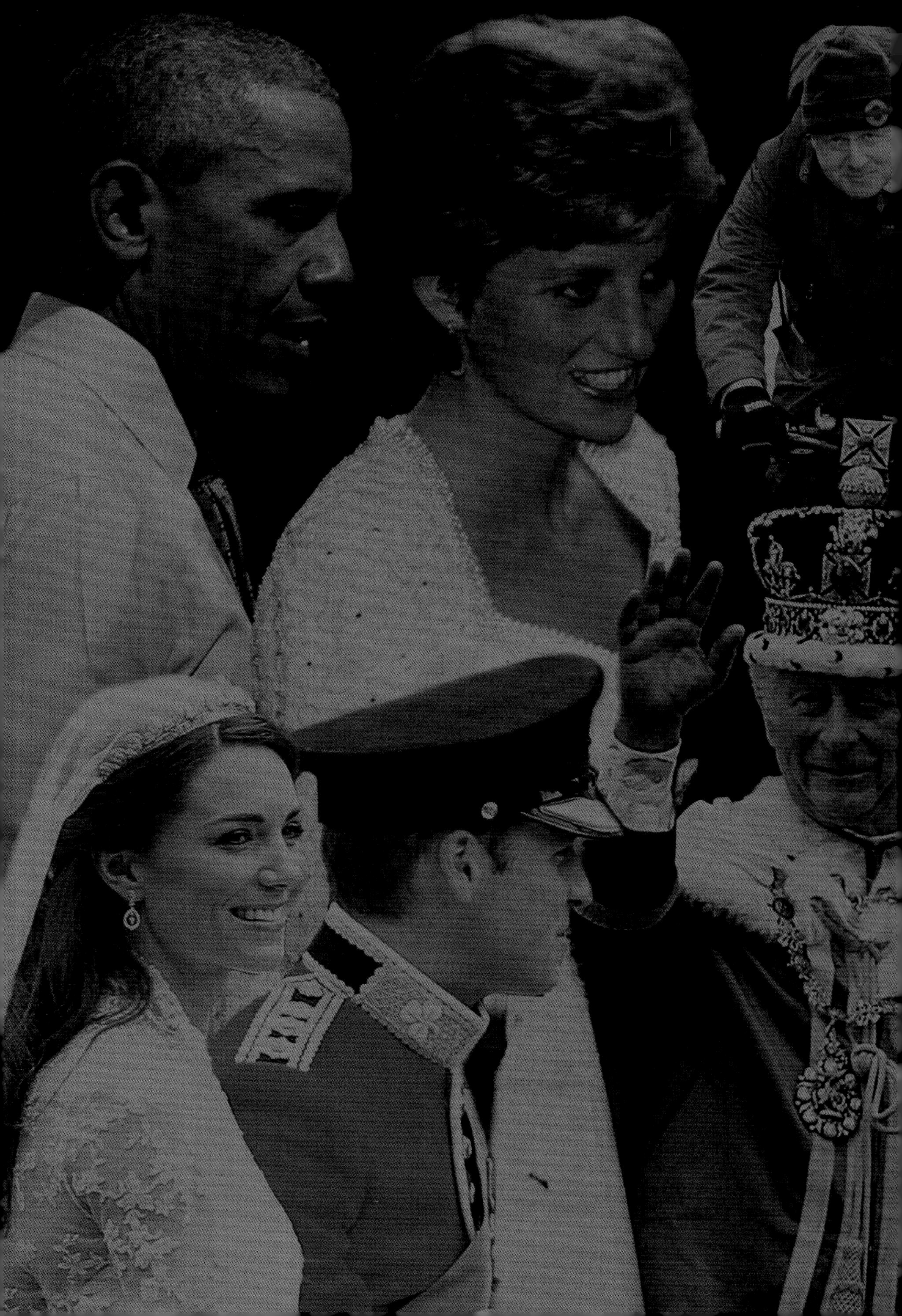

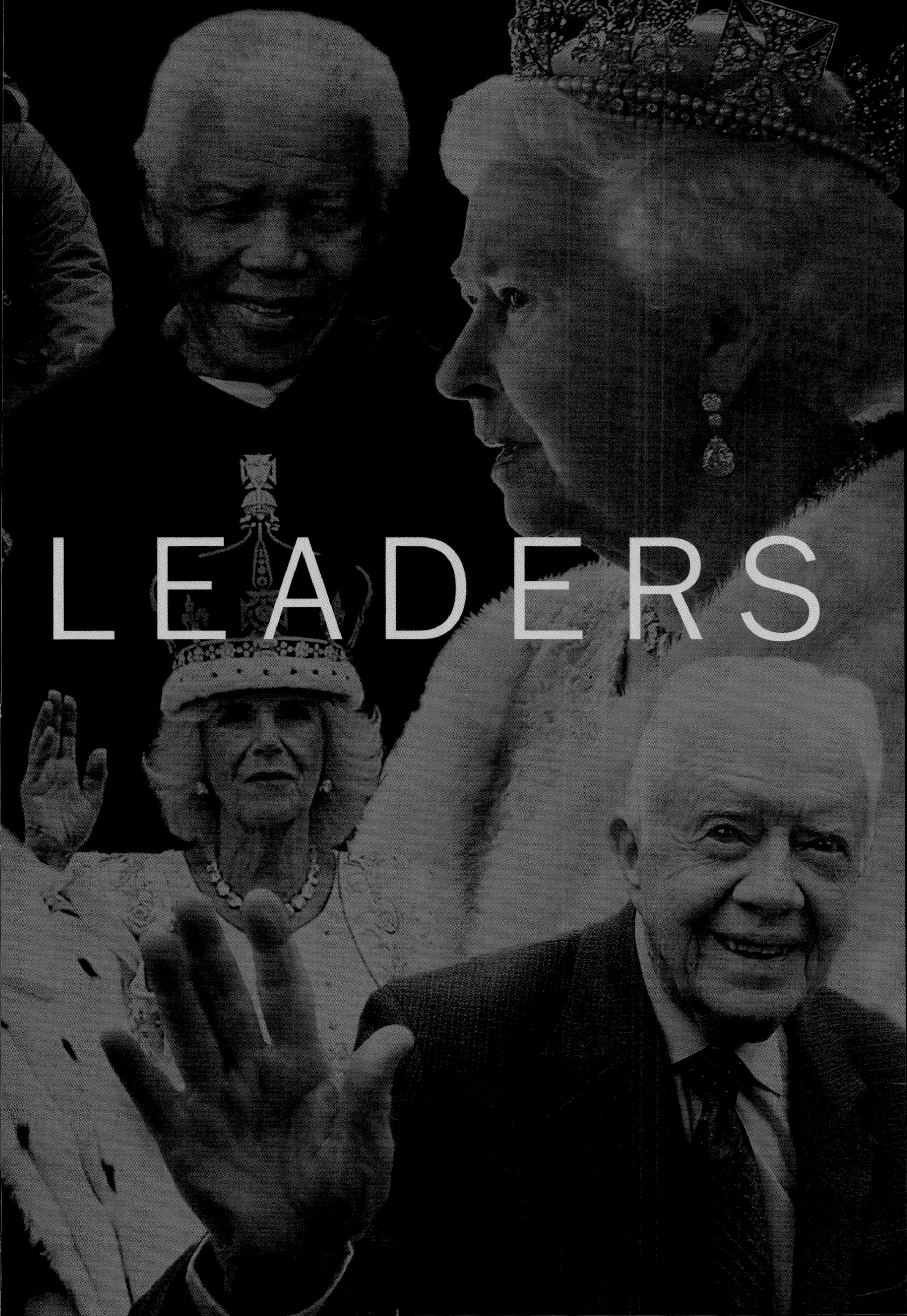

LEADERS

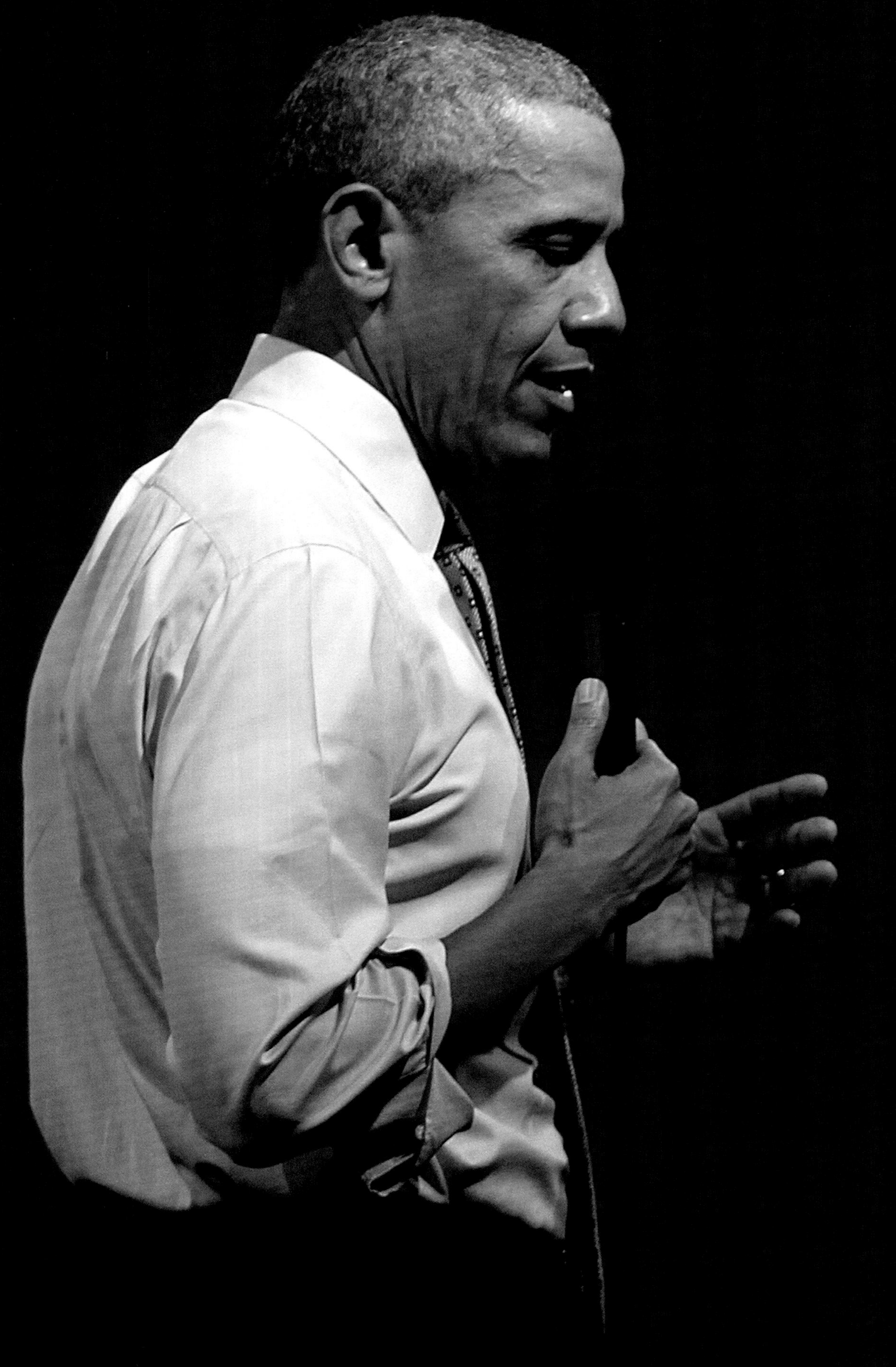

BARACK OBAMA

April 2016

Photographing a US president is like trying to catch sunlight in a net – everything about it feels impossible. With security details tighter than a drum, mazes upon mazes of restricted zones, and blacked-out cars galore, getting close can feel like more of an exercise in futility than an actual possibility. But sometimes, fortune favours those who are willing to take a chance, and for me that chance presented itself when Obama came to London. His agenda was packed with appearances: a stop at the iconic Globe Theatre, followed by a speech at the Royal Horticultural Halls in Victoria. I had no official pass, no golden badge, no scheduled slot in the grand machinery of presidential optics. Just a vague sense that I might be able to catch a glimpse of him arriving. *Why not try my luck?* I thought.

When I reached Vincent Square, it became immediately clear that this was going to be no easy task. The streets were utterly shut down, cordoned off into a sterile zone; every possible route of entry swarmed with Secret Service agents. These are the typical fortresses important people command. Most would turn around and head for the pub at that point, but there's a certain thrill in almost getting told "No", and I wasn't ready to give up quite yet.

Approaching the entrance of the Halls, I could feel the odds stacking up against me. There were metal detectors, security checks, and layers of people whose sole job was to keep opportunists like me out. But armed with nothing more than my camera, lenses, and a well-worn press card, I continued. Through the scanners I went – no alarms sounded – and I found myself face-to-face with a friendly American press officer. Obviously, my name wasn't on the list. She checked twice. And yet, instead of sending me on my way, she asked for my press credentials. I handed them over with the smile of someone who belonged there. A few minutes passed, which in situations like these usually feels like an eternity. When she finally came back, instead of the polite brush-off I was expecting, she handed me a White House press pass. *A White House press pass*. I held it like it might vanish if I blinked too hard. It was as if the gates of Olympus had creaked open.

Inside the Royal Horticultural Halls, I had free rein to move about, snapping shots from different angles as Obama, ever the excellent orator, addressed the crowd of young leaders. The speech was, as expected, inspiring – a natural blend of humility and gravitas that only a man like Obama could pull off. I watched him as much as I photographed him. For all the barriers he carried with him, he was perhaps the president that felt most like an ordinary citizen. There was something about his demeanour that invited you in, even with 30 guards in the wings. When listening to him, you felt like you were part of something far bigger than any one room.

"Photographing a US president is like trying to catch sunlight in a net – everything about it feels impossible."

The world can decide to be generous sometimes. These moments of access are fleeting but must be seized when there's even a flicker of a chance to get in. What's inside could change your life.

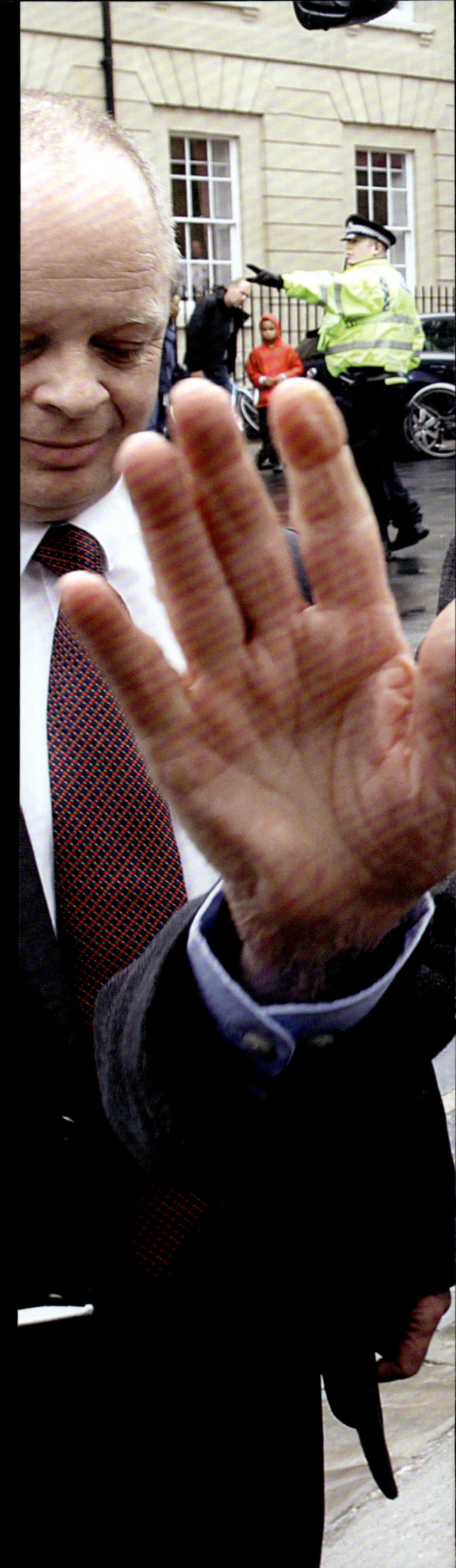

Jimmy Carter
Sheldonian Theatre,
University of Oxford
May 2014
Attending an Evening with the Elders event

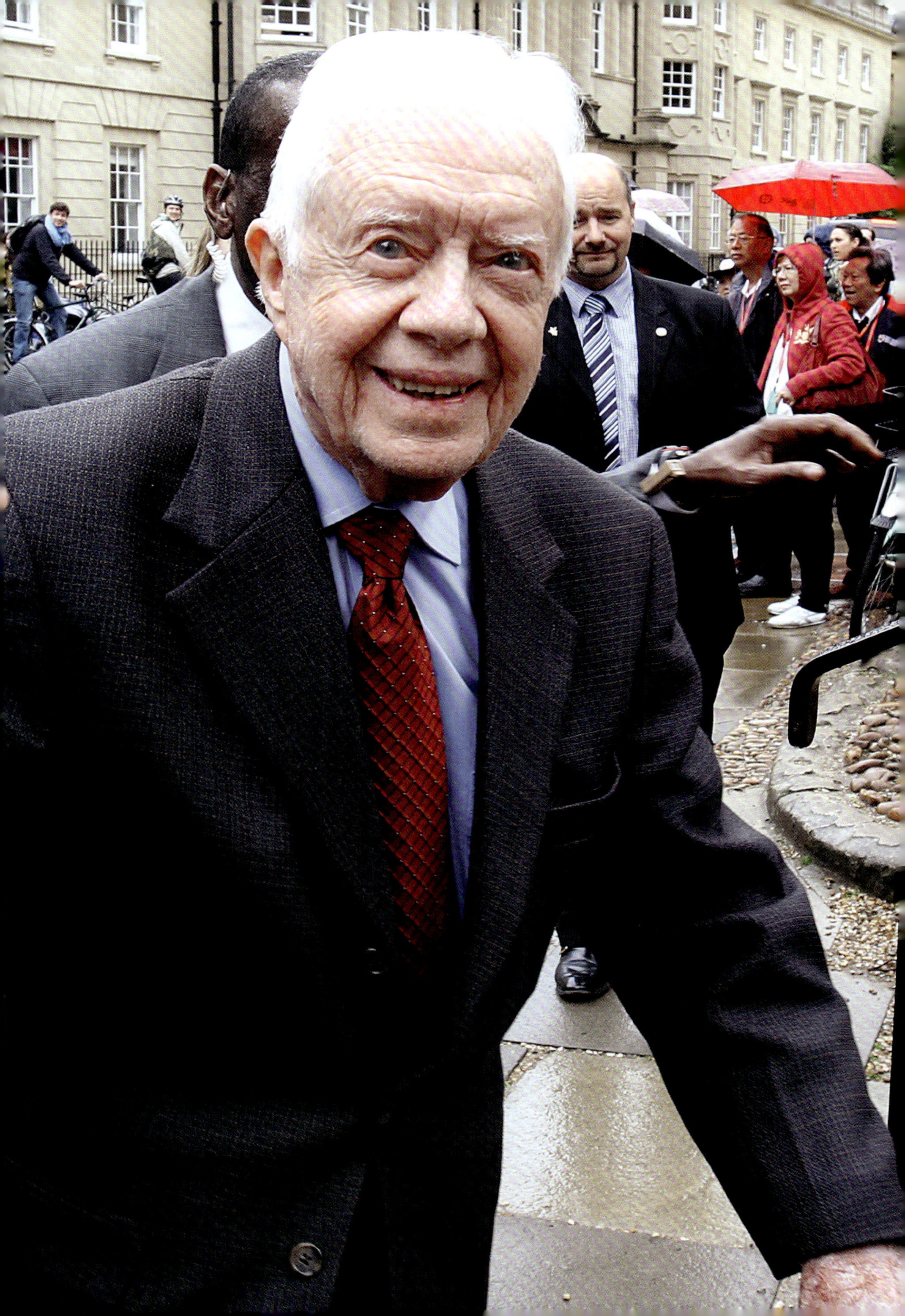

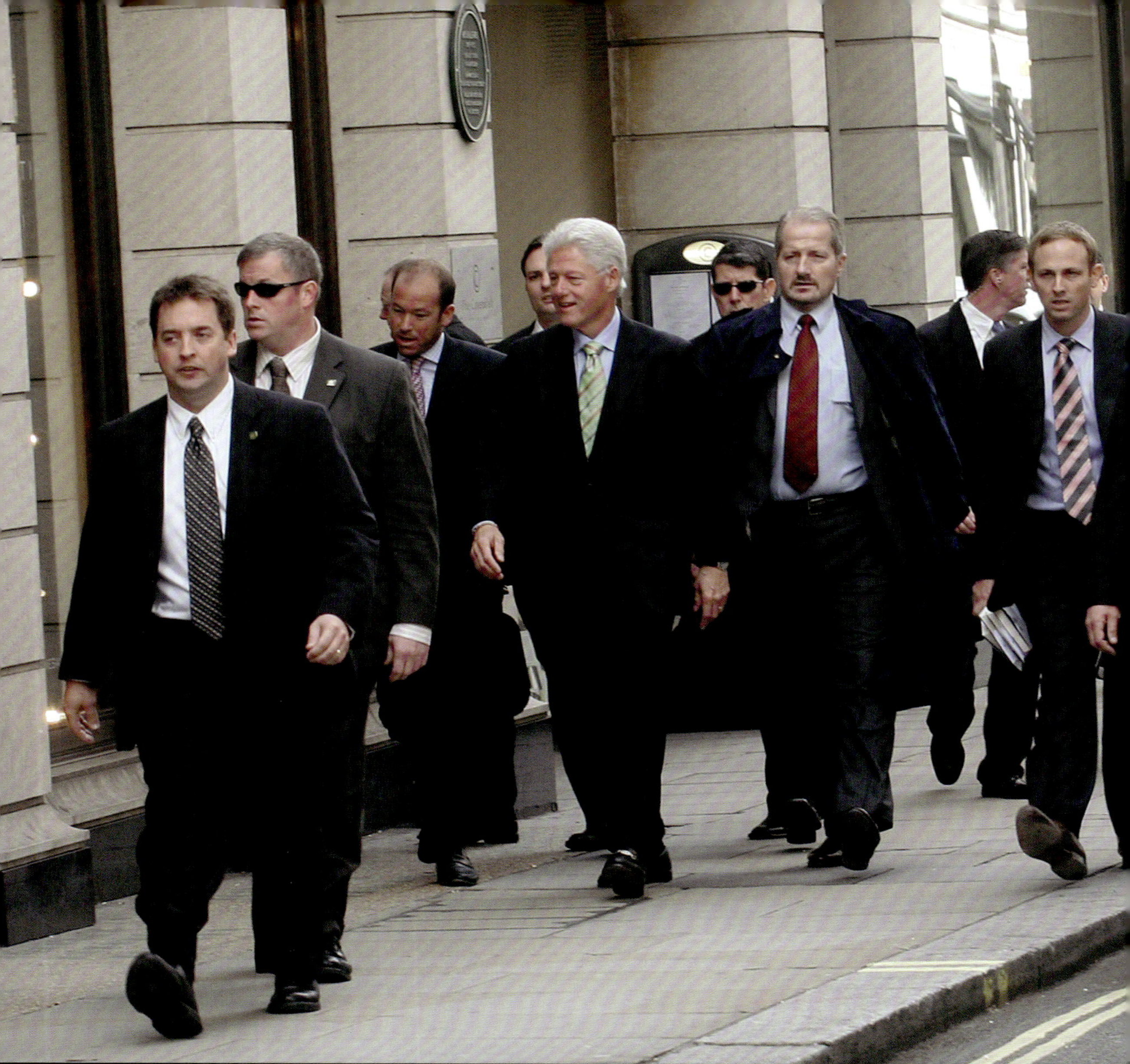

There are days when a photographer has to lean on instinct rather than chase the obvious, and the 12 July 2004 was certainly one of those days for me. Former President Bill Clinton, the silver-tongued son of Arkansas, was in town, ready to sign copies of his autobiography *My Life* at Waterstones in Piccadilly. The bookshop swarmed with media from both sides of the Atlantic, and the streets were lined with hundreds of onlookers, all pressing towards the glass, eyes wild for a glimpse. You couldn't move for lenses, elbows, and the constant hiss of journalistic urgency.

Security, as you'd expect around a former US president, was airtight. I knew the typical Clinton shot would get buried among hundreds of identical images. No, what I wanted was something different – something exclusive. And, luckily, I had a hunch. I happened to know where he was staying, a detail that hadn't yet reached the bustling crowd at Waterstones. With a warm London day in play, and the proximity of the hotel to the bookshop, I wondered, *Would he walk it?* It seemed likely, so I made my way to his address and waited, as any patient photographer would, hoping my intuition was sharper than the rest. It didn't take long. The door to the building swung open and, like clockwork, the street was flooded with Secret Service agents; stepping out from the middle of them all, with the kind of easy confidence that most people would lack if they were being flanked by 30 guards, was Clinton. He smiled, waved at the small crowd gathering and, much to my delight, started walking.

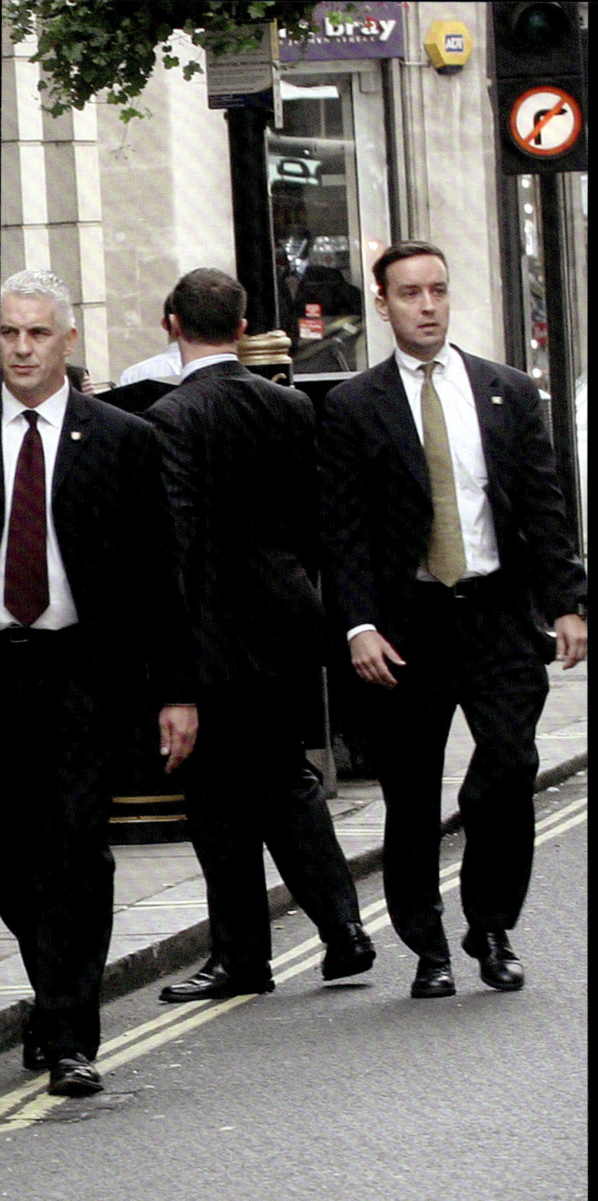

BILL CLINTON

July 2004

"The next morning, my instincts were vindicated. Four of my shots hit every front page, each accompanied by the headline, 'All the President's Men'."

I kept my distance, of course; no sense in ruffling the feathers of the Secret Service. From a safe space, I observed him, feeling a bit more like a fellow tourist than a photographer on duty. Clinton, seemingly enjoying his London stroll, stopped occasionally to indulge in a spot of window shopping, much to the amazement of passers-by who did comical double-takes as they realised who had just wandered past.

He didn't seem to mind me taking pictures. If anything, he looked rather comfortable with it, knew what I was after – not the staged signing desk or podium grin, but this long walk down Jermyn Street, swarmed by his phalanx of suited protectors. Thirty dark blurs orbiting one man in light blue. The geometry of it. The oddity. The power. By the time the crowd caught wind and surged towards Waterstones, it was over. He slipped into the building, swallowed by the flash-frenzied front. But I already had all I needed.

The next morning, my instincts were vindicated. Four of my shots hit every front page each accompanied by the headline, "All the President's Men". It was a clean sweep. Later, I received a request from Mr Clinton's team for four prints of the image. A few weeks after sending them over, one of the prints made its way back to me with a message signed in black ink: "To Greg, Great Photo. Many Thanks – Bill Clinton." It sits above my desk now – yes, as a trophy, but also as proof that, sometimes, you follow your gut down a quiet street and history will decide to walk beside you.

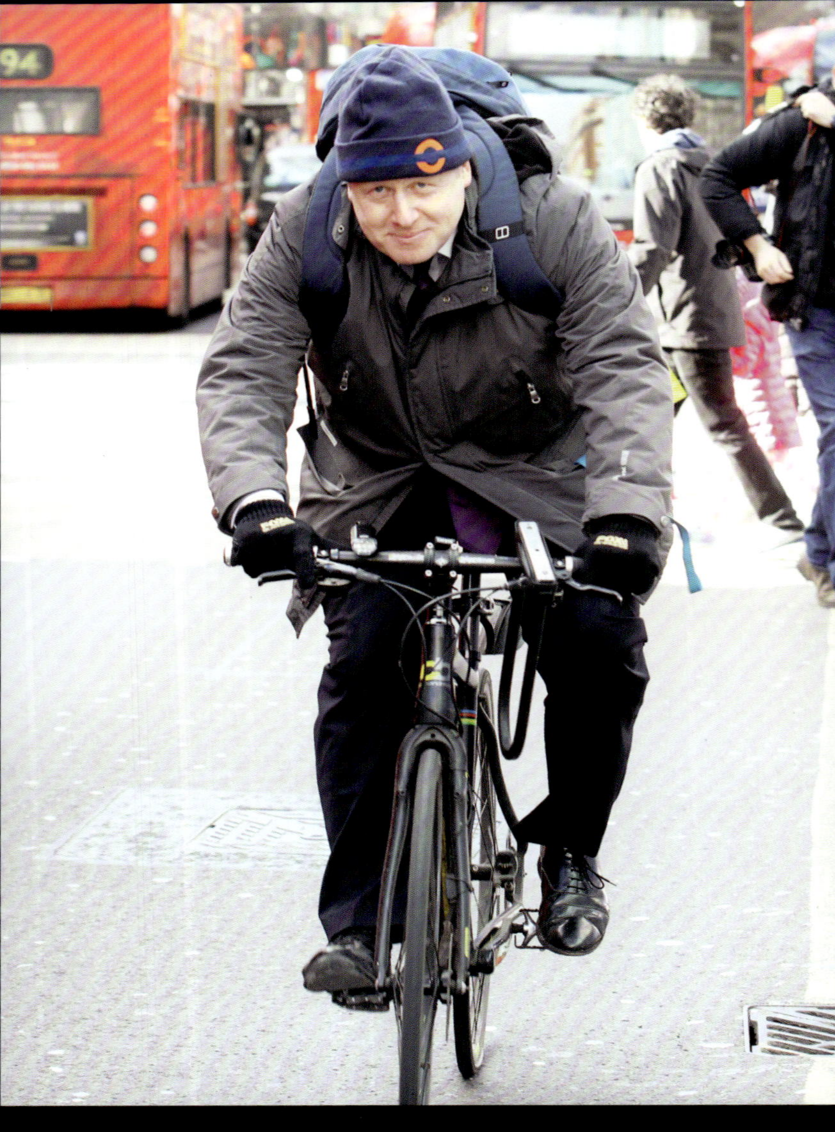

Boris Johnson
Bond Street
February 2016

Tony Blair and
Arnold Schwarzenegger
10 Downing Street
June 2007

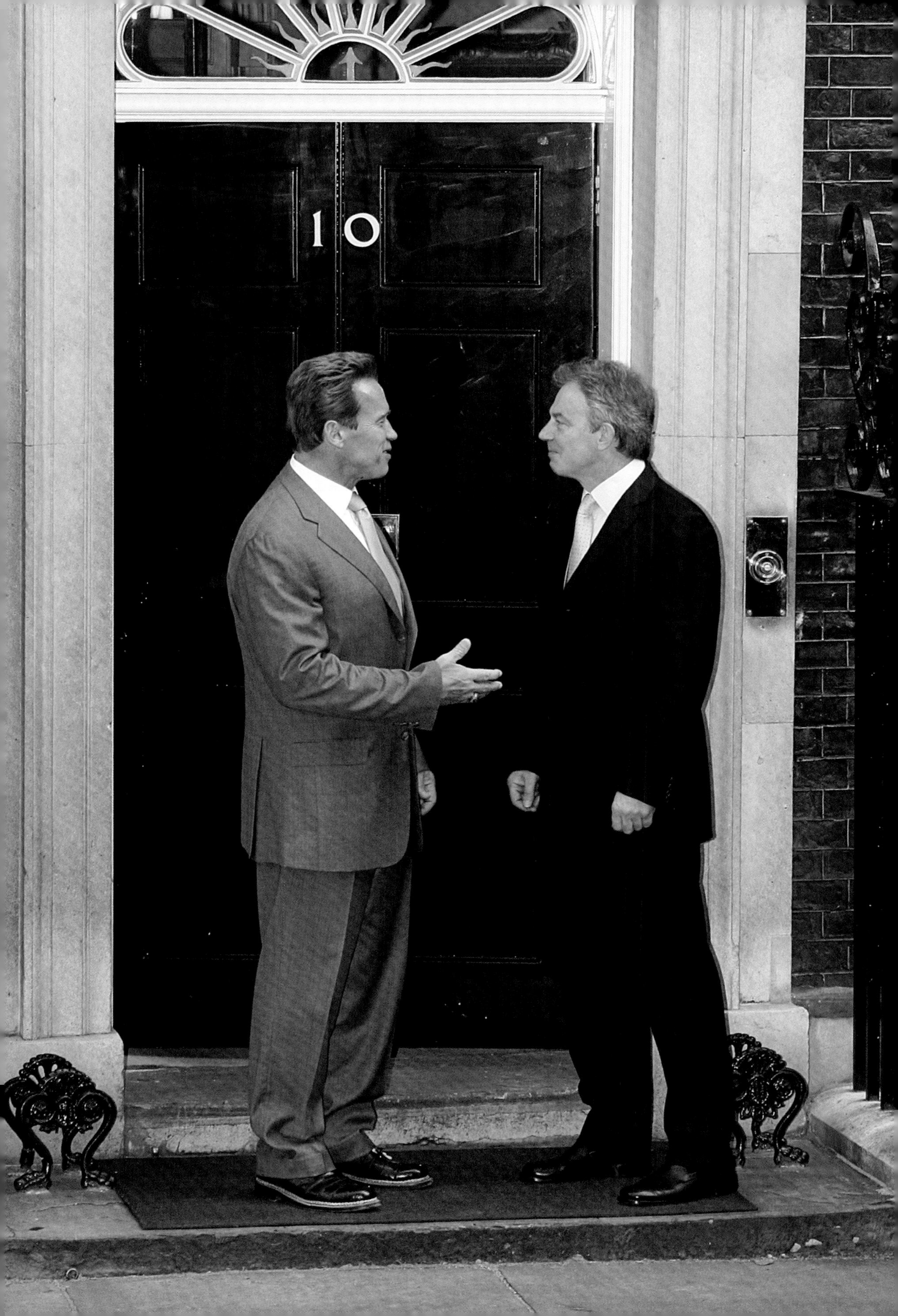
10

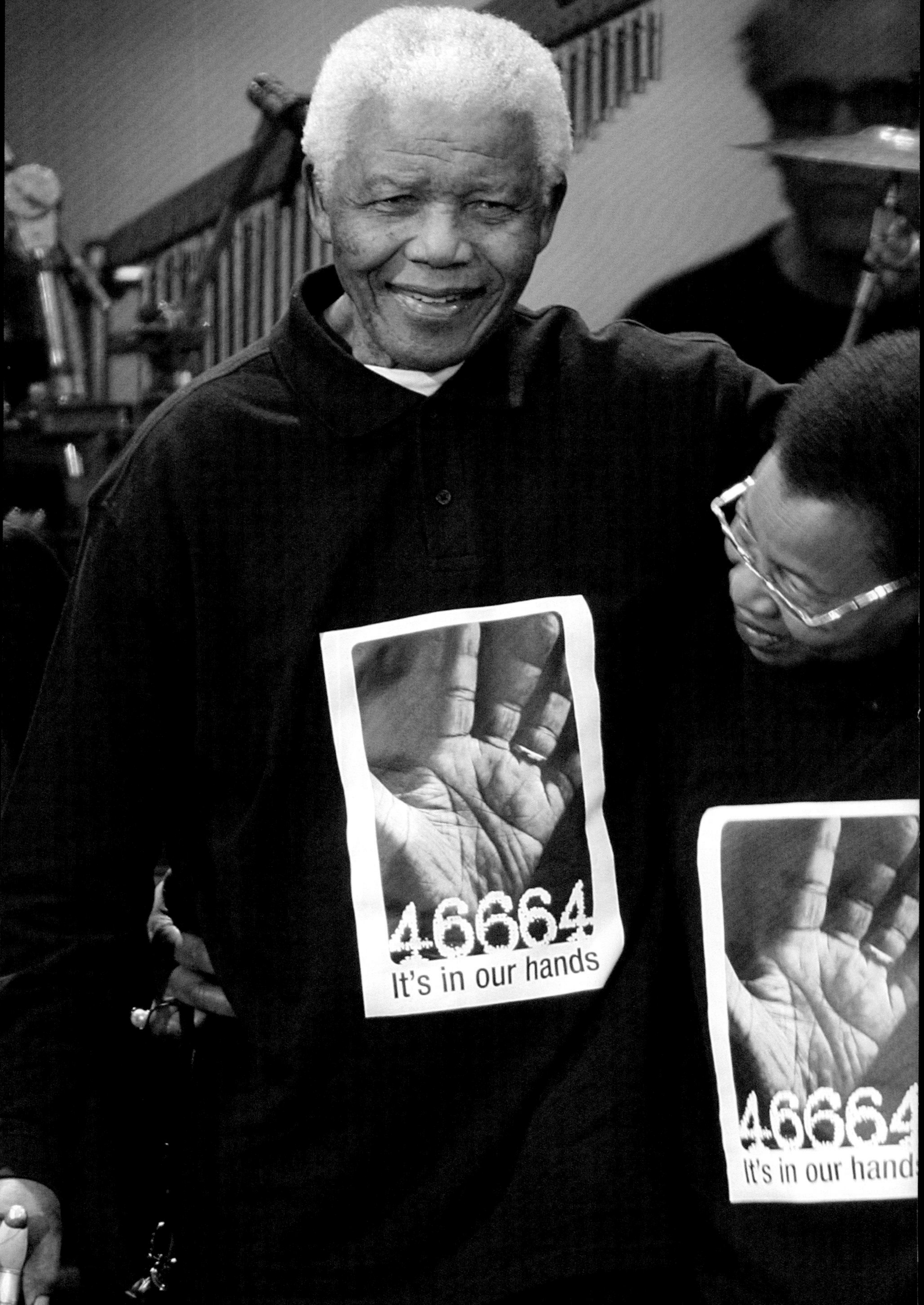
46664
It's in our hands
46664
It's in our hands

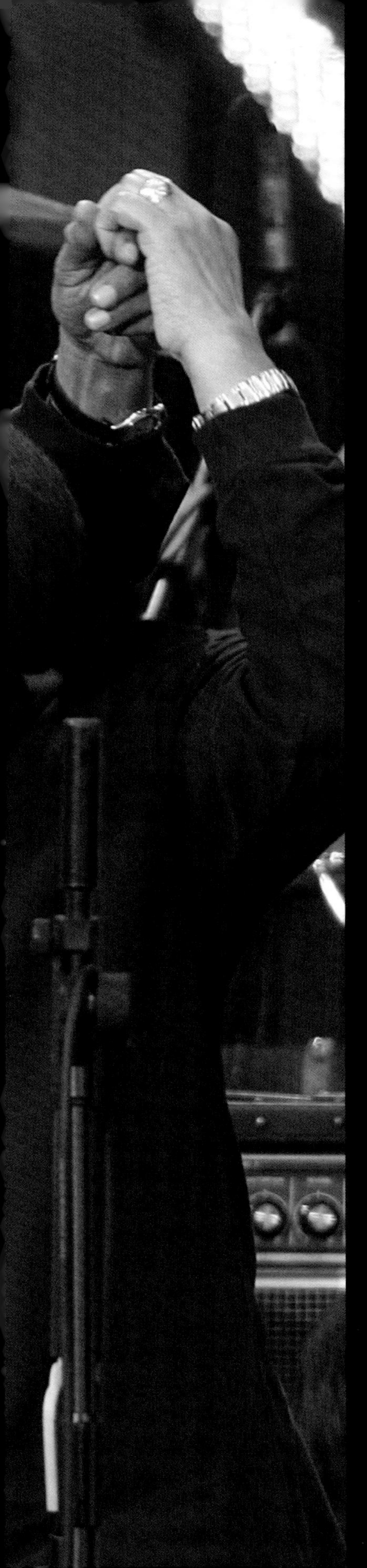

Nelson Mandela
and Graça Simbine
Hyde Park
June 2008
His 90th birthday tribute concert

Diana, Princess of Wales
Shaftesbury Theatre
May 1991
Leaving the premiere of 'L.A. Story'

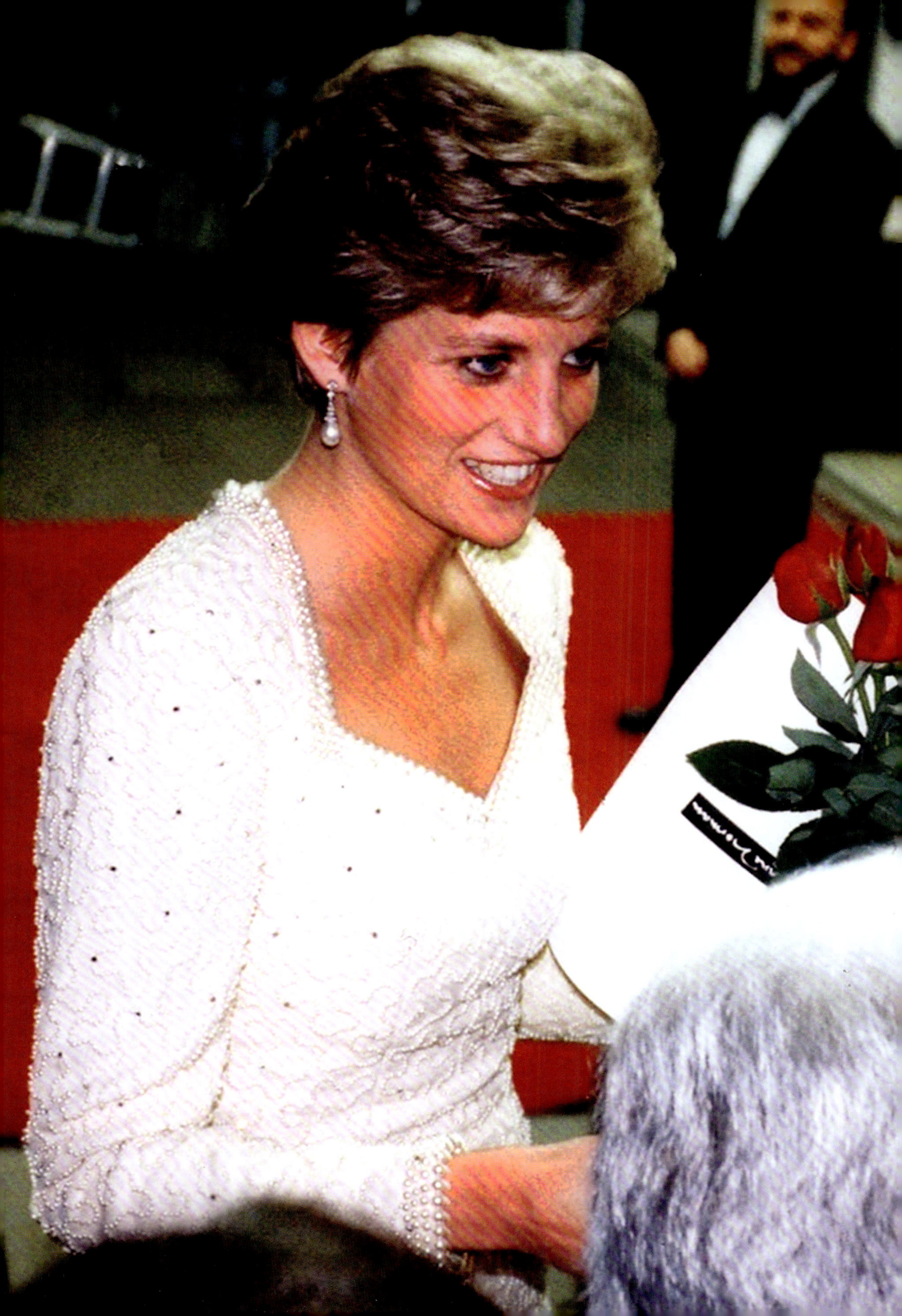

THE PRINCE and PRINCESS of WALES
April 2011

"But now, the real test lay ahead: the kiss. The balcony shot. The shot that would define every photo editor's front page."

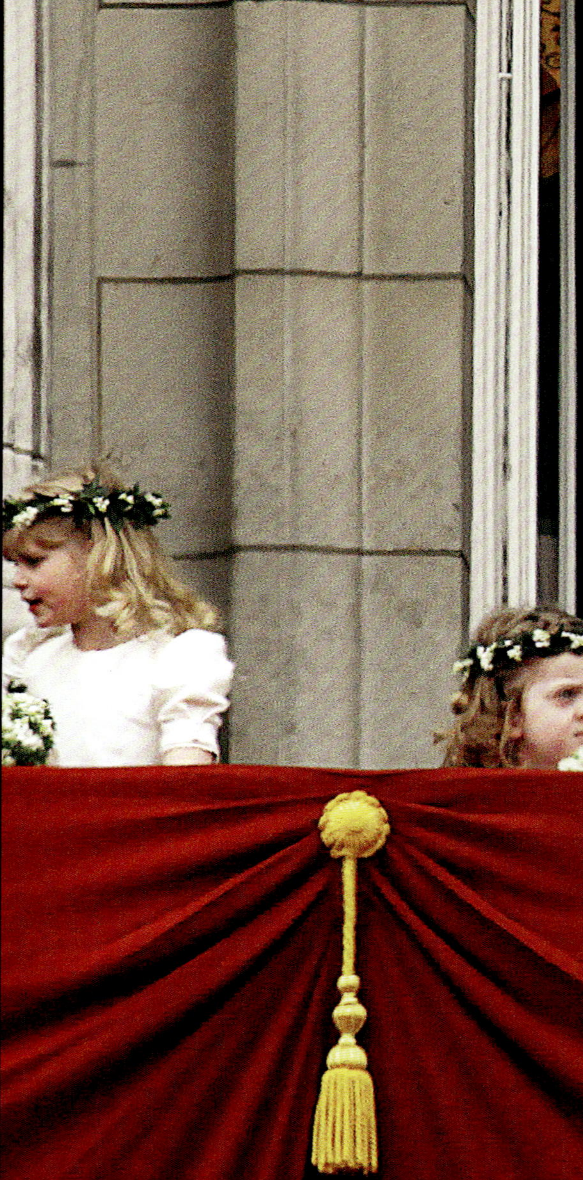

History was being written. The Royal Wedding was the crown jewel of the calendar for those of us behind the lens, the culmination of weeks filled with pre-dinners and gatherings of European royalty. Everything else was a prelude to today.

Unlike many of my colleagues, who had camped out in their trenches for days with foldable chairs and flasks, I trusted my instincts and opted for a different approach. Call it luck or experience, but I felt that the crowd might offer me the angle that I needed. So, at 6am, with my bag packed and a stepladder strapped to my back, I pedalled through the early morning hush of Hyde Park. The streets were still quiet – the calm before the royal storm. I parked my bike in St James's and made my way to The Mall, hoping to secure a prime spot amidst what would soon become a tidal wave of spectators.

It paid off. To my surprise, the crowd was still manageable, and I found myself at the front. With my stepladder set up and gear at the ready, I settled in, waiting for the first round of guests and dignitaries to glide past on their way to Westminster Abbey. Soon enough, the excitement stirred as Kate herself appeared, accompanied by her father. Grace doesn't photograph easily – it's too fluid, too intangible. But my lens didn't need direction that day. It moved of its own accord, capturing the dress, the veil, the soft resolve on her face. Everything about her passed as if she'd stepped out of a Renaissance painting.

By then, the crowd had swelled. Over a million people surged together along The Mall, a single

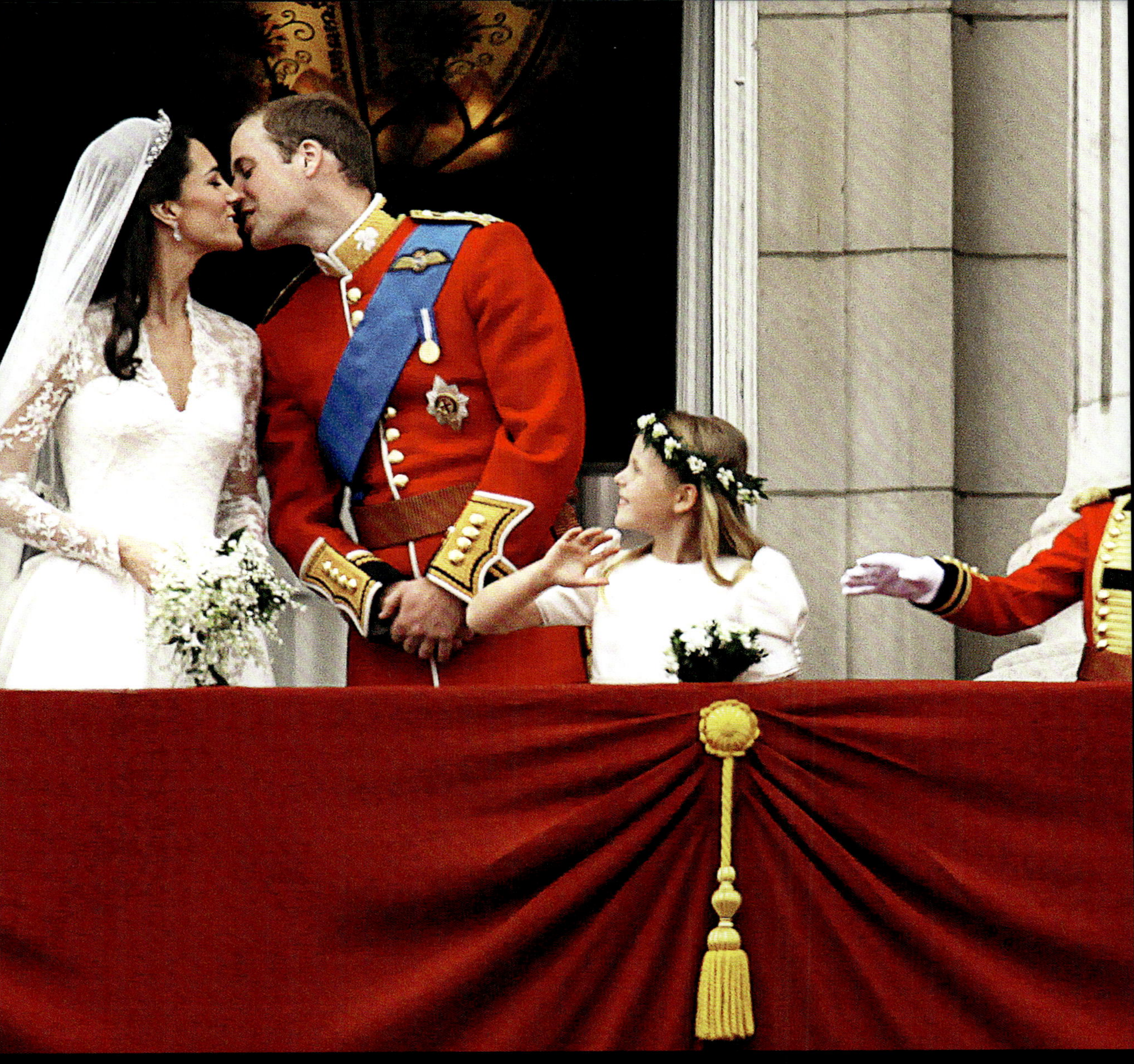

living, breathing mass of faces, flags and fervour held aloft by centuries of pageantry. The carriage followed, gold-trimmed, open-topped, straight out of Cinderella's private collection, and the central couple waving in unison as they passed by like a dream on wheels. The British do pomp and pageantry like no other, and that day, we really outdid ourselves. I'd covered royal events before, but nothing of this magnitude. Every inch of space had been claimed. But now, the real test lay ahead: the kiss. The balcony shot. The shot that would define every photo editor's front page. And I was far from the gates. Getting there felt like moving upstream through liquid joy – babies on shoulders, old women waving miniature flags, men in Union Jack suits cheering themselves hoarse. But there are ways. There are always ways. I won't reveal them all!

Somehow I made it, front and centre, the palace gates towering above, the balcony poised in stately silence. They emerged, the newlyweds, standing there together, the moment everyone had been waiting for. And then it happened – the kiss. It was brief, modest, maybe even shy, but perfect, made mighty by the awe-filled collective holding of breath by the nation. Click. One frame. Eternal.

The crowd's cheers could have burst hearts. The couple, as radiant as ever, waved to the masses before retreating inside. Moments later, a vintage Aston Martin pulled out, the couple inside, with "Just Married" scrawled on the back. It was a spell of a day, grandiose and intimate, breathless, bound by love. A fairy tale, shared by us all.

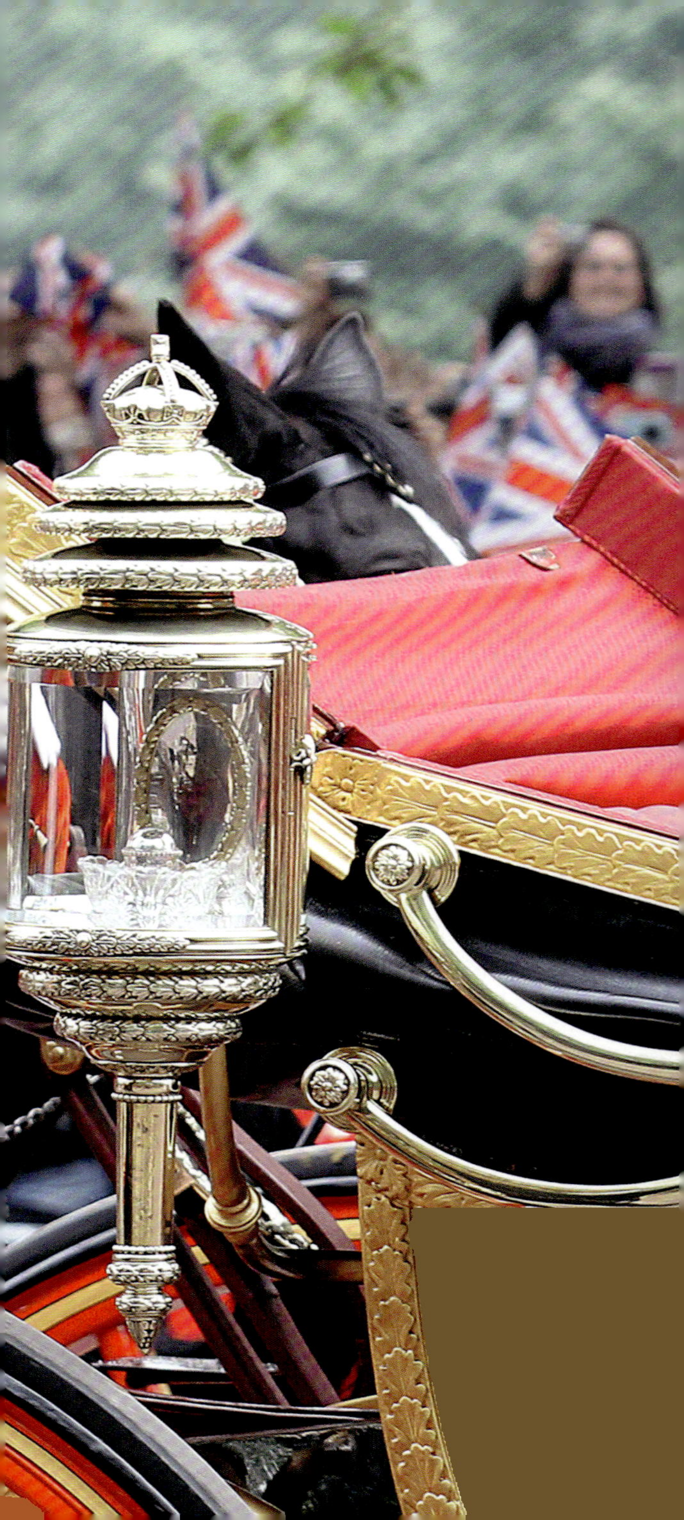

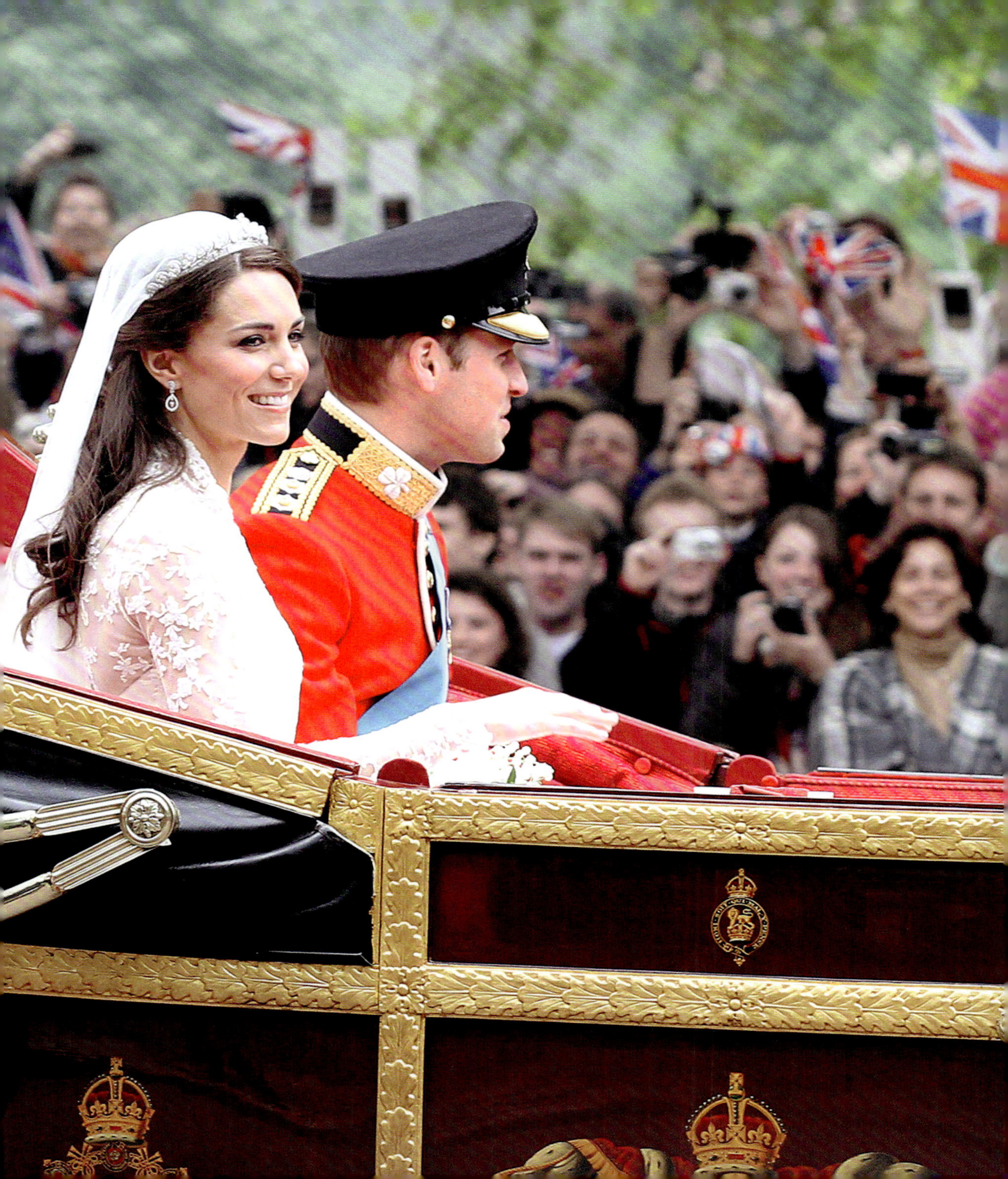

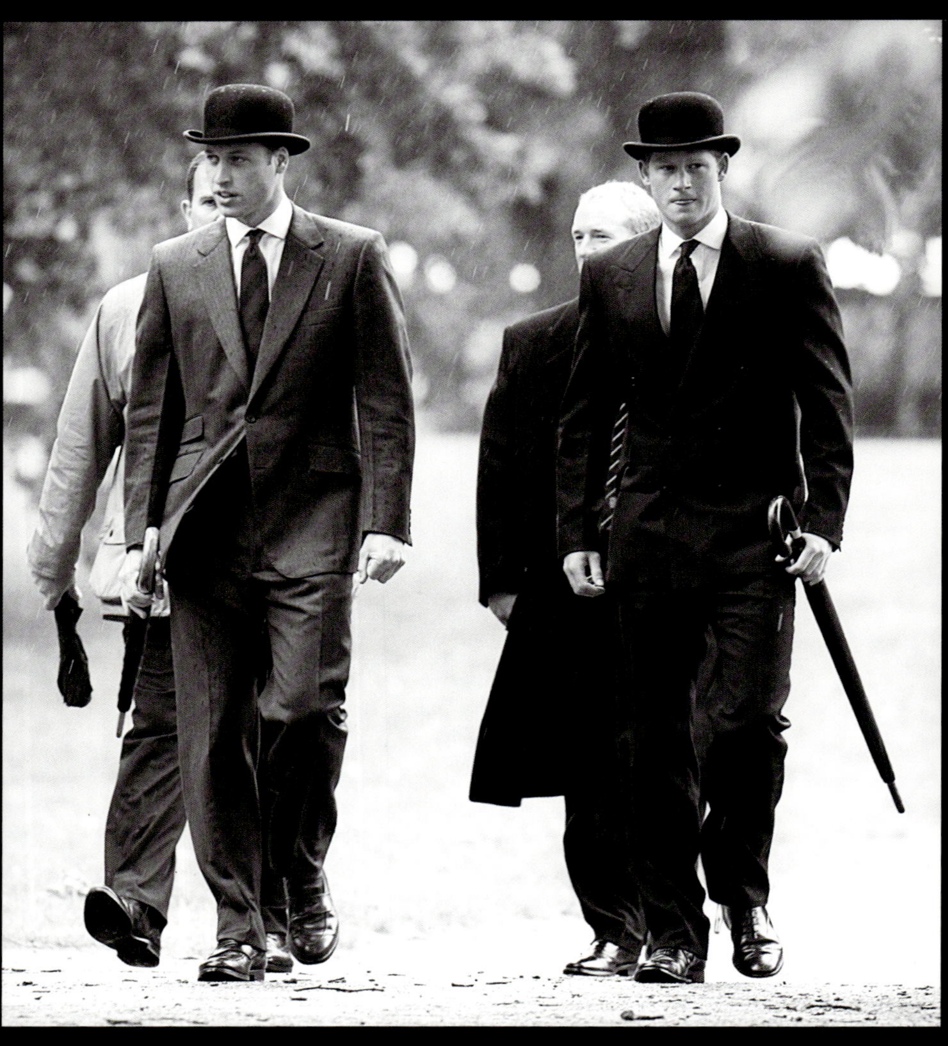

William, Prince of Wales
and Prince Harry, Duke of Sussex
Hyde Park
May 2007
Attending the Combined Cavalry Old Comrades Memorial Parade

Prince Harry, Duke of Sussex
and Meghan, Duchess of Sussex
The Mall
June 2018
Trooping the Colour

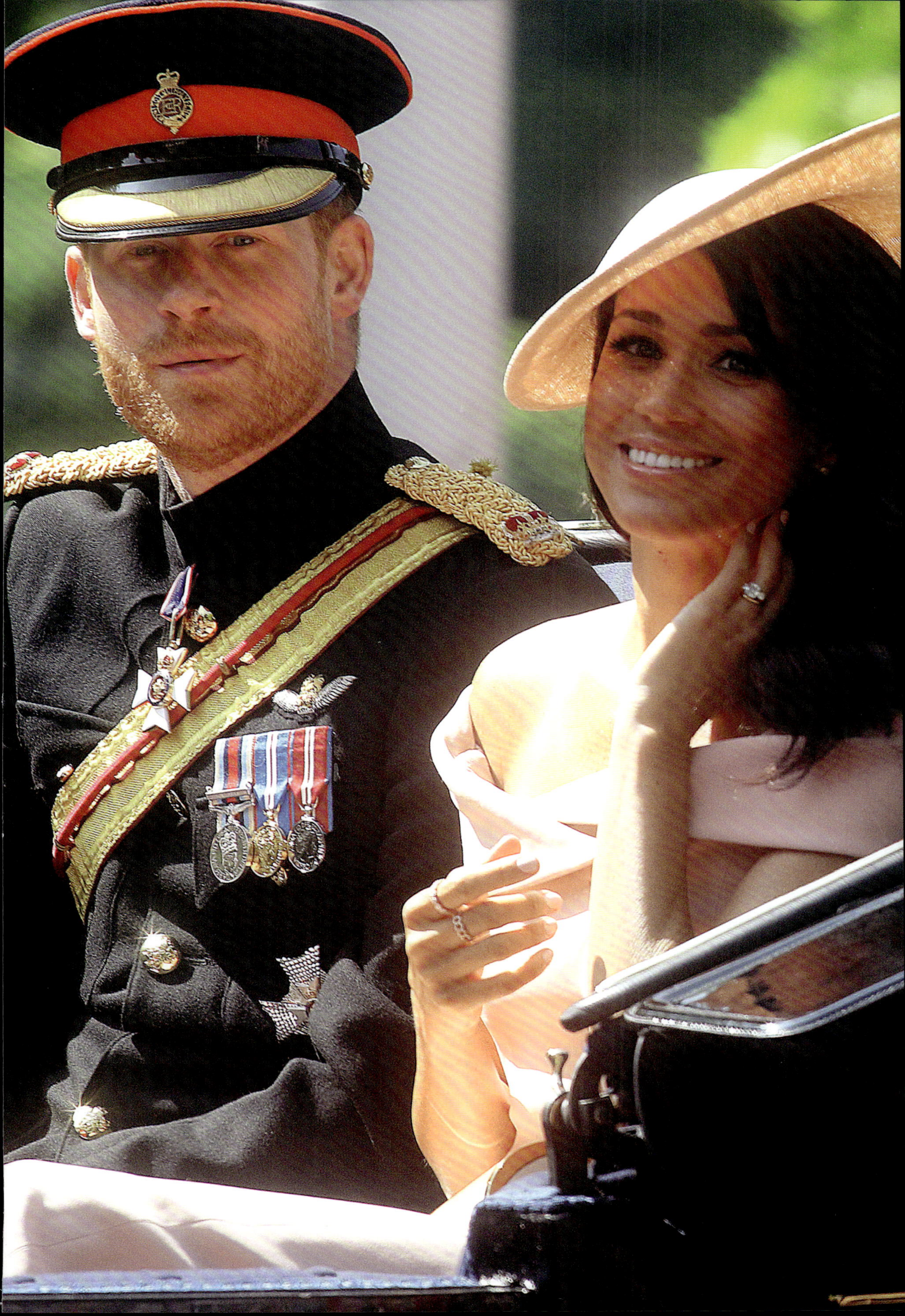

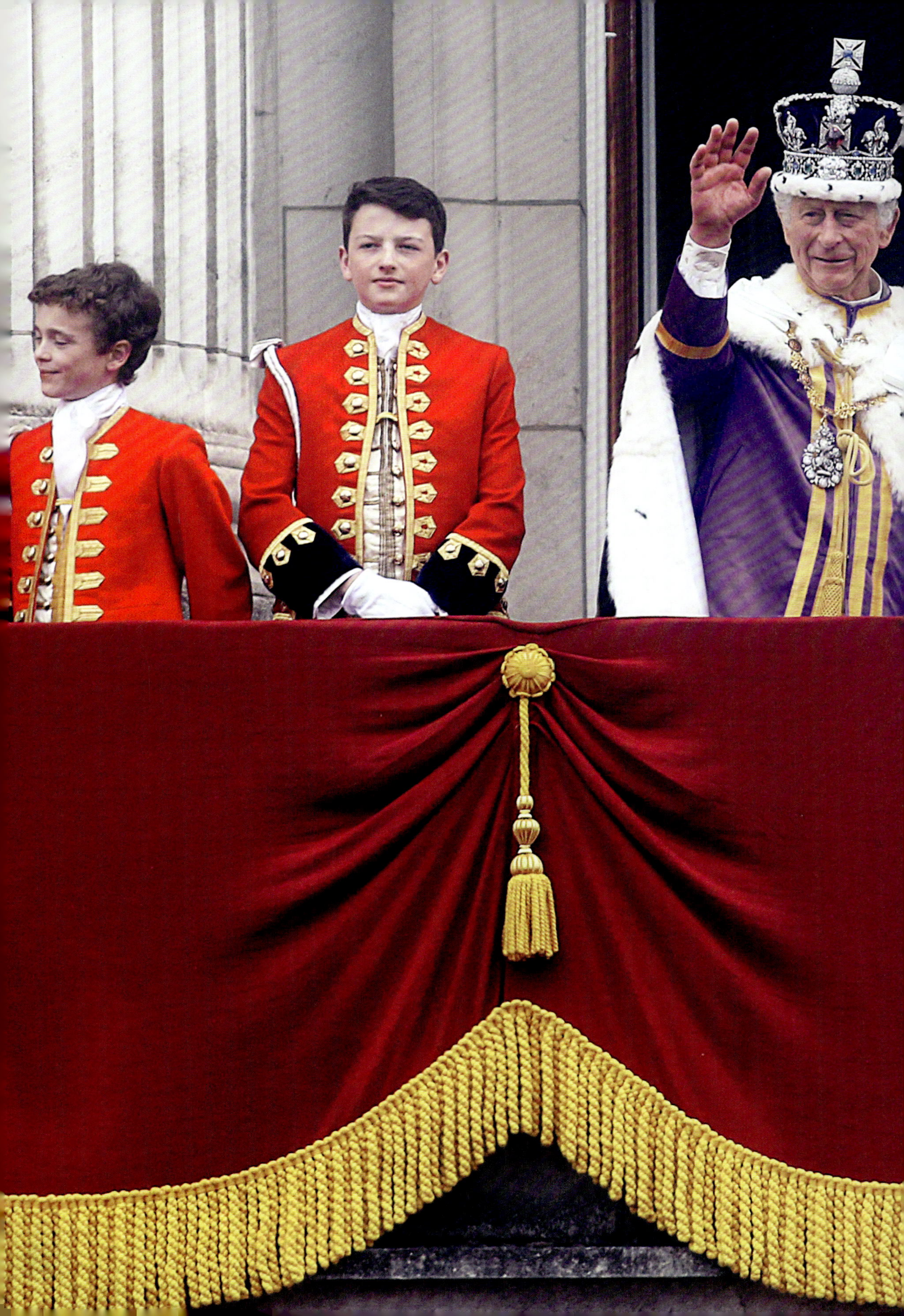

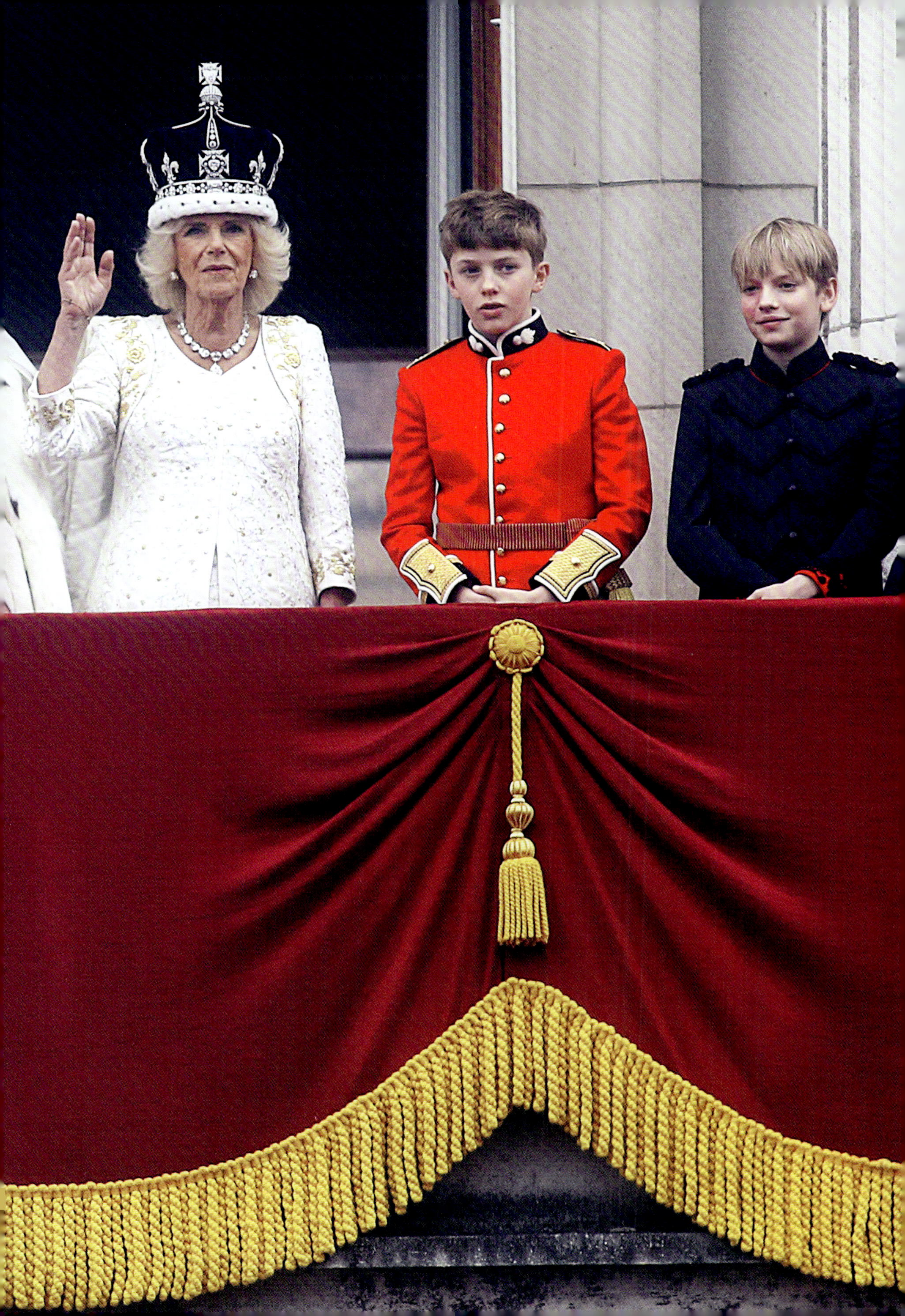

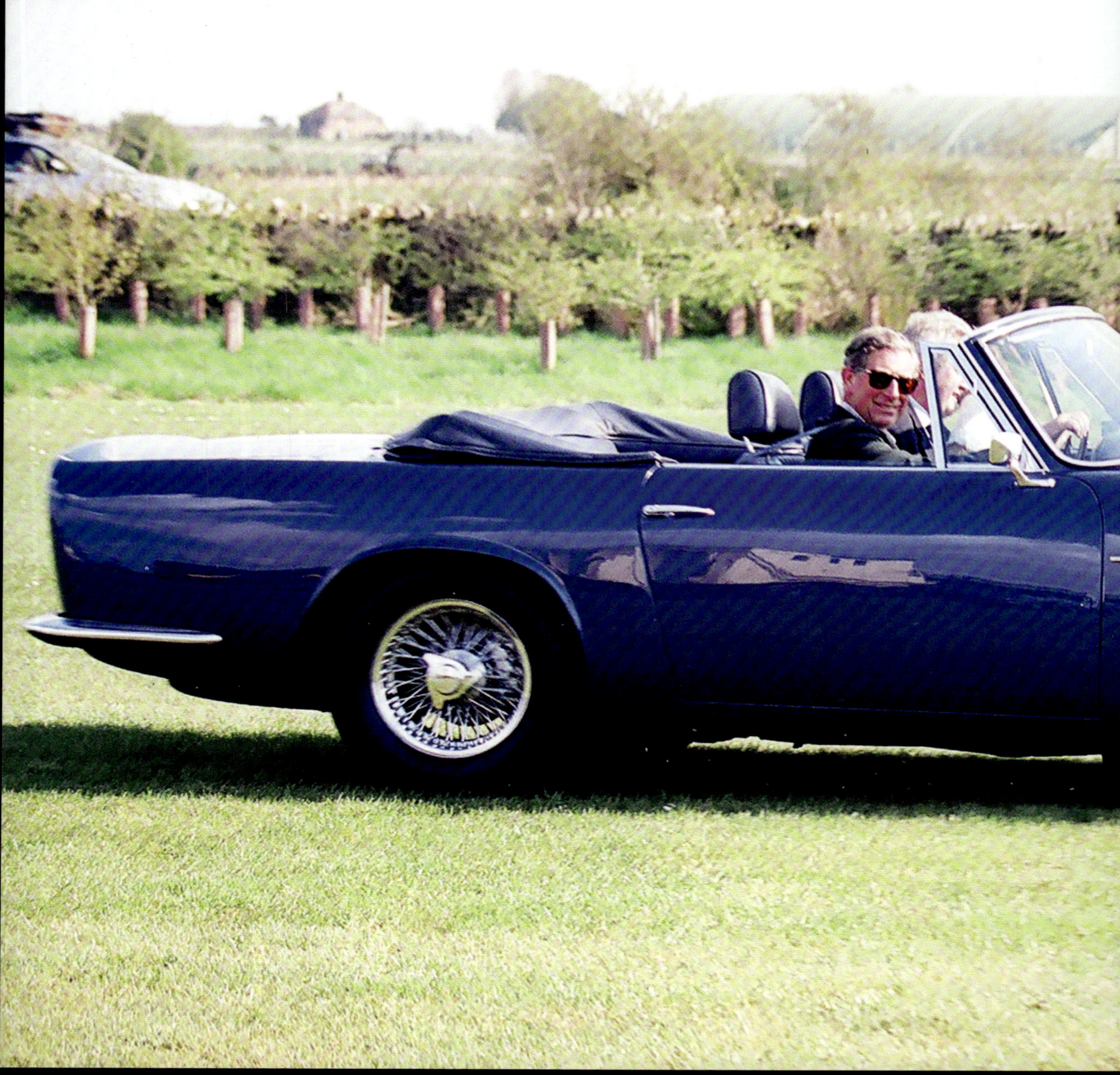

Prince Charles (now King Charles III)
Cirencester Polo Club, Gloucestershire
May 1999

Previous pages:
King Charles III and Queen Camilla
Buckingham Palace
May 2023

Following pages:
Queen Elizabeth II and
Prince Philip, Duke of Edinburgh
Tower of London
October 2014

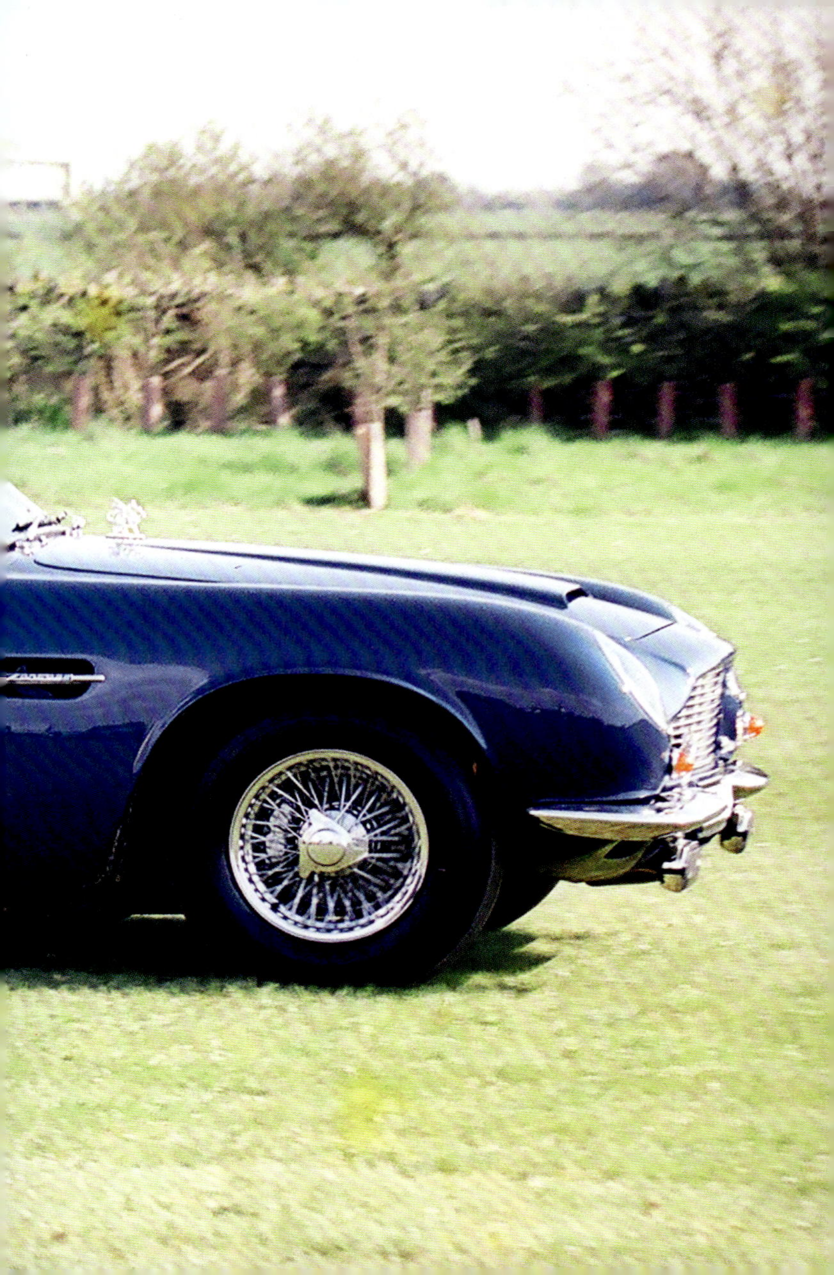

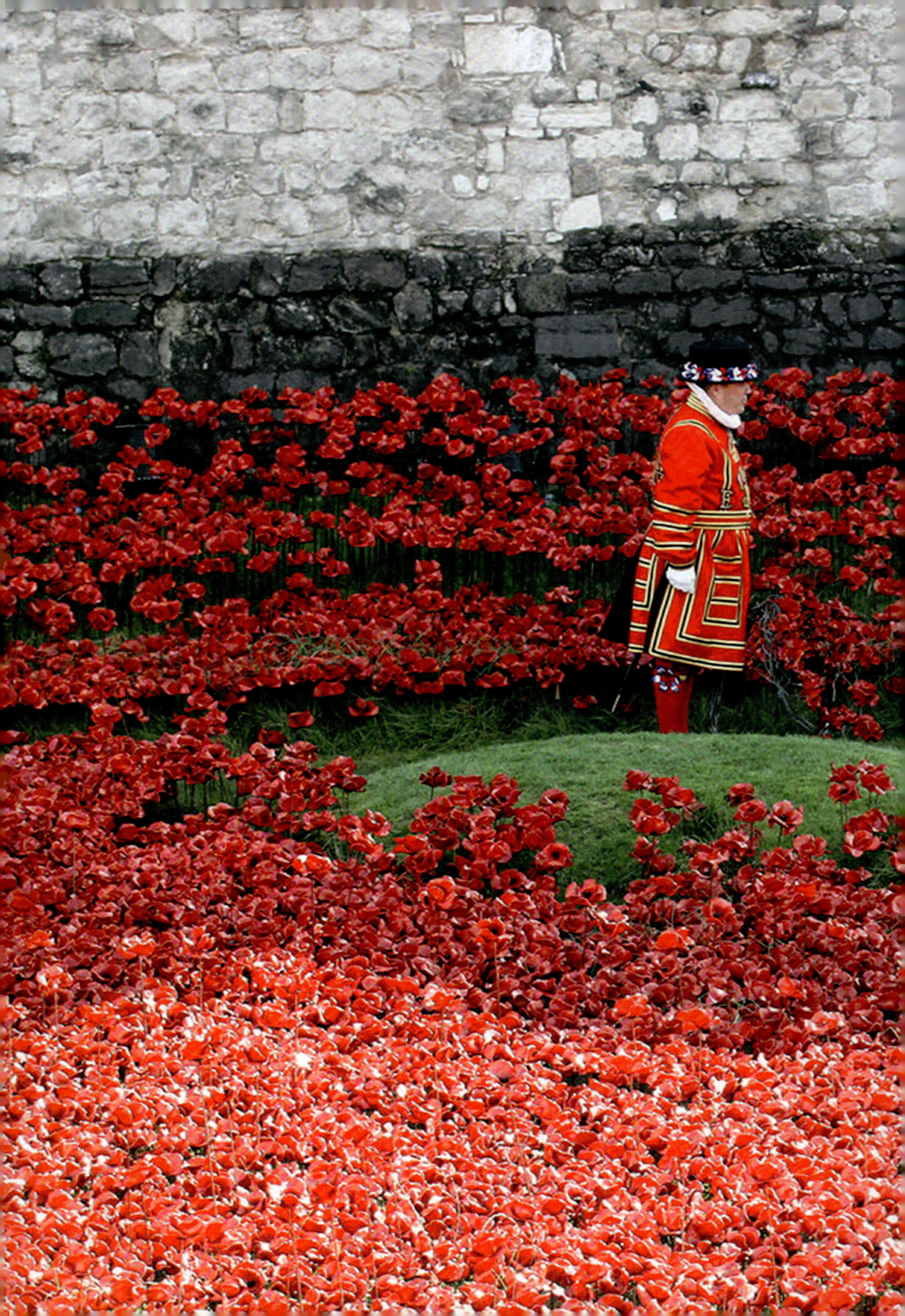

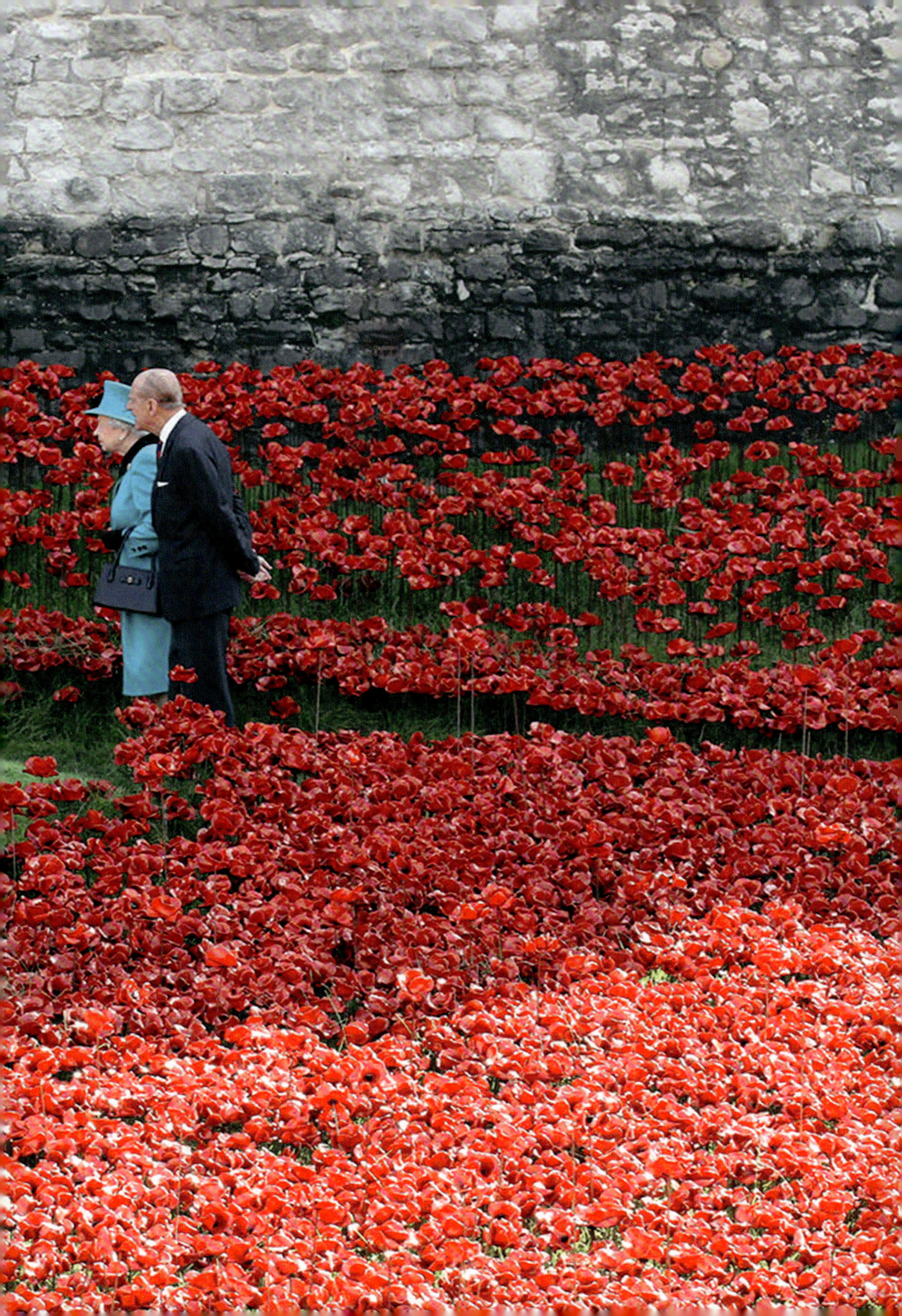

QUEEN ELIZABETH II

June 2015

As a photographer, one of the most common questions I encounter is: "What is your favourite picture that you've ever taken?" I have my share of favourites, but if asked what my proudest achievement is, it would undoubtedly be my portrait of Queen Elizabeth II that I call *Stamp of Approval*. This was a long, arduous project that began in 2003 and unfolded over years of persistence.

The journey started on a crisp morning as I prepared to cover the State Opening of Parliament for the first time. I was both excited and nervous, unfamiliar with the event's intricacies. I quickly found my position, eager to capture the iconic moment when The Queen would pass in her glass-covered, gilded carriage, drawn by four majestic horses. The competition was fierce, and every other photographer was vying for the same angle.

In that moment, an idea began to form. I remembered the most famous image of her: the effigy by artist Arnold Machin that graced our currency and postage stamps – a powerful representation of her legacy. This portrait had been etched in the public's memory since John Hedgecoe photographed her in 1966 for the definitive stamp, based on the renowned Penny Black design. It had remained unchanged throughout her reign. Knowing this, I felt compelled to capture something just as memorable.

However, the challenge was immense. The Queen only rode in one direction during the parade, which meant I would only have a handful of frames to work with each year. Undeterred, I returned year after year, trying different angles, desperate to capture that elusive side-on shot that would mirror Machin's portrait. Each time, I walked away with images of The Queen looking every way but the way I needed.

Twelve years later, in 2015, everything aligned. As the carriage approached, I readied myself with a 300mm lens attached to a monopod, heart racing. I locked in on her, my finger poised on the shutter. The carriage sped past, and I fired off a series of shots – one, two, three, four, five – each one revealing another hurdle. The first shot? Nothing. The second? The coach rider's leg blocked my view. The third? A nice frame of

"There it was! My heart skipped as I zoomed in on the image displayed on my camera's screen."

her slightly head-on. The fourth? A bar obscuring part of her face. And then I stopped dead in my tracks.

There it was! My heart skipped as I zoomed in on the image displayed on my camera's screen. It was pin-sharp, exactly the frame I had been searching for all those years. The moment was surreal – I had finally done it! Racing home, I printed it large and hung it on my living room wall, staring at it in disbelief. It was perfect. Yet a fear crept in: if I shared it with the press, someone might replicate it. So, I kept it under wraps.

Years later, I read that The Queen was retiring her carriage and crown in favour of a car. A bizarre idea struck me – what if I shared my portrait with her? I printed a small copy, penned a letter expressing my admiration, and sent it to Buckingham Palace. Everyone around me chuckled at my belief that The Queen was going to read my letter, but I felt certain; after all, I knew the power of a great picture.

Days later, an envelope arrived with a big red crown stamped on it. I picked it up off the hall floor and rushed to the kitchen, carefully boiling the kettle to steam open the letter – a trick I'd seen in a film once. It was from her private secretary – she had seen my picture! The letter requested a signed, exhibition-size print to be added to the Royal Photographic Collection for posterity. I could hardly believe it! I jokingly told my family that The Queen had asked for my autograph. The thought alone was enough to keep me buoyed for weeks. The Royal Photographic Collection, housing about 500,000 images accumulated by monarchs and stored in climate-controlled rooms at Windsor Castle, included some of the most renowned photographers of all time. Yet mine was different – I hadn't been commissioned. I had captured this moment on my own, fuelled by sheer determination and passion.

That is why this image holds a special place in my heart: it represents not just a photographic achievement, but a culmination of 12 long years of dedication, creativity, and the thrill of achieving the impossible. Above all, it encapsulates Queen Elizabeth II, one of the most beloved leaders of our time.

"The Royal Photographic Collection, housing about 500,000 images accumulated by monarchs and stored in climate-controlled rooms at Windsor Castle, included some of the most renowned photographers of all time. Yet mine was different – I hadn't been commissioned. I had captured this moment on my own, fuelled by sheer determination and passion."

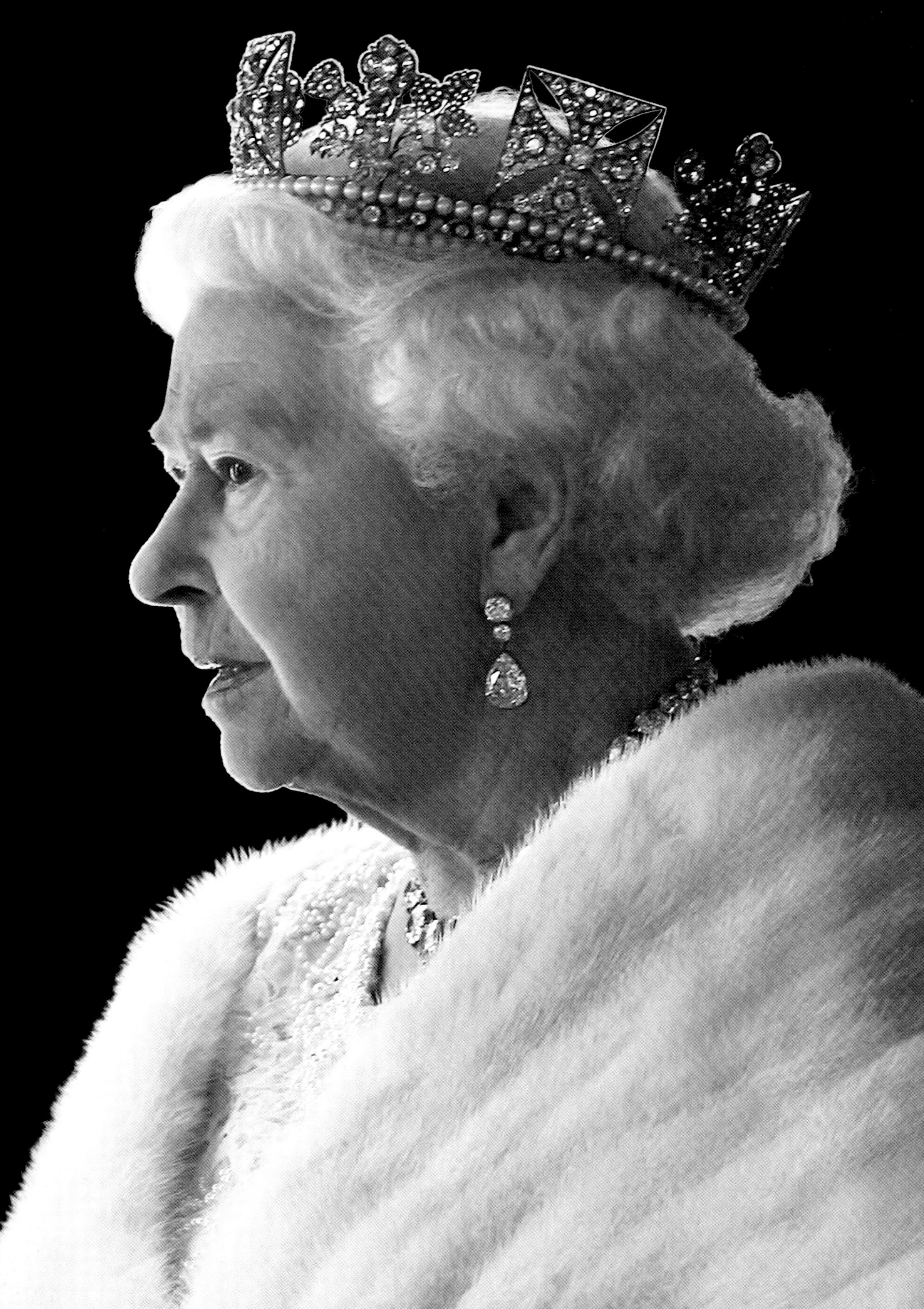

ISBN: 978 1 78884 353 9

A CIP catalogue record for this book is available from the British Library

We have made every effort to correctly identify the dates and locations in this book. Any errors are wholly unintentional. Greg Brennan is represented by Iconic Images Gallery, London.

Publisher: James Smith
Senior editor: Alice Bowden
Head of design: Mariona Vilarós Capella
Designer: Stephen Reid
Production manager: Simon Walsh
Reprographics manager: Corban Wilkin

EU GPSR Authorised Representative:
Easy Access System Europe Oü, 16879218
Address: Mustamäe tee 50, 10621 Tallinn, Estonia
Email: gpsr@easproject.com Tel: +358 40 500 3575

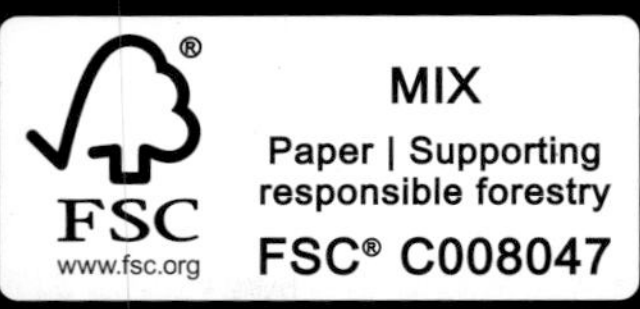

Printed in China by C&C Offset Printing Co. Ltd
for ACC Art Books Ltd., Woodbridge, Suffolk, UK

www.accartbooks.com

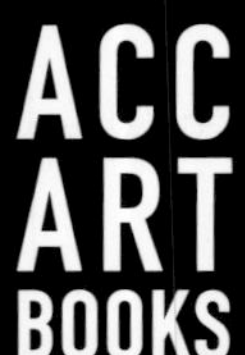

ACKNOWLEDGEMENTS

'I would be remiss to make an acknowledgements section without mentioning this book's secret (but just as essential) third author. Susana is the foundation upon which everything stands. There would be no book without her. Thank you for everything – your belief in me and your endless patience. This work, like everything I do, has your unseen fingerprints all over it.

To my mother, father, sisters, nieces and nephews – your enduring love and support have been my constant harbour. Thank you for picking me up after every fall. I carry you with me on every assignment. And on the other side of the pond, to Jose, Rosa, and all the rest of the family, for welcoming me as one of their own. To Dan, Tim, Rocky, Sean and Steve, for all their help and support over the years. And to Anna, whose courage in the face of unimaginable circumstances has taught me so much about the human spirit.

To all colleagues in the media, to Rav and Stephen and Ellie, all the picture desks and editors - thank you for your trust and belief in the power of the images we create together. This industry demands everything, and you've helped make the sacrifices worthwhile.

My deepest gratitude to Carrie and the entire team at Iconic Images for championing my work with such dedication and passion, giving my photographs a life beyond what I could have imagined. To Stephen, who has given this book its visual soul - thank you for your sensitivity, taste and patience in shaping how these images live on the page. And to James, Alice, and the rest of the team at ACC Art Books – thank you for your meticulous care in bringing these pages to life, and for honouring the stories these images tell.

For those I've lost but who continue to guide me: Johnny and Margaret, Benigno, Bill and Billy, and of course our much-loved Missy, whose unconditional love was the purest I will ever know.

And finally, to all the celebrities featured within these pages – thank you for your trust in those vulnerable moments, for allowing my lens to witness your humanity beyond the spotlight. These images exist because you let down your guard, if only for a moment.'

THE BIG SHOT

PHOTOGRAPHS BY GREG BRENNAN

WRITTEN BY DYLAN BRENNAN

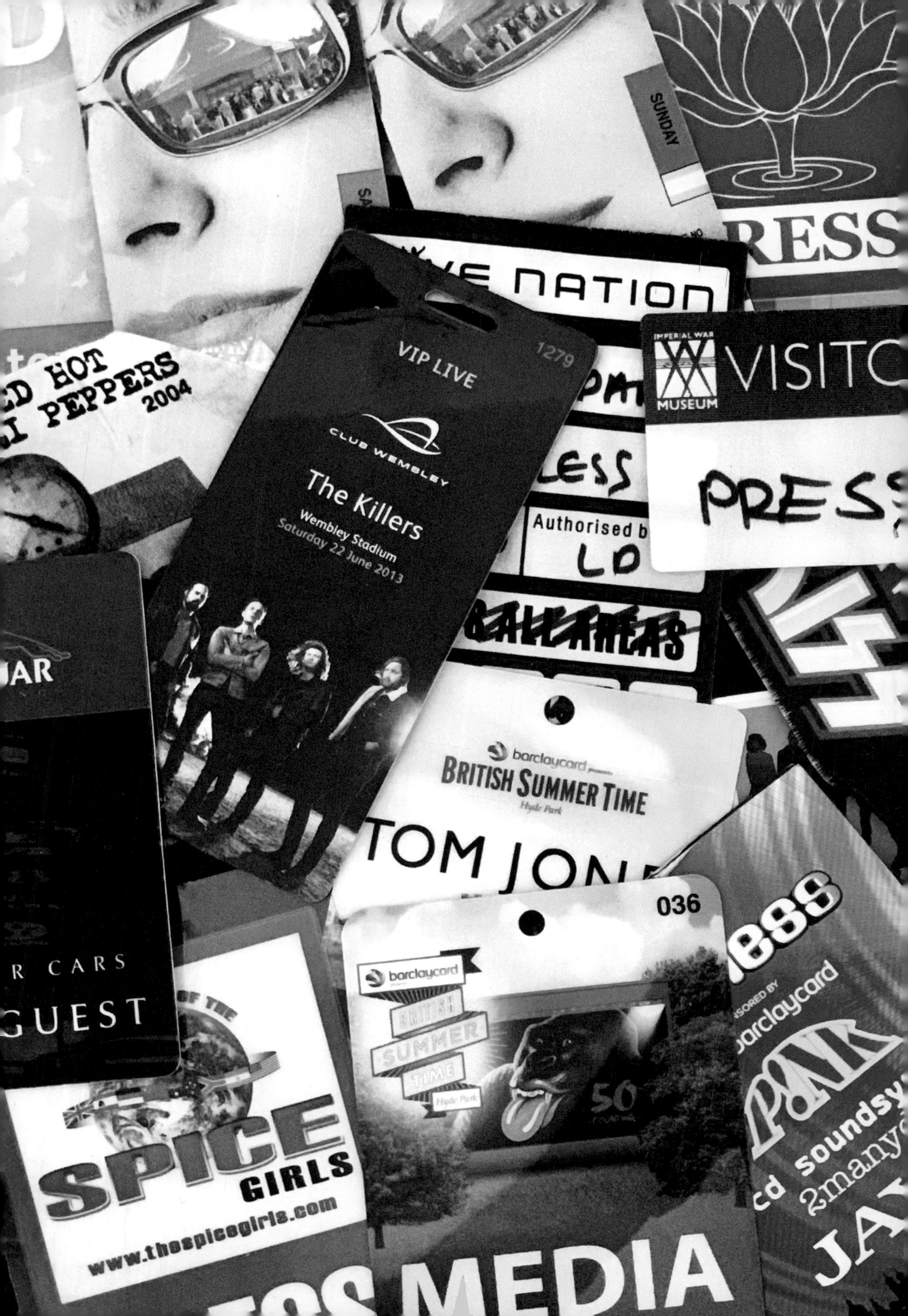

SUNDAY
RESS
VE NATION
IMPERIAL WAR MUSEUM
VISITO
PRESS
ED HOT
I PEPPERS
2004
VIP LIVE
1279
CLUB WEMBLEY
The Killers
Wembley Stadium
Saturday 22 June 2013
LESS
Authorised b
LD
ALL AREAS
AR
barclaycard presents
BRITISH SUMMER TIME
Hyde Park
TOM JON
036
barclaycard
BRITISH SUMMER TIME
Hyde Park
50
R CARS
GUEST
SPICE GIRLS
www.thespicegirls.com
barclaycard
soundsy
2many
JA
MEDIA